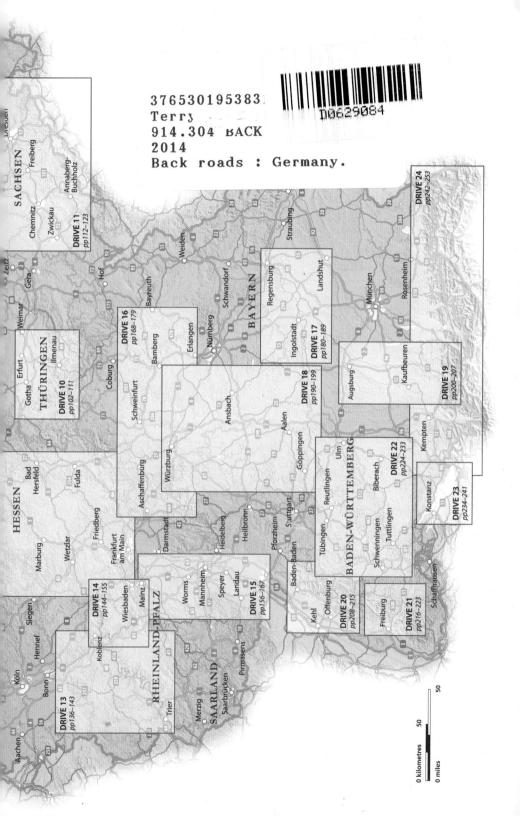

EYEWITNESS TRAVEL

BACK ROADS
GERMANY

EYEWITNESS TRAVEL

BACK ROADS GERMANY

CONTRIBUTORS

Jürgen Scheunemann, James Stewart,
Neville Walker, Christian Williams

DK

Above Punting on the Neckar river, Tübingen, Baden-Württemberg

LONDON, NEW YORK,
MELBOURNE, MUNICH AND DELHI
www.dk.com

MANAGING EDITOR Aruna Ghose

EDITORIAL MANAGER
Sheeba Bhatnagar

DESIGN MANAGER Kavita Saha

PROJECT EDITOR Arundhti Bhanot

EDITORS Beverly Smart,
Parvati M. Krishnan

PROJECT DESIGNER Mathew Kurien

DESIGNER Kaberi Hazarika

PICTURE RESEARCH
Taiyaba Khatoon, Shweta Andrews

DTP DESIGNERS Rakesh Pal,
Azeem Siddiqui

CARTOGRAPHY MANAGER
Uma Bhattacharya

CARTOGRAPHY
Jasneet Arora, Mohammad Hassan

ILLUSTRATOR
Arun Pottirayil

Printed and bound in China by
South China Printing Co.Ltd

First American Edition, 2011
14 15 16 10 9 8 7 6 5 4 3 2 1

Published in the United States by
DK Publishing, 345 Hudson Street,
New York, NY 10014

Reprinted with revisions 2014

Published in the UK by
Dorling Kindersley Limited.

A catalog record for this book is available from
the Library of Congress.

ISBN 978 1 4654 1015 3

Jacket: Road bridge over Lake Sylvenstein with
mountains in the background, Bavaria

CONTENTS

Below Upper gate of the Schloss Harburg along the
Romantic Road, Lower Saxony

Below Seventeenth-century Schloss Wachsenburg,
Drei Gleichen, Thuringia

Above Outdoor café and the Rathaus with its small turrets, Stralsund, Mecklenburg-Vorpommern

Above Vineyards surrounding Bernkastel-Kues, Rhineland-Palatinate

Above Bustling town center, Füssen, Bavaria

Below Half-timbered houses, old town, Tangermünde, Saxony-Anhalt

Below Sign along the route between Quedlinburg and Bad Harzburg

Title page Scenic road around village Bayrischzell, Bavaria
Half title page Lake Konstanz, Baden-Württemberg

About this Book

Located in the heart of Europe, Germany offers its visitors a diverse experience. Historic monuments, evocative landscapes, scenic towns and romantic medieval cities await those driving through this fascinating country. From the green marshes and pristine sandy coasts of the north to the mountainous and wooded regions of the south, the 24 leisurely drives in this book take you on a trip through a hospitable country while showing charming, lesser-known places off the beaten track.

The delightful landscape ranges from the windy Baltic Coast to the remote valleys of the Black Forest and from rolling green pastures to dramatic mountain peaks. Travellers will discover reminders of Germany's riveting past, delve into the alluring multicultural life of its cities, enjoy fine traditional cuisine and marvel at the country's beautiful natural vistas. Expect delightful surprises around every bend, packed with the sights, sounds and flavours of the real Germany.

Getting Started

The front section of the guide provides all the practical information needed to plan and enjoy a driving holiday in Germany. It includes an overview of when to go and how to get there, advice on bringing your own vehicle or renting one and details of any documentation required. The motoring advice ranges from driving rules to road conditions, buying petrol to break-down or accident procedures – the kind of background knowledge that will help to make driving stress free. There is information on money, opening hours, communications, health and safety and other practical matters, as well as advice on accommodation and dining options, to ensure that you experience the very best of Germany's hospitality. A language section at the back lists essential words and phrases, including key driving-related vocabulary.

The Drives

The main touring section of the guide is divided into 24 scenic drives, ranging in duration from one to six days. All the tours can be undertaken in a standard vehicle, and no special driving skills are required. Each drive

begins with a list of highlights and a clearly mapped itinerary. There is useful advice on the best time of year to do the drive, road conditions, market days and major festival dates. The tour pages contain detailed descriptions of each stop on the route, linked by clear driving instructions. Side panels highlight information on the most authentic places to stay and eat. Tinted boxes feature background information and interesting anecdotes.

Each drive features at least one mapped town or countryside walking tour, designed to take a maximum of two hours at a gentle pace with stops along the way.

The tours are flexible: they can be linked to create a longer driving holiday; others can be shortened into day trips while based in a region.

Using the Sheet Map

A pull-out road map of the entire country is attached at the back of this guide. This map contains all the information you need to drive around Germany and to navigate between the tours. All motorways, major roads, airports – both domestic and international – plus ferry ports are clearly identified. This makes the pull-out map an excellent addition to the drive itinerary maps within the book. The pull-out map also has a comprehensive index for easy location of sights. The map is further supplemented by a clear distance chart so you can gauge the distances between the major cities.

Top left Outdoor café, Oberammergau, Bavaria **Top right** Imposing Burg Hohenzollern, Baden-Württemberg **Centre left** Lake Titisee, Baden-Württemberg **Centre right** Back road to Immenstadt, Bavaria **Below left** Half-timbered houses, Tangermünde, Hesse **Below right** Sandy beach, Sylt, Schleswig-Holstein

Above Roadside viewpoint looking towards the Willibaldsburg, Eichstätt, Bavaria

Introducing Germany

Germany is a country of marked contrasts and this is nowhere more apparent than in its geographic diversity. Modern cities of glass and steel sit only a few minutes away from thickly wooded forests dotted with romantic castles. Germany's combination of multicultural cities, historic architecture and charming medieval villages set in breathtakingly beautiful countryside make it an ideal holiday destination. The country's main road network is extensive and well maintained, but it is the smaller roads that lead into the heart of the region. Here, through castles, villages and magnificent palaces, Germany's rich history is waiting to be discovered. Take a break to sample some exceptional wines – the most famous vineyards are in the western part of the country, especially the Pfalz and Rheinhessen regions – or take time to admire the natural landscape, from the stunning beauty of the German Alps to the myriad glacial lakes in the Müritz Nationalpark.

When to Go
The itinerary for each of the drives suggests the best times of the year to make the trip, based on the region. Visits to cities and historic buildings are best made in the spring or early autumn as it can get very hot in summer. However, July and August are the ideal months for a vacation by the sea or one of the numerous lakes. Winter offers skiing in the Alps, southern Germany, the Black Forest or the Harz Mountains. The country also hosts numerous events throughout the year, which makes a visit worthwhile during any seasons. In autumn, visitors can participate in traditional folkloric festivals such as Freimarkt in Bremen, which is held in mid-October. In December, festive Christmas markets are held all over the country. They are particularly charming in southern German cities with historic town centres and are good places to pick up souvenirs and presents.

Times to Avoid
In late July and August, it can get rather hot, especially in the southwestern regions. The busiest period is during the school holidays, which see a great surge in traffic levels. These are set independently in each state and take place in early April (Easter holidays), July and August (summer holidays) and October (autumn holidays). Roads can get particularly busy around Easter and national public holidays. To enjoy a stress-free trip, it is best to avoid driving at these times of the year. A visit to northern and eastern Germany between November and late February can be unpleasant due to harsh winter winds and low temperatures. Ice, rain and sleet make it challenging to drive and sightseeing difficult.

Festivals
Nearly every town and village hosts a parade, street shows, concerts and fairs. These include folk festivals connected to local traditions, such as the asparagus or grape harvest. In April and May, the first spring fairs are held. It is also time for the solemn observance of Easter. In June, a number of classical music events take place and July is a popular month for lively wine and beer festivals. January and February are the Carnival season while December is synonymous with Christmas celebrations.

National Public Holidays
New Year's Day (1 Jan)
Epiphany (6 Jan)
Good Friday, Easter Sunday and Monday
Labour Day (1 May)
Reunification of Germany Day (3 Oct)
All Souls Day (1 Nov)
Christmas (25/26 Dec)

Additional public holidays are held in some states and regions.

Left Panoramic view of Berchtesgaden from Hochlenzer in the German Alps

Above Half-timbered buildings, Limburg an der Lahn, Hesse

Getting to Germany

A popular destination, Germany is well connected to the rest of the world. Every large city in the country has an airport, most of which offer international flights. The increase in the number of low-cost flights has made it much easier to travel to Germany from various European cities. Travellers from outside Europe may find it cheaper to fly via London to take advantage of the many budget flights available from the UK. All the major US airlines also operate regular flights to Germany. Car rental services are well established at all the big airports in the country.

Above Germany's efficient budget air carrier, German Wings

Arriving by Air

Germany's most important airports are **Frankfurt am Main**, **Munich** and **Düsseldorf**, from where connecting flights can be made to other German cities. If coming from outside Europe, visitors are most likely to arrive at one of these major airports.

The largest German airports are Frankfurt am Main and Munich. The gigantic airport in Frankfurt comprises two huge terminals, which are connected by a fast overground railway. The airport in Munich is somewhat smaller, but still very popular. Among the busiest airports are Düsseldorf, Cologne-Bonn and Berlin, which is also where Schönefeld airport is located. Most airports are 20–40 km (12–25 miles) outside the nearest city and connected to the centre by local transport or Autobahn. International hubs such as Frankfurt, Munich and Düsseldorf offer long-distance train connections.

Germany's national carrier is **Lufthansa**, which operates regular, scheduled flights to destinations all around the world. **British Airways** offers regular, scheduled flights from London (Heathrow and Gatwick) to major German destinations as well as from several regional airports in the UK. Germany and the US are well connected through direct flights from major US cities such as New York, Washington DC, Boston, Chicago, San Francisco and Los Angeles. **Air Canada** operates daily flights from Canadian hubs to Frankfurt and Munich in arrangement with Lufthansa. Other carriers that offer flights to Germany are **Delta Airlines**, **Qantas** and **United Airlines**. Travelling to Germany by air and then renting a pre-booked car is certainly the best option for tourists from North America, South Africa, New Zealand and Australia.

In addition to Lufthansa, there are a number of other smaller carriers in Germany including **Air Berlin** and **German Wings**. These often offer cheaper fares than Lufthansa on internal routes, as well as providing air links with small airports such as Augsburg, Dortmund and Erfurt.

Arriving by Sea

There are ferry ports in many coastal cities, including Kiel, Lübeck, Rostock, Travemunde and Sassnitz. The major operators are **DFDS Seaways**, **Scandlines**, **Finnlines** and **Color Line**. Visitors travelling to Germany by car from the UK will first have to decide which ferry crossing to use (unless using the Eurotunnel). The shortest crossings are from Dover to Ostende in Belgium, or to Calais, in France. However, these will also require a fairly lengthy road trip. The Holland route of Harwich to Hook is useful for those starting their trip in Germany's northern region. Travellers coming from Ireland should first connect with a ferry service from Dublin to England before taking one of the options mentioned above. The latest provision to make a journey from the UK to mainland Europe by car is by using the Eurotunnel from Folkestone to Calais. The car is carried by train in just 35 mintues.

Arriving by Rail

Long-distance trains called EuroCity (EC) trains connect all important German cities with major European destinations. There are also overnight trains (City Night Line) from various European cities such as Amsterdam, Copenhagen, Belgrade, Budapest, Prague, Rome, Venice and Vienna. **Eurostar**'s high-speed passenger service also offers many cheap options for travelling by train.

The **Deutsche Bahn**, Germany's national railway company, operates highly modern, high-speed trains, the InterCity Express (ICE). The long distance ICE network is also linked to the international airport hubs of Frankfurt and Düsseldorf. However, ticket rates in the express trains are quite expensive. Seat reservations are recommended during the tourist season and public holidays.

Train tickets can be bought and reservations made through travel agents or at the railway station at the *Reisezentrum*, which also acts as an information centre. Tickets can also be reserved by telephone or through the Internet, where a detailed timetable can be viewed to plan an itinerary. **Eurail Passes**, such as the Eurail Global Pass, which allows unlimited first-class travel in 24 countries, are also a good option.

Arriving by Coach

Travelling to Germany by coach is not a very enjoyable experience as the distances are often long and fares not cheap when compared with low-cost airlines. **Eurolines** is the provider of international coach services to Germany. A hop-on, hop-off bus service, **Busabout**, serves Berlin, Dresden, Munich and Stuttgart.

Most towns have a bus station located in the town centre called ZOB *(Zentraler Omnibus Bahnhof)*, where timetables can be obtained and tickets purchased. It is best to enquire at the tourist information centre for travel details.

Below far left Airport display board showing destinations and timings *Below left* Ferry transporting vehicles, Konstanz *Below centre* Aerodynamically designed InterCity Express *Below* Airlines check-in counter, Berlin

DIRECTORY

AIRPORT INFORMATION

Berlin Schönefeld
0180 500 01 86;
www.berlin-airport.de

Berlin Tegel
0180 500 01 86;
www.berlin-airport.de

City Airport Bremen
0421 559 50;
www.airport-bremen.de

Cologne-Bonn
02203 40 40 01;
www.airport-cgn.de

Dresden
0351 881 33 60;
www.dresden-airport.de

Hamburg
040 50 75 25 57;
www.airport.de

Hannover
0551 97 70;
www.hannover-airport.de

Leipzig
0341 224 11 55;
www.leipzig-halle-airport.de

Nürnberg
0911 937 00;
www.airport-nuernberg.de

Stuttgart
01805 948 444;
www.flughafen-stuttgart.de

ARRIVING BY SEA

Color Line
www.colorline.com

DFDS Seaways
www.dfdsseaways.com

Finnlines
www.finnlines.com

Scandlines
www.scandlines.com

ARRIVING BY RAIL

Deutsche Bahn
01805 99 66 33;
www.bahn.de

Eurail Passes
www.eurail.com

Eurostar
www.eurostar.com

ARRIVING BY COACH

Busabout
www.busabout.com

Eurolines
www.eurolines.com

Practical Information

Germany is a country that is particularly well prepared to receive visitors. Public services operate smoothly and efficiently, and the health system is good. Every town, large and small, has a tourist information centre that can offer guidance on finding accommodation and information about local restaurants, attractions and activities. Germany is a safe country to travel in and its police are highly trained to deal with any emergency. Communication networks are good and almost all banks have ATMs.

Above Police patrol van

Language

Although all Germans do speak German, many of them use dialects that are sometimes almost incomprehensible, especially to foreigners with limited knowledge of German. The most difficult dialects to understand are probably those of southern Germany, particularly Bavarian and Schwabian, but Frisian and Saxon dialects are also likely to cause communication problems, even for German-speaking visitors. However, English is usually understood, particularly in larger cities and in places frequented by foreign tourists.

Passports and Visas

Citizens of EU member states, the US, Canada, Australia and New Zealand do not need a visa to visit Germany as long as their stay does not exceed three months. However, visitors from South Africa do need a visa. Nationals from most other countries require a Schengen Visa, named for the 1995 Schengen Agreement that abolished passport controls between Austria, Belgium, Denmark, Finland, France, Germany, Iceland, Italy, Greece, Luxembourg, the Netherlands, Norway, Portugal,

Spain and Sweden. This visa is valid for stays of up to 90 days. Visitors should check with the German embassy or consulate in their own country prior to travelling or visit the **Federal Foreign Office** website and search for "visa agreements".

Most embassies, including those of the US and the UK, are located in Berlin but consulates can be found in other major cities.

Travel Insurance

All travellers are strongly advised to take out travel insurance that offers cover for a broad range of possible emergencies. It is mandatory for all foreign visitors to have a medical insurance policy with sufficient protection on a visit to Germany.

In addition to medical insurance, a comprehensive policy will normally cover the holder for loss or theft of luggage and other belongings, such as passports and money, damage or injury to a third party, personal accidents and delayed or cancelled flights. Most policies also cover legal costs up to a certain limit. A standard policy will not cover hazardous or extreme sports, so anyone planning to go surfing, skiing or rock-climbing must check their policy; extra cover

can usually be added for a small premium. Most credit card companies offer insurance for lost luggage; one is also entitled to compensation in case of flight delays and cancellation.

Health

Germany poses no serious health hazards for travellers and no vaccinations are required before entering the country. Ticks are prevalent in rural areas, especially during the summer months. Avoid long grass, keep to paths and wear long trousers and stout shoes.

Those who require prescribed medication should ensure that they take enough to cover their stay, as it may not be available locally. Citizens of EU member states can obtain free medical assistance in Germany if they hold a European Health Insurance Card (EHIC). Travellers can obtain the card by applying online via the website of their national health authority before leaving home. To call an ambulance in the event of an emergency, dial 19222 plus the area code if using a mobile phone or simply 112 without the area code if calling from a pay phone. Pharmacies (*Apotheke*) can

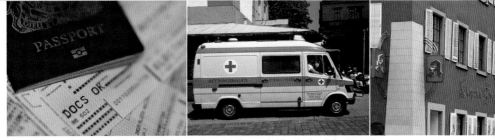

Above left European Union passports **Above centre** Ambulance **Above right** Pharmacy building, Konstanz, Baden-Württemberg

be identified by a sign bearing a large red "A". They are usually open from 8am to 6pm and also have a list of doctors in the area.

Personal Security

As in other countries, visitors are far safer in towns and villages than in big cities, where vigilance is needed against pickpockets and petty thieves. One should be particularly cautious in crowded places, such as railway platforms and on trains and buses, as well as at popular tourist sights. Leave passports, jewellery and expensive items in the hotel safe and keep valuables such as cameras and audio equipment concealed under clothing when walking around. Park the car in a safe car park. Report thefts and burglaries immediately to the police. The German police can be recognized by their green or blue uniforms. There are motorized police units *(Verkehrspolizei)* that patrol German cities by car, motorcycle, bicycle and even on horses. To telephone the **Emergency Services** (fire and police), dial 110. There are emergency buttons on the platforms of the public transport systems in the bigger cities. Contact the local **lost property** office *(Fundbüro)* – there is one located in every German city – to report lost

property. The railway network, Deutsche Bahn, has its own lost property offices, as do the urban transport systems in individual towns. In the event of a more serious problem, such as the loss of a passport, visitors should approach their consulate. Officials at the consulate can help travellers to get a new passport or obtain legal advice. In some circumstances, they may even finance the purchase of a ticket home.

Disabled Travellers

Germany is well prepared to receive disabled travellers. Large museums and historic monuments have special ramps or lifts for people who are confined to wheelchairs. Offices and banks are also accessible to wheelchair users, and there are usually lifts at railway stations and larger underground stations. Most public transport vehicles have been adapted to take wheelchair passengers. Many hotels, especially the higher grades, offer suitably equipped bedrooms. Contact **NatKo** for further information.

Below far left Pharmacy shop, Zwickau, Saxony
Below left Cyclists in Baden-Württemberg
Below centre Fire brigade alarm button
Below Popular tourist centre, Neustadt an der Weinstrasse, Rhineland-Palatinate

DIRECTORY

EMBASSIES AND CONSULATES
Australia
Wallstrasse 76–79, 10179 Berlin; 030 880 08 80; www.australian-embassy.de

Canada
Leipziger Platz 17, 10117 Berlin; 030 20 31 20; www.kanada-info.de

New Zealand
Friedrichstrasse 60, 10117 Berlin; 030 20 62 10; www.nzembassy.com

Republic of Ireland
Jägerstrasse 51, 10117 Berlin; 030 22 07 20; www.embassyofireland.de

South Africa
Tiergartenstrasse 18, 10785 Berlin; 030 22 07 30; www.suedafrika.org

United Kingdom
Wilhelmstrasse 70, 10117 Berlin; 030 20 45 70; www.britischebotschaft.de

United States of America
Pariser Platz 2, 14191 Berlin; 030 830 50; www.usembassy.de

PASSPORTS AND VISAS
Federal Foreign Office
www.auswaertiges-amt.de

HEALTH
Ambulance
112 or 19222 (when dialling the second number, dial the area code if using a mobile phone)

PERSONAL SECURITY
Emergency Services
For Fire and Police dial 110

Lost Property
Fundbüro der Deutschen Bahn; 0900 199 05 99; Zentrales Fundbüro Berlin; Platz der Luftbrücke 6, Berlin; 030 75 60 31 01

DISABLED TRAVELLERS
NatKo (Nationale Koordinationsstelle Tourismus für Alles)
Fleher Strasse 317a, 40223 Düsseldorf; 0211 336 80 01; www.natko.de; www.cometogermany.com

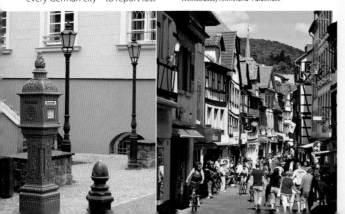

Communications

Postal and telecommunications services are very well developed in Germany. German phone numbers have area codes up to six digits long, beginning with 0 followed by a local number of five to nine digits, depending on the region. When dialling within the country, use the full area code.

Public telephones are serviced by Deutsche Telekom. Some accept coins, others require credit cards, or phonecards, which can be purchased at post offices. Coins of smaller denominations are not accepted; unused coins are returned, but no change is given. Card-operated phones are located at central locations in cities as well as at airports and train stations. It might be useful to have a mobile phone when travelling in Germany, especially in remote areas. Travellers should discuss their requirements with their domestic network provider beforehand. Charges vary according to the facilities and coverage offered. Be aware that roaming charges are higher than at home. If from an EU country, tariffs should be less than 50 cents per minute; outside the EU, they may be substantially higher. A money-saving option would be to buy a local SIM card in Germany.

Deutsche Post operates most postal services in Germany. Post offices are usually open Mon–Fri from 8am to 6pm and 8am to noon on Saturdays. Internet cafés can be found in all bigger cities and most hotels offer Internet services to their guests. An increasing number of hotels, restaurants and cafés provide Wi-Fi access to their customers.

Banks and Money

The Euro (€) has been Germany's currency since 2002. There are seven denominations of Euro banknote: the grey €5, the pink €10, the blue €20, the orange €50, the green €100, the yellow €200 and the purple €500. There are eight coins: €2 and €1, 50 cents, 20 cents, 10 cents, 5, 2 and 1 cents. The 2- and 1-Euro coins, are both silver and gold in colour. The 50-, 20- and 10-cent coins are gold. The 5-, 2- and 1-cent coins are bronze.

ATM machines can be found all over the country, but it is best to check with your bank or credit card company for fees. Travellers can change foreign currency at a bank or at exchange bureaus called *Wechselstuben*. There are no restrictions on the amount of foreign currency that can be brought into Germany. When changing cash, a commission may be charged for the transaction. It is best to check this before undertaking an exchange.

Most banks are open Mon–Fri from 9am to 3:30 pm with a lunch break from noon to 1pm. However, in larger cities they may keep longer opening hours. Exchange bureaus are located at airports and train stations as well as at many places that are frequented by tourists. It is advisable to take advantage of the services of the Reise Bank, which has branches at airports and railway stations. It is common to use travellers' cheques when

Above Old clock face on half-timbered building, Limburg an der Lahn, Hesse

travelling in Germany, even though taking money out at ATMs is more popular. One can cash cheques at banks and exchange bureaus.

Sign for Photography Museum, Deidesheim

Credit cards can be used for payments almost everywhere but be aware that many restaurants, supermarkets and smaller shops might not accept this form of payment. Credit card companies and banks are increasingly vigilant against fraud, so it is wise to let them know that you will be using the card abroad, so that they do not put a block on further use. It is also a good idea to carry another card as a back up.

Tourist Information

A very well-developed network of tourist information centres exists in Germany. These are usually run by the city or regional tourist authority and can be found all over the country. Tourist information centres have different names in Germany, such as *Touristeninformation*, *Fremdenverkehrsamt* or *Fremdenverkehrszentrale*. They provide information on opening

Above left Old-fashioned telephone booth **Above centre** Posters advertising events **Above right** Street vending machine for telephone cards

hours of monuments and museums, accommodation, organized excursions and city tours. They also sell or give away useful material about city attractions, such as guidebooks, maps and postcards and may be able to find and book a hotel room. The website of **German National Tourist Office** is also a useful source of travel information. Many cities also sell a Welcome Card, which allows the user 2–5 days free use of public transport and discounted access to museums.

Opening Hours
The opening hours of shops, offices and other businesses depend to a great extent on the size of the town. In larger cities, the usual office opening hours are Mon–Sat from 9am to 6pm. Supermarkets and other shops often have longer opening hours (mostly until 8pm). In smaller towns, however, nothing tends to open until 10am. Shops everywhere are usually closed on Sundays. Museums and historic monuments are also usually open from 9am to 6pm. However, some places might be closed on a particular day, often Monday, so check opening hours before arranging a visit.

Time
Germany uses Central European Time, which is GMT plus one hour. There is Daylight Saving Time between the end of March and the end of October, when the clocks move forward one hour on the last Sunday in March and back on the last Sunday in October.

Electricity
Germany's electrical system provides 220V, except in some hotel bathrooms, where a lower current is provided as a standard safety measure. UK 220V appliances can be plugged into German sockets with an adaptor. However, US 110V appliances will need a transformer.

Smoking in Public
Due to the federal system of government, the law on smoking in Germany varies from state to state. However, smoking is completely banned on public transport and in hospitals, airports, public and federal buildings, including the Parliament. However, there are differences between the German states when it comes to smoking in bars and restaurants. In some places, such as small pubs and bars, or during late hours, the ban is not observed at all.

DIRECTORY

COMMUNICATIONS
International Access Codes
Australia: 0061

Ireland: 00353

UK: 0044

US and Canada: 001

TOURIST INFORMATION
German National Tourist Office
*Beethovenstrasse 69; 60325 Frankfurt;
069 97 46 40; www.germany-tourism.de*

Below far left Information centre, Landshut, Bavaria **Below left** One of the many banks in Germany **Below centre** Notice board outside Reiskrater Museum, Nördlingen, Bavaria **Below centre right** Signpost along the road to Bad Harzburg, Lower Saxony **Below** Tourist information office in Würzburg, Bavaria

Driving in Germany

Driving is one of the best ways to explore Germany. The road conditions are among the best in the world and a well-developed network of Autobahns (motoways) and major roads allows access to almost every corner of the country. However, it is the scenic drives away from the urban centres, through Germany's beautiful landscapes that provide a unique experience. To make the most of your trip, it is best to know the basics of driving in Germany before setting off.

Above Driving along limestone cliffs, Altmuhl Valley, Bavaria

Insurance and Breakdown Cover

If you are travelling in your own vehicle, make sure that your insurance is valid in Germany, so that in the event of an accident, any damage will be covered. When renting a car, insurance is usually included in the rate. However, you should check the details of the rental company's policy. Most UK motoring services such as the **Automobile Association (AA)** and **Royal Automobile Club (RAC)**, offer insurance for assistance, breakdown and recovery in Germany. European breakdown and repatriation cover is also available with the **Allgemeiner Deutscher Automobil Club (ADAC)**.

What to Take

In order to drive in Germany, EU drivers must hold a valid driving licence and carry the registration documents and insurance policy for the vehicle. Driving licences from America and Australia are recognized in Germany. However, citizens of non-European countries should carry an International Driving Permit. Several agencies (www. drivers.com) are authorized to issue the permit, including the automobile association of the driver's home country.

Seat belts are compulsory in Germany, and there must be a warning triangle in the car, in case of a breakdown. Also, every registered vehicle must carry a first-aid kit that includes disposable surgical gloves and a thermal blanket. If you rent a car, make sure that such a kit is provided with the car.

Road Systems

Germany is famous for the Autobahn – a well-developed network of toll-free motorways. The prefix "A" on a blue sign indicates the Autobahn. Besides the motorways, there are well-maintained major roads (Bundesstrasse), which can be distinguished by the prefix "B"on a yellow sign.

Speed Limits and Fines

There is no specific speed limit for driving on the Autobahn, although many sections of it recommend a speed of 130 kph (81 mph). On major roads, the speed limit is 100 kph (62 mph), and inside a city and in built-up areas, it is 50 kph (31 mph). There are mobile speed cameras and radars (quite often at construction sites) and heavy fines may be imposed if you exceed these speed

limits. As a rule, the most severe fines, including the possible revoking of a driving licence, begin at exceeding 30 kph (19 mph) over the speed limit. Fines can also be incurred for tailgating and parking in prohibited areas. In both cases, your car hire company will bill you for any ticket that is sent to them, along with an administration fee.

Do not drink and drive. The law is stringent and penalties high. The legal limit is 0.5 mg, but if you are stopped for another traffic offence, the limit drops to 0.3 mg. The police can impose a fine on the spot. It is also illegal to use a mobile phone while driving. This also applies if the car is standing but the engine is running. If caught, drivers will be fined €60. However, bluetooth headsets are allowed.

Rules of the Road

Driving is on the right in Germany and seat belts must be worn at all times by the driver and all passengers, front seat and back. Knowing the general rules of the road is important. Be aware that overtaking other cars is only allowed in the left lane. Under no circumstances should you ever

Above left Deer and cow crossing sign **Above centre** Motorway to Limburg an der Lahn, Hesse **Above right** Sign for the Romantic Road, Southern Germany

overtake on the right lane. There is no sign indicating otherwise, but there is a strict *rechts vor links* rule, meaning that a car or any other vehicle coming from a street on your right has the right of way.

Germans usually drive very fast and quite aggressively. In the event of an accident on the motorway, or if a traffic jam necessitates an abrupt reduction in speed, drivers should turn on their flashing emergency lights to warn other drivers.

Distances are indicated in kilometres. Most road signs are internationally understood, though there are some signs which are specific to Germany. For example, on Autobahns, a yellow triangular warning sign with a row of cars indicates a possible traffic jam. On mountain roads, a sign showing a tyre wrapped in a chain, accompanied by the word *Schnee*, warns of difficult road conditions due to heavy snowfall requiring snow chains. A yellow sign with the word *Umleitung* indicates a diversion. A horizontal blue arrow with the word *Einbahnstrasse* refers to a one-way street. A special rule concerns the so-called Low Emission Zones or Green Zones implemented in 32

cities throughout the country. One is only allowed to access such a zone if the vehicle carries an Emissions Badge *(Umweltplakette)*. If entering a Green Zone with a vehicle that does not display such a badge, you could be fined €40. Visitors can obtain a sticker permitting entry into environmental (pollution-controlled) zones from car dealers, repair centres and garages in Germany. It can also be ordered online at *www.umweltplakette.de*

Buying Petrol

Germany has a good network of filling stations *(Tankstelle)*. Petrol *(Benzin)* and diesel are also widely available. Leaded petrol is no longer sold but you can purchase a lead substitute additive and add it to the fuel tank. Fuel in Germany is quite expensive. Prices can vary substantially and are among the highest in Europe. On smaller roads, and in more remote areas, it might sometimes take more time to find a petrol station, so make sure that you have enough fuel when travelling through less densely populated regions. Visit *www.benzinpreis.de* for the latest updates on fuel prices in Germany.

DIRECTORY

INSURANCE AND BREAKDOWN COVER

Automobile Association (AA)
0800 085 2721 (UK) or +33 825 09 88 76 (from abroad); www.theaa.com

Allgemeiner Deutscher Automobil Club (ADAC)
0185 101 112 (information); 01805 222 222 (breakdown service)

Royal Automobile Club (RAC)
+44 020 7930 2345; www. royalautomobileclub.co.uk

COMMON ROAD SIGNS

Anfang
Start

Ausfahrt
Exit

Gefahr
Danger

Halt
Stop

Steinschlag
Falling rocks

Zentrum
Town centre

Below far left Street sign indicating speed limit **Below left** Road along vineyards, near Nierstein, Rhineland-Palatinate **Below centre** Painted sign to a guesthouse **Below centre right** Road junction, Marburg, Hesse **Below** Winding road through Lower Saxony

Road Conditions

Most roads in Germany are well surfaced and usually well marked. However, the Bundesstrassen, or state roads, do vary in quality. In the north and west, and the touring areas of the Rhine Valley, Black Forest and Bavaria, the roads are well paved and in good condition.

The well-established network of motorways allows you to travel to most regions within a few hours. Regular maintenance work on the roads can generate problems, especially during the busy holiday season from July to mid-September. German-speaking drivers can listen to the radio for regular updates on the traffic situation or obtain information on traffic conditions by visiting the website www.verkehrsinfo.de

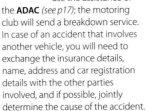

Parking and access road signs

Taking a Break

If you are feeling tired, or lost, it is a good idea to pull over and take a break. There are numerous sign-posted rest areas along motorways and major roads where you can park the car, stretch your legs and consult a map. Such places also often have clean public facilities. Motorways also have service stations at regular intervals, where you can stop for fuel and simple German food such as *Wiener Schnitzel* and *Currywurst*. On minor roads, and in remote areas, petrol stations may be few and far between.

The scenic landscape can sometimes be a distraction for drivers, so it is best to stop and admire the views. Parks and areas with nature trails also make good picnic stops.

Breakdown and Accident Procedures

If you have a problem on the Autobahn, you can use one of the yellow pillars with emergency buttons located along the road to call for help. In case of a breakdown or accident, move the car safely off the road, turn on hazard lights and put out a warning triangle; it is compulsory to carry one and use it. Car hire companies will normally supply a number to call in case of an emergency or problems with the vehicle. Usually they use the assistance of the **ADAC** *(see p17)*; the motoring club will send a breakdown service. In case of an accident that involves another vehicle, you will need to exchange the insurance details, name, address and car registration details with the other parties involved, and if possible, jointly determine the cause of the accident.

In the case of a serious accident, the police are quick to arrive at the scene and provide support. For minor accidents, the police do not always appear, but you can call the emergency number 112 to ask for assistance if you have problems with the other party involved in the accident. Circumstances can be confusing at the time of an accident, so do not admit fault, accept liability or give money to any party, which is illegal in Germany. If possible, take down details from any independent witnesses. It is also wise to take photographs of any damage to the vehicle, as well as the scene of the accident.

Parking

Lack of parking space can be a problem in cities. Using one of the multi-storey car parks *(Parkhaus)* is a convenient option, although they are expensive. A green or red sign in front of the car park will indicate whether there is an empty parking space. You pay for the number of hours that you park the car. Parking in city centres is often limited to 2 to 3 hours. Payment can be made with coins or (rarely) credit card to an automatic parking-ticket machine, which will issue receipts that are placed on the inside of the windscreen. There are also parking meters with a timer that allow parking for up to 2 hours. In many large cities, there are "Park and Ride" areas outside the centre. It is possible to park your car here to take advantage of the well-developed public transport system.

It is never worth leaving your car in a prohibited area – a traffic warden will impose a fine and

Left Typical yellow road sign indicating route and distance **Right** Slow-moving traffic in Pottenstein, Bavaria

arrange for the vehicle to be towed away. Retrieving an impounded car is expensive and difficult.

Maps

It is always helpful to have a map with you when driving through Germany. Free tourist maps are widely available but they are seldom useful for back roads driving. The best option is to buy an up-to-date road atlas that provides detailed maps of all regions of Germany. You can usually purchase road maps at petrol stations, bookshops and tourist information centres.

Caravans, Camper Vans and Motorhomes

Camping in Germany is a great way to experience the country and enjoy its green landscapes. Caravans and motorhomes (RVs) are subject to the same rules of the road as other vehicles. There are many well-maintained camp sites in the country that are ideal for a tour with a caravan, camper van or motorhome. These are generally open from April to September, although many are open year round.

Most camp sites accept the Camping Card International (CCI), a document that can be used as a form of identity and is accepted by many camp sites as security in lieu of a passport. Many camp sites also offer discounts on presentation of the CCI.

When driving a caravan outside cities, do not exceed speeds of 70 kph (43 mph) and 100 kph (62 mph) on motorways. The traffic police are strict about speeding, so be aware that you might have to pay a heavy fine if caught driving too fast. The websites of the **German National Tourist Office** and **Eurocampings** offers up-to-date information about most camp sites in Germany. It enables you to search for your desired camping location and gives detailed information about sites.

Transporting Bicycles, Roof Racks and Caravans

Bicycle carriers, roof racks and caravans must be strongly attached to the car. You can either fix the bicycle behind the vehicle or on top of the car. If you are using a roof rack, make sure that the weight of the items you want to transport is evenly distributed on the rack. As far as caravans are concerned, make sure that the items inside are properly secured so that nothing moves around in case of braking or defensive driving action.

DIRECTORY

CARAVANS, CAMPER VANS AND MOTORHOMES

Eurocampings
www.eurocampings.co.uk

German National Tourist Office
www.germany-tourism.co.uk

Below far left Driving through the town of Weilburg, Hesse **Below left** Transporting a bicycle on a car **Below centre** Camping sign near Pottenstein, Bavaria **Below centre right** Signpost to the walk around Blaubeuren, Baden-Württemberg **Below** Road patchwork on the isolated stretch to Havelberg, Saxony-Anhalt

Motorcycles

The drives presented in this guide are also ideal for a motorcycle trip. The well-maintained roads that crisscross Germany's countryside allow one to enjoy a feeling of freedom while discovering beautiful vistas. To rent a bike, get in touch with one of the major rental services well in advance as rental stations do not always have them available.

AdMo Tours is a national motorbike rental chain where motorcycles and dirt bikes can be booked for short periods. Several brands are available for hire, including BMW, Harley, Suzuki and many more.

It is mandatory for motorcyclists and passengers to wear protective helmets at all times. Drivers must have a valid driving licence to cover a motorcycle or moped, and an insurance policy.

The rules of the road are the same for motorcyclists as for other drivers, although you should take additional safety precautions. Go slow when filtering or driving between traffic lanes. Give other vehicles a wide berth when overtaking them, and be aware that they might not always see you. Motorcycles must have rear number plate lighting.

Driving with Children

Drivers must ensure that all passengers under the age of 14 wear seat belts or sit in an approved child restraint. Make sure that their seat belts are always fastened. This is not only obligatory by law but also important for their safety. Babies must never be placed in a rear-facing child seat in the passenger seat if there is an active airbag fitted, as it

can cause serious injury or death to the child in a crash. Children, under the age of 12, have to be seated in a special child car seat. In this case, it does not matter if the child is seated on the back seat or on the front seat. However, there is an exception to this rule for children who are shorter than 150 cm (93 inches). Children below this height have to sit in the back seat.

Remember to request any necessary child seats in advance when making your car hire booking.

Disabled Drivers

There are a number of parking concessions for disabled drivers in Germany. Visitors from non-EU countries who wish to apply for temporary parking permits should get in touch with the local council or the district authority. Germany's **Federal Ministry of Transport, Building and Urban Affairs** can advise travellers on this matter. Applicants have to provide a disability ID and a passport-sized photograph. Medical documentation regarding their disabled status might also be required. Parking for disabled drivers can be found in all public areas, indicated with a sign displaying a wheelchair.

Car and Camper Van Hire

Most of the big international car hire companies, such as **Budget**, **Avis**, **Sixt** and **Hertz**, have offices at airports, railway stations and more expensive hotels, and offer a wide range of vehicles. The ADAC, Germany's and Europe's largest automobile club, offers rental services for tourists who do not want to bring their own vehicle to

Above Motorcycles parked outside a café, Hollandische Viertel, Postdam, Brandenburg

Germany. You can call the ADAC service number *(see p17)* to find out how to arrange the booking.

To rent a vehicle, it is necessary to present a passport and a driving licence. Drivers must be over 18, however, check before you make your reservation regarding "age restrictions". It's recommended that you book in advance, especially during peak season – you will often get a better rate. Rental rates usually include unlimited mileage, but do double check. Consider renting a smaller car than you may be used to at home, as they are much easier to handle on narrow country roads than big SUVs. If you need a child seat, it should be booked in advance as well.

Third-party insurance is compulsory and is included in the rate. Some rental agreements also include Collision Damage Waiver (CDW), which limits your liability for damages to the rental car, theft loss cover and personal injury insurance; others charge additional fees for these items. Be sure to read your agreement carefully so that you fully understand what your coverage and liabilities are. Some drivers may be able to use insurance from a personal

Left Road gritter clearing snow from the road **Right** Taxis parked in the old town centre, Landshut, Bavaria

credit card to claim CDW, but check carefully with your credit card company beforehand to make sure they will cover your trip abroad, and be prepared to show proof of cover.

Driving in Winter

If driving through Germany during the winter, you should buy or rent chains (if there is heavy snow) or at least the essential winter tyres. From December to March, roads in mountain areas can be coated with snow and ice. Motorways are kept clear, but minor roads may be closed completely, and access to other roads may only be permitted for vehicles fitted with snow chains.

When hiring a car, make sure you get winter tyres along with the car, even though many companies offer just regular summer tyres. Note that car hire companies usually charge extra for snow chains. Make sure that the tyres are in good condition. In case of an accident, if the car does not have adequate tyres, the insurance cover may not remain valid. The maximum speed possible with snow chains is 50 kph (30 mph). In Germany, winter tyres are not mandatory, but on the spot fines can be imposed if the vehicle is not equipped for winter weather

conditions. In other words, fines can be levied for not enough windshield cleansing fluid or use of the wrong sort of tyres. Bring plenty of warm clothes, a blanket, food and water during winter travel in case of major delays on the Autobahn, or if travelling under hazardous conditions in mountainous areas. Always reduce your speed in adverse conditions, as you will need a longer braking distance, and poor visibility gives less time to react.

In high-altitude regions and mountainous areas, you may encounter ice and snow in winter. Slow down, especially for curves and turns, and keep your actions steady and deliberate to avoid sliding out of control. If the car skids, take your foot off the accelerator – do not brake – and turn the wheel into the skid until the car corrects itself. Watch out for ice, especially on bridges and overpasses, which freeze up first. If you hit a patch, do not brake or turn the wheel, but keep as straight as possible and coast over it.

When conditions reduce light levels, dipped headlights should be used. Turn on fog lights whenever visibility is less than 100 m (328 ft).

DIRECTORY

MOTORCYCLES
AdMo Tours
www.admo-tours.com

DISABLED DRIVERS
Federal Ministry of Transport, Building and Urban Affairs
+ 49 (030) 18 300 3060

CAR HIRE
Avis
01805 21 77 02; www.avis.de
Budget
01805 21 77 11; www.budget.de
Hertz
01805 33 35 35; www.hertz.de
Sixt
01805 25 25 25; www.sixt.de

Below far left Camper van parked on the road between Wildsteig and Rottenbuch, Bavaria **Below left** Motorcycles at Schloss Rheinsberg, Bradenburg **Below centre** Bicycle secured to a motorhome **Below centre right** Well-maintained road to Bad Harzburg, Lower Saxony **Below** Downtown shopping street in Neustadt an der Weinstrasse, Rhineland-Palatinate

Where to Stay

Germany, like many other countries, has numerous hotels converted from palaces, castles and other historic buildings. The range of prices for a night's accommodation is wide, and depends on the services offered and the location of the establishment. Lodgings can be particularly expensive in the centres of larger cities. However, smaller towns located in the tourist areas often have rooms to rent at reasonable rates. Set amid country landscapes, charming, family-run hotels offering comfortable rooms and local specialities reflect the unique character of Germany's back roads.

SCHLOSS HAIGERLOCH

Above Logo of Schloss Haigerloch, a luxurious three-star hotel, Baden-Württemberg, *see p232*

Hotels

Hotels in Germany are categorized according to the number of stars awarded for facilities, and not the standards of service. However, the star rating is no guide to the more subjective charms of a hotel, such as the style of decor or the kind of regional cuisine served. In larger cities, it is not difficult to find accommodation in deluxe hotels that are often part of an international chain. Away from the cities, high prices generally apply to rooms in comfortable hotels in beautiful locations or those provided within historic palaces or villas. There are many smaller hotels too, offering good, affordable lodgings. Often the name *Schlosshotel* indicates a hotel within a palace. Many of these hotels are members of organizations such as **Historic Hotels of Europe**, who can provide further information.

A hotel labelled *Garni* suggests that there is no restaurant on the premises, only a dining room where breakfast is served. *Apartmenthotels* offer suites with equipped kitchens or a kitchen annexe.

Guesthouses

Guesthouses *(Gasthof)* can be found throughout the country, usually located in private houses that function as traditional bed and breakfast places. Often labelled as *Pension* or *Hotelpension*, the distinction between a small hotel, a pension and a private B&B varies from region to region. Quite popular, they offer good value for money. Located in smaller towns and villages, they are cheaper than hotels; however, the standards of service and facilities offered are also lower. The rooms are usually cozy and comfortable, and equipped with TV and a bathroom. Guests can also expect a large German breakfast in most guesthouses.

Youth Hostels

Youth hostels *(Jugendherberge)* represent the cheapest option for a stay and can be located in almost every town as well as major tourist areas in Germany. Some are housed in very attractive historic buildings. While they offer cheap lodging, the standards are still surprisingly good.

Accommodation is usually provided in double or triple rooms, as well as in dormitories. In order to stay at a youth hostel, guests must carry a membership card of the Youth Hostels Association (YHA), which can be obtained from the association in their home country. Prices vary between €12 and €25 per day, depending on the choice of room and the region where the hostel is located.

Camping

Summer is the best time for a camping trip to Germany, as most camp sites close between November and March. These sites are well equipped, and usually have access to a shared kitchen, bathroom and laundry facilities, as well as refuse stations. Most offer power connections. Some also feature playgrounds and restaurants and organize sports activities. A lot of camp sites also have additional cabins apart from pitches for tents, motorhomes or caravans. Visitors should reserve a spot well in advance if visiting during the busy summer season, especially at popular destinations.

Left Four-poster bed in Burghotel auf Schönburg, Rhineland-Palatinate, *see p151* **Right** Oberhof resort close to Thuringian forest

Self-catering

Along the country roads, spectacular natural backdrops provide perfect settings for a picnic. Supermarkets are usually well stocked and offer all that travellers will need for an enjoyable outing, such as a great variety of food and camping crockery. Be sure to check the opening hours for supermarkets and convenience stores as very few are open at night or on Sundays, and almost none for 24 hours. Outdoor markets, often held on Saturdays or Wednesdays, are also a good place to pick up fresh produce that is easily transported.

Booking

Reservations for accommodations can be made directly with the hotel by telephone, Internet, letter or fax. Visitors can also contact the local tourist office and ask them to make the arrangements. The office can also provide information about rooms in private homes as well as advice on the availability of other accommodation options in the area. A written confirmation may be required to make a reservation, along with a credit card number. It is also best to inform the establishment concerned if arriving late or if delayed.

Facilities and Prices

With a wide range of accommodation on offer – from the basic to the luxurious – the facilities available generally reflect the price paid. Luxuries such as swimming pools and saunas are more often available in high-end hotels. For simple accommodation in beautiful surroundings, guesthouses are a good option. However, prices are also heavily influenced by other factors, such as the time of year.

In resort areas, prices are highest in summer, while in larger cities, spring and autumn are more expensive. Prices may also double if a city or region is hosting a special event. This is especially the case for commercial fairs and cultural festivals. In cities, hotels situated in the centre are particularly costly, as are establishments housed within historic palaces or charming villas. However, many hotels offer reductions at weekends.

Below far left Burg Stahleck alongside Rhine river, Bacharach, Rhineland-Palatinate, *see p152* **Below left** Camp site, Pottenstein, Bavaria **Below centre** Atlantic Hotel Sail City, Bremerhaven, Bremen, *see p36* **Below centre right** Village guesthouse, Blaubeuren, Baden-Württemberg **Below** Schloss Tangermünde, Saxony-Anhalt, *see p70*

DIRECTORY

ACCOMMODATION AND RESERVATIONS

Deutsche Zentrale für Tourismus
Beethovenstrasse 69, 60325 Frankfurt;
069 97 46 40;
www.deutschland-tourismus.de

Hotel Reservation Service (HRS)
Blaubach 32, 50676 Cologne;
0221 207 76 00;
www.hrs.com

Historic Hotels of Europe
www.historichotelsofeurope.com

YOUTH HOSTELS

Deutsches Jugendherbergswerk DJH Service GmbH
Bismarckstrasse 8, 32756 Detmold;
05231 740 10;
www.jugendherberge.de

CAMPING

Deutscher Camping Club e.V.
Mandlstrasse 28, 80802 Munich;
089 380 14 20;
www.camping-club.de

PRICE CATEGORIES

The following price bands are based on a standard double room in high season including tax and service:

Inexpensive – under €70
Moderate – €70–€150
Expensive – over €150

Where to Eat

Each region of Germany can be distinguished by its cuisine. Menus increasingly feature local produce and there are markets where one can stock up on gourmet delights. Many establishments specialize in regional fare, which although heavy, is appetizing. In addition, ethnic cuisine, notably Italian, Greek, Thai, Turkish, Chinese and Indian, is popular throughout the country and can be enjoyed even in smaller towns. Some fine restaurants run by master chefs serve European cuisine of the highest quality.

Butcher's sign listing items on sale

Practical Information

Most restaurants are open from noon but sometimes close for a break between 3 and 6pm, while cafés open from 9am. Many are closed for one day during the week. On Sundays, brunch is served in most places until 2pm. During the lunch period, between noon and 2pm, many establishments offer a fixed-price menu that is cheaper than in the evenings. Dinner is usually served from 7pm. Calling to make a reservation is recommended in popular city restaurants.

The cost of a meal depends on the location. While a three-course meal in some restaurants may cost €10, it will be more expensive in the downtown areas of larger cities. In more upscale restaurants, expect to pay up to €70. Alcoholic drinks can be quite costly, but beer, the national drink, is cheap. In general, the prices on a menu include service and tax, but it is common to leave a tip of around 10 per cent of the total bill. Restaurants usually take credit cards and display the logos of accepted cards at the entrance.

In most good restaurants, the menu is written in German and English, and sometimes also in French. In cafés and less expensive restaurants, the menu may be hand-written in German, in which case the staff may help with a translation.

Restaurants

The term *Restaurant* is used to define both upmarket restaurants offering fine cuisine at steep prices and popular local establishments serving affordable food. For regional cuisine, visit one of the many *Ratskellers* found in the cellars of old town halls all across Germany, which serve *Sauerkraut* (fermented shredded cabbage) and regional specialities at affordable prices.

They usually have atmospheric interiors that are well adapted to the vaulted, dark spaces of the historic cellars. *Weinstuben* (wine bars) or *Bierstuben* (beer bars) also offer great local food such as seasonal vegetables in a Hollandaise sauce or with dumplings, accompanied by local beverages. A *Gasthaus* refers to a rather simple restaurant serving good regional cuisine in a family atmosphere. Self-service venues offering snacks are known as *Imbiss*. These can vary from a stall serving baked sausages and cans of drink to kiosks with an

extensive choice of salads and fast food. These kiosks are often run by immigrants. In fact, in most large German towns, there are numerous kiosks serving Arabic, Turkish, Chinese and American food. For a sandwich or a healthy salad, visitors can also try the restaurants or cafeteria facilities in department stores, which are usually self-service.

Cafés and Bars

The term café has a number of connotations in Germany. Often, this is a place that offers good breakfast options in the morning and serves mostly international cuisine from noon onwards. Sometimes, a café will have a selection of cakes on display. In addition, at any time of the day and evening, customers can have coffee or ice cream. Many of these establishments turn into bars in the evening, when alcoholic drinks are served and live music is played.

A typical venue to have a drink in Germany is the *Kneipe*, which is best compared to an English pub in terms of its atmosphere. A wide range of alcoholic drinks is available here, and sometimes, loud music is played. The most commonly served beer is Pils, a bottom-fermented

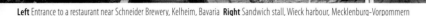

Left Entrance to a restaurant near Schneider Brewery, Kelheim, Bavaria **Right** Sandwich stall, Wieck harbour, Mecklenburg-Vorpommern

pilsner lager. Brown ales are also popular. Schwarzbier, a top-fermented brown ale, is increasingly popular, as is Weizenbier, a bitter top-fermented beer. A small number of dishes such as *Strammer Max* (a slice of toast covered with ham and fried egg) are usually offered and customers can often enjoy indoor games such as pool, darts or table football.

Local Markets

Lively markets are held at designated locations in the centres of towns and villages all across the country. Shopping at these markets is the best way to sample local flavours. A good introduction to the specialities of the region; they have lively atmosphere and offer a great choice of fresh, high-quality food. Farmers come to these markets to sell their fresh produce.

Many farmers also have shops on their farm, where they sell their goods. When driving through regions known for their agricultural produce, keep an eye out for fresh fruit and vegetables, honey, wine or even sausages on sale. Each driving tour notes the location and days of the week for markets around the region. Other great places to visit are

bakeries. A *Bäckerei* specializes in bread and rolls, while a *Konditorei* mainly makes pastries, cakes and sometimes chocolates. Germans make excellent breads, often organic, from various grains. Bread in Germany is of two kinds: rolls (*Brötchen*) and loaves (*Brot*). Delicatessens where one can find high-quality sausages, cheese, meat and fish are also worth a visit. Special deli counters can be also be found in major supermarkets. However, prices can be quite high here. All kinds of fresh meats and sausages can also be bought at butchers' shops (*Fleischern*), easily found in any city or town.

Picnics and Outdoor BBQs

There are many nice locations especially designated for picnics in Germany. These are usually situated in pleasant green areas and equipped with outdoor tables and litter bins. Most towns have a shop or a delicatessen where one can grab picnic supplies such as cold cuts, sliced cheeses, breads and salads. Traditional German potato salad and pasta dishes are often sold in convenient deli-style plastic containers for easy carrying on a road trip.

Below far left Atmospheric *Weinstube*, Würzburg, Bavaria **Below left** Cafés outside the Rathaus, Lübeck, Schleswig-Holstein **Below centre** Wine bar, Tüchersfeld, Bavaria **Below centre right** Roadside sausage stall, Rostock, Mecklenburg-Vorpommern **Below** Local market, Münsterplatz, Freiburg, Baden-Württemberg

The Flavours of Germany

Germany is home to a variety of cuisines, with significant differences in culinary traditions between its regions. However, the country is unified by its love of meat, bread, sausages and beer. Though traditional meals can be high in calories, a new generation of chefs is improvising German classics to create "nouvelle" dishes. Fresh produce can be found at the many farmers' markets and charming stores across the country and home-made breads and cheeses and locally caught fish are usually of a high standard.

Pilsner, the popular bottom-fermented lager

Northern Coast

Northern German food is meant to sustain fishermen during long, cold days, and to this end, is full of starches. The hardships of life in the northern coast are reflected in the hearty and filling cuisine of this region, much of which makes use of ocean fish such as halibut or plaice, or freshwater fish such as trout. The popularity of *Matjes*, salted herrings with cream and onions, served with baked potatoes, has spread from the northern cities to the rest of the country. Warming stews and soups, such as *Pichelsteiner Eintopf*, a one-pot dish with meat, potatoes and vegetables cooked in broth for the harsh winter months, are readily available as is potato salad, which is served hot or cold with chopped pickle relish or onions. Potatoes, often cooked with bacon, are by far the most popular side dish in the region.

Rhineland and Southwestern Germany

This part of Germany, with its wine-growing regions along the rivers Rhine, Mosel and Neckar, is known for its superb, often French-influenced, gourmet feasts. Swabian food is rich, traditional German cuisine. Pasta and bread feature largely in a Swabian meal including *Maultaschen*, large pasta parcels containing meat, cheese or vegetables served in soup or butter, or *Spätzle*, a type of pasta, which in Bavaria is made with beer instead of water. Swabian food is often referred to as "wet" food, since it is often drenched in sauce or melted butter. The Pfalz, a region of southwestern Germany, is famous for its *Pfälzer Saumagen*, sow's stomach filled with sausage, herbs and potatoes. The Franks, inhabitants of Franconia, part of Bavaria, produce perhaps the finest gingerbread in the country, as well as *Nürnberger Rostbratwürstchen* (small spicy roast sausages), and dishes using rare types of fish, such as sheatfish.

Saxony and Thuringia

Thüringer Bratwurst, a spicy roasted sausage served with mustard, originates from this east German region, as does *Sauerbraten*, roast beef marinated in vinegar. Meat is not the only option, however, as Thuringian food is heavily influenced by the wide variety of vegetables grown. Excellent asparagus, cabbage and cauliflower dishes are also served.

Saxony is widely known for its cakes, or *Stollen*; there are strict requirements which must be met for a cake to be considered an authentic *Dresdner Stollen*, including where it is made geographically. These cakes are usually served on or around Christmas. Another cake originating in Saxony is *Baumkuchen*, a multi-layered, pyramid-shaped cake covered in a chocolate glaze. Thuringia is more likely to offer *Bechkuchen* (sheet cakes), such as *Streusel-Kuchen*, a German crumb cake.

Bavaria

Much of southeastern Germany's cuisine is heavily influenced by Eastern Europe, as demonstrated by the goulash dishes and dumplings that regularly feature on the menu. *Knödel*, for example, are boiled dumplings made in a variety of ways with several types of filling, such as liver, onions, or egg; *Semmelknödel* are bread-based dumplings with onion and egg and *Leberknödel* are liver dumplings. Bavarian food, which the world identifies with Germany,

Above left Pretzels garnished with poppy seeds **Above centre** Wine shop on Cremerstrasse, Wetzlar, Hesse **Above right** *Spritzgebaeck*, chocolate-dipped biscuits

is filling and hearty; beer and pretzels, white sausages, *Sauerkraut* (dish made from fermented cabbage) and roast pork are fixtures of the traditional Bavarian menu. The *Weisswurst* (white sausage) has its origins in Munich, where several "rules" were made for its consumption, including not eating it after midnight.

Breads
Germany is home to an incredibly large variety of breads, including pretzels, *Laugenbrötchen* (salty sourdough rolls), *Semmel* (milk-dough rolls), *Berliner Landbrot* (mild rye breads), *Mehrkornbrotchen* (mixed grain rolls) and many more. Bakeries are ubiquitous, so freshly-baked bread and rolls are always available, and in many regions, such as Swabia, there's no meal without bread. German breakfasts consist mainly of different types of bread and toppings such as jam or cheese.

Beer
Beer is more than the most popular beverage in Germany – it is a way of life, with many regional specialities and locally produced brews available throughout the country. Bavaria, a major brewing centre, is home to brands that are known the world

over for quality and taste, such as Beck's, Löwenbräu and Bitburger. Brown ales are popular, particularly in the south, but the most commonly drunk beer is Pils, a bottom-fermented lager.

Wine
Germany is renowned for its delicious white wines, particularly those made from the Riesling grape. Among the most highly prized are those from the Rheingau region. Lovers of red wine can try Assmannshausen Spätburgunder, produced from the Pinot Noir grape. German wines are largely categorized into three groups according to their quality: the lowest is *Tafelwein*, then *Qualitätswein* and the highest is *Qualitätswein mit Prädikat*. The term *Trocken* indicates a dry wine, *Halbtrocken*, semi-dry and *Suss*, the sweet variety. Excellent sparkling wines known as Sekt, are also produced in Germany.

Below far left Tourist market, Lübbenau, Brandenburg **Below left** Traditional beer wagon, Ettal, Bavaria **Below centre** Allgau cheese factory, Immenstadt, Bavaria **Below centre right** Grape vines, Reichenau, Baden-Württemberg **Below** Typical German loaves, Bavaria

ON THE MENU

Backhendl
Roast chicken

Bratwurst
Grilled sausage

Currywurst
Sausage served with tomato ketchup and curry powder

Eis
Ice cream

Forelle
Trout

Eisbein
Boiled pigs' trotter

Käsekuchen
Cheesecake

Kuchen
Cake

Rindfleisch
Beef

Salat
Salad

Schinken
Ham

Suppe
Soup

Vorspeise
Starter

Wiener Schnitzel
Thin cutlet in breadcrumbs

Wurstsalat
Sausage salad

Oldenborch • Mol. • Beuezenborg • Neustat • Furstberg
Lunenborg • Elbis A. • Domic • Parleberg • Wistock • MARCA • Ang
Bremen • Dannenberg • Wilsenack • Gransoe • Nest
Caselingen • Delm: ehorst • Verden • Vlczen • Osterborg • Sehusen • Nawen • Bocow • Pernow
Cloppen borch • Wil: ehuse • Alden • Zeel • Soltwedel • Warpen • Hauelberg • Ratenaw • Berlin • Mo.
Hoi • Aller A. • Burgdorf • Garleben • Tanger • mund • Spadaw • Kopenick • Belicz
Quakenbrugge • Nienborg • Lein A. • Brau nswijg • Stendel • Elbis • NO • Brandeborg • Luben
Witlag • Minden • Hanofer • Helmstat • Magdeborg • Zerbst • VA • Luca
ALIA • Osen brug • Engern • Heru ord • Hildesheim • Halberstat • SAXO • Wittenberg • LVZA
Tecklen borg • Bilfelt • Lemgow • Hamelen • Bokelem • Goslar • NI • Schlieben • Hertz
Rauensburg • Brakel • Boden werd • Gandersheim • Stalberg • Eisleben • Hall • A. • Finsterwald
Lippe • Palborn • Huren • Nort hufen • Dibe • Leypzig • Torga • Cami
la Geiko • Nort heim • Sunderhusen • Saltzquele • Sul fl. • Strelin • Meißen
ndorn • HAS • Warborg • Gottingen • TVRING • Weis • Dres
Waldeck • Ferster • Munden • sefels • Grim • Pir
Dreis • Cassel • Cappel • Grutzberg • Erffurt • Nawburg • MISNIA • emitz
Marpurg • Homburg • Spange berg • Gotha • IA. • Iena • Alden borg • Zuckaw • Shneberg
Dullemberg • Cronberg • Hirsfeld • Vach • Isenach • Weida • Anneberg
nach • Wielmust • Giessen • SIA. • Aursperch • Ilmenaw • Salfeld • Plawen • Iochimstal • Laun
Weilburg • Buzbach • Fuld • Eiffelt • Solburk • Hock • Olsnicz
Boppart • Gelnhausen • Neustat • Coburg • Staffelstein • Eger • Elebogen • Rolicz: an. R.
S Guer • Fridberg • Hamelburg • Schwein furt • Hasfurt • Deutschen • Sacz • Pilser
Wesel • Ments • Gemund • Culmbach • Reid • Dachaun • BO
Oppehe: • Franc fort • Neust • Hasfurt • Bamberg • Benaw • Tamdo • Neu
Creutz: at • Geraw • Wert • Wirtzburg • Potenstain • Weiden • Taindo • Su
nach • Darstat • heim • Haslach • Forchaim • Wald munche • Glatti
Wor mbs • Miltenburg • Rotingen • Kitzing • CO • Hersbruk • Naburg • Chamb • Koczing
Heidelberg • AN • Onsbach • Nurenberg • Am berg • Neuburg • Lengenfelt
Speir • Wimpfen • FR • Rotenburg • NIA. • Straubinge • Teckendo
andaw • Neccar fl • Hall • Guntzen hausen • Kelheim • rf
Rhei: • Aschberg • Canstat • Dinken: spuhel • Weißen burg • Newmarck • Regensburg • Vilshouen
zab ern. • Pfortzen • Stukgart • Eslingen • Norlin gen • Aichstet • Meck mul • Eckefeld • Scherdi
Wildbat • WIRTEN • Tu: • Geppingen • Ingolstat • Neustat • Meienburg • Otingen • Brunau
Strasburg • BERG • bingen • Blauburen • Donaw fl. • Isereck • Landshut • Ried
Offenburg • Rotenburg • Vlm • SVE • Burgaw • Kindfelt • Frifingen • BA
Rinow • Dornheim • Babling • V • Zusmar • Augs • Dachaun • Arding • Burck hufen
Retwijl • Riedlin • Biberach • hufen • purg • Munchen • Waßer • Freberg
Brisach • ge • Ochsenhusen • IA. • Delcz • burg • VA
Friburg • Grefin gen • Vberin: gen • Memmingen • Lands • Carls • Ail • Rosen • Salczburg • Ruct
Badenwiler • Schafhusen • berg • berg • bling • haim • Reichenh • Werb
Basel • Vsna • Kempte • Fuße • Weil • Au • Rickz: • Bischo
Lauffen berg • Costen • Lindau • Ereuberg • hen • Kopfstein • Schwacz • buhel • S. Vit

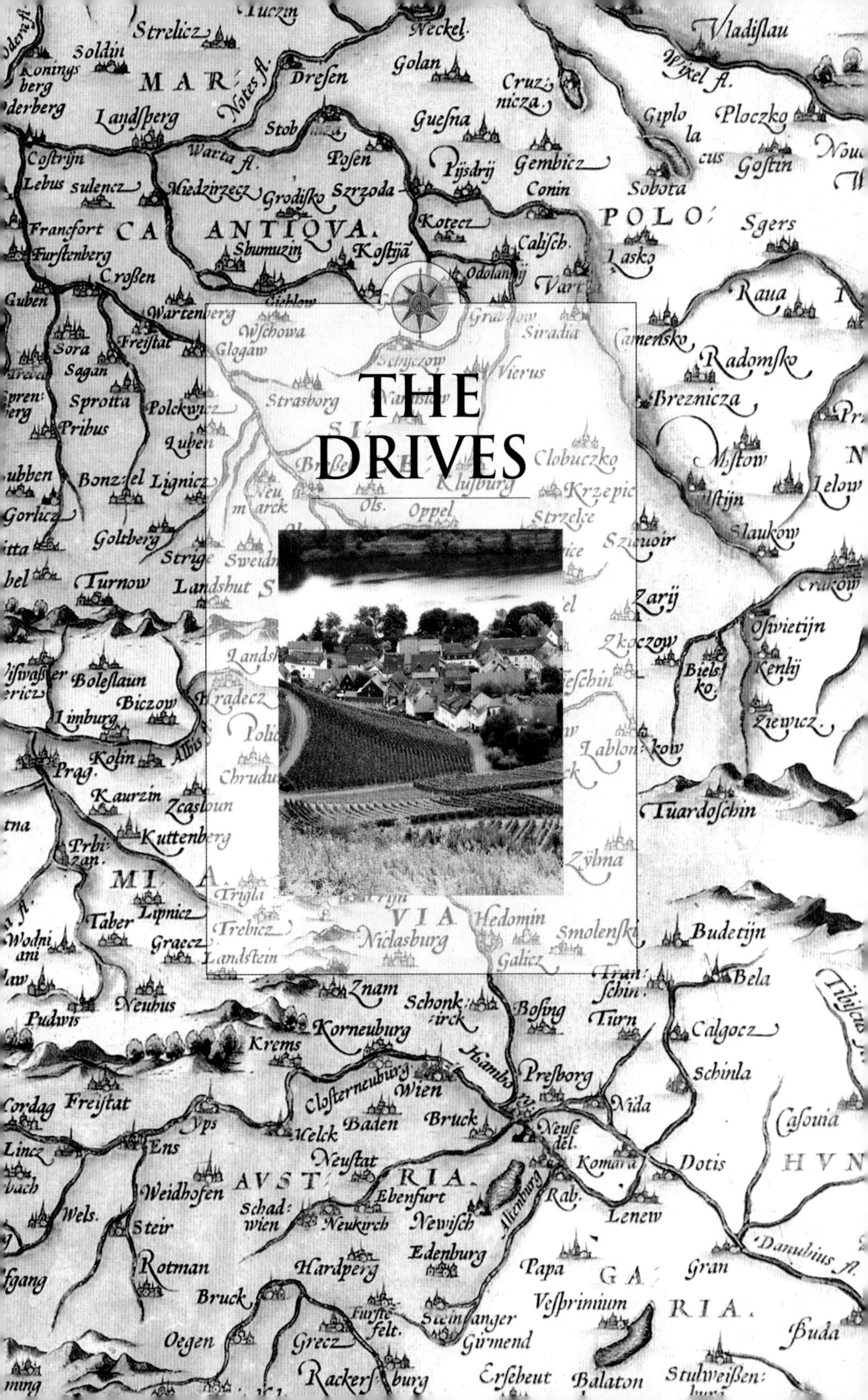
Strelicz
Neckel.
Vladislau
Soldin
Konings berg
MAR
Notes fl.
Dresen
Golan
Cruz nicza.
Wixel fl.
derberg
Landsperg
Stob
Guesna
Giplo la cus
Ploczko
Costrijn
Warta fl.
Posen
Pijsdrij
Gembicz
Gostin
Lebus
sulencz
Miedzirzecz
Grodisko
Szrzoda
Conin
Sobota
Francfort
CA
ANTIQVA.
Kotecz
POLO
Sgers
Furstenberg
Sbumuzin
Kostijn
Calisch.
Lasko
Crossen
Odolanij
Vart
Guben
Wartenberg
Raua
Wschowa
Siradia
Camensko
Sora
Freistat
Glogaw
Vierus
Radomsko
Sagan
Sprotta
Polckwicz
Strasborg
Breznicza
Pribus
Luben
Clobuczko
Mstow
Bonzel
Lignicz
Brsle
Klusburg
Lelow
Krzepic
Gorlicz
Neu marck
Ols.
Oppel
Strzelce
Goltberg
Strige
Sweidn
Szieuoir
Slaukow
Turnow
Landshut
Zarij
Landsh
Zkoczow
Oswietijn
Boleslaun
Hradecz
Teschin
Bielsko.
Kenlij
Biczow
Limburg
Ziewicz.
Kolin
Albis
Polic
Lablonkow
Prag.
Chrudu
Kaurzin
Zcaslaun
Tuardoschin
Kuttenberg
Prbizan.
Zylma
MI
A
Trigla
Taber
Lipnicz
VIA
Hedomin
Wodniani
Trebicz
Smolenski
Budetijn
Graecz
Niclasburg
Landstein
Galicz
Bela
Transchin.
Znam
Pudwis
Neuhus
Schonkirck
Bosing
Turn
Calgocz
Korneuburg
Krems
Hamb
Presborg
Schinla
Closterneuburg
Wien
Cordag
Freistat
Nida
Yps
Baden
Bruck
Casouia
Melck
Neuse del.
Lincz
Ens
Neustat
Komara
Dotis
HVN
AVST
RIA.
bach
Weidhofen
Schad wien
Ebenfurt
Alienburg
Rab.
Lenew
Wels.
Steir
Neukirch
Newisch
Edenburg
Danubius fl.
Rotman
Hardperg
Papa
GA
Gran
fgang
Bruck
Furste felt.
Steinanger
Vesprimium
RIA.
Oegen
Grecz
Girmend
Buda
Rackersburg
Ersebeut
Balaton
Stulweissen

THE DRIVES

Dramatic North Sea Coast

Lüneburg to East Frisia & the East Frisian Islands

Highlights

- **Architectural splendour**
  Take a walk in the once-rich Hanseatic city of Lüneburg, with its charming churches and houses

- **Flowering orchards**
  Enjoy the scenic Altes Land, one of the most beautiful fruit-growing regions in Europe, when the cherry and apple trees are in full bloom

- **Lively medieval city**
  Visit the market square of Bremen, with its stunning Renaissance town hall and the Roland statue, both of which are UNESCO World Heritage Sites

- **Island adventures**
  Explore the remote and pristine landscape and beaches of the East Frisian Islands

View across East Frisia to Norderney, one of the Frisian Islands

Dramatic North Sea Coast

The sweeping, green marshy lowlands of northern Germany form the backdrop to this picturesque drive. Beginning at Lüneburg, the route traverses the state of Lower Saxony (Niedersachsen) to Germany's far northwest, East Frisia (Ostfriesland). It continues through scenic villages set in fields of heather and orchard blossoms in the Altes Land (Old Land) to reach some outstanding medieval city centres such as the one in the Hanseatic city of Bremen, whose grand Gothic and Renaissance landmarks are reminders of its remarkable former wealth. The drive also explores fascinating natural landscapes such as the North Sea tideland nature reserve and the East Frisian barrier Islands (Ostfriesische Inseln).

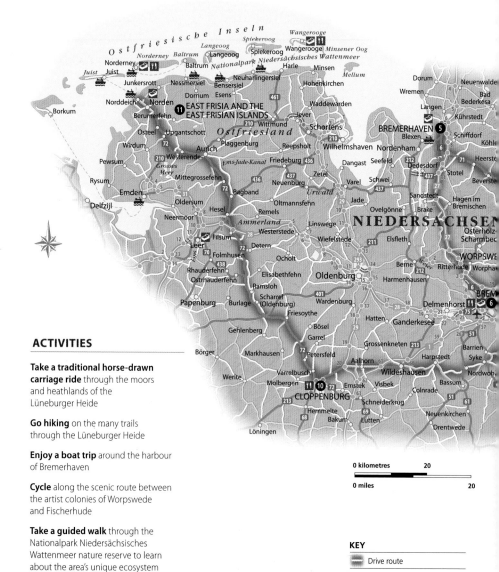

ACTIVITIES

Take a traditional horse-drawn carriage ride through the moors and heathlands of the Lüneburger Heide

Go hiking on the many trails through the Lüneburger Heide

Enjoy a boat trip around the harbour of Bremerhaven

Cycle along the scenic route between the artist colonies of Worpswede and Fischerhude

Take a guided walk through the Nationalpark Niedersächsisches Wattenmeer nature reserve to learn about the area's unique ecosystem

0 kilometres   20

0 miles   20

KEY

▨ Drive route

Above Tranquil landscape on the way to the East Frisian Islands, *see p39*

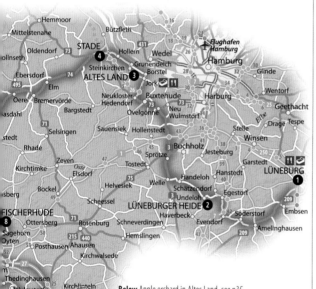

PLAN YOUR DRIVE

Start/finish: Lüneburg to East Frisia and the East Frisian Islands.

Number of days: 3–4 days, allowing half a day to explore Bremen.

Distance: 500 km (311 miles).

Road conditions: All roads along this drive are in very good condition.

When to go: For warm and dry weather, the best time to visit this region is between late May and mid-August. It is particularly lovely in late April when cherry and apple orchards blossom.

Opening times: Most shops and attractions are open from 9am to 6pm, Monday to Friday.

Main market days: Lüneburg: Wed & Sat; Bremen: Mon–Fri; Verden an der Aller: Tue & Fri.

Shopping: Lüneburg's historic old town, an area with limited vehicular traffic, is ideal for shopping. Bremen's malls, such as the Lloyd Passagen and the Domshof Passagen, offer a good range of stores for shoppers.

Major festivals: Lüneburg: Lüneburger Sülfmeistertage (medieval festival), Oct; Bremen: Breminale (cultural festival), Jun; Freimarkt (general fair), Oct.

Below Apple orchard in Altes Land, *see p35*

DAY TRIP OPTIONS

Spend a day on a family visit to the city of Lüneburg for a **walking tour** through the historic city centre or take a horse-drawn carriage ride through the nearby Lüneburger Heide. Art enthusiasts can visit the **artist colonies** of Worpswede and Fischerhude, with their marvellous **art museums**, before visiting the Deutsches Schifffahrtsmuseum and the Deutsches Auswandererhaus in Bremerhaven. **Nature lovers** can experience a full day of **marsh walks** and **beach life** in the Nationalpark Niedersächsisches Wattenmeer on one of the lovely East Frisian Islands. For full details, *see p39*.

Right Lush apple orchards in Jork, Altes Land
Below left Stately Rathaus on Am Markt,
Lüneburg **Below right** Outdoor cafés in Stade

VISITING LÜNEBURG

Parking
The most convenient car parks are at
the train station and the Rathaus.

Tourist Information
*Rathaus, Am Markt, 21335; 04131 207
66 22; www.lueneburg.de*

WHERE TO STAY

LÜNEBURG

Bergström *moderate*
This four-star hotel offers comfortable
rooms. Facilities include a pool and a
gym. Pets are allowed.
*Bei der Lüner Mühle, 21335; 04131 30 80;
www.bergstroem.de*

Bremer Hof *moderate*
A perfect starting point for sightseeing,
this hotel serves
traditional as well as innovative dishes
from northern Germany.
*Lüner Strasse 12–13, 21335; 04131
22 40; www.bremer-hof.de*

ALTES LAND

Altes Land *moderate*
The attractive Altes Land combines
village charm with modern comforts.
Its restaurant features regional cuisine.
*Schützenhofstrasse 16, 21635 Jork;
04162 914 60; www.hotel-altes-land.de*

STADE

Parkhotel Stader Hof *moderate*
Built in 1990, this well-known first-class
hotel has 100 rooms and 6 suites.
*Schiffertorsstrasse 8, 21682; 04141
49 90; www.parkhotel-staderhof.de*

Zur Hanse *moderate*
Surrounded by mansions, this private
hotel provides modern and
comfortable rooms.
*Am Burggraben 4, 21680; 04141 952 40;
www.altstadt-hotel-stade.de*

① Lüneburg
Lower Saxony; 21335
This former salt-mining hub and
Hanseatic city was once one of
the richest in Germany. Lüneburg's
past wealth is evident in the
splendid gables that line the streets
of its old town. One of the city's
three Gothic churches, the
Johanniskirche, has a 108-m (354-ft)
high brick steeple that leans more
than 2 m (6 ft) from the perpen-
dicular. Built between 1300 and
1370 and restored in 1420, it is
considered a major example of
north German brick architecture.
  The city's most important
monument is the **Rathaus** *(closed
Mon)*, located in Am Markt. This town
hall, parts of which date back to
the 13th century, is one of the most
architecturally interesting town
halls in northern Germany. Its council
chamber features Renaissance
woodwork by 16th-century artist
Albert von Soest, and the **Museum
im Rathaus** holds a remarkable
collection of municipal silverware.
To the left of the town hall, the
Schroederstrasse is lined with
good restaurants, cafés and bars.
Stroll on Ilmenaustrasse, which
runs past the old port on the Ilmenau

river. On Lüner Strasse stands the
Altes Kaufhaus, a former herring
warehouse with a superb Baroque
façade. This striking building was
formerly used to load salt on to
ships. A walk across the historic
heart of the city leads to
Michaeliskirche, with its beautiful
basilica, consecrated in 1409.
  🚗 *From Lüneburg take the B209
towards Amelinghausen, then
follow the road to Soderstorf. Take
Schulstrasse towards Evendorf and
then Evendorf Dorfstrasse to Egestorf,
then get on to Schätzendorfer Strasse
in the direction of Hanstedt. In
Schätzendorf, turn left to Undeloh.*

② Lüneburger Heide
Lower Saxony; 21274
Situated south of Hamburg,
between the Elbe and Aller rivers,
the Lüneburger Heide is a remote,
enticing heathland and nature reserve.
The half-stepped terrain also serves
as grazing land for a special breed of
sheep, the Heidschnucken. Starting
at the pretty village of **Undeloh**, this
area can easily be explored on foot,
by bike or horse-drawn carriage
(Mühlenstrasse 2, Bispingen; 05194 830).
The highlight is the traditional village
of **Wilsede**, whose tranquil scenery

🚗 *From Jork, continue driving to Borstel then turn left to Grunendeich. Follow Mittelnkirchen to Steinkirchen and carry on to Hollern. Follow the river and take Altländer Strasse to Stade.*

❹ Stade

Lower Saxony; 21680
A medieval Hanseatic town located to the west of Hamburg, Stade has retained most of its characteristic half-timbered buildings, the most attractive of which can be found along the old harbour, **Alter Hafen**. Located in a granary built during the time of the Swedish occupation in the 17th century, **Schwedenspeicher-Museum** *(closed Mon)* houses exhibits on the history of the town. Nearby, a building at Am Wasser West 7 displays the **Kaufmann Collection** *(closed Mon)*, comprising works of artists from Worpswede *(see p38)*. Other attractions are the **Bürgermeister-Hintze-Haus** at Am Wasser West 23 and the **Rathaus**, both of which date from the 17th century. Stade also has its share of grand churches such as the 14th-century Gothic **St Wilhadi** *(closed Sun)* and the 17th-century **St Cosmas und Damian** *(closed Sun)*.

🚗 *Take the B74 and continue past Elm. Turn right on to the B71 to Bremervörde passing Heerstedt to reach the A27. Cross the A27 to get on to Weserstrasse to reach Bremen's deep-water harbour, Bremerhaven.*

Baroque portal, Rathaus, Stade

and quaint houses set among trees is a reminder of its bucolic past. Not far from here is the **Wilseder Berg**, the highest point of the moraine region, which offers a panoramic view of the countryside.

🚗 *From Undeloh, head to Handeloh. Continue on Handeloher Strasse to Welle. Turn right on to the B3 and cross the A1. Continue on this road then turn left on to the B73 and pass Neukloster Hedendorf. Turn right on Jorker Strasse to Jork.*

❸ Altes Land

Hamburg; 21635
The flat floodplains of the **Altes Land** along the banks of the lower Elbe teem with cherry and apple orchards. The area is particularly lovely between April and May when the trees are in bloom and the whole countryside turns into an ocean of white and pink. In the midst of these natural surroundings, charming red-brick houses with thatched roofs and decorated gables await the visitor. There are a number of villages to be discovered, such as **Neuenfelde**, **Borstel**, **Steinkirchen**, **Hollern** and **Jork**, with many Baroque churches that are worth visiting. The unofficial capital of the Altes Land, Jork offers some delightful restaurants. Neuenfelde attracts visitors with its pretty rose gardens; another draw is the historic windmill of Hollern-Twielenfleth.

Left Half-timbered houses along the Alter Hafen, Stade **Below** Moorlands covered in heather, Lüneburger Heide

---

EAT AND DRINK

LÜNEBURG

Elrado-House *moderate*
Situated in the heart of Lüneburg, off the market square, this homely steakhouse is the ideal place at which to dine after a walking tour. Enjoy good food in a friendly, rustic setting. *Am Markt 4, 21335; 04131 39 04 03; www.elrado-house.de*

Mama Rosa *moderate*
This Italian restaurant is both a trattoria and a gourmet food-and-wine store. Visitors can enjoy a light breakfast in the morning, lunch in the sun and drink a cappuccino in the afternoon or a glass of wine in the evening with Italian antipasto and a selection of home-made pasta dishes. *Bei der Abtsmühle 1, 21335; 04131 30 83 07; www.mama-rosa-lueneburg.de*

Zum Heidkrug *expensive*
The menu at this well-known gourmet restaurant, changes according to the season and the creative ideas of its Michelin-starred chef. *Am Berge 5, 21335; 04131 241 60; www.zum-heidkrug.de; closed Sun & Mon*

ALTES LAND

Die Mühle Jork *moderate–expensive*
The chefs at this upmarket restaurant offer culinary twists, such as pork fillets with pear, and red wine and butter ice cream. The home-made cakes and pies are a treat. *Am Elbdeich 1, 21635 Jork-Borstel; 04162 63 95; closed Tue & Jan*

STADE

Barbarossa *expensive*
This cozy restaurant in an old townhouse is located next to the harbour, so the seafood, such as freshly harvested oysters from Sylt Island, is particularly good. The cuisine is excellent, as are the wines. *Salzstrasse 25, 21682; 04141 28 84; www.barbarossa-stade.de; closed Sun*

Knechthausen *expensive*
Savour home-made pasta, antipasto, meat and fish dishes and delightful desserts in the Knechthausen's peaceful ambience. It has a superb wine selection, too. *Bungenstr 20–22, 21682; 04141 453 00; www.knechthausen-stade.de; closed Sun*

Eat and Drink: inexpensive, under €20; moderate, €20–€40; expensive, over €40

⑤ Bremerhaven
Bremen; 27501

Bremen's harbour, Bremerhaven, is worth visiting for its museums. Designed by renowned architect Hans Scharoun, the **Deutsches Schiffahrtsmuseum** *(Nov–mid-Mar: closed Mon; mid-Mar–end Oct: open daily)*, or the German Maritime Museum, includes an open-air museum and a harbour museum. This site features both originals and models of a wide range of ships. The most attractive exhibit here is the *Seute Deern*, the last great German sailing ship. The **Deutsches Auswandererhaus**, a museum, recounts the German emigrant experience of the 19th century with costumed models and replicas of the cabins and family histories written in the travellers' own words. ⌂ *Return to the B6, which meets the A27. Continue on the A27, then turn right on the B6 to reach Bremen.*

⑥ Bremen
Bremen; 21895

A prosperous city on the Weser river with a colourful 1,200-year history, Bremen is Germany's oldest port still in use today. The magnificent town hall and the grand old statue of Roland, both on the market square, represent its main tourist attractions and are listed as UNESCO World Heritage Sites.

Above Statue of Roland in the Marktplatz, Bremen **Below right** Atlantic Hotel Sail City, Bremerhaven **Below far right** Fishing boat in Bremerhaven

VISITING BREMEN

Parking
Parking is available at Parkhaus Pressehaus on Langenstrasse.

Tourist Information
Hauptbahnhof, 28195; 0421 30 800 10; www.bremen-tourismus.de

WHERE TO STAY

BREMERHAVEN

Atlantic Hotel Sail City *expensive*
Housed in a magnificent building on the waterfront, this hotel offers exceptional comfort and good service at fair prices.
Am Strom 1, 27568; 0471 30 99 00; www.atlantic-hotels.de

BREMEN

Ringhotel Munte am Stadtwald *moderate*
This traditional family hotel with its spacious spa and indoor pool is ideal for relaxation. The hotel has two restaurants – Wels, which offers gourmet fish and game dishes, and Del Bosco that serves Italian cuisine.
Parkallee 299, 28213; 0421 220 20; www.hotel-munte.de

Park Hotel Bremen *expensive*
A member of the Leading Hotels of the World, the luxurious Park Hotel lives up to high standards with its 177 individually styled rooms and suites.
Im Bürgerpark, 28209; 0421 340 80; www.park-hotel-bremen.de

A two-hour walking tour

Exit the car park and continue on Langenstrasse, then turn left on Am Markt to the **Marktplatz** ①, the heart of the city. The town hall, the cathedral and the Roland statue dominate this impressive square. The statue of Roland, a knight of Charlemagne who is considered the city's protector, was erected in 1404. Roland's sword of justice symbolizes the judiciary's independence, and its engraved motto confirms the emperor's edict conferring town rights on Bremen. The second monument on the square is the statue of the Bremen Town Musicians, famous protagonists of a Grimm fairy tale.

Statue of the Bremen Town Musicians

Constructed in 1953, local legend has it that touching the front hooves of the donkey will make wishes come true. From here, turn right on to Am Dom to visit the Gothic town hall, the **Rathaus** ② *(daily guided tours)*. Built between 1405 and 1410, the edifice has a Renaissance façade that dates to the early 17th century. Inside the great hall, a lovely fresco from 1932 portrays Solomon's court. Walk along Am Dom to the 11th-century **Dom** ③ *(open daily)*, which stands nearby. The façade of this Romanesque cathedral features two spires. Inside are historic treasures such as the stone bas-reliefs dividing the western choir stalls. In the second eastern chapel,

Above left Street musicians in the seaport city of Bremen **Above right** View of Bremen and the Weser river

visitors can see the oldest Bremen sculpture of *Christ the Omnipotent*, dating back to 1050. Return along Am Dom and turn left on to Am Markt to the Mannerist **Schütting** ④, a former meeting place for merchants, with a Renaissance façade. Head south and walk along Am Markt, which becomes **Böttcherstrasse** ⑤. This lively street was transformed into a Gothic-cum-Art Nouveau fantasy in the 1920s by artists commissioned by the coffee magnate Ludwig Roselius. Don't miss the golden bas-relief at the entrance to the street. There are also attractions such as the Paula-Modersohn-Becker art museum. Return to the Rathaus and walk along Am Dom, turn right on to Balgebrückstrasse, left on to Dechanatstrasse and then turn right to reach the **Schnoorviertel** ⑥, located in the eastern quarter of the city centre. A historic area with many houses dating from between the 15th and 18th centuries, this district boasts a collection of art galleries and restaurants. Continue on this road, which becomes Stavendamm, turn right on to Tiefer, which becomes Martinistrasse, to return to the car park.

🚗 **Cross the A27 and get on to Hauptstrasse, which becomes Falkenberger Landstrasse. Turn left on to Worphauser Landstrasse in the direction of Worphausen. Continue on this road, which becomes Ostendorfer Strasse. Turn left on Hemberg Strasse to Worpswede.**

Bremen Town Musicians

A famous fairy tale, the *Bremen Town Musicians* was written by the Brothers Grimm. In the story, a donkey, a dog, a cat and a rooster leave their farms when their owners decide to kill them. They meet by coincidence and decide to travel to Bremen, a town known for its free-spirited society, to make a living as musicians. On the way, they encounter some robbers in a cottage and frighten them away with their disharmonious music. The robbers abandon the cottage and the animals live there forever.

EAT AND DRINK IN BREMEN

Port Speicher XI *moderate*
The Speicher XI offers home-style cooking. Visitors can enjoy pizzas, pastas and a huge selection of drinks. The harbour museum is just next door.
Am Speicher XI 1, 28217; 0421 61 94 10; www.port-speicherxl.de

Meierei *expensive*
This restaurant serves mainly Mediterranean cuisine and offers a great selection of mostly Italian wines. In summer, visitors can dine on the terrace.
Im Bürgerpark, 28209; 0421 340 86 19; www.meierei-bremen.de; closed Mon

Restaurant Luv *expensive*
Traditional cooking is given a creative twist in this restaurant – the seafood is highly recommended. Diners can also sit outside by the promenade along the Weser river.
Schlachte 15–18, 28195; 0421 165 55 99; www.restaurant-luv.de

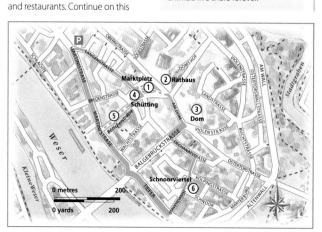

Eat and Drink: inexpensive, under €20; moderate, €20–€40; expensive, over €40

Above left Village cottage with a thatched roof, Elisabethfehn Above right Verden an der Aller town centre Below Norderney, one of the many East Frisian Islands

CYCLING IN WORPSWEDE

Rent a bike *(Fahrradladen Worpswede; www.fahrrad-eyl.de)* and enjoy exploring the quaint village of Worpswede.

WHERE TO STAY IN EAST FRISIA AND THE EAST FRISIAN ISLANDS

Haus Norderney *moderate*
A modern B&B, offering 10 individually decorated rooms.
Janusstrasse 6, 26548 Norderney; 04932 22 88; www.hotel-haus-norderney.de

Ostfriesenhof *moderate*
This first-class hotel has wonderful views of the East Frisian landscape.
Groninger Strasse 109, 26789 Leer; 0491 609 10; www.ostfriesen-hof.de

Villa im Park *expensive*
This four-star hotel in a villa offers single or double rooms, 8 suites and 9 apartments, all with extra-long beds.
Dorfplatz 16, 26486 Wangerooge; 04469 870 80; www.vip-wangerooge.de

7 Worpswede
Lower Saxony; 27726
Situated northeast of Bremen, the small village of Worpswede is a must-see for art lovers. A number of famous painters, notably Fritz Mackensen, Otto Modersohn, Hans am Ende, Fritz Overbeck and Heinrich Vogeler, lived here from 1889 until the end of World War II. The greatest of them all was perhaps Paula Modersohn-Becker, one of the most important exponents of early Expressionism. The **Grosse Kunstschau** and the **Worpsweder Kunsthalle** *(closed Mon)*, where the work of the founding members of the colony is displayed, are worth a visit. Most of the paintings on display highlight the scenic beauty of northern Germany, showing moorland, birch trees and marshlands under wide open skies. Visiting poets such as Bohemian-Austrian Rainer Maria Rilke helped establish the legendary reputation of this hamlet. Even today, many painters live in Worpswede, and the village is proud of its cultural scene.

🚗 *Take the Kirchdamm to Grasberg and then the Speckmannstasse to Fischerhude.*

8 Fischerhude
Lower Saxony; 27726
Another attraction for art lovers is nearby Fischerhude, which nestles in the Wümme river lowlands, surrounded by waterways and drainage canals that frame the captivating meadows and fertile fields. With its idyllic farmhouses, many of which are centuries old, this village leaves the visitor with a distinct impression of the region's lifestyle as it was hundreds of years ago. At the end of the 19th century, Fischerhude also became an important cultural colony, attracting artists such as Heinrich Breling, the landscape painter Otto Modersohn, the sculptor Clara Rilke-Westhoff and the author Diedrich Speckmann.

🚗 *Leave Fischerhude following signs to Sagehorn and then on to Oyten. Take the A1 towards Bremen, then the A27 southeastwards, and then Hamburger Strasse to Verden an der Aller.*

9 Verden an der Aller
Lower Saxony; 27238
The town of Verden an der Aller is known for its attractive churches, such as the **Johanniskirche**, the **Andreaskirche**, and the Lutheran cathedral, the **Dom**, all of which adorn the town centre. The cathedral's hall features a multi-sided presbytery and a passageway dating from between 1268 and 1311. The town's horse riding and racing tradition is honoured in the **Deutsches Pferdemuseum** *(closed Mon)*, which features a vast collection of equestrian artifacts. North of the cathedral, the Domherrenhaus

Where to Stay: inexpensive, under €70; moderate, €70–€150; expensive, over €150

houses the **Historisches Museum** *(closed Mon)*, which displays exhibits on the town's history.

🚗 *Take the minor road to Syke via Thedinghausen. Follow signs to Nordwohlde, turning right to Harpstedt. Drive to Wildeshausen and take the B213 to Cloppenburg. Follow signs to the Museumsdorf.*

⑩ Cloppenburg

Lower Saxony; 49661

The market town of Cloppenburg is famous for its interesting open-air museum, **Museumsdorf** *(open daily)*, a re-creation of a medieval village. Attractions include half-timbered houses, windmills and a small 17th-century church. Also worth a visit are the megalithic graves of **Visbek** *(04445 89 00 35; www.visbek.de)* to the east of Cloppenburg, which date from 3,500 to 1,800 BC. The main attraction is the 80-m (263-ft) grave known as Visbeker Bräutigam (Visbek groom) and the 100-m (321-ft) Visbeker Braut (bride).

🚗 *Take the B72 and drive through Aurich to join B210, then turn left, taking B72 following signs to Norden. Here, several ports serve as the springboard to the Frisian Islands.*

⑪ East Frisia and the East Frisian Islands

Lower Saxony; 26506

With its unique landscape and lovely beaches, East Frisia is a perfect place to end a tour of northern Germany. Meadows dotted with windmills characterize the countryside. Along the North Sea Coast extends the belt of several East Frisian Islands: Norderney, Baltrum, Langeoog, Spiekeroog and Wangerooge. All around them is the **Nationalpark Niedersächsisches Wattenmeer**, listed as a UNESCO World Heritage Site. A popular excursion here is the "Watt Walk" to the wetlands that are formed when mud is deposited by tides. This tour by local experts *(Ostfriesland Tourism; Ledastrasse 10, 26789 Leer; www.ostfriesland-tourism. com)* includes an introduction to the unique ecosystem. Tours on horse-drawn carriages are also a delightful way to explore this nature reserve. The **Moor und Fehnmuseum** *(Apr–Oct: open Tue–Sun)* in Elisabethfehn, south-east of the town of Leer, is also worth a visit. The museum is dedicated to the extraction of peat and exhibits the world's largest plough.

Above Mudflats at low tide, East Frisia **Below** Exhibits in the Grosse Kunstschau, Worpswede

EAT AND DRINK

VERDEN AN DER ALLER

Pades *expensive*
Enjoy French, Italian and regional food in an old townhouse or in its backyard. *Grüne Strasse 15, 27283; 04231 30 60; www.pades.de; closed Mon*

CLOPPENBURG

Margaux *moderate*
This pleasant restaurant in Hotel Schäfer offers top-class German cuisine in a relaxed ambience. *Lange Strasse 66, 49661; 04471 24 84; www.schaefers-hotel-cloppenburg.de; closed Mon & Tue*

EAST FRISIA AND THE EAST FRISIAN ISLANDS

Kruse *moderate*
A congenial restaurant, Kruse offers a great variety of high-quality local fish. *Anna Strasse 15–17, 26486 Wangerooge; 04469 14 14; www.fischrestaurant-kruse.de*

Weisse Düne *moderate*
The Weisse Düne serves typical island specialities such as marinated crabs with home-made dip and pickled *Matjes* herring; *Wiener Schnitzel* (veal coated in breadcrumbs) is also available. *Weisse Düne 1, 26548 Norderney; 04932 93 57 17; www.weisseduene.com*

DAY TRIP OPTIONS

Centrally-located Bremen is a good base for day trips along this route.

A day in Lüneburg
Visit historic Lüneburg ①, then take a horse-drawn carriage tour through Lüneburger Heide ②.

From Bremen take the A1 in the direction of Hamburg and then the A250 to

Lüneburg. Follow signs from Lüneburg.

History beckons
Visit the art museums in Worpswede ⑦ and Fischerhude ⑧ and enjoy exploring these scenic villages. Next, stop at Bremerhaven ⑤ to take a tour of its museums .

From Bremen take the A27 to Ritterhude. Follow instructions to Worpswede and

Fischerhude. Bremerhaven can be reached via the A27.

Island life
Spend a day relaxing at the beaches of the East Frisian Islands ⑪.

From Bremen take the A28 and B27 to Norden-Norddeich where the coastal road leads to the different ports with access to the East Frisian Islands.

Eat and Drink: inexpensive, under €20; moderate, €20–€40; expensive, over €40

Wonders of Schleswig-Holstein
Wedel to Husum

Highlights

- **Ancient seaport city**
  Admire the unique red-brick Gothic architecture of Lübeck, once home to German writer Thomas Mann

- **Little Switzerland**
  Explore the moraine hills of Holsteinische Schweiz, dotted with scenic lakes and quaint villages

- **Sailor's paradise**
  Visit the historic naval city of Kiel, which hosts the Kieler Woche, the largest maritime festival in northern Europe

- **Pristine beaches and spas**
  Enjoy the white sand beaches and superb spas at Germany's popular resort-island, Sylt

Sandy beach in the pretty village-resort of Kampen, Sylt

Wonders of Schleswig-Holstein

Situated between the Baltic and the North seas and bordered by the Elbe river and Denmark, Schleswig-Holstein is the northernmost state in Germany. A predominantly maritime region, it offers endless white sand beaches and impressive lakes. The stops along this route include a visit to the historic old town of Lübeck, an architectural gem and a UNESCO World Heritage Site, and to the lovely lakes around Plön. The drive traverses pretty, tree-lined country roads through a largely agricultural region, where the pace of life is more relaxed, pausing at the charming towns of Holstein's Switzerland. The trip also weaves in a visit to the city of Kiel, which hosts the annual Kieler Woche, the biggest maritime festival in northern Europe.

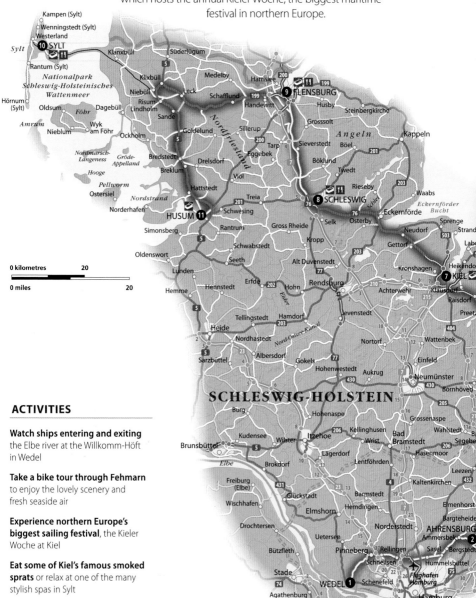

ACTIVITIES

Watch ships entering and exiting the Elbe river at the Willkomm-Höft in Wedel

Take a bike tour through Fehmarn to enjoy the lovely scenery and fresh seaside air

Experience northern Europe's biggest sailing festival, the Kieler Woche at Kiel

Eat some of Kiel's famous smoked sprats or relax at one of the many stylish spas in Sylt

Above Glorious countryside of Holsteinische Schweiz, *see p46*

KEY

Drive route

PLAN YOUR DRIVE

Start/finish: Wedel to Husum.

Number of days: 3 days, allowing a day to explore Lübeck.

Distance: 524 km (326 miles).

Road conditions: The roads in this region are in good condition.

When to go: The drive is best enjoyed between May and September.

Opening times: Most shops and attractions are open from 9am to 6pm, Monday to Friday.

Main market days: Lübeck: Mon & Thu; Kiel & Flensburg: Wed & Sat.

Shopping: Marzipan, a popular sweet, is a must-buy from the Café Niederegger located in Lübeck's charming old town.

Major festivals: Kiel: Kieler Woche (Kiel week), Jun; Travemünder Woche, (sailing race and cultural festival), Jul; **Sylt**: Kampener Literatur-und Musiksommer, (literature and music festival), Jul–Aug.

DAY TRIP OPTIONS

Those interested in **history** can head to Flensburg and then enjoy beach life at Sylt. Visit the town of Lübeck and stop at Fehmarn to admire its **scenic beauty**. For full details, *see p47*.

Below left Seventeenth-century Schloss in Eutin, Holsteinische Schweiz, *see p46* **Below right** Scenic island of Fehmarn on the Baltic sea, *see p45*

VISITING LÜBECK

Parking
Parkhaus Mitte, in the centre of the town, is the best spot for parking.

Tourist Information
Welcome Center; Holstentorplatz 1, 23552; 045188 997 00; www.luebeck-tourism.de; open daily

WHERE TO STAY

LÜBECK

Ringhotel Jensen *moderate*
One of the oldest hotels in the old town, this family-run place has individually designed rooms with modern facilities. *An der Obertrave 4–5, 23552; 0451 70 24 90; www.hotel-jensen.de*

Radisson Blu Hotel Lübeck *expensive*
The modern Radisson Blu has all the amenities of an upmarket business hotel. Its homely interior has a distinctive maritime touch. The hotel also offers an indoor pool and a fine German restaurant. *Willy-Brandt-Allee 6, 23554; 0451 14 20; www.senatorhotel.de*

FEHMARN

Die Strandburg *moderate*
This well-equipped four-star hotel has upmarket holiday apartments in different sizes. *In der Strandburg, 23769; 04371 86 96 66; www.strandburg.com*

IFA Fehmarn *moderate*
A three-star hotel with a beachfront complex and 422 apartments. It also offers wellness and spa services. *Burg, Südstrandpromenade 23769; 04371 890; www.ifa-fehmarn-hotel.com*

Above Old mill beside a pond in the town of Ahrensburg **Below** Picturesque old town and canal in Lübeck

❶ Wedel
Schleswig-Holstein; 22880

Situated on the Elbe river's right bank, Wedel was once an important cattle market. A reminder of this is the **Roland of Wedel** monument that stands in the Marktplatz as a symbol of market law. The town's main attraction is the **Willkomm-Höft** (welcome point) on the Elbe. Vessels arriving here have been traditionally greeted with flag signals since 1952, while the national anthem of the country of origin of the ship is played.

🚗 *Take Pinneberger Strasse to Pinneberg. Head to Schnellsen via Rellingen. Take the B432, then B433 to Hummelsbuttel. Get on to Poppenbutteler Weg. Take Saseler Damm/Saseler Chaussee to Ahrensburg.*

❷ Ahrensburg
Schleswig-Holstein; 22926

Located in the Tunneltal, Ahrensburg is part of the Hamburg metropolitan area. The town's highlight is the Renaissance **Schloss Ahrensburg** *(Mar–Oct: closed Mon & Fri; Nov–Feb: open Wed, Sat & Sun)*, which dates back to 1595. The building has four prominent corner towers and luxurious interiors.

🚗 *Head to the A1, cross it to reach Stubben then get on to Labenz. Take Klein Kinkrade then Hauptstrasse to Sierksrade. Take the B208 to Ratzeburg.*

❸ Ratzeburg
Schleswig-Holstein; 23909

Ratzeburg is situated on an island in the Grosser Ratzeburger See. In 1143, Heinrich der Löwe (Henry the Lion) became the ruler of the town and was responsible for the construction of the Romanesque **Dom** *(May–Sep: open daily; Oct–Apr: closed Mon)*. An early example of brick architecture, the cathedral features decorative elements in the southern vestibule.

🚗 *Return to Harmsdorf and continue on the B207 to Lübeck.*

Statue in the town of Ratzeburg

---

❹ Lübeck
Schleswig-Holstein; 23552

By the end of the Middle Ages, Lübeck had become one of the richest and most powerful Hanseatic towns in Europe. Today, it is renowned for its unique *Backsteingotik* (north German Gothic brick architecture) and seven towers. The town was also home to Nobel Laureate Thomas Mann, one of the most famous figures in the German literary world.

A two-hour walking tour
Exiting the car park at the end of Wallstrasse, turn right on to Holstenstrasse to the **Holstentor** ①, or Holsten gate. Based on Flemish designs, the gate was built by Hinrich Helmstede at the end of the 15th century. Continue on Holstenstrasse to the 14th-century **Petrikirche** ② *(closed Mon)*, or Church of St Peter, Lübeck's only five-naved church. Turn left into Schlusselbuden to visit **Marienkirche** ③ *(open daily)*, which houses great art treasures. From here, turn left into Mengstrasse to the **Schabbelhaus** ④, a charming patrician house with stepped gables. Return to Schlusselbuden and continue along Mengstrasse to the Gothic **Buddenbrookhaus** ⑤ *(open daily)*,

once the home of Thomas Mann. It now houses a museum dedicated to the Mann family. Next, turn right on to Breite Strasse to the 13th-century **Rathaus** ⑥ *(open Mon–Sat, guided tours)*, Germany's most famous brick town hall. Return along Breite Strasse to the 15th-century **Jakobikirche** ⑦, a Baroque church on the right. Turn right into Koberg then left into Grosse Burgstrasse to the **Burgtor** ⑧, an ancient gate that bears testimony to the town's historic fortifications. Return to Grosse Burgstrasse to the **Heiligen-Geist-Hospital** ⑨, a Gothic brick building, notorious for its spiky towers. Continue into Konigsstrasse, turn left on to Mühlenstrasse, then right on to Dankwartsgrube, and left again into Pferdemarkt for the **Herz-Jesu-Kirche** ⑩, on the right. This 19th-century church houses a memorial to four clergymen who were executed during the Third Reich for resisting the Nazi regime. Across the parade square stands the **Dom** ⑪ *(open daily)*, built in the 12th and 13th century. Highlights include a triumphal cross sculpted from an oak tree. Get on to St Annen-Strasse to visit **Kunsthalle St-Annen** ⑫, or St Anne's Museum *(open daily)*, which is housed in an Augustinian convent. Return to Kohlmarkt turning left on Holstenstrasse for the car park.

🚗 *Take the A1 to Ratekau and then past Neustadt to take the B501 to Heiligenhafen. Then turn on to the B207 to Fehmarn.*

Thomas Mann

Thomas Mann, one of Germany's most influential writers, was awarded the Nobel Prize for literature for his works *Buddenbrooks* and *Der Zauberberg* (The Magic Mountain) in 1929. An anti-fascist, Mann emigrated to Switzerland in 1933 and to the US in 1939. Disowned by his country, he became the leading voice of *Exilliteratur*, the exiled German literature that was outlawed by the Nazi regime.

❺ Fehmarn
Schleswig-Holstein; 23769

This Baltic Coast island is renowned for its serene beaches, pristine landscape and some 2,200 hours of sun per year. The best way to explore Fehmarn is on foot or a bike. Visitors can also relax at one of several wellness spas *(www.inselwellness-fehmarn.de)* or play golf on one of the prettiest golf courses in Germany. The biggest village is **Burg auf Fehmarn**, home to the **St Nikolai Kirche**, or St Nikolai church. To the southwest of the island stands the 37-m (121-ft) tall lighthouse **Flügge**, which offers panoramic views of the island.

🚗 *Take the B207 then the A1 to Oldenburg. Turn on to the B202 to Lütjenburg then the B430 to the town of Plön, in Holsteinische Schweiz.*

Above left Tranquil shore of the island of Fehmarn **Above right** Cycling on a narrow road in Fehmarn

BIKING IN FEHMARN

Bikes can be rented at **Conny's** *(Breite Strasse 46; 04371 13 03; www.fehmarn-fahrrad.de)*. Visitors can also get maps at the **tourist office** *(Sudstrand-Promenade 1; www.fehmarn.de)*.

EAT AND DRINK

RATZEBURG

Der Seehof *moderate*
This charming family-owned restaurant and hotel offers international and regional dishes.
Lüneburger Damm 1–3, 23909; 04541 86 01 01; www.der-seehof.de

LÜBECK

Schiffergesellschaft *expensive*
Located in a beautiful historic building, this popular restaurant serves great beer and seafood. Book in advance.
Breitestrasse 2, 23552; 0451 767 76; www.schiffergesellschaft.com

Wullenwever *expensive*
One of the best restaurants in town, the Wullenwever serves local cuisine, with Mediterranean and maritime influences.
Beckergrube 71, 23552; 0451 70 43 33; www.wullenwever.de; closed Sun & Mon

FEHMARN

Aalkate Lemkenhafen *moderate*
Housed in a historic building from the 18th century, this restaurant offers eel specialities. These and other fish are smoked according to old local recipes and best enjoyed with a North German draft beer.
Königstrasse 20, 23769; 04372 532; www.aalkate-original-fehmarn.de; closed Jan & Feb

Restaurant Altes Zollhaus *moderate*
A simple restaurant serving typical regional seafood dishes, often featuring freshly caught fish.
Westermarkelsdof 11, 23769; 04372 991 635; www.zollhaus-fehmarn.de; closed Sun & Mon

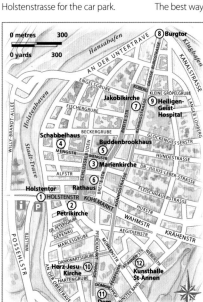

Eat and Drink: inexpensive, under €20; moderate, €20–€40; expensive, over €40

Right Nord-Ostsee-Kanal, Kiel **Below** Port of Flensburg

WHERE TO STAY

AROUND HOLSTEINISCHE SCHWEIZ

Restaurant Hotel Stolz *moderate*
Located in a historic building, this hotel offers superb views.
Markt 24, 24306 Plön; 04522 503 20; www.hotel-restaurant-stolz.de

KIEL

Hotel Kieler Yachtclub *expensive*
With views over the Kieler Förde, this hotel offers 21 rooms and suites.
Hindenburgufer 70, 24105; 0431 881 30; www.hotel-kyc.de

SCHLESWIG

Ringhotel Strandhalle Schleswig *moderate*
A modern hotel with harbour views.
Strandweg 2, 24837; 04621 90 90; www.hotel-strandhalle.de

FLENSBURG

Hotel Flensburger Hof *moderate*
This hotel provides comfortable rooms.
Süderhofenden 38, 24937; 0461 707 16 70; www.flensburgerhof.de

SYLT

Dorint Söl'ring Hof *expensive*
Enjoy romantic views over the sea at this thatch-roofed resort.
Am Sandwall 1, 25980; 04651 83 62 00; www.soelring-hof.de

HUSUM

Romantik-Hotel Altes Gymnasium *expensive*
A country hotel with a wellness area.
Süderstrasse 2-10, 25813; 04841 83 30; www.altes-gymnasium.de

⑥ Holsteinische Schweiz
Schleswig-Holstein; 24301

The area's low moraine hills, which reach a height of 164 m (538 ft), and 140 lakes are the reasons why this area is known as Holstein's Switzerland. The best way to explore this region is on a bike tour. The main centre of this holiday area is **Plön** on the Grosser Plöner See or Lake Plön. **Preetz**, an old shoemakers' town and **Bosau**, home to a Romanesque church, are nearby. Visit the town of **Eutin**, referred to as the "Weimar of the North" because of its pretty buildings. Eutin's brick **schloss** contains Rococo stuccowork and paintings by German artist Johann Heinrich Wilhelm Tischbein (1751–1828), which were inspired by the *Iliad* and the *Odyssey*, epic poems written by Homer.

🚗 *Take the B76 to Kiel. To reach the beach resort of Laboe, follow the B502 to the north.*

⑦ Kiel
Schleswig-Holstein; 24103

Schleswig-Holstein's capital Kiel marks the beginning of the **Nord-Ostsee-Kanal**, or Kiel Canal, which was built at the end of the 19th century to connect the Baltic Sea and the North Sea. Germany's main submarine base during World War II, this town is now known for its beautiful coastline of tiny beaches and inlets. Every summer, the town attracts yachtsmen for the famous **Kieler Woche** or Kiel Week *(www.kieler-woche.de)*. A walk along the Schweden-Kai embankment leads to the **Nikolaikirche**, which has a Gothic altar, and to the **Rathaus** or town hall. About 6 km (4 miles) from the town is the **Schleswig-Holsteinisches Freilichtmuseum** *(Apr–Oct: open daily; Nov–Mar: open Sun)*, an open-air museum with exhibits on German rural architecture. Around 18 km (11 miles) from Kiel is the beach resort of Laboe. Visit the **U-Boot Museum**, which tells the history of Germany's feared submarine fleet in World War II.

🚗 *From Kiel, take the B76 to Eckernförde and on to Schleswig.*

⑧ Schleswig
Schleswig-Holstein; 24837

A principal seat of the Vikings, Schleswig became a bishopric as early as 947. The town's main attraction is **Schloss Gottorf** *(Apr–Oct: open daily; Nov–Mar: closed Mon)*, which served as the residence of the dukes of Schleswig-Holstein from 1544 to 1713. This castle houses a regional museum, **Schleswig-Holsteinisches Landesmuseum**, and the **Archäologisches Landesmuseum**.

Where to Stay: inexpensive, under €70; moderate, €70–€150; expensive, over €150

Also visit the **Dom** *(open daily)*, which displays the Bordesholmer altar, a masterpiece of Gothic carving. Stroll around the fishermen's district of **Holm** and visit the **Viking Museum Haithabu** *(Apr–Oct: open daily; closed in winter)*, which sheds light on the days when the Vikings used Schleswig as their headquarters.

🚗 *Take the B76, which becomes Bundesstrasse and then Schleswiger Strasse to Flensburg.*

⑨ Flensburg
Schleswig-Holstein; 24901
Germany's northernmost town, Flensburg was an important trading centre in the 16th century. The town's trademark northern gate, the **Nordertor**, dates from 1595. Visitors can explore the fascinating **Schiffahrtsmuseum** *(closed Mon)* or maritime museum. The town is home to four outstanding churches – the **Marienkirche** features a Renaissance altar; nearby **Heilig-Geist-Kirche**, or Church of the Holy Ghost, belongs to the town's Danish community; the **Nikolaikirche** houses an amazing Renaissance organ and the **Johanniskirche** has a superb painted ceiling. About 9 km (6 miles) from the town centre stands the

historic 16th-century **Schloss Glücksburg** *(May–Oct: open daily; Nov–Apr: open Sat & Sun)* with massive corner towers. West of the town is **Seebüll**, where Expressionist painter Emil Nolde (1867–1956) lived and worked.

🚗 *Continue on the B199 to reach Niebull. Take the car-train Niebull-Westerland to reach the island of Sylt.*

⑩ Sylt
Schleswig-Holstein; 25980
The North Frisian Islands lie scattered in the North Sea 6 km (4 miles) off Schleswig-Holstein. Sylt, the largest island is 40-km (25-mile) long. Known for its posh villas, vibrant nightlife and Michelin-starred restaurants its highlights include sandy beaches, red cliffs and the "Watt", the expanse of mudflats in **Nationalpark Schleswig-Holsteinisches Wattenmeer**. Relax at one of Sylt's many spas *(Arosa Sylt; www.resort.a-rosa.de; Budersand; www.budersand.de)* before visiting **Westerland**, the main town. Stroll down Friedrichstrasse to a seafood restaurant, or take a detour to visit the neighbouring **Kampen**, an affluent resort. Also explore the nearby **Amrum** and **Helgoland**, Germany's only deep-sea islands.

🚗 *Take a car train from Westerland to Niebüll then take the B5 to Husum.*

⑪ Husum
Schleswig-Holstein; 25813
A medieval seaport with a colourful North Sea harbour, Husum has a delightful old town. The town's central market square is filled with charming 17th- and 18th-century buildings. Husum was home to the German poet and writer Theodor Storm (1817–88) whose residence **Theodor Storm Haus** *(Apr–Oct: open daily; Nov–Mar: open Tue, Thu, Sat)* now houses a small museum that displays exhibits related to the author's life.

Above Red cliffs in Kampen, Sylt **Below** Sandy beach in Kampen, Sylt

DAY TRIP OPTIONS
A great range of day trips is possible along this route.

Museum and beaches
Head to Flensburg ⑨ to tour its maritime museum, then continue on to Sylt ⑩ to laze on its sandy

beaches before heading to one of the upmarket restaurants for dinner.

Continue on the B199 to Niebüll. Take the Niebüll-Westerland car-train to Sylt.

Culture and landscape
Visit Lübeck ④ to admire its rich

architectural heritage. Next, stop at Fehmarn ⑤ to enjoy the spectacular views of the coast before relaxing at one of the town's several wellness spas.

Take the A1 and then the B501 to Heiligenhafen and the B207 to Fehmarn.

Eat and Drink: inexpensive, under €20; moderate, €20–€40; expensive, over €40

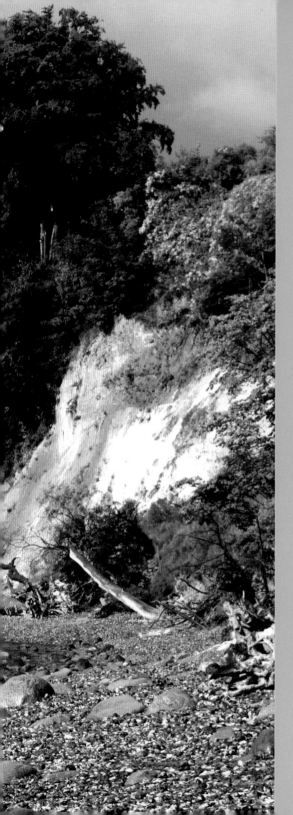

The Baltic Coast

Bad Doberan to Usedom

Highlights

- **Historic Gothic port**
  Explore Stralsund, a UNESCO World Heritage Site, where gorgeous medieval architecture forms a backdrop to everyday life

- **Leisurely beach life**
  Relax in a wicker *Strandkörb*, found on powdery white sand beaches throughout the region

- **Island playground**
  Escape to Rügen, a beautiful island that boasts *belle époque* villas, steam trains and chalk cliffs

- **Gourmet delights**
  Savour fresh fish at the harbour, served smoked straight from the boat, at Greifswald

White chalk cliffs at the Nationalpark Jasmund, Rügen

The Baltic Coast

Decorative Gothic brickwork in cozy old towns, beautiful beaches with their distinctive *Strandkörbe* (wicker chairs) and restaurants serving fresh fish are what make the Baltic Coast a popular holiday destination for Germans, even though it is yet to be discovered by foreign visitors. Going eastwards along the coastline and to the islands of Rügen and Usedom, this tour takes drivers through unspoiled scenery. The route starts inland in the spa town of Bad Doberan, then goes through Stralsund and Greifswald, ports of the medieval Hanseatic League. The tour also takes visitors to the *belle époque* resorts of the Kaisers on the islands of Rügen and Usedom and through former fishing villages on the Fischland peninsula, now transformed into fashionable resorts.

ACTIVITIES

Take a historic steam train to the seaside resort of Kühlungsborn from Bad Doberan

Browse for art in the ateliers of Ahrenshoop on the Fischland Peninsula

Walk under the Baltic Sea through glass tunnels at the Ozeaneum in Stralsund

Take a boat trip along the north coast from Göhren to Sassnitz

Stroll along white chalk cliffs above a sparkling jade-coloured sea at the Königstuhl on Rügen

See where the space race began in the Historisch-technisches Informationszentum at Usedom

KEY

Drive route

Above Lighthouse along the coast, Rügen, *see pp54–5*

PLAN YOUR DRIVE

Start/finish: Bad Doberan to Usedom.

Number of days: 5–6 days, allowing one day to explore Rügen.

Distance: 456 km (283 miles).

Road conditions: There are excellent single lane and dual-carriageway B-roads, except on Rügen, which has some short cobbled stretches.

When to go: The best time to visit for a beach holiday is between June and early September, though Rügen and Usedom can get busy between July and August. Christmas and New Year is the high season for visitors.

Opening times: Most shops are open from 9am to 5pm, Monday to Friday. Other attractions can be visited from 9am to 5pm, Tuesday to Sunday; they are generally closed on Mondays.

Main market days: Rostock: daily; Stralsund: Tue & Fri; Greifswald: Tue–Fri.

Major festivals: Warnemünde: Warnemünder Woche Regatta (boat races), 1st two weeks of Jul; Hanse Sail (maritime festival), 1st or 2nd weekend of Aug; **Stralsund:** Wallensteintage (folk festival), 3rd weekend of Jul; **Rügen:** Störtebeker Festspiele (theatre festival), Jun–Sep.

DAY TRIP OPTIONS

Culture lovers can stay in Bad Doberan to visit the graceful Münster. **Nature enthusiasts** can drive to Rostock and its **beach resort**, Warnemünde, a **chic art village** and a **bird-watcher's treat**. Families may prefer historic Stralsund, with its **fine beaches**, and a drive to the island of Rügen and the **charming town** of Greifswald. For full details, *see p57*.

Above Universitätplatz lined with colourful buildings, Rostock **Below left** Gothic Rathaus in Stralsund **Below right** Cistercian Gothic Münster in Bad Doberan

BAD DOBERAN TRAIN RIDE

The Mecklenburgische Bäderbahn Molli runs from Alexandrinenplatz terminus to the coastal resorts of Heilgendamn and Kuhlungsborn from late April to October as well as in winter. *038293 431331; www.molli-bahn.de*

WHERE TO STAY

BAD DOBERAN

Hotel Friedrich-Franz-Palais *moderate*
The Duke of Mecklenburg's former guesthouse for aristocrat spa-goers offers pretty rooms.
August-Bebel-Strasse 2, 18209; 038203 779290; www.hotel-friedrich-franz-palais.de

FISCHLAND

Seezeichen *expensive*
The Seezeichen, a stylish spa hotel, has a terrace overlooking the sands.
Dorfstrasse 22, 18347 Ahrenshoop; 03822 06 79 70; www.seezeichen-hotel.de

STRALSUND

Pension Peiss *moderate*
A friendly home-away-from-home, this pension has colourful modern rooms.
Tribseer Strasse 15, 18439; 03831 30 35 80; www.altstadt-pension-peiss.de

① Bad Doberan
Mecklenburg-Lower Pomerania; 18209
Chinoiserie park pavilions, Neo-Classical buildings and a historic steam train *(daily)* to the seaside resort of Kühlungsborn, 6 km (4 miles) away from the town, are reminders of Bad Doberan's days as a fashionable health spa established in 1801 by the Duke of Mecklenburg, Friedrich Franz. Prior to this, the town's only claim to fame was its graceful Gothic **Münster** *(open daily)*. The church's rich medieval furnishings attest to the wealth of the Cistercian Order; the gilded high altar dating from 1300 is said to be the oldest wing altar in the world.

🚗 *Turn left out of the Münster car park to join the B105 to Rostock. Follow signs to Zentrum, then to "City" car park in Lange Strasse.*

② Rostock
Mecklenburg-Lower Pomerania; 18055
Industrialization after World War II turned Rostock into Germany's largest Baltic port and the biggest city in the state. However, it still has historic monuments and is a popular beach resort. One of the highlights of the city is the 15th-century **Marienkirche** *(open daily)* on Lange Strasse. Behind the church's altar is a contemporary astronomical clock, whose clockwork apostles parade in front of Jesus when the clock strikes noon. Post-war rebuilding has returned some of the city's sights to their former glory. These include the **Neuer Markt** opposite the church, with its multicoloured gabled houses, the town hall and **Kröpeliner Strasse**, the shopping high street. To get to the beach, return down Lange Strasse to find the B103 to **Warnemünde**. The fish restaurants and boutiques of this seaside suburb are as much of a surprise as its powder-fine beach dotted with wicker chairs or *Strandkörbe*.

🚗 *Continue on the B103 for the ferry at Passagierkai across the Warnow to Hohe Düne. Drive to Niederhagen, turn right towards Rostock at Rövershagen, then take the B105 towards Ribnitz. After 10 km (6 miles), turn left to reach the Fischland peninsula.*

③ Fischland
Mecklenburg-Lower Pomerania; 18347
Artists acclaim the unspoiled rural landscapes of this peninsula, which extends parallel to the coast. In 1880, an artist's colony was founded in the fishing village of **Ahrenshoop**, which is now a chic seaside retreat. **Kunstkaten** *(closed Mon)* holds art exhibitions in a traditional art house and a retrospective art museum is scheduled to open in 2012. Drive through the woods of Darss and beyond Prerow am Darss to **Zingst**, whose coastal marshes host middle Europe's largest crane roost in spring and autumn. Zingst also has a museum on the peninsula's culture *(closed Mon)*.

🚗 *Take the main road to Barth then follow signs to Löbnitz to take the B105 to Stralsund. Turn towards the Altstadt on to the B96 and follow signs to the Ozeaneum car park.*

❹ Stralsund

Mecklenburg-Lower Pomerania; 18439

An exquisite skyline hints at Stralsund's architectural wealth. Ringed by water, its Gothic core has impressed visitors for centuries, from the merchants who came to trade in one of the most powerful medieval ports in the Baltic to the UNESCO inspectors who awarded it World Heritage Site status in 2002.

A one-hour walking tour

From the car park, walk to the old harbour to see the windjammer **Gorch Fock** ① *(open daily)*, which is permanently moored here for tours. Among the 19th-century warehouses along the seafront is the **Ozeaneum** ②, where visitors can walk through the spectacular glass tunnels at the North and Baltic Sea aquariums and explore the auditorium, which has life-size models of whales. Behind it and across the Fährkanal, merchants' gabled houses line the **Fährstrasse** ③, which linked

Portal of the Nikolaikirche, Stralsund

the hubs of medieval life in Stralsund: port and government. Carl Wilhelm Scheele, the 18th-century scientist who discovered the existence of oxygen, was born at No. 27–28, which now hosts exhibitions.

Continue down the street to **Alter Markt** ④ to see one of the finest ensembles of Gothic architecture in the Baltic – the 14th-century Rathaus (town hall) with its rosetted façade to let strong winter winds through; St Nikolaikirche *(open daily)*, whose Novgorod altar depicts fur traders hunting squirrels to sell to a Hanseatic League merchant; and Wulflam Haus, built for a wealthy patrician family. It is also possible to see reminders of the two centuries of Swedish rule that followed the Thirty Years' War – Commandantenhaus, the grey Baroque governor's residence with its Swedish coat of arms and, inside the town hall, a bust of the Swedish King Gustav Adolf. Walk south from Alter Markt, on to the high street, **Ossenreyerstrasse** ⑤; the bookshop at No. 14 is thought to be the town's oldest secular building, dating from 1258. Continue right, around the corner on to Apollonienmarkt, then turn right into Mönchstrasse to reach the 13th-century **Kloster**

St Katharinen ⑥. Now deconsecrated, it houses an aquarium *(open daily)* and a culture museum *(Feb–Oct: open daily; Nov–Jan: closed Mon)* with a muralled refectory. The museum ticket also provides access to the Gothic house of a merchant at No. 38 on Mönchstrasse and a museum of Mecklenburg folk culture at No. 23 on Böttcherstrasse. For an image of Stralsund in its prime, walk south-wards down Mönchstrasse to **Marienkirche** ⑦ on Neuer Markt. The town's largest church has lovely stellar vaulting as well as views out to sea from its octagonal tower *(open daily)*. A ten-minute walk between the historic houses on Frankenstrasse off Neuer Markt leads back to the harbour and to the car park near the Ozeaneum.

🚗 **Return to the B96 and follow signs to Insel Rügen. Drive across the suspension bridge, then turn right towards Putbus. Parking is on the Markt.**

VISITING STRALSUND

Parking
Ample parking is available at the Ozeaneum car park on Hafenstrasse.

Tourist Information
Alter Markt 9, 18349; 03831 246 90; www.stralsundtourismus.de

EAT AND DRINK

ROSTOCK

Borwin *moderate*
Located by the harbour, Borwin has a beach-shack atmosphere that belies an excellent fresh fish menu.
Am Strande 2, 18055; 03831 490 75 25; www.borwin-hafenrestaurant.de

Chezann *expensive*
Creative dishes such as spiced tuna on avocado chutney plus duck with Calvados (brandy) are served in this stylish bistro and restaurant.
Mühlenstrasse 28, 18119 Warnemünde; 0381 510 77 77; www.chezann.de; open Tue–Sun dinner

FISCHLAND

Elisabeth's *expensive*
In the former home of artist Elisabeth von Eicken, this hotel restaurant serves Mecklenburg and fine, modern dishes.
Dorfstrasse 39, 18347 Ahrenshoop; 038220 6797 24; closed Mon

STRALSUND

Zur Kogge *moderate*
This 19th-century inn serves good-value Baltic fish.
Tribseer Strasse 25, 18439; 03831 28 58 50; closed Mon

Eat and Drink: inexpensive, under €20; moderate, €20–€40; expensive, over €40

Top Viewpoint on a cliff in the Nationalpark Jasmund, Rügen **Above** Neo-Classical hunting castle, Jagdschloss Granitz

BOAT TRIPS

Reederei Ostsee Tour (www.reederei-ostsee-tour.de), **Adler Schiffe** (www.adler-schiffe.de) and **Weisse Flotte** (www.weisse-flotte.de) ferries ply along the north coast from May–Oct.

VISITING RÜGEN

Tourist Information
Alleestrasse 35, 18581 Putbus; 038301 431; Heinrich-Heine-Strasse 7, 18509 Binz; 038393 14 81 48.

WHERE TO STAY IN RÜGEN

Panorama Hotel Lohme moderate
This small hotel on a cliff has classic modern decor and great sea views.
An der Steilküste 8, 18551 Lohme (2 km/ 1 mile north of Königsstuhl car park); 038302 91 10; www.lohme.com

Cerês expensive
This five-star hotel brings metropolitan style to the traditional seafront.
Strandpromenade 24, 18509; 038393 666 70; www.ceres-hotel.de

⑤ Rügen
Mecklenburg-Lower Pomerania; 18556, 18546, 18609

Two centuries of tourism have not marred the appeal of Germany's largest island (926 sq km/357 sq miles). Whether exploring its rural villages, relaxing in beach resorts in belle époque villas, riding a vintage steam train or strolling along chalk cliffs, Rügen's appeal is timeless and simple.

① Putbus
Putbus's **Markt**, with its Neo-Classical theatre and smart Circus, would not look out of place in a city. In this large village, however, it appears almost aristocratic. Prince Wilhelm Malte I had hoped to create a Prussian St Tropez when he unsuccessfully planned the village as a health spa in 1809. Unfortunately, his castle was blown up with dynamite in the 1960s – the story goes that a local mayor wanted to impress East Germany's Communist rulers – although the orangery and park remain, as does the colonnaded **Badehaus**, or bathhouse, which lies 2 km (1 mile) away, near Lauterbach. From here, it is possible to take a boat trip to the Vilm Island Nature Reserve.
🚗 Drive through Putbus towards the seaside town of Binz. Beyond Nistelitz village, turn left at the T-junction, then turn right to reach the Jagdschloss Granitz car park.

② Jagdschloss Granitz
A Neo-Classical hunting castle of Prince Wilhelm Malte I, Jagdschloss Granitz (May–Sep: open daily; Oct–Apr: closed Mon) crowns the Tempelburg Hill, the highest point in east Rügen. Climb up the castle's 38-m (125-ft) high tower for a sweeping panorama of the Baltic Sea. An apocryphal tale explains this curiosity as the prince's ruse to settle a land dispute – Swedish rulers agreed he could own whatever he saw from his castle.
Spread along the coast beyond, **Binz**, Rügen's premier seaside resort, is renowed for its ornate villas and fine beach.
🚗 Head through Binz to Sassnitz to take the B96 to the Nationalpark Jasmund and the Königsstuhl car park in Hagen village. Visitors can either take the bus to

The Rasender Roland
The Rasender Roland (open daily; www.ruegensche-baederbahn.de), or Racing Roland, is a steam-powered narrow-gauge railway that plies on Rügen and provides an enjoyable change from travelling by car. The steam locomotives whistle out of Putbus station northwards through the fields at 30 kph (19 mph), pause at Jagdschloss Granitz and Binz en route before terminating an hour later in Göhren in east Rügen.

Königsstuhl, or opt for a pleasant 3-km (2-mile) stroll.

③ Königsstuhl
A lovely road from Sassnitz cuts through the **Nationalpark Jasmund**, a landscape of spacious beech woods that cover white chalk sea cliffs. Romantic artist Caspar David Friedrich (1774–1840) immortalized the scenery in his etchings and oils, so popularizing the Königsstuhl (open daily) that in 1865 Kasier Wilhelm I himself inspected the chalk bluff with his daughter Princess Viktoria. Königsstuhl literally means "king's stool", a name derived from the tradition that Rügen's early rulers followed to prove themselves worthy by climbing the 118-m (388-ft) high cliff. For a

better view, walk 500 m (547 yards) south to the **Victoriasicht** viewpoint or to the beach via steep steps.

🚗 *Continue down the road to rejoin B96 then head towards Altenkirchen. Turn right to reach the car park at Putgarten. Tourist trains leave every 10 mins for Kap Arkona and Vitt, otherwise it is a 2 km (1 mile) walk.*

Strolling the Stubbenkammer

The Königsstuhl is the most accessible of the Stubbenkammer cliffs that line Rügen's east coast. Marked by a blue stripe, the Hochuferweg path is a beautiful clifftop trail that leads south to Sassnitz. This 8-km (5-mile) long path, with beech woods on one side and a shifting emerald-jade sea on the other, passes the Kollicker Ort navigation light before proceeding through Ernst, Moritz, Arndt, Sicht and the Wissower Klinken viewpoints. Another hour's walk leads to Sassnitz, from where there are taxis or buses back to Königsstuhl.

④ **Kap Arkona**

Two lighthouses *(open daily)*, the smaller by the 19th-century Prussian architect Karl Friedrich Schinkel, afford a view over the rapefields that cover the cliffs of Kap Arkona, the wind-blown tip of Rügen. A 2-km (1-mile) path around the cape returns to the car park via the earthworks of the **Jaromarsburg** *(open daily)*, a fortified temple of the Slavic tribes who occupied Rügen until the 12th century. Continue on the path to **Vitt**, an idyllic ancient fishing hamlet cupped in a dell behind the beach, where Slavic runes number some houses. Do not miss the folk mural in the village's 19th-century chapel.

🚗 *Return to Altenkirchen, then go to Wiek, and take the car ferry, Wittower Fähre. Drive to Gingst, then join the B96 at Samtens, and past Stralsund, join the B105 to Greifswald. Parking is available at the Zentrum, by the harbour and at the Markt.*

Above left Steam train on the narrow-gauge Rasender Roland **Above right** Beautiful white sand beach at Binz **Below** White chalk cliff at Kap Arkona, Rügen

EAT AND DRINK IN RÜGEN

Zum goldenen Anker *inexpensive*
Housed in a pretty, historic inn, this restaurant in Kap Arkona serves seasonal Baltic fish.
Vitt 2, 18556; 038391 121 34; www.gasthof-vitt.de

Strandhalle Binz *moderate*
Well known for Mecklenburg dishes as interpreted by gourmet chef Toni Münsterteicher, this restaurant is housed in a vintage seaside hall in Binz and has an eclectic decor.
Strandpromenade 5, 18609; 038393 315 64; www.strandhalle-binz.de; closed early Jan–late-Mar

Eat and Drink: inexpensive, under €20; moderate, €20–€40; expensive, over €40

Right Visitors enjoying a walk on the pier in Ahlbeck, Usedom **Below left** Ruins of the 13th-century Cistercian monastery, Greifswald **Below right** Alter Speicher – the half-timbered granary in Wolgast

WHERE TO STAY

GREIFSWALD

Kronprinz *moderate*
This old-fashioned four-star hotel near the cathedral has spacious but spartan rooms with reassuringly formal service.
Lange Strasse 22; 03834 79 00; www.hotelkronprinz.de

USEDOM

Villa Oasis *moderate*
Built for a Berlin industrialist, this is an Art Nouveau villa with elegant rooms and personal service. Some rooms are in a smaller lodge in the garden.
Puschkinstrasse 10, 17424 Heringsdorf; 03837 826 50; www.villa-oasis.de

⑥ Greifswald
Mecklenburg-Lower Pomerania; 17489
This former Hanseatic town is situated 5 km (3 miles) from the Bay of Greifswald. Caspar David Friedrich (1774–1840), the Romantic painter, drew inspiration from the town's **Altstadt**, with its gabled houses and picturesque spires. Representations of the Gothic merchants' houses on the Markt and the cathedral with its striking twin-bulbed tower can be seen on his canvases in the excellent **Pommersches Landesmuseum** *(closed Mon)*, which also has displays on regional history. Drive 2 km (1 mile) east on Wolgaster Strasse to Wiek, a pretty harbour scented with the smell of smoking fish, then on to Eldena and the ruins of a 13th-century Cistercian monastery, another favourite subject of the artist.

🚗 *Continue past Eldena to Kemnitz, then to Pritzwald to reach the B111 to Wolgast. Parking is available on Platz der Jugend opposite St Petrikirche.*

⑦ Wolgast
Mecklenburg-Lower Pomerania; 17438
Now peaceful after being wrecked by war for centuries, the "Gateway to the island of Usedom" is an ideal stop on the drive. Visitors can walk behind the 14th-century parish church, **St Petrikirche**, which has part of an early Slavic temple next to the rear portal and a copy of 16th-century artist Hans Holbein's *Totentanz* frieze, into the cozy Altstadt. Rebuilt after being burnt down by Peter the Great of Russia in 1713, the old town clusters above a small harbour where grain ships docked in the 19th century.

Other highlights include the **Alter Speicher**, an 80-m (262-ft) long half-timbered granary, one of the largest buildings in the old town and the family home of Philipp Otto Runge (1777–1810), the famous Romantic painter.

🚗 *Continue on the B111 over the bridge on to Usedom. Turn left after 5 km (3 miles) to reach Peenemünde.*

⑧ Usedom

Mecklenburg-Lower Pomerania; 17424
The island, named after the village of Usedom and separated from the mainland by the Peenestrom Strait, is the second largest in Germany, covering an area of 445 sq km (172 sq miles). Renowned for its great natural beauty, Usedom boasts white beaches, forests, peat bogs and bays overgrown with rushes in the south. The island is linked to the mainland by two drawbridges near Anklam and Wolgast.

Historically, the most interesting spot on the island is the **Historisch-technisches Informationszenytum** *(Apr–Sep: open daily; Oct–Mar: closed Mon)* at Peenemünde, located in military territory. On 3 October 1942, Luftwaffe scientists successfully launched a rocket here after seven years of testing. Originally intended for a jet plane, the

Replica of a V-2 Vergeltungswaffen at Peenemünde

technology was hijacked by the Nazis to develop the V-1 and V-2 *Vergeltungswaffen* (vengeance weapons) – flying bombs that were used to attack London in 1944. The museum documents this breakthrough in science and its post-war consequences.

Return to the B111 junction and then turn left to reach **Heringsdorf**. Park near the tourist office. The largest resort in Usedom spreads out behind a silvery sand beach with continental Europe's longest pier (508 m/555 yards). In the late 19th century, this was the playground of Prussia's elite, as is evident in the palatial summer residences on Delbrückstrasse promenade. Visitors can either walk or drive 2 km (1 mile) eastward to **Ahlbeck**, a smaller town and an elegant beach resort with villas, hotels and boarding houses gathered around a turreted pier.

DAY TRIP OPTIONS

Both Bad Doberan and Stralsund make good bases from which to explore the region.

Art, old and new
With Bad Doberan ❶ as a base, visit the Münster, its Gothic altars steeped in medieval mystery, then tour the Marienkirche in Rostock ❷ and the beach at Warnemünde. Drive to the art colony beach resort of Ahrenshoop on Fischland ❸ for lunch and some window shopping. Later, stroll on an unspoiled beach, then either admire

Prerow am Darss's museum or, in spring and autumn, go bird-watching at Zingst.

Take the B105 to Rostock and then the B103 to Warnemünde. Follow the driving instructions through Ahrenshoop to Zingst, then take the B105 back to Bad Doberan.

Culture and coast
In Stralsund ❹ explore the Alter Markt's fine ensemble of Gothic buildings before driving to Rügen Island ❺ for a clifftop stroll at the

Königsstuhl, the ideal way to work up an appetite for lunch on the beach at Binz. Leave the car at the car park in Jagdschloss Granitz, a Neo-Classical castle, and make the return trip to Putbus, Rügen's first resort, by vintage steam train. End the day relaxing at the beach resort of Binz, which is near the castle.

Take the B96 to Sassnitz, then follow driving instructions to Königsstühl and in reverse to Binz. Take the B196 to Bergen to rejoin th B96 for Stralsund.

Land of a Thousand Lakes

Wismar to Neustrelitz

Highlights

- **Grand ducal palace**
  Marvel at the pomp of Schwerin's Schloss and visit the orangery where Duke Paul Friedrich Franz II tended his plants

- **Water wonderland**
  Enjoy cruising on the lakes, aboard a steam launch from Waren or on a canoe in the Müritz-Nationalpark

- **Abundant birdlife**
  Try to spot nesting ospreys and sea eagles around the towns of Federow and Speck

Camp site among the trees on the banks of a tranquil lake in Schwerin

Land of a Thousand Lakes

Numerous glacial lakes give the heart of Mecklenburg-Lower Pomerania (Mecklenburg-Vorpommern) its nickname, the "Land of a Thousand Lakes". This aquatic mosaic encompasses everything from small freshwater seas to myriad minor pools in the Müritz-Nationalpark, where astonishing birdlife is as much a part of the scenery as sweeping vistas. This tour takes drivers from coast to country: from the cobbled lanes of the medieval port of Wismar to Schwerin, the capital of the state, with its enchanting castle, then east into the state's rustic heart around Güstrow, finally ending at Neustrelitz, the former Residenzstadt of a duchy.

ACTIVITIES

Hunt for "Swedish Heads" in the medieval lanes of Wismar

See the work of Ernst Barlach, the Expressionist sculptor, in Güstrow

Board a vintage steamship for a cruise from Waren

Go canoeing in the Müritz-Nationalpark

Go bird-watching around Speck in the Müritz-Nationalpark

Above Buildings lining the Markt in Wismar, *see p62* **Below left** Waters of Schweriner See, *see p63* **Below right** Display at a museum near Müritzsee, *see p64*

Map

u Heinde
Gross
Wüstenfelde
108
Matgendorf
Dalkendorf Thürkow Karnitz
Alt-Sührkow
Teterow
ross
kern 108 Remplin Malchin
104
Hohen Bristow
Demzin
BURG Gielow Scharpzow
CHLITZ **5**
Demzin
Ziddorf *Malchiner* Rothenmoor
See
108 Moltzow Schwinkendorf Faulenrost
Vollrathsruhe
Marxhagen
lohen Alt Varchentin
Vangelin Schönau Gross Lehsten
Grabowhöfe Baumgarten Gievitz
Torgelower Klein Plasten
Jabel *See* Marihn
ossentiner 108 192
lütte Möllenhagen
Kölpinsee 192 Waren Kargow Gross
Vielen
Göhren Klink Federow Ankershagen Peckatel
Lebbin
Müritzsee Speck 193
Specker Kratzeburg Adamsdorf
See **6**
MÜRITZ- Dalmsdorf Blumenholz
NATIONALPARK Granzin 96
Boek
Blankenförde NEUSTRELITZ **7**
Roggentin Userin
Gross
Quassow 198

0 kilometres   10
0 miles   10

KEY

Drive route

Start/finish: Wismar to Neustrelitz.

Number of days: 2–3 days, allowing half a day to explore Wismar.

Distance: 250 km (155 miles).

Road conditions: Roads are good except in the Müritz-Nationalpark, where a section of paved track and unsurfaced road can be tricky in winter when it snows. Roads are well signposted outside the national park.

When to go: Late spring to autumn is a good time to visit the region. Visitors should not miss the spectacular annual crane migration in mid-October. Most facilities in the park close from November to April, and small lakes often freeze in winter.

Opening times: Most shops are open from 9am to 5pm, Monday to Friday. Attractions are open from 9am to 5pm, but are generally closed on Mondays.

Main market days: Wismar: Tue, Thu & Sat; **Schwerin:** Wed & Fri; **Güstrow:** Tue, Thu & Sat; **Waren:** Tue & Thu.

Major festivals: Wismar: Hafentage (harbour festival), 2nd weekend in Jun; **Schwerin:** Schlossfestspiele (music festival), Jun–Jul; Altstadtfest (old town festival), mid-Sep.

DAY TRIP OPTIONS

History and architecture lovers can visit Güstrow's **palace** and Wismar's **monuments**, while outdoor enthusiasts can stay in Waren in the Müritz-Nationalpark to enjoy a **lake cruise**, **walks** and **bird-watching** around Speck and then drive to nearby villages to go **canoeing**. For full details, *see p65*.

Above left Impressive Marienkirche in Wismar
Above right Schweriner See shore

① Wismar

Mecklenburg-Lower Pomerania; 23952
A provincial town on the Baltic Sea, Wismar is worth a visit for its faded
grandeur and historic charm. Renovation has repaired the damage
wreaked by World War II to restore something of the looks of the
town's golden ages. It was declared a World Heritage Site in 2002.

A 90-minute walking tour

Take Grünestrasse near the car park
and turn left onto Dankwarstrasse to
reach the cobbled **Markt** ①. A showpiece of restoration work, this is one
of the largest market squares in north
Germany. To the north of the square
is the Neo-Classical Rathaus, which
houses a museum (open daily) in its
cellar with displays on the town's
history. Cross the main shopping
street, Hegede, behind the tourist
office, to reach the town's Gothic
quarter. Only an archdeacon's house
on the corner of Sargmacherstrasse
and the massive tower of
Marienkirche ② remain from before
the Allied bombing raids in 1945. Take
a tour up the 80-m (262-ft) tower (open
daily), which has displays on medieval

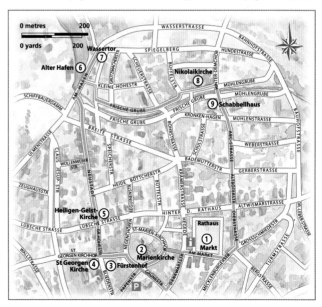

Swedish Heads

Wismar's unofficial mascots, these brightly painted moustachioed figures have lions' heads for hats. One bust is in the Markt, two more are near the mouth of the old port, all replicas of two "Swedish Heads" that stood at the harbour mouth during the Swedish occupation. One theory behind the name suggests that the original busts came from an 18th-century Swedish merchant ship.

construction techniques. A little further, on Vor dem Fürstenhof, is the **Fürstenhof** ③. An Italian-style palace for the dukes of Mecklenburg, this Mannerist building has terracotta friezes that retell the stories of the Trojan Wars and the Prodigal Son.

Further down this road stands **St Georgen Kirche** ④, the largest church in Wismar. The Grosse Hohe Strasse leading northwards from the church portal threads down to the cobbled Lübsche Strasse, once a mercantile thoroughfare. On its junction with Neustadt is the **Heiligen-Geist-Kirche** ⑤ (open daily), a fine example of a hospital church.

Take Neustadt from beside the church and continue down it to cross the Grube – Germany's first urban canal, dug in the mid-1200s – and to get to the ring road and the **Alter Hafen** ⑥. The port may look familiar to film buffs as it was featured in the classic silent movie *Nosferatu* (1922). Opposite is the **Wassertor** ⑦, the last of the gateways in the town's medieval fortifications. Return to the Grube and follow it eastwards to the **Nikolaikirche** ⑧. This bulky late-Gothic basilica was once the church of medieval seafarers and, despite its size, managed to survive World War II's air raids. View glazed friezes on its façade before marvelling at the 37-m (121-ft) high interior with original frescoes. Continue alongside the Grube and then cross it on Schweinsbrücke or "pig bridge". Here stands the **Schabbellhaus** ⑨, a Dutch Renaissance mansion whose museum (closed Mon) contains one of the original "Swedish Heads" among many paintings and curios. Continue southwards on ABC-Strasse to reach the Markt, then take Dankwarstrasse and Grünestrasse back to the car park on Papenstrasse.

🚗 *Take Dr-Leber-Strasse, then join the B106 to Schwerin. Follow signs for Am Schloss car park opposite the palace.*

② Schwerin

Mecklenburg-Lower Pomerania; 19053

Picturesquely situated amidst several lakes, the state capital's main attraction is hard to miss. The ducal **Schloss**, bristling with towers and topped with a gilded turret like a crown, looks like something out of *Cinderella*. Duke Paul Friedrich Franz II's inspiration for the renovation of his dynastic residence came from the Loire's Chambord Chateau. The palace's showrooms (open daily) revel in ancestral pomp. Across the palace footbridge is the state museum, **Staatliches Museum** (closed Mon). Highlights include 17th-century Flemish art and works by Rembrandt. After the visit, enjoy a cruise (www.weisseflotteschwerin.de) on the Schweriner See.

🚗 *Drive around the lake to follow signs to Ludwigslust, then to the B321. In Zippendorf, park at Am Strand.*

③ Zippendorf and Muess

Mecklenburg-Lower Pomerania; 19063

About 3 km (2 miles) from Schwerin's city centre, the lakeside suburb of Zippendorf is a great place to relax on the beach or stroll around the lake. About 2 km (1 mile) from here lies another suburb, Muess. Its open-air museum, **Freilichtmuseum** (mid-Apr–Oct: closed Mon), provides a glimpse of rustic Mecklenburg.

🚗 *Continue west on the B321 past Crivitz and turn left to Goldberg. Get on to the B192 to Dobbertin, turn right to Güstrow and follow signs to Zentrum. Turn left on to Wallensteinstrasse to park near the Schloss.*

Above View of Wismar's old town and canal **Below** Ducal Schloss, on an island on Lake Schwerin

EAT AND DRINK

WISMAR

Zum Weinberg *moderate*
This former Renaissance hall of a wine merchant is located behind the town hall and serves gutsy Mecklenburg dishes such as green kale and bacon or *Rippenbraten* (pork stuffed with fruit). *Hinter dem Rathaus 3, 23966; 03841 28 35 50; www.weinberg-wismar.de*

SCHWERIN

Die Orangerie *moderate*
Palm leaves and wicker seats highlight the interiors of Die Orangerie, which serves Mediterranean light lunches and sumptuous coffee and cake. *Schwerin Schloss, Lennéstrasse 1, 19053; 03855 25 29 15; closed Nov–Mar*

Weinhaus Woehler *moderate*
Named after the wine trader who opened a cellar here in 1819, this fine restaurant serves a good selection of fish and meat dishes. The house speciality is Sauerfleisch (pickled meat). *Puschkinstrasse 26, 19055; 0385 55830*

Right Dom in the town of Güstrow

VISITING MÜRITZ-NATIONALPARK

Tourist Information
Schlossplatz 3, 17237 Hohenzieritz;
039824 25 20; www.mueritz-
nationalpark.de

Nationalpark Informationshaus,
17192 Federow, 17192; 03991 66 88 49;
www.nationalpark-service.de

Boat Rental
Charterpoint Müritz Grosse;
Burgstrasse 1, 17192, Waren; 03991 16
55 59; www.charterpoint-mueritz.de

WHERE TO STAY

BURG SCHLITZ

Burg Schlitz *expensive*
Housed in Count Schlitz's Neo-Classical
palace, this hotel has rooms decorated
with Biedermeier furnishings.
Hohen Demzin, 17166; 03996 127 00;
www.burg-schlitz.de

AROUND MÜRITZ-NATIONALPARK

Kleines Meer *moderate*
Situated near the waterfront, this
friendly hotel is decorated in calm
neutral colours.
Alter Markt 7, 17192 Waren (3 km/
2 miles north of Müritz-Nationalpark);
03991 64 80; www.kleinesmeer.de

Below left Back road to Waren **Below
right** Baroque town church in Neustrelitz
Bottom Gently rolling countryside, Güstrow

④ Güstrow
Mecklenburg-Lower Pomerania; 18273
The old town in Güstrow is dominated
by its 16th-century **Schloss** *(Apr–Oct:
open daily; Nov–Mar: closed Mon)*, built
by the Italian architect Franz Parr.
Highlights include its banquet hall
with striking stucco hunting scenes.
Among its glass and antiques is the
Menagerie series that Flemish artist
Maerten de Vos (1532–1603) created
at the height of the Age of Exploration.
The nearby **Dom** contains the tombs
of the palace's founder, Duke Ulrich,
and his two wives. This early-Gothic
basilica has a bronze angel by Ernst
Barlach, Germany's finest Expressionist
sculptor. His work can also be seen in
Gertrudenkapelle (Gertrude Chapel)
(closed Mon) and **Atelierhaus** *(closed
Mon)*, 3 km (2 miles) east of Güstrow.
🚗 *From the car park, return to
the main road and turn left onto
Goldberger Strasse. Turn right onto
Plauer Strasse for the B104. In
Teterow, take the B108 to Burg Schlitz.*

⑤ Burg Schlitz
Mecklenburg-Lower Pomerania; 17166
Nicknamed "Mecklenburg Switzerland"
due to its low moraine hills, the municipality of Hohen Demzin is known for
its palaces, the grandest of which is
the Neo-Classical Burg Schlitz. Built
in the 1820s for Count Schlitz, it is now
a luxury hotel that stands within beautifully landscaped parkland. Near its

chapel is the Secessionist nymph
fountain, cast in 1903 for a Berlin
department store. A copy of the fountain stands in New York's Central Park.
🚗 *Continue south on the B108 to
Waren; drive into Zentrum for car
parks around the harbour.*

⑥ Müritz-Nationalpark
Mecklenburg-Lower Pomerania; 17192
Covering an area of 322 sq km
(124 sq miles), the Müritz-Nationalpark
is famous for its birdlife and boating
facilities. Foreign visitors, however,
have not yet discovered the tiny
glacial lakes, forests and abundant
birdlife of this sparsely populated and
quiet backwater destination.
   A half-timbered town on the north
shore of the Müritzsee (Lake Müritz),
Waren is an ideal base for tourists
with its beaches, hiking and boating
options *(03991 153 40; www.mueritz-
fisch.de)*. At 115 sq km (44 sq miles),
Müritzsee is Germany's largest lake
after Constance. Visitors can find a
bench at the harbour and enjoy the
bustle as motorboats and small
yachts tie up at the wharf or embark
on a cruise on the lake *(Weisse Flotte
Muritz, Kietzstrasse 17; 03991 12 26 68;
www.mueritzschiffahrt.de)* aboard a

Winged Wonders
Renowned for its birdlife, the Müritz-
Nationalpark is a popular destination
for those who want to spot the
ospreys and sea eagles that breed
here. Visitors can get information
about sightings from the park
centre at Federow where there is an
observation station. The spectacular
avian show in the second half of
October should not be missed.
Thousands of cranes can be seen
migrating south. The marshland
around the Rederangsee, south of
Federow, is a favourite roosting area.

vintage steamer. The **Müritzeum** *(03991 633 680; www.mueritzeum.de)*, at the eastern edge of the old town, houses the nation's largest freshwater aquarium and has displays on ecology.

Return from the centre to locate brown signs for the Müritz-Nationalpark on the B192. After 1 km (half a mile) turn right, following parking signs on Meckleburger Strasse and head to **Federow**. Visitors can pick up maps from the park centre in Federow *(May–Oct: open daily)* and then continue to the hamlet of **Speck** on the banks of the Specker See (Lake Speck); it is possible to spot ospreys on a 2.5 km (1.5 mile) circuit of the lake. Another walk ascends to a viewing platform on the Käflingsberg Hill; the trail head is just over 1 km (half a mile) from the end of the paved road.

For a long walk, continue walking on the track beyond Speck, then turn left at the crossroads to the farming villages of **Granzin** and **Dalmsdorf**, where residents sell smoked fish by the roadside. Canoes can be hired *(Kormoran Kanutouing Granzin 38, 17237 Kratzeburg-Granzin; www.kormoran-kanutouring.de)*, between April and early October to view the scenery around the lake.

🚗 *Return to Waren and turn right onto the B192. At Möllenhagen, turn right again following signs to Ankershagen, Peckatel and Blumenholz. Turn right onto the B96 and take the Neustrelitz/Kiefernheide exit to Neustrelitz.*

❼ Neustrelitz
Mecklenburg-Lower Pomerania; 17235
Designed in the 1730s as the Residenzstadt, or residence town, of a minor Mecklenburg duchy, the origins of Neustrelitz as a custom-built capital are evident in its unique and symmetrically designed Markt or marketplace, with streets that radiate like spokes from the corners. Visitors can better appreciate the square's perfect geometry from a viewing platform in the Baroque town church and then take the Schlosstrasse to the **Schloss**. This ducal palace was destroyed in World War II but its gardens retain their naturalistic English style as designed by Peter Josef Lenné, the great Prussian garden designer of the 19th century. The orangery also remains intact and is now a restaurant. Its interiors were designed by the 19th-century master architect Karl Schinkel and Prussian court sculptor Christian Daniel Rauch.

Above Reed beds in the Muritzsee, renowned for its birdlife **Below** Nymph fountain, Burg Schlitz

EAT AND DRINK

GÜSTROW

Café Küpper *inexpensive*
A few steps from the Schloss, the small Café Küpper offers excellent soups, snacks and gateau.
Domstrasse 15, 18273; 03843 68 24 85

BURG SCHLITZ

Wappensaal *expensive*
Housed in the spectacular Neo-Classical hall in Burg Schlitz , this restaurant serves French and Italian cuisine with an Asian touch. Book in advance.
Schlosshotel Burg Schlitz, 17166; 03966 12 700; open Wed–Sun, closed Feb

AROUND MÜRITZ-NATIONALPARK

Fischerhof *inexpensive*
Located behind the high street off the main square, this small courtyard restaurant specializes in fresh Müritzsee fish.
Neuer Markt 19, 17192 Waren (3 km/ 2 miles north of Müritz-Nationalpark); 03991 66 98 15

NEUSTRELITZ

Luisenstube *moderate*
Situated just off the Markt, this cozy restaurant serves freshwater fish.
Seestrasse 8, 17235; 03981 20 07 77

DAY TRIP OPTIONS
Schwerin and Waren are both good bases for making day trips.

Historical romance
In Schwerin ❷, visit Staatliches Museum then drive east to Güstrow ❹ for lunch. Explore the Dom and schloss and head to Wismar ❶ to view more architectural wonders. End

the day on Zippendorf's ❸ beach.

Take the B104 northwards from the Schloss in Schwerin to Güstrow. Return on the B104 to Prüzen, turn right to Bützow and head to Steinhagen, Neukloster. Then turn right onto the B192. Go left at Zurow to the B105 to reach Wismar. Follow the driving instructions to reach Zippendorf.

Outdoor escapes
Spend a day in Waren and explore the Müritz-Nationalpark ❻. Visit the park centre in Federow or go on a hike up the Käflingsberg. Drive to Granzin to go canoeing before strolling around the Schloss gardens of Neustrelitz ❼.

Follow instructions to Neustrelitz. Retrace the route to Waren.

Eat and Drink: inexpensive, under €20; moderate, €20–€40; expensive, over €40

History and Revolutions Along the Elbe

Havelberg to Lutherstadt Wittenberg

Highlights

- **Magnificent churches**
  Tour the impressive churches that dot the banks of the Elbe river

- **School of modern design**
  Visit the Bauhaus design school, the inspiration behind modern art and architecture

- **Charming country gardens**
  Wander around the landscaped gardens of Wörlitz in the heart of eastern Germany

- **Historic town**
  Delve into history at Lutherstadt Wittenberg, a lovely getaway with relics of the Protestant Reformation

The picturesque central lake at Wörlitz gardens, Dessau

History and Revolutions Along the Elbe

This tour loosely follows the Elbe, a major river that runs through Saxony-Anhalt (Sachsen-Anhalt), a state dotted with historic sights. In the 7th century, the river formed a natural frontier between Germans in the west and Slavic tribes in the east. In the 10th century, however, the German Saxons made a concerted effort to secure the border and colonize and Christianize the east, to which end, they built a series of great churches and abbeys in Magdeburg, Havelberg and Jerichow. With the border secured, river trade helped settlements flourish – in particular the town of Tangermünde, whose half-timbered core has been wonderfully preserved. Further south along the Elbe, the small town of Lutherstadt Wittenberg is renowned as the birthplace of Protestantism. History is not the only attraction on this route: large portions of the Elbe are part of a UNESCO-designated biosphere reserve that offers good hiking, as do the wonderful country gardens of Wörlitz.

Above Scenic road to Havelberg, *see p70*

ACTIVITIES

Enter the zany world of architect Friedensreich Hundertwasser at the Grüne Zitadelle building in Magdeburg

Take a boat trip on the Elbe river

Explore the palatial Wörlitz gardens on foot or by gondola

Climb the stairs of Lutherstadt Wittenberg's castle tower for glorious views of the town

KEY

Drive route

Above Central lake, Wörlitz gardens, *see p72*
Below Magnificent late-Gothic gate, Neustädter Tor, Tangermünde, *see p70*

PLAN YOUR DRIVE

Start/finish: Havelberg to Lutherstadt Wittenberg.

Number of days: 3 days, allowing half a day to explore Lutherstadt Wittenberg.

Distance: 222 km (138 miles).

Road conditions: All major and minor roads are well paved and well signposted.

When to go: The month of June is the best time to visit.

Opening times: Most attractions open daily. Shops are open from 9am to 5pm, Monday to Friday, but close early on Saturdays. Shops and services are closed on Sundays. Restaurants generally close around 10pm.

Main market days: Magdeburg: Mon–Sat; **Lutherstadt Wittenberg:** Thu.

Shopping: In Lutherstadt Wittenberg, look out for *Lutherbrot*, a tasty gingerbread with chocolate and sugar icing.

Major festivals: Havelberg: Pferdemarkt (horse market), early Sep; **Lutherstadt Wittenberg:** Luther's Hochzeit (Luther's wedding festival), late Jun; Reformationstag (Reformation day), 31 Oct.

DAY TRIP OPTIONS

The northern part of this tour along the Elbe will appeal to **history buffs** who wish to see the great Saxon churches built as missionary outposts. The southern part of the Elbe, which takes in the Bauhaus School and the landscaped gardens of Wörlitz, will engage those interested in **design and architecture**. Exploring Lutherstadt Wittenberg, associated with the **Protestant Reformation**, can take a whole day. For full details, *see p73*.

Above left View of the old town from Dom St Marien, Havelberg **Above right** Half-timbered houses lining the streets of Tangermünde **Below** Gothic Dom St Mauritius und St Katharina, Magdeburg

WHERE TO STAY

TANGERMÜNDE

Schloss Tangermünde *moderate*
Located in the castle, this is the town's most prestigious lodging. Facilities include a sauna and steam room. The restaurant here is also the best in town.
Auf der Burg, Amt 1, 39590; 039322 73 73; www.schloss-tangermuende.de

MAGDEBURG

Hotel Ratswaage Magdeburg *moderate*
Situated in the city centre, this large hotel has 174 rooms, several bars, a restaurant, an indoor pool and a sauna.
Ratswaageplatz 1–4, 39104; 0391 592 60; www.ratswaage.de

Hotel Stadtfeld *moderate*
This peaceful hotel has simple rooms and offers free wireless Internet.
Maxim-Gorki-Strasse 31–37, 39108; 0391 50 66 60; www.hotelstadtfeld.de

Residenz Joop *moderate*
This bed-and-breakfast is an easy walk from the town centre.
Jean-Burger-Strasse 16, 39112; 0391 626 20; www.residenzjoop.de

Herrenkrug Parkhotel *expensive*
Lovely four-star hotel offering spacious and modern rooms. There is also a fine spa and a reputed restaurant.
Herrenkrug 3, 39114; 0391 850 80; www.herrenkrug.de

AROUND BAUHAUSGEBÄUDE

Bauhaus Dessau *inexpensive*
The design school has turned its former student dormitories into guest rooms, some equipped with kitchens.
Gropiusallee 38, 06846; 0340 650 80; www.bauhaus-dessau.de

① Havelberg
Saxony-Anhalt; 39532

Havelberg's old town occupies a small island in the Havel river close to its confluence with the Elbe. This town was founded as a Christian missionary outpost in 948 by Emperor Otto I, who sensed a perfect defensive position in heathen Slav territory. Medieval houses still cluster in the old town, and above them looms the sombre **Dom St Marien** *(open daily)*, built between 1150 and 1170. The cathedral was destroyed in a huge fire in the 13th century, and its present appearance is the result of Gothic additions to its Romanesque core, with impressive results. Its most remarkable feature is a 14th-century stone choir screen carved with scenes from the New Testament.

🚗 *Turn right in the direction of Genthiner Strasse and stay on the B107 to Jerichow. Turn right at the town entrance to the Abbey car park.*

② Jerichow Abbey
Saxony-Anhalt; 39319

Like the Dom at Havelberg, Jerichow Abbey *(closed Mon)* was built during a spate of mid-12th-century ecclesiastical expansion. This Premonstratensian convent was founded in 1144, making it one of northern Germany's oldest brick buildings. The **abbey museum** displays the brick building methods that became typical of the region as it was settled in by the Germans.

🚗 *Drive along the B107, turn left on to the B188 westwards to Tangermünde.*

Leave the B188, going south on Arneburger Strasse. Bear right on Lindenstrasse, left on Grete-Minde to park on Lange Strasse.

③ Tangermünde
Saxony-Anhalt; 39585

Statue of Grete Minde, Tangermünde

Central Tangermünde is a snapshot of the early 17th century – almost all the half-timbered houses along its central cobblestoned Lange Strasse replaced those lost in a fire in 1617. The fire was blamed on an innocent Grete Minde, who was thought to want revenge after the town's court refused her inheritance. She was soon after burned as a witch, but is now celebrated by a bronze statue that stands to the left of the **Rathaus**, one of the few buildings to escape the blaze. Built in the 1430s, it bristles with gables and ornamentation. A stroll down Kirchstrasse reveals a series of timber-framed houses en route to the

late-Gothic **St Stephanskirche**, completed at the end of the 15th century. The church was built by Charles IV, King of Bohemia, who used the town as his second royal residence after Prague. Behind the church are the remains of his castle, which was destroyed in 1640 by a Swedish campaign in the Thirty Years' War.

🚗 *Turn left to Lüderitz on to the B189, which becomes the B71 in Magdeburg. Follow signs to Zentrum then the Dom to reach the Domplatz for on-street parking.*

Friedensreich Hundertwasser
The Grüne Zitadelle in Magdeburg was the last work of Austrian architect and designer Friedensreich Hundertwasser (1928–2000). Inspired by Antonio Gaudí and Gustav Klimt, Hundertwasser is famed for his rejection of straight lines in favour of unruly shapes, bright colours and chaotic designs. Fascinated by spirals, he called straight lines "the devil's tools".

❹ Magdeburg
Saxony-Anhalt; 39104

Established as a trading post by Charlemagne in the 9th century, Magdeburg became the main residence of Emperor Otto I in the 10th century. The town was brutally sacked in 1631 by Catholic imperial forces, while World War II levelled most of it. However, Magdeburg is not without reminders of its glorious past. The most impressive is the Gothic **Dom St Mauritius und St Katharina** *(open daily)* with distinctive octagonal turrets and spires. Its construction began in

1209, vastly enlarging an earlier monastery church founded by Otto I in 926. Look out for the emperor's tomb, sculptor Ernst Barlach's contemplative 1929 memorial to the dead of World War I and the sculpture of the *Magdeburger Virgins* (1240), illustrating the Parable of the Ten Virgins. In contrast, the most celebrated new building is the **Grüne Zitadelle** *(tours: daily)*. With its playful curves and colours, this apartment complex, designed by Austrian architect Friedensreich Hundertwasser, is a key landmark.

🚗 *Turn right along Ernst-Reuter-Allee and continue on the Brückstrasse, which becomes the B1, on to the B184. In Dessau, turn right on Rosslauer Allee then right on to Antoinettenstrasse, which becomes Puschkinallee, then left on Gropiusallee to the car park.*

❺ Bauhausgebäude
Saxony-Anhalt; 06846

Built in 1925 in Dessau, the **Bauhaus School** continues to be a design school. The work of architect Walter Gropius, this white concrete building is famed for the Bauhaus logo beside its car park and the innovative balconies at the back of the building. Its small museum, **Ausstellung im Bauhaus** *(open Mon–Fri)*, has displays showcasing the application of Bauhaus theory to many areas of art and design. The front desk also sells tickets to the other Bauhaus attractions: the **Meisterhäuser** (masters' houses) and the **Törten**, a 1920s prototype housing estate, 7 km (4 miles) southeast of central Dessau.

🚗 *Go back to Puschkinallee, turn right and follow the street to the T-junction with Friedrichstrasse. Turn left then right on to Kavalierstrasse. Turn left to Vockerode, and at the T-junction, turn left to Wörlitz. Turn left on Seespitze and follow signs to the car park.*

Bauhaus
The Bauhaus movement was begun in 1918 by painter Max Pechstein to utilize art for revolutionary purposes. One of its members, architect Walter Gropius, founded the design school at Weimar, though it later moved to Dessau. At odds with the Nazis during World War II, many members went into exile in the US.

Above Striking Grüne Zitadelle complex, Magdeburg **Below** Elegant Meisterhäuser, the masters' houses, Bauhausgebäude

EAT AND DRINK

HAVELBERG
La Dolce Vita *inexpensive*
This restaurant offers superb town views from its terrace and serves Italian dishes and delicious ice cream.
Domplatz 2, 39539; 039387 20 83 40

TANGERMÜNDE
Alte Brauerei *moderate*
The food at this restaurant is good, with various salads, steaks and fish dishes on offer.
Lange Strasse 34, 39590; 039322 441 45

MAGDEBURG
Le Frog *moderate*
A popular brasserie in the town's main park, Stadtpark, Le Frog's beer garden often hosts live music. The menu includes local game, wild mushrooms and good salads.
Heinrich-Heine-Platz 1, 39104; 0391 531 35 56; www.lefrog-md.de

Kornhaus *moderate*
Housed in an elegant Bauhaus building, this restaurant serves German and Mediterranean cuisine.
Kornhausstrasse 146, 39104; 0340 65 01 99 63

Petriförder *moderate*
A large restaurant in a pleasant riverside location with an extensive international menu that includes standard Italian options.
Petriförder 1, 39104; 0391 597 96 00

Die Saison *expensive*
The restaurant of the Herrenkrug Parkhotel serves the best food in Magdeburg. Gourmet treats include red mullet fillet and prawns on mussel risotto and broccoli rabe, as well as a variety of delicious desserts.
Herrenkrug 3, 39114; 0391 850 80

Eat and Drink: inexpensive, under €20; moderate, €20–€40; expensive, over €40

Above Serene lake and 18th-century country gardens of Wörlitz

The 56-km (35-mile) Gartenreichtour Fürst Franz hiking and biking trail travels through the nearby UNESCO biosphere reserve. Signposted from Wörlitz car park, the closest point of interest along the route is the fishing village of Vockerode and the adjacent royal woodland park, Sieglitzer, both around 6 km (4 miles) to the west of Wörlitz. www.woerlitz-information.de; www.dessau-tourismus.de

WHERE TO STAY

WÖRLITZ

Pension Zum Hauenden Schwein *moderate*
This traditional place has clean and bright rooms and a good wine bar.
Erdmannsdorffstrasse 69, 06786; 03490 53 01 90; www.zumhauendenschwein.de

LUTHERSTADT WITTENBERG

Alte Canzley *moderate*
The former chancellery building has now been revamped to create a spotless, upmarket hotel. Facilities include a sauna.
Schlossstrasse 3, 06886; 03491 42 91 90; www.alte-canzley.de

Stadthotel Lutherstadt Wittenberg Schwarzer Baer *moderate*
A central hotel in a 500-year-old building with free parking.
Schlossstrasse 2, 06886; 03491 420 43 44; www.stadthotel-wittenberg.de

Stadtpalais *moderate*
The most exclusive hotel in town has modern luxuries, including a sauna.
Collegienstrasse 56/57, 06886; 03491 42 50; www.stadtpalais. bestwestern.de

⑥ Wörlitz
Saxony-Anhalt; 06786
Many splendid residences set in landscaped gardens were built around Dessau in the 18th and 19th centuries. Of these, the most impressive is Wörlitz, where Gothic follies and mock Classical statues dot manicured lawns, while swans and rowing boats bob on a tranquil lake. Prince Leopold III of Anhalt, along with his court architect Friedrich Wilhelm von Erdman, built the gardens in the second half of the 18th century. At the centre stands the Neo-Classical Schloss Wörlitz *(open daily)* with its muted Baroque decor. Behind the palace, the central lake spreads out and gondola tours pass beneath an array of bridges around the lake. Other park attractions include the **Gotisches Haus**, the prince's Neo-Gothic residence, the mock Italian landscape **Insel Stein** and a **synagogue** *(all open daily)* modelled on the Temple of Vesta in Rome.

🚗 *Turn left on Erdmannsdorff Strasse then right on Dorfstrasse on to Wittenberger Strasse to join the B2. Turn right at the B187, then left at Elsterstrasse and right on Am Hauptbahnhof to exit on Lutherstrasse. Turn left at Neustrasse for the car park.*

⑦ Lutherstadt Wittenberg
Saxony-Anhalt; 06886
Clinging to a scenic stretch of the Elbe, the tidy little town of Lutherstadt Wittenberg is named after its most famous resident, Martin Luther, who came here in 1508 and sparked the Protestant Reformation. It now basks in this golden era, celebrating the homes and graves of those who together created the "Protestant Rome."

A two-hour walking tour
From the Neustrasse car park turn left onto Mittelstrasse and follow it to Collegienstrasse where, beside a small park, lies the **Lutherhaus** ① *(Apr–Oct: open daily; Nov–Mar: closed Mon)*, formerly the Augustinian monastery into which Luther entered on arriving in the town. Dissolved during the Reformation,

Exterior detail, Lutherhaus

one of the monastery's wings served as the Luther family residence. Today it contains a collection of Reformation relics: Luther's desk, pulpit and first editions of many of his books. Outside the Lutherhaus, and on the corner of Lutherstrasse and Am Hauptbahnhof, grows an old oak, the **Luthereiche** ②, which was planted in 1830 on the spot where Luther displayed his

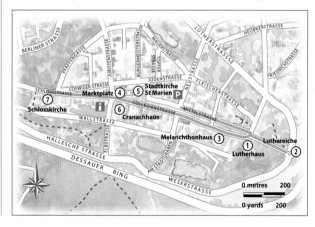

Left Impressive interior of the Gothic Schlosskirche, Lutherstadt Wittenberg
Below Luthereiche outside the Lutherhaus, Lutherstadt Wittenberg

VISITING LUTHERSTADT WITTENBERG

Parking
The most convenient place to park is the outdoor car park on Neustrasse at the corner of Mittelstrasse, though there is plenty of on-street parking in the vicinity, if this is full.

Tourist Information
Schlossstrasse 16, 06886; 03491 49 86 10; www.wittenberg.de

EAT AND DRINK

WÖRLITZ

Gastwirtschaft im Küchengebäude moderate
Located in the old kitchens of the Schloss, this restaurant is the only real option inside the park grounds.
Schloss Wörlitz, 06786; 03495 02 23 38

Pension Zum Hauenden Schwein moderate
This pension has a good traditional wine bar and restaurant.
Erdmannsdorffstrasse 69, 06786; 03490 53 01 90

LUTHERSTADT WITTENBERG

Wittenberger Kartoffelhaus inexpensive
An old-fashioned dark-wood pub specializing in potato preparations.
Schlossstrasse 2, 06886; 03491 41 12 00

Alte Canzley moderate
An excellent organic restaurant, with a menu featuring pork roast with beans and Bohemian-style dumplings.
Schlossstrasse 3, 06886; 03491 42 91 90; www.alte-canzley.de

Marc de Cafe moderate
The fabulous cakes, coffee and relaxed atmosphere here encourage lingering.
Pfaffengasse 5, 06886; 03491 695 80 85

---

conviction in 1520 by publicly burning the papal bull threatening his excommunication. Further along Collegienstrasse from the Lutherhaus is the Renaissance **Melanchthonhaus** ③ *(closed Mon)*, the former house of Humanist Philipp Melanchthon, Luther's closest associate and the author of *Augsburg Confession,* a statement of belief that became the Protestant constitution. Further on, Collegienstrasse ends at the **Marktplatz** ④, where 19th-century statues of Luther and Melanchthon stand. To their right, an alley cuts through a row of townhouses to the **Stadtkirche St Marien** ⑤ *(open daily),*

Luther's Living Room
Look out for Luther's living room in the Lutherhaus. Left as bare as it was in 1535, it is easy to imagine his students gathered here for the religious conversations that were later compiled in the book *Table Talk.* Luther's views on many religious and social matters are candidly outlined in the book.

where Luther married Katharina von Bora and their six children were baptized. This church dates from 1300 and contains an altar (1547) painted by the artist Lucas Cranach the Elder and his son. On the southern side of the Marktplatz is the **Cranachhaus** ⑥, once the residence of the artist. A few doors to the right is his former studio, the Galerie im Cranachhaus *(open daily).* Further left, Schlossstrasse leads to the old palace and the Gothic **Schlosskirche** ⑦ *(open daily).* On 31 October 1517, Luther is said to have pinned his 95 theses on its door, which has since been replaced with a bronze door with the theses inscribed in Latin. His tombstone lies below the pulpit, opposite that of Melanchthon. The stairs up the Schlossturm (castle tower) next door offers pretty views over the town. Take the Schlossstrasse to Collegienstrasse, turn left into Mittelstrasse to the car park.

DAY TRIP OPTIONS
A variety of day trips are possible along this route, taking in ecclesiastical outposts, trading towns and landscaped gardens. Also discover Lutherstadt Wittenberg's many links with the Protestant Reformation.

The ecclesiastical frontier
Visit the red-brick abbeys and churches at Jerichow ❷ and Havelberg ❶ and then wander around the half-timbered houses of

Tangermünde ❸. The last two can also be reached by sailing up the Elbe on a day trip from Magdeburg ❹.

Take the B1 and turn left on to the B107 to Jerichow and then Havelberg.

Landscape and architecture
Follow the tour from Magdeburg ❹ to the Bauhaus design school ❺. Next, head for the charming, English-style gardens of Wörlitz ❻. If the weather is bad, visit the other

Bauhaus buildings in Dessau; if it is fine, enjoy a picnic in Wörlitz.

Follow the driving instructions from Magdeburg.

In the footsteps of Reformation
Children will love the Lutherhaus, as it offers plenty of engaging audio-visual games. Be sure to climb the stairs of the Schlossturm and then relax with coffee and cake at Marc de Café.

Take the B184 and then the B187.

Eat and Drink: inexpensive, under €20; moderate, €20–€40; expensive, over €40

Prussian Splendour

Schloss Charlottenburg to Filmpark Babelsberg

Highlights

- **Lakeside palaces**
  Discover the palaces and gardens around the scenic lakes and forests to the southwest of Berlin

- **Royal retreat**
  Explore Park Sanssouci – Frederick the Great's retreat and one of Europe's most beautiful royal complexes

- **Cultural haven**
  Visit the characterful Dutch and Russian quarters in Potsdam, the historic lakeside state capital

- **Regional cuisine**
  Enjoy typical, hearty Berlin and Huguenot cuisine with a beer in one of Potsdam's many traditional restaurants

Sculpture in the palace gardens of Park Sanssouci

Prussian Splendour

Potsdam, the historical residence of the Prussian royals, is one of Germany's most attractive cities. Visitors from all over the world come to see its pretty royal summer castle, Schloss Sanssouci, built for the Prussian king, Frederick the Great. This is a tour through the countryside between Berlin and Potsdam, with beautiful landscapes, inviting lakes and extravagant Prussian residences. Its highlights are the Schloss Charlottenburg, Schloss Glienicke and its surrounding lakes, and the breathtaking Potsdam palaces and the churches in the historic city.

KEY

Drive route

Below Avenue leading to the Neues Palais, Park Sanssouci, *see pp78–9*

PLAN YOUR DRIVE

Start/finish: Schloss Charlottenburg to Filmpark Babelsberg.

Number of days: 1–2 days, allowing half a day to explore Park Sanssouci.

Distance: 36 km (23 miles).

Road conditions: The roads along this drive are in very good condition.

When to go: The best time to visit the region is between late spring and early autumn.

Opening times: Most attractions open daily, while shops are open from 9am to 5pm, Monday to Friday.

Major festivals: Park Sanssouci: Potsdamer Schlössernacht (night of Potsdam's palaces), Aug; Hollandisches Viertel: Potsdamer Tulpenfestival (tulip festival), Apr.

1 Schloss Charlottenburg

Berlin; 14059

The Charlottenburg castle *(closed Mon)* was designed as a summer home for Sophie Charlotte, Elector Friedrich III's wife. Construction of the **Altes Schloss** *(closed Mon)*, the old castle, designed by the German architect Johann Arnold Nering (1659–95), began in 1695 and the **Neuer Flügel** *(closed Tue; under restoration until April 2014)*, or new wing, was added in the 18th century. The interior of the building was fully restored after World War II.

The **Nering-Eosander-Bau** *(closed Mon)*, the palace in the Altes Schloss, contains the suites of Friedrich III and his wife. Its highlights include the Oak Gallery and the early 18th-century palace chapel. The Neuer Flügel is famous for its **Goldene Galerie**, a huge golden ballroom, and for its paintings by Watteau, Chardin and Pense *(guided tours only)*.

The park behind the castle was originally French Baroque, but was reconstructed after World War II. Full of interesting buildings, it is open to visitors all year round and offers a scenic refuge for city dwellers, joggers and families.

Golden griffin sculpture, Klein Glienicke

🚘 *Take the A115 towards Potsdam and turn on to Spanische Allee, which becomes Wannseebadweg, following signs to Strandbad Wannsee.*

2 Strandbad Wannsee

Berlin; 14129

The public lido Strandbad Wannsee *(17 Apr–25 Sep: open daily)*, was constructed at the beginning of the 20th century and is big enough to accommodate 40,000 people on its artificial sandy beach. Its buildings, including the changing rooms, eateries and bathrooms, were built in the straightfoward, functional *Neue Sachlichkeit*, or New Objectivity style, spearheaded by the architect Martin Wagner. Alternatively, stroll down Wannseebadweg to explore the nearby **Schwanenwerder Island**, which is home to some stunning villas.

🚘 *Return to the A115 towards Potsdam and take the exit to Wannsee. Follow the B1 and continue westwards to reach Klein Glienicke.*

3 Klein Glienicke

Berlin; 14129

For centuries, the Hohenzollern Dynasty, who first ruled as Prussian electors and kings and later as emperors, transformed the sandy glades, pine forests and lakes south-west of Berlin into picture-perfect *Kulturlandschaft* – man-made landscapes of parks and palaces. Among the most brilliant of these is Klein Glienicke, built for Prince Karl of Prussia in the early 19th century. The vast park comprises the **Schloss Glienicke** *(Apr–Oct: closed Mon; Nov–Mar: open Sat & Sun, guided tours only)*, the **Jagdschloss Glienicke**, or Glienicke Hunting Lodge, and a number of smaller buildings. The palace and park were declared a UNESCO World Heritage Site in 1990.

The simple Neo-Classical façade of the charming **Schloss Glienicke** has a solemn dignity about it that was once admired by Goethe *(see p108)*. Inside, the atmosphere is rich, with many lovely paintings, colourful walls and rooms that are elegantly appointed with the architect Schinkel's furnishings and lit by bright, golden chandeliers. The proportions are perfect, giving the entire ensemble a particularly harmonious look.

The adjoining park has a mock monastery, or Klosterhof, a coach house, and the **Grosse Neugierde**, a Neo-Classical pavilion that offers splendid views of the Havel river.

🚘 *Return to the B1 and then continue on it towards Potsdam. Once in the city, follow the signs towards Park Sanssouci.*

Above Impressive entrance to the Schloss Charlottenburg, Berlin

WHERE TO STAY

AROUND SCHLOSS CHARLOTTENBURG

Pension Dittberner *moderate*
Sophisticated comfort is provided here. Sculptures, paintings and posters in the rooms create a welcoming atmosphere for art lovers.
Wielandstrasse 26, 10707 Berlin (3 km/ 2 miles southeast of the castle); 030 881 64 85; www.hotel-dittberner.de

Schlosshotel im Grunewald *expensive*
This beautiful and serene luxury hotel has a gourmet restaurant, bar and spa and is set in a former country estate.
Brahmsstrasse 10, 14193 Berlin (6 km/ 4 miles southwest of the castle); 030 89 58 40; www.schlosshotelberlin.com

EAT AND DRINK

AROUND SCHLOSS CHARLOTTENBURG

Kleine Orangerie *moderate*
This inviting café, set right next to the Schloss, offers tea, coffee and cake, but is most popular for its beer garden and tempting Sunday breakfast buffet.
Spandauer Damm 20, 14059 Berlin (west of the castle); 030 322 20 21; www. kleineorangerie.de; closed Mon in winter

KLEIN GLIENICKE

Blockhaus Nikolskoe *moderate*
Commissioned by Friedrich Wilhelm III according to a Russian design, this historic restaurant has a changing menu of traditional regional cuisine.
Nikolskoer Weg 15, 14109 Berlin; 030 80 529 14; www.blockhaus-nikolskoe.de

Ludwig & Werner *expensive*
The restaurant in Schloss Glienicke serves modern versions of traditional German dishes. Enjoy views of the sunset from the terrace in summer.
Königstrasse 36, 14109 Berlin; 030 805 40 00; www.schloss-glienicke-berlin.de; closed Mon & Tue

---

Eat and Drink: inexpensive, under €20; moderate, €20–€40; expensive, over €40

VISITING PARK SANSSOUCI

Parking
Ample parking space is available
at Neues Palais outside the entrance
to the park.

Tourist Information
*An der Orangerie 1, 14469; 0331 969
42 00; closed Mon*

WHERE TO STAY

AROUND PARK SANSSOUCI

Hotel am Luisenplatz *moderate*
A harmonious and unique ambience
awaits guests at this very stylish hotel
located in the historic downtown of
Potsdam. The rooms and suites of this
four-star hotel are elegantly appointed.
*Luisenplatz 5, 14471 Potsdam (2 km/
1 mile south of the park); 0331 97
19 00; www.hotel-luisenplatz.de*

Steigenberger Hotel Sanssouci
moderate–expensive
The Steigenberger Hotel Sanssouci,
whose striking 1950s Anglo-American
design contrasts sharply with the
surroundings, is both pleasant and
very conveniently located for guests.
*Allee nach Sanssouci 1, 14471 Potsdam
(2 km/1 mile south of the park);
0331 909 10; www.steigenberger.
com/Potsdam*

Below top Outdoor exhibits in Filmpark
Babelsberg **Below** Schloss Cecilienhof in
the Neuer Garten, Park Sanssouci

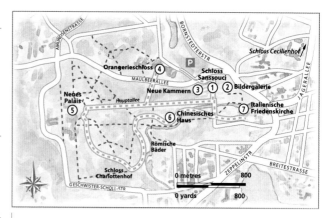

❹ Park Sanssouci
Brandenburg; 14469

A vast collection of ornate gardens, water features and follies,
Park Sanssouci is also home to fantastic Neo-Classical, Baroque
and Rococo palaces and pavilions. The first building on the site
was the enchanting Schloss Sanssouci, built for the Prussian King
Frederick the Great in 1745. Over the next 150 years, the park was
transformed into one of the finest royal complexes in Europe.

A two-hour
walking tour

**Fountain head at
the Neues Palais**

Arrive early at Park
Sanssouci in order to
avoid the crowds. Georg
Wenzeslaus von Knobelsdorff
(1699–1753) built this lavish
complex between 1745 and
1747. From the car park,
walk to the surprisingly small **Schloss
Sanssouci** ① *(open Tue–Sun; Nov–Mar:
guided tours only)*, which served the
art-loving Frederick the Great as a
retreat from wars and daily politics.
Start the tour through the park at
this magnificent Rococo palace, set
atop beautiful terraced lands with
grapevines. To the east of the palace
stands the **Bildergalerie** ②, home to
the king's collection of 17th-century
Italian and Dutch paintings, including
works by Caravaggio, Rubens and Van
Dyck. To the west of the palace is the
massive **Neue Kammern** ③ *(Apr–Oct:
open Tue–Sun; closed Nov–March)*, the
new chambers, formerly used as a
guesthouse by the royal family.
   Cross the Maulbeerallee and follow
signs to **Orangerieschloss** ④ *(Apr:
open Sat & Sun; May–Oct: closed Mon)*,
which dates back to 1860 and now
houses the tourist information centre
for the park. The **Neues Palais** ⑤

(closed Tue), or New Palace, is
much larger and grander
than Schloss Sanssouci. It is
accessed by following
Hauptallee, the straight
avenue that runs through
Park Sanssouci. This palace
was built after the Seven
Years' War (1756–63) as a
symbol of the strength and stability of
Frederick's reign in the wake of the
conflict. Highlights of this palace
include the Grotto Hall where marble
walls and columns are decorated
with marine motifs. The upper gallery has paintings by 17th-century
masters and the theatre is still used to
host performances of classical music.
   Take the path to the south of the
Neues Palais to Schloss Charlottenhof,
*(May–Oct: open Tue–Sun, guided tours
only)*, a palace built in 1826 during the
reign of Frederick William IV by
architect Karl Friedrich Schinkel in
typical Neo-Classical style. From here,
walk to the neighbouring Römische
Bäder *(May–Oct: closed Mon)*, or Roman
Baths, and the **Chinesisches Haus** ⑥
(May–Oct: closed Mon). Designed in an
imitation Chinese style that was
fashionable in 1757, this Rococo tea
house was once used to host royal tea
parties. An exhibition of exquisite

porcelain is now housed here. Walk eastwards from here and across the canal to the **Italienische Friedenskirche** ⑦, home to a 12th-century Byzantine mosaic. This Neo-Romanesque church is modelled on the Basilica of San Clemente in Rome. Walk back to the main avenue and then follow signs back to the car park.

Visitors can also opt for a detour to Schloss Cecilienhof *(closed Mon)*, built for Crown Prince Wilhelm in 1913. It is located in the Neuer Garten, or New Garden, a section of the park that borders on Heiliger See. The palace is famous for having hosted the Potsdam Conference in 1945, when the heads of the Allied nations discussed the fate of post-war Germany. To reach the palace from Schloss Sanssoucci, walk east on Voltaireweg, then Reisterweg and Alleestrasse, or take Bus No. 603 from outside Park Sanssouci.

🚗 *From Schloss Sanssouci follow signs towards Babelsberg and then to Alexandrowka to reach the Russische Kolonie.*

⑤ Russische Kolonie and Holländisches Viertel
Brandenburg; 14467
A short drive from the Neuer Garten, Russische Kolonie, the Russian colony, is a charming residential area known for its wooden log cabins, each with an enchanting little garden. It was built in 1826 for the singers of a Russian choir – a present from Tsar Alexander I of Russia to Prussia. In turn, the Prussian king built the Russian-style houses so

that the choir would feel more at home in Potsdam. Follow the B2 to the **Holländisches Viertel**, or Dutch quarter. It has 134 red-brick gabled houses along cobblestoned alleys that were built by Dutch craftsmen in the first half of the 18th century, during the reign of Friedrich Wilhelm I.

🚗 *Follow signs southeastwards to the Filmpark Babelsberg.*

⑥ Filmpark Babelsberg
Brandenburg; 14482
This film park was laid out on the site where Germany's first films were produced in 1912. The major films created in these studios were *Metropolis*, by the Austrian-American filmmaker Fritz Lang, and *Blue Angel*, which turned the actress Marlene Dietrich into a star. The film park was also used for the production of Nazi propaganda films during Hitler's rule. Today, it is one of Europe's largest studio complexes and the source of blockbusters such as Quentin Tarantino's *Inglourious Basterds*. Visitors can admire some of the sets as well as stuntmen in action.

Above left Picturesque path flanked by trees leading to Neues Palais, Park Sanssouci
Above right Red-brick gabled house in Holländisches Viertel **Below** Neo-Classical Schloss Charlottenhof, Park Sanssouci

EAT AND DRINK

AROUND PARK SANSSOUCI
Maison Charlotte *expensive*
Tucked away in an old building in the Dutch Quarter, Maison Charlotte is an old wine bar with an excellent wine list and robust German-French cuisine. The traditional country-style cooking uses seasonal produce from France.
Mittelstrasse 20, 14467 Potsdam (2 km/1 mile east of the park); 0331 280 54 50; www.maison-charlotte.de

Restaurant Friedrich-Wilhelm *expensive*
This charming Michelin-starred restaurant with a great terrace, located in the five-star hotel Bayrisches Haus, offers creative German nouvelle cuisine. Reservation is recommended and the dress code is formal.
Elisenweg 2, 14467 Potsdam (7 km/4 miles southwest of the park); 0331 550 50; www.bayerisches-haus.de; closed Sun & Mon

RUSSISCHE KOLONIE AND HOLLÄNDISCHES VIERTEL
Restaurant Juliette *expensive*
At the heart of the historic Dutch Quarter lies the charming French Restaurant Juliette. Guests can enjoy carefully prepared French cuisine and an extensive wine list.
Jägerstrasse 39, 14467 Potsdam; 0331 270 17 91; www.restaurant-juliette.de; closed Mon & Tue

Eat and Drink: inexpensive, under €20; moderate, €20–€40; expensive, over €40

Grand Old Prussian Avenues

Schloss Rheinsberg to Freilandmuseum Lehde

Highlights

- **Sleepy rural haven**
  Explore the picturesque Schloss Rheinsberg, once the retreat of kings, writers and poets

- **Sobering memorial**
  Take a sombre tour of the former concentration camp of Sachsenhausen

- **Tropical paradise**
  Enjoy an unlikely getaway provided by a Zeppelin hangar at Tropical Islands

- **Punts and Sorbs**
  Go punting on the mellow waterways of the Spreewald and discover the culture of the Sorbs, Germany's only indigenous ethnic minority

Sunlit stretch of tree-lined avenue to Chorin, Brandenburg

Grand Old Prussian Avenues

Around Berlin, scores of venerable, tree-lined Prussian avenues slice through the flat countryside to connect a series of varied attractions. Amid the forested rolling hills between Brandenburg and Mecklenburg-Western Pomerania in the north is Rheinsberg, a pretty town with a modest palace that was once a favourite of Frederick the Great. A short drive south is the former concentration camp of Sachsenhausen. More pleasant reminders of the past lie to the east, including the 13th-century monastery at Chorin and a remarkable Prussian ship hoist at Niederfinow. To the south, the leafy hills around Buckow are perfect for hiking, while the myriad waterways that crisscross the UNESCO-designated biosphere reserve of Spreewald can be explored in a punt. The Spreewald region also bears remnants of the Sorbian culture that prevailed before the 10th-century German conquest.

ACTIVITIES

Cruise the lakes around Rheinsberg in a rowing boat or kayak

Experience being lowered in a boat by an old Prussian ship hoist at Niederfinow

Explore the scenic woodlands around Buckow

Luxuriate, **swim**, **slide and play** in the warm temperature inside an old Zeppelin hangar in Tropical Islands

Go punting or paddling on the Spreewald waterways

Savour the famous Spreewald gherkin in the region that produces 40,000 tonnes (44,092 tons) of the pickled cucumbers per year

KEY

 Drive route

0 kilometres 10

0 miles 10

Below left Beautiful scenery en route to the Tropical Islands, *see p87* **Below right** Colourful boats and canoes, perfect for exploring Lübben, *see p87*

Above Broad avenue to Chorin, *see p85*

PLAN YOUR DRIVE

Start/finish: Schloss Rheinsberg to Freilandmuseum Lehde.

Number of days: 3 days, allowing half a day to explore Buckow.

Distance: 300 km (186 miles).

Road conditions: Generally well paved and straight minor roads.

When to go: Summer is best for attending music festivals and visiting Buckow and the Spreewald region. In winter, allow plenty of time in the warmth of Tropical Islands.

Opening times: Most attractions open daily, while shops usually open from 9am to 5pm, Monday to Friday but close early on Saturdays. Shops and services are closed on Sundays. Restaurants generally close around 10pm.

Main market days: Schloss Rheinsberg: Wed & Sat; **Lübben:** Wed & Fri.

Shopping: In Rheinsberg, look out for traditional pottery with its trademark dark blue and cream glazes.

Major festivals: Schloss Rheinsberg: Rheinsberger Musiktage (music days), May/Jun; Kammeroper Schloss Rheinsberg (opera festival), late Jun/mid-Aug; **Kloster Chorin:** Choriner Musiksommer (classical music festival), Jun; **Buckow:** Literatursommer (literary summer festival), May–Aug.

DAY TRIP OPTIONS

Families will enjoy **boating** in Spreewald before taking a splash in Tropical Islands. **History enthusiasts** can head to the **monastery** in Chorin followed by a visit to the **ship hoist** at Niederfinow and later, take a **walk** around Buckow. Visitors could also begin with an exploration of the Sachsenhausen before unwinding in Rheinsberg. For full details, *see p87*.

Right Schloss Rheinsberg, one of the town's main attractions **Below** Grim exterior of the former concentration camp at Sachsenhausen

BOATING AROUND RHEINSBERG

Much of Rheinsberg's charm lies in its adjacent tranquil wooded lakes. These can be explored with **Reederei Halbeck** *(033931 386 19; www. schiffahrt-rheinsberg.de)*, who operate half-day cruises of local lakes from the quay behind the palace. They also rent out rowing boats and kayaks.

WHERE TO STAY

AROUND SCHLOSS RHEINSBERG

Zum Jungen Fritz *inexpensive*
This centrally located inn has cheerful hosts and tidy rooms. Free passes to the local gym are also provided.
Schlossstrasse 8, 16831 Rheinsberg (west of Rheinsberg); 03393 140 90; www.junger-fritz.de

Der Seehof *moderate*
A mid-18th-century former farmhouse just north of Schloss Rheinsburg, offering bright rooms with lake views.
Seestrasse 18, 16831 Rheinsberg (north of Rheinsberg); 03393 140 30; www.seehof-rheinsberg.de

Pension Holländermühle *moderate*
This comfortable B&B has a novel location in a 100-year-old windmill, just a couple of minutes' drive south of Schloss Rheinsberg.
Holländer Mühle 01, 16831 Rheinsberg (21 km/13 miles south of Rheinsberg); 03393 123 32; www.hollaender-muehle.de

AROUND KLOSTER CHORIN

Waldsee Hotel *moderate*
Beautifully situated in the woods north of the monastery grounds, this family-run hotel has simple, floral rooms.
Neue Klosterallee 12, 16230 Chorin (south of Chorin); 03336 653 10; www.waldseehotel-frenz.de

AROUND THE SCHIFFSHEBEWERK

Am Schiffshebewerk *moderate*
A guesthouse with clean and spacious en suite rooms located in quiet, rural surroundings. Famous for traditional meals and home-made cakes.
Hebewerkstrasse 43, 16248 Niederfinow (north of Niederfinow); 03336 27 00 99; www.hotel-schiffshebewerk.de

❶ Schloss Rheinsberg
Brandenburg; 16831

According to Frederick the Great, king of Prussia, his happiest days were spent in the Schloss Rheinsberg *(closed Mon)*, located in a sedate little town of the same name. Here, in the early 18th century, he studied for the throne, wrote flute sonatas and gave occasional concerts. Later, the palace served as a sanatorium. It has since been renovated and has become a popular attraction with lovely gardens; some of the elegant palace rooms can be visited. Highlights include the Spiegelsaal (mirror hall), with its dizzying ceiling fresco by court painter Antoine Pesne, and the Baroque Muschelsaal (shell hall) with its maritime theme. The north wing of the palace houses the **Tucholsky Literaturmuseum** *(closed Mon)*, which examines the life of pacifist and left-wing journalist Kurt Tucholsky (1890–1935).

🚗 *From Schlossstrasse, drive towards Herzberg to reach Köpernitz. At*

Rheinsberg and Kurt Tucholsky

The picturesque setting of Rheinsberg provided Kurt Tucholsky with inspiration for his novel *Rheinsberg: Ein Bilderbuch für Verliebte* (Rheinsberg: a Picture Book for Lovers), a cheerful love story laced with criticism of bourgeois thought and nationalism. This made it one of the books burned by the Nazis once they came to power, though by then Tucholsky had already left Germany. He died in exile, in Sweden, before the World War II he had predicted broke out.

Köpernitz, turn left in the direction of Gransee. From here, turn right and get onto the B96 to Nassenheide. Take the exit towards Oranienburg-Nord then turn left on Granseer Strasse towards Sachsenhausen. Turn left on to the Friedrichsthaler Strasse, and almost at the roundabout, exit onto Sophie-Scholl-Strasse, which becomes Aderluch. Turn left on Schäferweg to reach the car park at the former camp gates.

❷ Gedenkstätte Sachsenhausen
Brandenburg; 16515

A poignant reminder of one of the most oppressive regimes of the 20th century, the Gedenkstätte Sachsenhausen, or memorial *(open daily; museums: closed Mon)*, portrays the atrocities that occurred here when it was converted into a concentration camp during World War II. The Sachsenhausen became a model for most other Nazi camps. Though it was never designated a full-blown

"death camp", around half of its 220,000 prisoners were killed. Inside, several museums detail the lives and fates of the prisoners and document the horrors of systematic executions. Take a tour of the hall that examines the Soviet Special Camp (1945–50) which existed here after World War II when the Russians imprisoned 60,000 suspected Nazis and killed at least 12,000 of them, although most of them were probably innocent.

Turn left from the car park on Strasse der Nationen and then right on to Strasse der Einheit. Take the B273 to Wandlitz, then turn left in the direction of Bisenthal and continue towards Eberswalde. In Eberswalde, turn right on to the B167, then left over the canal towards Angermünde. Finally, turn left into the signed cloister car park.

❸ Kloster Chorin

Brandenburg; 17279
Founded in 1258 by Cistercian monks, Chorin cloister *(open daily)* is studded with decorative brick-work. One of the grandest red-brick structures in Germany, its scale is impressive even today; it is hard to imagine what its impact would have been in the 12th century. Dissolved in 1542, the monastery slowly crumbled until the 19th century, when its slender arches, graceful windows and step gables were renovated during the Romantic movement. The surrounding parkland beside a pretty lake offers an idyllic walk.

Return via Angermünder Strasse and just before Eberswalde, turn left

on *Oderberger Strasse which becomes Macherslust, then turn right on to Hebewerk Strasse. Park at car park beside the ship hoist.*

❹ The Schiffshebewerk

Brandenburg; 16248
A huge iron sentinel perched amid rolling green hills, the Schiffshebewerk (ship hoist) has a framework of gigantic girders designed for lifting boats 36 m (118 ft) between the Oder river and the Oder-Havel canal, two vital regional waterways. The ship hoist cuts the process of transferring giant barges from several tedious hours to just 20 minutes. On its completion in 1934, it was the largest of its kind and remains impressive, particularly when viewed from the upper platform *(open daily)*, a vantage point which provides good views. It is also possible to be a part of the experience by being lifted or lowered in a boat, such as those belonging to Fahrgastschiffahrt Neumann *(03334 244 05; www. finowkanalschiffahrt.de)* whose ticket booth is in the Schiffshebewerk car park information kiosk. An adjacent visitors' centre *(open daily)* details the construction of the hoist and of a new structure that is planned for 2015.

Turn left out of the car park, then at the T-junction turn left briefly on to the B167 then right following signs to Prötzel. In Prötzel, turn left on to the B168, then right at a roundabout to Bollersdorf. Shortly after Bollersdorf turn right to Buckow and then left on Schulstrasse to reach the public car park.

Above Sculptures adorning the garden, Schloss Rheinsberg **Below** Pretty red-brick Kloster Chorin

EAT AND DRINK

AROUND SCHLOSS RHEINSBERG

Schlosshotel Rheinsberg *moderate*
An elegant dining option featuring an inventive regional menu with the occasional exotic Asian touch. Try the local speciality *Zander* (a perch-like fish), served with sesame rice and carrot.
Seestrasse 13,16831 Rheinsberg (north of Rheinsberg); 03393 13 90 59; www.schlosshotel-rheinsberg.de

Other options
For a unique local gastronomic experience, pay a visit to **Eisfabrik** *(Kurt-Tucholsy-Strasse 36, 16831)*, an ice-cream maker with a wide range of highly unusual yet refreshing flavours, which include garlic, parsley and radish.

AROUND KLOSTER CHORIN

Alte Klosterschänke *moderate*
This traditional restaurant, a short walk from the monastery, uses fresh, seasonal and local organic produce. The excellent *Klosterpfanne* (cloister pan) combines three types of pan-fried poultry with baby carrots, sweetcorn and mashed potato.
Amt Chorin 9, 16230 Chorin (south of Chorin); 03336 653 01 00; www.alte-klosterschaenke-chorin.de; Jan–Feb: open Sat & Sun, Mar–Oct: open daily, Nov–Dec: open Wed–Sun

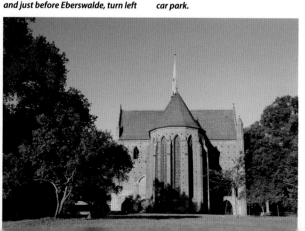

Above Brecht-Weigel-Haus, Bertolt Brecht's summer retreat

VISITING BUCKOW

Parking
The car park lies just off Schulstrasse.

Tourist Information
Wrezener Strasse 1a; 03343 36 59 82; www.maerkischeschweiz.eu; open daily

WALKING AROUND BUCKOW

For a long walk around Buckow take the 7.5-km (5-mile) path bordering the Schermützelsee. It is well marked and takes about two hours to complete.

WHERE TO STAY

BUCKOW

Zur Märkischen Schweiz *inexpensive*
A reasonably priced traditional inn.
Hauptstrasse 73, 15377; 03343 34 64

Bergschlösschen *moderate*
This late 19th-century villa offers comfortable rooms with valley views.
Königstrasse 38, 15377; 03343 35 73 12

TROPICAL ISLANDS

Tropical Islands *inexpensive–expensive*
Visitors can rent a tent or stay in a lodge on the islands. It is also possible to sleep on the beach.
Tropical-Islands-Allee 1, 15910, Krausnick, 15910; 03547 760 50 50; www.tropical-islands.de

AROUND LÜBBEN

Hotel Schloss Lübbenau *moderate*
Lübbenau's palace has elegant *fin-de-siècle* rooms and a relaxing spa.
Schlossbezirk 6, 03222, Lübbenau (south of Lübben); 03542 87 30; www.schloss-luebbenau.de

Zur Bleiche *expensive*
A boutique hotel with luxurious suites.
Bleichstrasse 16, 03096, Burg im Spreewald (southeast of Lübben); 03560 36 20; www.hotel-zur-bleiche.com

Where to Stay: inexpensive, under €70; moderate, €70–€150; expensive, over €150

⑤ Buckow
Brandenburg; 15377

With its rolling hills, trickling streams and languid lakes, the sleepy little spa town of Buckow has long been a popular getaway from Berlin. Poet and playwright Bertolt Brecht was among those drawn here, spending several summers in an idyllic lakeside cottage. The house now makes an interesting stop on a walk around the three lakes between which Buckow nestles.

A 90-minute walking tour

From the car park turn left down to Schulstrasse, left again along Hauptstrasse and then look for a right turn down Erlenweg to the lovely lakeside promenade. Follow this around the Buckowsee lake, turn right at a junction in the path to arrive at the **Brecht-Weigel-Haus** ① *(open Wed–Sun)*, where the artist couple Brecht and his wife, Helene Weigel, spent many summers in the mid-1950s. It is now a memorial to their time spent here. The interior of the house displays rustic furnishings alongside photo exhibits and the famous covered wagon used in Brecht's play *Mother Courage and Her Children*. From the house, follow Werderstrasse uphill then turn left up Bertolt-Brecht-Strasse, which climbs steeply to offer superb lake views. Buckow's ritziest homes are found here. Most are attractive **pre-World War II villas** ② built with Art Nouveau touches. Turn left down Ringstrasse and left again on to the shores of the Schermützelsee, Buckow's largest lake. Here, **Strandbad Buckow** ③, a popular swimming beach, provides facilities as well as opportunities for renting rowing boats *(www.buckow-online.de/freizeit/sport/sport.html)*. The hour-long lake tours by Seetours *(Apr–Oct: open daily; 033433 232)* also begin from here.

A signposted path behind and uphill from the beach leads up the side of **Schlossberg** ④, a small hill that provides pretty views of the town. This leads back down to follow the banks of Griepensee to a small bridge beside the **Schweizer Haus** ⑤, a visitors' centre that has a series of information boards and interactive displays about the local ecology and hiking routes. It faces Lindenstrasse, which leads to Königstrasse and into **Buckow's centre** ⑥, with its smattering of shops. Return to the car park by walking left along Hauptstrasse and turning left again into Schulstrasse.

🚗 *Return to the B168 and continue to Müncheberg then to Beerfelde. Follow the B168, bypassing Fürstenwalde, then turn right on to Hauptstrasse, following signs to Alt Schadow. Take Lubbener Strasse, which becomes Dorfstrasse to Schlepzig. Turn left, go past Krausnick-Gr. Wasserburg then turn right to the car park at the Tropical Islands.*

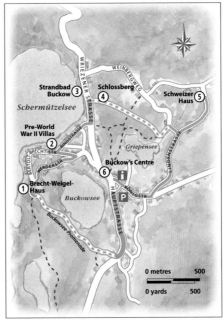

Strandbad Buckow ③
Schlossberg ④
Schweizer Haus ⑤
Schermützelsee
Pre-World War II Villas ②
Griepensee
Buckow's Centre ⑥
Brecht-Weigel-Haus ①
Buckowsee
Buckowsee-Promenade

WRITZENER STRASSE
WEINBERGWEG
BRECHT STR
BERTOLT BRECHT STR
WERDERSTR
RINGENSTR
LINDENSTRASSE
KÖNIGSTR
HAUPTSTRASSE

0 metres   500
0 yards   500

⑥ Tropical Islands
Brandenburg; 15910

Occupying a former Zeppelin hangar, Tropical Islands *(open daily)*, is a landscaped indoor park complex which contains plenty of water-based attractions, such as pools, lagoons, whirlpools, waterfalls and saunas as well as a number of restaurants. Enjoy the lush landscape and look out for the tropical birds that luxuriate in the constant 27º C (81º F) temperature of the complex.

🚗 *Return to Krausnick-Gr. Wasserburg and head to Schlepzig. From here turn right, then right again to get on to the B87 to park at the harbourside car park in Lübben.*

⑦ Lübben
Brandenburg; 15907

The largest Spreewald town, Lübben bustles with hotels and restaurants. Its most popular attraction is the pretty Schloss *(Apr–Oct: closed Mon; Nov–Mar: open Wed–Sun)*, which houses a regional history museum. Behind the palace is the attractive Schlossinsel, an artificial archipelago with gardens and a leafy maze. Nearby, the busy harbour area buzzes with punts, or *Kahn*, which cruise the surrounding waterways. A number of operators *(www.bootsverleihpetrick. de)* offer tours as well as canoe or kayak rentals.

🚗 *From the car park turn left on to the B87 then left again, following signs to Lübbenau. From Lübbenau turn left at Dammstrasse and park in central Lübbenau for a 4 km (2 mile) walk to the Freilandmuseum.*

⑧ Freilandmuseum Lehde
Brandenburg; 03222

Popular for punting and canoeing trips, the village of Lehde is dominated by the Freilandmuseum Lehde *(Apr–Oct: open daily)*. This museum re-creates a traditional Sorbian village, using original houses and farmhouses. Take a look at the simple, rustic furnishings inside, including some memorable beds designed to sleep a whole family.

The Sorbs

Germany's only indigenous ethnic minority, the Sorbs, now just 60,000 in number, can trace their ancestry back to the Slavic Wends, who, in the 5th century, settled in the Lusatia swamps between the Oder and Elbe rivers. In the 10th century, this region was conquered and forcibly Germanized. Yet Sorbian is still spoken in the region, most street signs are bilingual and popular Sorbian festivals are still observed.

Above Canoes in the Spreewald town of Lübben **Below left** Open-air Freilandmuseum, set in Lehde

EAT AND DRINK

BUCKOW

Fischerkehle *moderate*
An elegant choice, famous for simple local dishes featuring fish and game. *Fischerberg 7, 15377; 03343 33 74; www.fischerkehle-buckow.de*

Stobbermühle *moderate*
A former watermill, this charming restaurant serves regional and national dishes. It is a favourite with locals, especially for its terrace in summer. *Wriezener Strasse 2, 15377; 0334 36 68 33*

LÜBBEN

Schlossrestaurant Lübben *moderate*
This restaurant offers superb views of the palace gardens and serves traditional Spreewald dishes. *Ernst-von-Houwald-Damm 14, 15907; 03546 40 78; www.schlossrestaurant-luebben.de; closed Mon*

Other options
Strubel's *inexpensive (Dammstrasse 3, 15907; 03542 27 98)* offers traditional cuisine with a local flavour. Try the local fish and its perch, eel and pike platter.

DAY TRIP OPTIONS

This route offers a wide range of day trips.

Spreewald delights

Begin the day by punting or canoeing in the canals of Lübben ❼, then indulge in water sports at the relaxing Tropical Islands ❻.

From Lübben, take the Frankfurter Strasse and then the Dorfstrasse to the Tropical Islands.

A monastery and a ship hoist

Tour the monastery at Chorin ❸ and explore the remarkable Schiffshebewerk ❹ at Niederfinow before visiting the peaceful woods and lakes at Buckow ❺.

From Chorin take the Angermünder Strasse to Britz, then turn on to Oderberger Strasse and further on to Coderberger Strasse, then An der Schleusentreppe and Hebewerk Strasse to Niederfinow. Take the B167 to Sternebech, which joins the B35. Then take the Hauptstrasse following signs to Buckow.

History and architecture

Visit the memorial at Sachsenhausen ❷ before heading to the delightful Schloss Rheinsberg ❶.

Take the B96 to Gransee. Take the Sonnenberger Strasse and then the Rheinsberger Strasse to Koppernitz, following signs to Rheinsberg.

Eat and Drink: inexpensive, under €20; moderate, €20–€40; expensive, over €40

Palaces and Castles of Münsterland

Kalkar to Münster

Highlights

- **Historical romance**
  Tour the grand moated castles of Münsterland, from swaggering Baroque palaces surrounded by trim gardens to grizzled stone castles whose painted halls hint at Renaissance courtly life

- **Cultural capital**
  Wander around Münster, a bustling, prosperous university town whose lanes abound with historic architecture

- **Country cooking**
  Sample hearty Westphalian fare, including smoked hams, strongly flavoured sausages and heavy stews, in rustic beamed inns

Sculptures in the expansive gardens of Schloss Nordkirchen

Palaces and Castles of Münsterland

The plains on the German-Dutch border see few visitors except those who stop by Westphalia's (Nordrhein-Westfalen) capital, the lively university city of Münster. Yet, with its short distances and straight roads, Münsterland provides perfect back roads touring. It is a sparsely populated landscape of half-timbered farmsteads, windmills and woods as well as of spires that soar above neat market squares. The countryside is dotted with numerous moated castles and manor houses on artificial islets – the hundred or so *Wasserschlösschen* (water castles) from a feudal past still largely privately owned by noble families. Starting at the historic town of Kalkar, this tour takes drivers to the architecturally rich city of Münster.

KEY

⊐ Drive route

PLAN YOUR DRIVE

Start/finish: Kalkar to Münster.

Number of days: 2 days, allowing half a day to explore Münster.

Distance: 156 km (97 miles).

Road conditions: The region has well-signposted roads. There is some congestion during rush hour in the short section of the road into Münster.

When to go: It is best to visit this region in late spring or summer, when palace gardens are in full bloom.

Opening times: Most restaurants are closed either on Mondays or Tuesdays.

Main market days: Kalkar: Thu; Xanten: Mon, Thu & Sat; Münster: Wed & Sat (produce and crafts market).

Major festivals: Münster: The Send (funfair and crafts market) early Mar, 3rd or 4th weekend in Jun & Sep.

Above Rapeseed flowers on the road to Schloss Lembeck, *see p91*

❶ Kalkar

North Rhine-Westphalia; 47546

Cafés and shops occupy the patricians' houses on Kalkar's cobbled Marktplatz, dominated by the 15th-century **Rathaus**. The square is a fine place to sit and soak up the atmosphere of this historic town. Highlights include **St Nikolaikirche** *(open daily)*, whose stunningly intricate altars date from Kalkar's golden age in the 15th and 16th centuries; the high altar was created by three craftsmen over 12 years.

🚗 *Leave the town on Altkakaren Strasse to the left of the church. Turn left at the roundabout on to the B57 towards Xanten. Parking is available in the Archäologischer Park and in Xanten's Ostwall and Markt.*

❷ Xanten

North Rhine-Westphalia; 46509

Located by the mighty Rhine river, Xanten was once a Roman metropolis known as Colonia Ulpia Traiana. Today's walled town was created around a memorial church, **Dom St Victor**. Built on top of the grave of the martyr St Victor, the church was first named *Ad Sanctos* (by the saints), which was soon shortened to Xanten.

On the outskirts of the town is the **Archäologischer Park** *(open daily)*, which, with its reconstructed Roman public buildings, hints at the scale of this 1st-century port, which housed 10,000 people. A museum by the baths has displays on the town's Roman past.

🚗 *Continue on the B57 and turn left towards Wesel. Follow the B58 through Wesel to turn left on to the B70 to Raesfeld. Park at the Schloss.*

❸ Schloss Raesfeld

North Rhine-Westphalia; 46348

The 17th-century moated palace of Count Alexander II von Velen, Schloss Raesfeld, was described as a "trumpet blast in stone", and is still an impressive edifice with a fine Baroque altar in its chapel. A riverside walk through the garden behind the palace leads to a ruined watermill.

🚗 *Drive through Raesfeld and take the B224 at the roundabout on the outskirts of the town. Turn left at Erle to reach Lembeck. Follow signs to the Schloss.*

Chateaux of Münsterland

Without a defensive hill anywhere on the plains of Münsterland, feudal rulers in the Middle Ages turned to water for protection. Broad moats were dug to encircle their *Wasserschlösschen*. More powerful cannons and peace rendered such defences obsolete in the 17th century, so aristocrats re-created their strongholds as chateaux-style status symbols. Around 100 of these remain within a 100-km (50-mile) radius of Münster, of which 40 are still owned by the original noble families.

❹ Schloss Lembeck

North Rhine-Westphalia; 46286

The formidable gatehouse of the moated Schloss Lembeck *(Mar–Nov: open daily)*, belies the Baroque elegance inside. The Westphalian court architect Johann Conrad Schlaun introduced Italianate style to the castle in the 17th century, when he redesigned the **Festsaal**, or Celebration Hall. Do visit the rhododendron park.

🚗 *Turn right from the entrance of the castle and left at T-junction on to the B58. Drive through Haltern, turn left in Lüdinghausen at the white signpost for "Burgen" and park at the castle.*

VISITING XANTEN

Parking
The town centre has limited parking space but there is ample parking at the Archäologischer Park.

Tourist Information
Kurfürstenstrasse 9, 46509; 02801 983 00; www.xanten.de; open daily

WHERE TO STAY

XANTEN

Van Bebber *moderate*
Housed in a Baroque townhouse, this friendly family hotel has spacious rooms with antique-style furnishings, as well as an excellent restaurant that specializes in game.
Klever Strasse 12, 46509; 02801 66 23; www.hotelvanbebber.de

AROUND SCHLOSS RAESFELD

Landhaus Keller *moderate*
Overlooking meadows and the Schloss, this hotel has relaxed country decor, spa facilities and a good restaurant.
Weseler Strasse 71, 46348 Raesfeld (northeast of the Schloss); 02685 608 50; www.landhaus-keller.de

EAT AND DRINK IN XANTEN

Café de Fries *inexpensive*
Savoury crêpes, waffles, salads and snacks are served in this café-cum-cake shop with a large terrace.
Kurfürstenstrasse 8, 46509; 02801 20 68; www.cafe-defries.de

Gotisches Haus *moderate*
One of Xanten's oldest inns, this atmospheric place is spread over four floors. In summer, the beer garden in its courtyard is open.
Markt 6, 46509; 02801 70 64 00; www.gotisches-haus-xanten.de; closed Mon

Eat and Drink: inexpensive, under €20; moderate, €20–€40; expensive, over €40

Above left Burg Vischering, a magnificent moated castle **Above right** Wooden doors of the Überwasserkirche, Münster **Below** Quiet road leading to Münster

WHERE TO STAY IN MÜNSTER

Hof zur Linde *moderate*
Located on the riverside in the Handorf suburb, the Hof zur Linde is a traditional hotel with modern furnishings and fittings.
Handorfer Werseufer 1, 48157; 0251 327 50; www.hof-zur-linde.de

Martinihof *moderate*
A simple but good-value modern hotel above a pub, the Martinihof is situated close to Prinzipalmarkt.
Hörsterstrasse 25, 48143; 0251 418620; www.hotel-martinihof.de

Mauritzhof *moderate*
A boutique hotel on the ring road around the city centre, the Maurtitzhof has a designer look that compensates for its compact standard rooms.
Eisenbahnstrasse 17, 48143; 0251 417 20; www.mauritzhof.de

Schloss Wilkinghege *expensive*
Historic style meets modern comfort in the individually decorated rooms of this 18th-century *Wasserschloss*.
Steinfurter Strasse 374, 48159; 0251 14 42 70; www.schloss-wilkinghege.de

⑤ Burg Vischering
North Rhine-Westphalia; 59348
Burg Vischering *(closed Mon)* is one of the oldest and best-preserved castles in Münsterland. Founded in 1270, it was extended in the 16th and 17th centuries. Across a drawbridge from agricultural outbuildings, the formidable U-shaped palace retains its loopholes (arrow slits in the walls) and battlements. The castle also has features of early Renaissance palaces with its Oriel windows, gables and the sandstone fireplaces inside its painted halls. Walk through the surrounding woodland for picture-postcard views of the castle reflected in the moat.
🚗 *Return to the B58 and follow signs to Nordkirchen. Follow signs from the town centre to "Wasserschloss". Parking is available at the castle.*

⑥ Schloss Nordkirchen
North Rhine-Westphalia; 59394
The vast, moated Schloss Nordkirchen, *(open Sun)* nicknamed the "Westphalian Versailles", is a perfectly symmetrical French Baroque castle. It was designed by the German architect Johann Conrad Schlaun (1695–1773) as an aristocratic status symbol. Now a

school of finance, it has Baroque gardens *(open daily)* sprinkled with white statuary.
🚗 *Return to Lüdinghausen to reach the B235. Past Senden, turn right towards Albachten. Once past Roxel, turn left to park at Burg Hülshoff.*

⑦ Burg Hülshoff
North Rhine-Westphalia; 48329
The writer and poet Annette von Droste-Hülshoff, the most celebrated member of the aristocratic Hülshoff Dynasty, was born at Burg Hülshoff in 1797. The castle's ground floor *(mid-Mar–Oct: open daily; Nov: open Wed–Sun)* is a shrine to the writer, who is viewed as Germany's very own Emily Brontë – both writers died unmarried and penned sombre tales steeped in their personal tragedies. There are splendid views of this Renaissance manor rising from its moat from the adjoining park, restored to re-create the gardens in which Hülshoff found inspiration.
🚗 *Return to Roxel, turn left on to Roxeler Strasse to Münster. Continue on Einsteinstrasse and Wilhelmstrasse, turn right at the B219 junction. Park in front of Schloss Münster.*

Revolution in Münster
Religious disaffection during the Reformation led to one of the most colourful episodes in Münster's history. A fundamentalist Anabaptist regime seized control of the city in 1534, with a Dutchman named Jan van Leiden at its head – money was made obsolete, property communal and polygamy a duty. However, the city was recaptured in 1535 and van Leiden and his lieutenants were executed and their bodies hung in cages from the Lambertikirche spire as a warning to others.

Where to Stay: inexpensive, under €70; moderate, €70–€150; expensive, over €150

⑧ Münster

North Rhine-Westphalia; 48143

Steeped in centuries of learning, the capital of Westphalia is the university city par excellence. World War II saw 90 per cent of the old town laid to ruins, but most of it has now been rebuilt. In 2004, the UN Environmental Programme hailed Münster as the world's most livable city. For visitors, its shops and fine cuisine add to its appeal and complement the impressive monuments and museums.

A 90-minute walking tour

The car park is located in the forecourt of **Schloss Münster** ①, the palace of Münster's Prince-Bishop rulers. Designed by the court's master-architect Johann Conrad Schlaun, the Baroque residence is now the main university building. From the car park, cross the road into Frauenstrasse. Turn left into Jüdefelderstrasse to the **Kuhviertel** ②, a cozy nest of lanes full of student drinking dens. Walk back to Frauenstrasse and turn left to the Gothic Liebfrauenkirche, the Church of Our Lady, popularly called **Überwasserkirche** ③, or church over water, after the Aa river behind it.

Continue down the road and cross the Aa to reach a cobbled lane framed by the twin spires of the **Dom St Paul** ④, built in the 13th century to replace the monastery that gave Münster its name. Inside is a beautifully painted 16th-century astronomical clock by painter Ludger Tom Ring and a frieze in the Romanesque

Detail on the door of the Schloss Münster

vestibule illustrating the labours of the months. Opposite the cathedral, the **Landesmuseum** ⑤ *(closed Mon)* displays art and sculpture from the medieval to the modern ages. It includes religious sculptures by Münster's Heinrich Brabender that survived the Anabaptist purges. Walk across Domplatz to Prinzipalmarkt, a former merchants' street that now has some of the finest shops. Ahead is the gabled Gothic **Rathaus** ⑥ *(closed Mon)* where the Catholic faction brokered a peace deal to end the Thirty Years' War. Walk down the main street to the 15th-century **Lambertikirche** ⑦. The three iron cages attached to its spire were used to display the executed Anabaptist revolutionaries. Turn right in front of the church to stroll down Salzstrasse. Go past the **Stadtmuseum** ⑧ *(closed Mon)* at No. 28, which has Anabaptist exhibits, to the Promenadenring parkland that circles the city. A stroll along the promenade leads back to the car park.

Above Thirteenth-century twin-spired Dom St Paul, Münster

VISITING MÜNSTER

Parking
The city's largest parking areas are at the Schloss on Schlossplatz. Central car parks on Königstrasse and Heinrich-Brüning-Strasse are busy at weekends.

Tourist Information
Heinrich-Brüning-Strasse 9, 48143; 0251 492 27 10; www.tourismus. muenster.de; closed Sun

EAT AND DRINK IN MÜNSTER

Café Kleimann *inexpensive*
Located opposite the Lambertikirche, Café Kleimann is an acclaimed *Konditorei* (cake shop).
Prinzipalmarkt 48, 48143; 0251 430 64; www.konditorkleimann.de; closed Sun

Pinkus Müller *moderate*
In the Kuhviertel is Münster's last surviving and oldest micro-brewery specializing in draft beers and regional cuisine such as veal ragout Töttchen.
Kreuzstrasse 4–10, 48143; 0251 451 51; www.pinkus-mueller.de; closed Sun

Kleiner Kiepenkerl *expensive*
This upmarket family-run inn offers regional fare such as sausage-platters. Tables are set on a terrace in summer.
Spiekerhof 47, 48143; 0251 434 16; www.kleiner-kiepenkerl.de; closed Mon

Kleines Restaurant im Oer'schen Hof *expensive*
Housed in a historic building, this hotel serves exquisite modern European cuisine.
Königstrasse 42, 48143; 0251 484 10 83; www.kleines-restaurant-im-oerschenhof.de; closed Sun & Mon

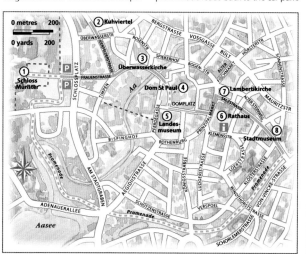

Eat and Drink: inexpensive, under €20; moderate, €20–€40; expensive, over €40

Mystical Mountains

Burg Falkenstein to Rammelsberger Bergbaumuseum

Highlights

- **Medieval towns**
  Wander around the lovely half-timbered towns of Quedlinburg and Goslar

- **Witches and folklore**
  Spark the imagination with tales of witches at the Hexentanzplatz and the Brocken

- **Delightful steam trains**
  Chug up the Harz mountain range to reach the Brocken on Europe's largest narrow-gauge network

- **Mining heritage**
  Explore the old mines that were for centuries a way of life in the Harz at the Rammelsberger Bergbaumuseum

Spectacular view along a hiking trail in the Bode Valley

Mystical Mountains

A popular outdoor retreat for northern Germans, the scenic Harz mountain range lies where Saxony-Anhalt (Sachsen-Anhalt), Thuringia (Thüringen) and Lower Saxony (Niedersachsen) meet. Soaring peaks are absent here, but thickly wooded mountains abound, with pretty villages and modest resort towns tucked between them. The Harz's highest peak, the Brocken, is also its centrepiece, not least for its long-standing mystical associations with witchcraft. Mining too has been an integral part of life here, and old mines have now been made into attractions, but the Harz is famous mostly for hiking and cycling opportunities in summer and tobogganing and skiing in winter. The old narrow-gauge railway network, complete with steam trains, is ideal for exploring the gateway towns of Quedlinburg and Goslar, both UNESCO World Heritage Sites.

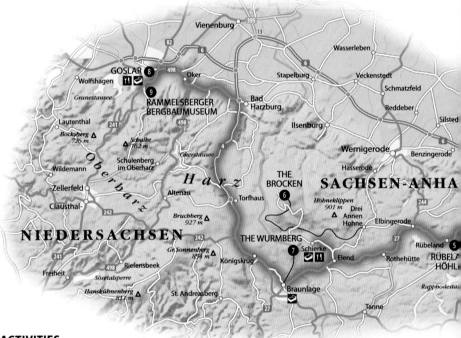

ACTIVITIES

Watch cuckoo clocks being made at the Harzer Uhrenfabrik in Gernrode

Hike in the deep and verdant Bode Valley for a picturesque view of the Harz mountains

Explore the atmospheric limestone caverns at the Rübeland Caves

Take a steam train to the top of the Harz mountains on the Brockenbahn railway

Enjoy skiing, tobogganing, hiking and mountain biking on the Wurmberg

Journey into the dark depths of the Rammelsberger silver mine near Goslar

Above Hillside surrounding the Hexentanzplatz, *see p99* **Below left** Pastel-coloured half-timbered houses in the town of Quedlinburg, *see p98* **Below right** Steam train to the Brocken peak, *see p99*

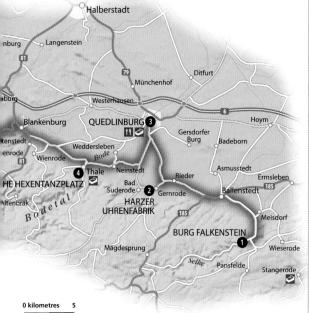

PLAN YOUR DRIVE

Start/finish: Burg Falkenstein to Rammelsberger Bergbaumuseum.

Number of days: 2–3 days, allowing half a day to explore Goslar.

Distance: 139 km (86 miles).

Road conditions: Well paved, though many roads through the mountains tend to be steep and winding.

When to go: It is possible to visit year round, but minor roads are occasionally snowbound from December to March. Winter is best for skiing and sledging.

Opening times: Most attractions open daily, while shops open from 9am to 5pm, Monday to Friday, but close earlier on Saturday. Most shops and services are closed on Sunday. Restaurants generally close around 10pm.

Main market days: Quedlinburg: Wed; **Goslar:** Tue & Fri.

Shopping: Look out for wood carvings such as marionettes of witches or cuckoo clocks at Harzer Uhrenfabrik. Local crafts are available at Goslar's Kunsthandwerkermarkt.

Major festivals: Quedlinburg: Musiksommer (classical music festival), Jun–Sep; **The Brocken**: Walpurgisnacht (witches' night), 30 Apr.

DAY TRIP OPTIONS

Using Quedlinburg as a base, **nature enthusiasts** can spend a day **hiking** in the southern Harz, then ride on the **steam train** up the Brocken. Those interested in **history** can explore Goslar's half-timbered old town before returning on a scenic route via the Rübeland Höhlen. For full details, *see p101.*

Above Aerial view of Burg Falkenstein and the surrounding forest **Below** Entrance to the Rübeland Höhlen

WHERE TO STAY

AROUND BURG FALKENSTEIN

Reit-und Sporthotel Nordmann *moderate*
A lovely country hotel whose facilities include a pool, a sauna and horse riding.
Deistrasse 23, 06543 Stangerode (19 km/ 12 miles west of Burg Falkenstein); 03474 295 30; www.nordmannharz.de

QUEDLINBURG

Am Brühl *moderate*
This country-house-style hotel in a half-timbered building on the edge of the old town serves regionally inspired food.
Billungstrasse 11, 06484; 03943 961 80; www.hotelambruehl.de

Schlossmühle *moderate*
A smart hotel with fine castle views from its snug, spotless modern rooms.
Kaiser-Otto-Strasse 28, 06484; 03943 78 70; www.schlossmuehle.de

AROUND THE HEXENTANZPLATZ

Ferienpark Bodetal *moderate*
Neat little holiday village at the foot of the Hexentanzplatz with a pool.
Hubertusstrasse 9–11, 06502 Thale (7 km/4 miles north of the Hexentanzplatz); 03947 776 60; www.ferienpark-bodetal.de

AROUND THE BROCKEN

Waldschlösschen *moderate*
A family-run hotel with modern rooms and impressive views over Braunlage. Its Art Nouveau restaurant serveslocal cuisine.
Hermann-Löns-Weg 1, 38889 Schierke (23 km/14 miles south of the Brocken); 03945 586 70

❶ Burg Falkenstein
Saxony-Anhalt; 06543
Sitting on a rocky outcrop, the stocky Burg Falkenstein *(Mar–Oct: open daily; Nov–Feb: closed Mon)* provides views over wooded hills and the eastern plains of Saxony-Anhalt, making it the most attractive castle in the Harz. Built between 1120 and 1180, it has since been expanded. Inside, the chapel is a highlight, as is the walk around its interiors, which include a museum. Falconry displays *(Mar–Oct: closed Mon)* are an added attraction.

🚗 *Follow signs to Ballenstedt and turn left on to the B185. At the T-junction, turn right to Rieder. In Gernrode, turn right on Bergstrasse to Lindenstrasse. Park in Harzer Uhrenfabrik.*

❷ Harzer Uhrenfabrik
Saxony-Anhalt; 06507
Woodcarving has long been a traditional craft in the Harz, which is known for its cuckoo clocks.

The Harzer Uhrenfabrik factory *(open daily)* is one of the few places in Germany where visitors can watch clocks being made. A few paces down Lindenstrasse lead to the **Stiftskirche St Cyriakus**. An early pioneer of the Romanesque style, it is one of the country's best preserved churches.

🚗 *Head back towards Rieder, but turn left on to Quedlinburger Strasse before the town of Quedlinburg. In Quedlinburg's town centre, turn left on to Steinbrücke, then left again on to Carl-Ritter-Strasse car park.*

❸ Quedlinburg
Saxony-Anhalt; 06484
Set in the rolling foothills of the Harz, the town of Quedlinburg dates back to its foundation as a fortress in 922, after which it became the favourite residence of Saxon emperors. The town flourished as a centre for dyes, paper production and engineering in the Middle Ages, when most of its half-timbered houses were built. Reached by continuing along Carl-Ritter-Strasse from the car park, then turning left up Finkenherd, the **Schlossberg** *(closed Mon)* is a knuckle of rock that served as the foundation for a 16th-century Renaissance castle constructed around the **Stiftskirche St Servatius** *(closed Mon)*, built between 1070 and 1129. The adjacent **Schlossmuseum** *(closed Mon)* has local treasures dating back to the Stone Age. To the right of the castle gates is a row of half-timbered houses with a courtyard that hosts the **Lyonel-Feininger-Galerie** *(closed Mon)*, where

the 1920s works of this Bauhaus artist are displayed. To the left of Carl-Ritter-Strasse, on Wordgasse, lies the **Fachwerkmuseum** (open Fri–Wed), Germany's oldest half-timbered house, built in 1310, now a construction museum. Turn left for a short walk to the Markt. One of its many attractive buildings is the Rathaus, parts of which date back to 1320.

🚗 *Leave Quedlinburg on Gernröder Weg, which becomes Suderöder Chausee, then turn right on Suderöder Strasse for Thale. In Thale, turn left, then right to Hexentanzplatz car park.*

Walpurgisnacht
Walpurgisnacht (30 April) probably began as a Celtic festival celebrating spring, but developed a reputation for black magic. Legends grew of witches and warlocks flying up to the Brocken to recount the past year's evil deeds before holding an orgy that included the devil himself. So powerful were these legends that for centuries church bells would toll on Walpurgisnacht to deter evil forces.

➍ The Hexentanzplatz
Saxony-Anhalt; 06502
The Hexentanzplatz, or "witches' dance place" probably began life as a spiritual place used for Celtic rituals and sacrifices. Later, it became known as an occult centre, where witches were said to gather before flying to the Brocken on Walpurgisnacht. Today, revellers arrive on the same night to enjoy the celebrations. A modest museum, the **Walpurgishalle** (May–Oct: open daily), explains pagan worship in German with vivid drawings and a ghoulish Germanic sacrificial stone.

Sculpture of a goblin, the Hexentanzplatz

🚗 *From Thale return to the T-junction and turn left. Continue on the same road and turn right on to the B81. In Blankenburg, turn left on to the B27 to the car park left beyond the caves.*

➎ Rübeland Höhlen
Saxony-Anhalt; 38889
Since its chance discovery by a 15th-century miner, the 600,000-year-old **Baumannshöhle** (closed Nov–Apr) has attracted visitors keen to tread in the footsteps of Stone Age inhabitants and Ice Age bears, some of whose skeletons remain here. The adjacent **Hermannshöhle** (closed Nov–Apr) has impressive stalagmites and stalactites.

🚗 *Continue on the B27, turn right at Elend and continue to Schierke; park at the railway station.*

➏ The Brocken
Saxony-Anhalt; 38879
The ascent of the Brocken (1,141 m/3,747 ft), the highest peak in the Harz, is a vital part of any Harz itinerary. The easiest way to reach the top is by the narrow-gauge Brockenbahn railway, which climbs steeply to a height of 1,125 m (3,691 ft). Trains depart from Schierke for the short journey. Here, the **Brockenmuseum** (open daily) displays exhibits on the mountain's geology and mythology. An easy 2.5-km (1.5-mile) path loops the summit, offering superb views.

🚗 *Return to the B27 and turn right. In Braunlage, turn right down Pfaffenstieg and right again on to the Wurmberg chairlift car park.*

Steam Trains in the Harz
Steaming through 140 km (87 miles) of track through the mountains, the **Harzer Schmalspurbahn** (www.hsb-wr.de) is the largest narrow-gauge network in Europe. Many of the steam trains are from the 1950s, but one has been in service since 1887. The railway lines link Quedlinburg, Nordhausen and Wernigerode with the Brocken. Round trips depart on Thursdays, Fridays and Saturdays.

Left Scenic train ride to the Brocken
Below Sixteenth-century Renaissance castle atop the Schlossberg, Quedlinburg

HIKING IN THE BODE VALLEY
The Hexenstieg or Witches' Trail along the Bode Valley, takes in spectacular scenery, passing gnarled trees that are centuries old. This path is best explored by first taking a bus No. 18 from Thale's train station to the village of Treseburg, then walking the 10 km (6 miles) back downstream, which takes between 2–3 hours. For a longer walk, take the chairlift to Hexentanzplatz, then walk the 10-km (6-mile) trail to Treseburg, stop for lunch, then return to Thale via the Hexenstieg – a walk of 4–5 hours. Maps are available at the tourist information office (Bahnhofstrasse 1, 06502 Thale; 03947 25 97).

EAT AND DRINK

QUEDLINBURG
Himmel und Hölle *inexpensive*
A cosy restaurant in a small hotel, Himmel und Hölle is known for its *Flammkuchen*, a pizza-like dish topped with cheese, onion and bacon.
Hölle 5, 06484; 03946 52 86 55

Theophano *expensive*
Tucked beneath the cellar arches of a 360-year-old half-timbered house, this restaurant serves modern regional cuisine with an international touch, as chef Sebastian Vogel and his team experiment with various cooking styles.
Kornmarkt 6, 06484; 03946 81 00 50; www.restaurant-theophano.de

AROUND THE BROCKEN
Bahnhofsbaude Schierke *inexpensive*
Dishes and hearty snacks from the Harz region are served here.
Auf dem Brocken, 38879 Schierke; 03945 55 83 45

Above Charming town of Goslar on the northwestern slopes of Harz Mountains

⑦ The Wurmberg
Lower Saxony; 38700

The Harz's second-highest peak, the Wurmberg (971 m/3,186 ft) is a venue for many outdoor sports *(open daily)*. In winter, the ski lift *(www.wurmberg-seilbahn. de)* of the resort town of Braunlage is used by snowboarders. In summer, the Wurmberg's chairlift carries hikers to a good selection of trails. Hiking from the summit to the base takes around 1.5 hours.

🚗 *Turn right on to Pfaffenstieg, left on to Am Amtsweg then right on Harzburger Strasse. Turn right on the B4, and in Bad Harzburg, turn left on to Harzburger Strasse. Take the B498 and get on to the B241 to Goslar. In Goslar, turn right and then left to the car park.*

⑧ Goslar
Lower Saxony; 38640

One of Germany's most attractive towns, Goslar is famous for its half-timbered houses. The discovery of silver in the 10th century made it one of Europe's leading towns but it fell into decline after the Duke of Braunschweig-Wolfenbüttel claimed the mine in 1532. Much of the town has been preserved, along with its Romanesque palace.

VISITING GOSLAR

Parking
The multi-storey car park on Bäckerstrasse on the eastern side of Goslar and the parking space near Kaiserpfalz are among the most convenient of several car parks.

Tourist Information
Markt 7, 38640; 05321 780 60; www.goslar.de; open daily

WHERE TO STAY

AROUND THE WURMBERG

Residenz Hohenzollern-Victoria-Luise *expensive*
Braunlage's smartest hotel lies on the sunny southern side of the Wurmberg and offers spacious rooms. It also has an international gourmet restaurant.
Doktor-Barner-Strasse 10–11, 38700 Braunlage (8 km/5 miles south of the Wurmberg); 05520 932 10; www.residenz-hohenzollern.de

GOSLAR

Altstadt-Hotel Gosequell *moderate*
This family-run hotel in the town's historic centre is housed in a restored heritage building. The restaurant serves local specialities.
An der Gose 23, 38640; 05321 34050

Kaiserworth *moderate*
A historic hotel in a former 15th-century guildhall near Goslar's marketplace, the Kaiserworth has rooms decorated in a range of styles. The restaurant has a seasonal regional menu.
Markt 3, 38640; 05321 70 90; www.kaiserworth.de

A two-hour walking tour

Exit the car park on Bäckerstrasse, turn right then left on to Fischemäker Strasse and follow it to Goslar's **Markt** ①, where a group of half-timbered buildings surround a 13th-century fountain on which Goslar's imperial eagle puffs out his chest. The old treasury building to the left is famed for its 18th-century carillon *(open daily)* in which parading figures tell the story of mining history. Opposite,

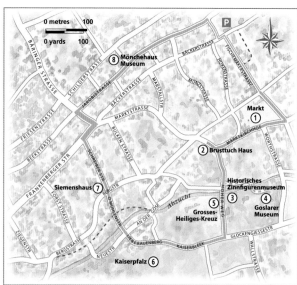

the 15th-century Rathaus with its Gothic gables looks most impressive at night. Behind it is the Romanesque market church or Marktkirche. The 16th-century half-timbered **Brusttuch Haus** ②, with its excellent woodwork, lies behind the church. From the left of the house, Hoher Weg leads to the **Historisches Zinnfigurenmuseum** ③ *(closed Mon; www.zinnfigurenmuseum-goslar.de)*, one of the best miniature tin figure museums in Germany. Just off Hoher Weg, a path to the left follows the Abzucht stream, which leads to the **Goslarer Museum** ④ *(closed Mon)*. Inside, the Goslarer Evangeliar, a jewel-encrusted book of gospels, and the Bergkanne, a stein with figures of miners, are displayed. Back to Hoher Weg, the **Grosses-Heiliges-Kreuz** ⑤ *(closed Mon)*, a former hospice, is now a crafts centre. At the end of Hoher Weg is the Domvorhalle, the vestibule of a church that once housed the Kaiserstuhl, the imperial throne. Down the street to the right is the **Kaiserpfalz** ⑥ *(open daily)*, the 11th-century imperial palace of Heinrich III. Later, it was used as a granary, until it was rescued by Kaiser Wilhelm I in 1868 for the Second Reich. Inside, the Ulrichskapelle is the resting place of

Heinrich III's heart in a gilt box. From Kaiserpfalz go left to Bergstrasse. On the opposite corner is the Baroque **Siemenshaus** ⑦ *(guided tours only)*, the family home of the Siemens industrialist family. A short walk from here to Jakobistrasse leads to **Mönchehaus Museum** ⑧ *(closed Mon)*, which displays the work of artists including Willem de Kooning. Continue down Jakobistrasse to the car park.

🚗 **Turn right on to Vogelsang, left on to Bäckerstrasse, then right on to Mauerstrasse and left on to Okerstrasse. Turn right on to the B241 and left on to Rammelsberger Strasse to the museum.**

⑨ Rammelsberger Bergbaumuseum
Lower Saxony; 38640

For a millennium the Rammelsberger silver mine formed Goslar's economic backbone. Closed down in 1998, it has since become the **Bergbaumuseum** *(open daily)* that chronicles the mine's history. Visitors can don overalls and tour the 18th- and 19th-century shafts.

Above left Fountain in the Markt, Goslar
Above right Outdoor cafés in Goslar with the Marktkirche looming behind **Below** Old mine at the Rammelsberger Bergbaumuseum

EAT AND DRINK IN GOSLAR

Die Worthmühle *moderate*
Harz's speciality restaurant, with rustic nooks and dishes such as wild boar and trout, serves excellent *Goslarer Gosebier*, a fruity local beer. *Worthstrasse 4, 38640; 05321 434 02; www.worthmuehle.de*

Aubergine *expensive*
A luxury restaurant serving French and Italian cuisine. Good for fresh fish and lamb. The mocha mousse dessert is a house speciality. *Marktstrasse 4, 38640; 05321 421 36; www.aubergine-goslar.de*

Other options
Goslar is filled with atmospheric cafés but look out for the Baroque-style **Café Anders** *(Hohe Weg 4, 38640; 05321 238 14)*, which offers home-made truffles and great Harz views.

DAY TRIP OPTIONS
Despite its many dark and remote corners, the Harz is compact and within range of day trips. Quedlinburg is a good base and is well served by the narrow-gauge railway.

Castles and caves
From Quelinburg ③, head to Thale and walk along the Bode Valley. If there is time to spare, the Harzer Uhrenfabrik ② at Gernrode is a good wet-weather option, along with the Burg Falkenstein ① or the Rübeland Höhlen ⑤.

Follow thr route to Thale and continue to the T-junction after Neinstedt. Turn right and head to Gernrode, then take the road to Ballenstedt and continue to Burg Falkenstein. For the caves, head from Thale to Blankenburg and on to the B27.

Magical Brocken
Enjoy a ride on the narrow-gauge trains from Quedlinburg ③ to the summit of the Brocken ⑥.

Quedlinburg's railway station is at the end of Bahnhofstrasse; from the market walk along Steinbrücke and then turn right down Bahnhofstrasse.

Picturesque Harz
Explore Goslar ⑧, a pretty town with 1,800 half-timbered houses and then head to the interesting Rammelsberger Bergbaumuseum ⑨ to visit the old silver mine and learn about the history of mining in this region.

Follow the route to Goslar, then the B241 to Rammelsberger Bergbaumuseum.

Hilltop Castles and Lush Landscapes

The Wartburg to Schloss Belvedere

Highlights

- **Iconic castle**
  Tour the Wartburg, whose fairy-tale looks match its romantic past

- **Sleepy towns**
  Walk around the half-timbered old towns of Schmalkalden and Arnstadt, nestled in wooded hills

- **Highland hiking**
  Escape to the hills in the Thuringian Forest to hike the trails, or to follow in Goethe's footsteps in a day-long expedition

- **Cultural jewel**
  Explore the museums and palaces of the UNESCO-listed town of Weimar

View of the town of Mühlberg from Burg Gleichen

Hilltop Castles and Lush Landscapes

Hilltop ski resorts, spa towns and the network of hiking trails through the Thuringian Forest (Thüringer Wald) have transformed the "green heart" of Germany into a holiday playground. Yet, thanks to its fragmentation into a patchwork of small duchies in the 16th and 17th centuries, Thuringia (Thüringen) is just as rich in history and art. References to luminaries such as composer Johann Sebastian Bach, reformer Martin Luther and writer and polymath Johann Wolfgang von Goethe appear regularly on a route that begins at a fairy-tale castle in Eisenach and winds deep into the Thuringian Forest, a wooded upland where cozy timber-framed towns and ducal palaces nestle beneath pine-clad hills. The route emerges from this timeless landscape to veer east towards its final stop, Weimar, a cradle of culture that appeals to head and heart alike.

0 kilometres   5

0 miles   5

ACTIVITIES

Hike into the high country on the 20-km (13-mile) stretch from Ilmenau or just take a walk around Grosser Inselsberg

Go skiing in winter and summer at Oberhof

Try Thuringian bratwurst, grilled over hot charcoal, available throughout the region

Explore Goethe's house in Weimar

KEY

Drive route

PLAN YOUR DRIVE

Start/finish: The Wartburg to Schloss Belvedere.

Number of days: 3–4 days, allowing half a day to explore Weimar.

Distance: 250 km (155 miles).

Road conditions: Roads are generally good in the Thuringian Forest. In winter, snow can be a problem.

When to go: The best time to visit is summer (June to August), when flowers carpet the meadows, festivals are in full swing and hiking is idyllic. The ski season is from mid-December to February.

Opening times: Most shops are open from 9am to 5pm Monday to Friday. Many museums in Weimar are closed on Mondays.

Main market days: The Wartburg: Wed & Thu; **Ilmenau:** Thu & Fri; **Arnstadt:** Tue, Fri & Sat; **Erfurt:** Mon–Sat; **Weimar:** Wed, Thu–Sun.

Major festivals: Erfurt: Krämerbrückenfest (merchant's bridge medieval festival), Jun; DomStufen-Festspiele (music/theatre festival), Jul–Aug; **Weimar:** Wine Festival, Aug; Weimarer Zwiebelmarkt (onion festival), Oct.

DAY TRIP OPTIONS

Meiningen is an ideal base for **outdoor activities** in the Thuringian Forest, with **skiing** in Oberhof and **walks** around Ilmenau. Visit Weimar to see **splendid art galleries**, and **aristocratic palaces**, then stop by Erfurt's **Gothic cathedral** and take a side-trip to Arnstadt. For full details, *see p111*.

Above left Straw bales on a meadow, Drei Gleichen, *see p108* **Above right** Shops and cafés on Krämerbrücke, Erfurt, *see p109* **Below** Sculpture at Dom St Marien, Erfurt, *see p109*

Above Bachhaus with its lovely garden, Eisenach **Below** The Wartburg, perched on top of a hill, Eisenach

VISITING THE WARTBURG

Parking
Park in the castle's car park. Alternatively, visitors can park in Eisenach's old town and take mini-trains or bus No. 10 from the main square.

Tourist Information (Eisenach)
Markt 24, 99817; 03691 792 30; www.eisenach.info

VISITING GROSSER INSELSBERG

Tourist Information
Tabarz, Theodor-Neubauer-Park 3, 99891; 03625 96 10 87

Hiking
03613 74 20; www.thueringen-tourismus.de

WHERE TO STAY

THE WARTBURG

Hotel auf der Wartburg *expensive*
This luxurious small hotel has individually styled rooms.
Auf der Wartburg, 62298; 03691 79 70; www.wartburghotel.de

SCHMALKALDEN

Patrizier *moderate*
A half-timbered building in the town centre, this hotel is decorated with floral wallpaper and antique-style furnishings.
Weidebrunner Gasse 9, 98574; 03683 60 45 14; www.stadthotel-patrizier.de

MEININGEN

Sächsischer Hof *moderate*
Elegant Biedermeier-style furnishings and spacious dimensions reflect this hotel's early 1800s vintage.
Georgstrasse 1, 98617; 03693 45 70; www.saechsischerhof.com

① The Wartburg
Thuringia; 99817
Clasped to a ridge south of Eisenach, the Wartburg *(open daily)* is a wellspring of German identity. The castle's Romanesque Palas, or Great Hall, is rich with 19th-century murals and mosaics. According to legend, medieval bards once battled for their lives in singing contests romanticized in Wagner's opera, *Tannhäuser*. The exiled Martin Luther hid here while translating the New Testament into German in 1521. In 1817, student fraternities from across the country gathered here to demonstrate for a united Germany. Drive to the old town of Eisenach on the B19 to pay tribute to Johann Sebastian Bach, by visiting the **Bachhaus** *(open daily)*, the museum built on what was thought to be the site of his birth.

🚗 *Follow signs for Naturpark-Route Thüringer Wald on the B7 then the B88. At Thal, take the B88 to Seebach, Tabarz and then Friedrichroda. Turn right at the T-junction and park on the main square.*

② Friedrichroda
Thuringia; 99894
Spa waters have attracted holiday-makers to Friedrichroda for the past two centuries. In 1835, Britain's Princess Victoria came here to take a cure and fell in love with Duke Albert of Saxe-Coburg-Gotha, her future husband. Tour the gardens of the Neo-Gothic **Schloss Reinhardsbrunn** *(May–Oct: open Sat & Sun)* where the two royals met. Return to Tabarz to visit the **Marienglashöhle** *(open daily)* grotto. It literally means "Mary's Glass Cave", which alludes to the gypsum crystals found here that were mined for altar decoration.

🚗 *Return to Tabarz, then turn left at the brown panorama symbol and drive through the town centre. Drive uphill, following signs to turn right towards Grosser Inselsberg.*

③ Grosser Inselsberg
Thuringia; 98599
A patchwork of woodland and meadow spreads out beneath one of the highest mountains in the Thuringian Forest. At 918 m (3,012 ft), it has forested hills to the south and foothills rolling north to Eisenach. Well known as a winter ski resort, Grosser Inselsberg is also a popular destination in summer. Adventure enthusiasts can try walking a section of the Rennsteig, Germany's most popular long-distance footpath, to climb to the summit or whizz downhill through the pine trees on a summer toboggan run *(Mar–Oct: open daily)*.

🚗 *Return to the main road and head to Brotterode. Turn left in the town centre, following signs to Schmalkalden. Parking is available in the Pfaffenwiese car park, past the roundabout.*

Forest Train to Gotha

A novel way to visit Gotha and Schloss Friedenstein *(see p109)* and do some sightseeing is on the Thüringerwaldbahn from Friedrichroda. The Thuringian Forest Train (tram No. 4) takes 50 minutes to cover the 20-km (12-mile) journey northwards to Gotha. Trams depart twice an hour in summer and once an hour in winter from Friedrichroda.

❹ Schmalkalden

Thuringia; 98574

So quaint are its timber-framed buildings that it is hard to believe that Schmalkalden was briefly the epicentre of European politics. An imperial meeting was convened here in 1537 to reconcile the continent's Catholic rulers with Protestant princes and Martin Luther. Up the high street from the town square, Altmarkt, a mosaic of historic buildings, is the red-beamed Lutherhaus, Martin Luther's residence during the Imperial Diet. The Reformation also changed **Schloss Wilhelmsburg** *(Apr–Oct: open daily; Nov–Mar: closed Mon)*. This castle's chapel was one of the first to represent Luther's elevation of the spoken word over decoration.

🚗 *Continue along Recklinghäuser Strasse, turn right at the T-junction to take the B19 to Meiningen. Drive into the centre, and at Sächsischer Hof hotel, turn right to park on Klostergasse or park past the Schloss in the Zentrum West car park.*

❺ Meiningen

Thuringia; 98617

A past life as the Residenzstadt or royal seat of the Saxe-Meiningen dukes lends Meiningen an aristocratic air. Romantic composers such as Franz Liszt and Johannes Brahms conducted the town's orchestra and its court theatre was acclaimed across Europe. Today, the town retains a reputation for ballet, theatre and classical music *(www.das-meininger-theater.de)*. The Ducal Riding Hall *(closed Mon)*, which stands next to Schloss Elisabethenburg *(closed Mon)*, displays backdrops from 19th-century theatre productions. Do not miss the castle's stuccoed café.

🚗 *Follow the one-way system to Neu-Ulmer-Strasse and turn left towards Suhl. In Rohr, follow signs to Benshausen, then to Zella-Mehlis on the B62. Take the Bahnhof Strasse then the Oberhofer Strasse, which becomes the Heinrich-Ehrhardt-Strasse to Oberhof and turn towards Oberhof-Sud to park beside the Haus des Gastes.*

❻ Oberhof

Thuringia; 98559

Spread over a ridge at an elevation of 860 m (2,822 ft), Oberhof is the main winter playground of the Thuringian Forest. Skiers and snowboarders have a choice of slopes, and non-skiers can swish downhill in rubber rings or on a toboggan. Skiing is possible even in summer, on a 2-km (1-mile) long circuit in the DKB-Skisport-Halle *(open daily; www.oberhof-skisporthalle.de)*. Visitors can also hike through the surrounding high meadows on circular trails; maps are available in the Haus des Gastes.

🚗 *Leave Oberhof via Crawinkler Strasse and follow signs to Ohrdruf. Turn right towards Crawinkel, then take the B88 to Ilmenau, via a short section of the A71. Leave the A71 at Ilmenau West to park beside Erfurter Strasse, just before the sign to the Rathaus.*

Above Scenic road to Oberhof, through the Thuringian Forest **Below left** Half-timbered building, Eisenach **Below right** Statue of Bach at Bachhaus, Eisenach

EAT AND DRINK

FRIEDRICHRODA

Brauhaus *inexpensive*
A 19th-century inn, Brauhaus offers country cooking, such as game roulade, and beers brewed in-house. It also has five rooms and a beer garden. *Bachstrasse 14, 99894; 03623 30 42 59; www.brauhaus-friedrichroda.de*

SCHMALKALDEN

Ratskeller *moderate*
Traditional dishes such as *Eisbeinsülze* (salted pork knuckle) and fresh trout are served here, inside the town hall. *Altmarkt 2, 98574; 03683 27 42*

MEININGEN

Die Posthalterei *expensive*
Housed within the Sächsischer Hof hotel, this is the finest restaurant in the Thuringian Forest. Specialities include local recipes with subtle Mediterranean and Asian flavours. **Kutscherstube** *moderate*, a sister inn, serves pub fare. Try the Thuringian *Klösse* (dumplings). *Georgstrasse 1, 98617; 03693 45 70; Die Posthalterei: open Wed–Sat, Kutscherstube: open daily*

Above Houses and shops around Krämerbrücke, Erfurt **Below** Schloss Wachsenburg above Holzhausen

WHERE TO STAY

ILMENAU

Berg-und Jagdhotel Gabelbach
moderate
Located midway along the Goethewanderweg path, this comfortable if rather dated spa hotel in the woodland south of Ilmenau is well placed for walkers.
Waldstrasse 23, 98693; 03677 86 00; www.gabelbach.com

ARNSTADT

Park *moderate*
This understated design hotel was renovated from a brick brewery in 2008 and has an attached microbrewery/restaurant. Located south of the old town, it provides free bikes for guests to explore the region.
Brauhausstrasse 1–3, 99310; 03628 60 74 00; www.hotelpark-arnstadt.de

ERFURT

Zumnorde am Anger *moderate*
Extra-large beds come as standard in the classic, modern rooms of this smart and efficient hotel in the city centre.
Anger 50–51,99084; 0361 568 00; www.hotel-zumnorde.de

⑦ Ilmenau
Thuringia; 98693
"I was always happy to spend time here," wrote JW Goethe, 18th-century playwright and philosopher, about this university town. Ilmenau returned the compliment by dedicating the **Goethe Stadtmuseum** *(closed Mon)* to the father of the German Enlightenment. The museum is located in the Baroque Amtshaus on the Markt, where a bronze of Goethe rests on a bench.

🚗 *Take the Bücheloher Strasse, following signs to Martinroda, Neusiss and Dosdorf to Arnstadt. Go straight over the roundabout into Plauesche Strasse towards the tower and park on Ried.*

⑧ Arnstadt
Thuringia; 99310
A medieval watchtower at Arnstadt's entrance hints at the charm of this old town at the forest's edge. Full of half-timbered houses and tangled lanes, it is a great place to explore. The **Markt** has a Renaissance town hall and the Bachkirche. Arnstadt was the home of the composer Johann Sebastian Bach, who, at the age of 18, scandalized the congregation of the Bachkirche with his contrapuntal style on the organ. In the **Schlossmuseum** *(closed Mon)* on Erfurter Strasse are 18th-century doll tableaus and porcelain displays.

🚗 *Return to the roundabout and turn left on to Lindenallee, following signs to Zentrum. Turn left at the roundabout on to Wachsenburgallee, then right and then left on to Ohrdrufer Strasse towards Gotha to reach Holzhausen.*

Johann Wolfgang von Goethe
The Frankfurt-born son of a wealthy family, Goethe (1748–1832) found fame at the age of 26 as the author of *The Sorrows of Young Werther*. This tale of obsessive love not only became the best seller of the early Romantic movement, but also led to Goethe's appointment as ducal adviser in Weimar in 1775. Yet, to label Goethe as just a writer is inadequate. Between court duties, he conducted scientific experiments, studied geology, designed palaces and gardens, collected antiquities and penned his masterpiece, *Faust*. Author Thomas Mann dubbed him "the greatest German of all".

⑨ Drei Gleichen
Thuringia; 99869
Three castles, collectively known as Drei Gleichen, crown the hills en route to Gotha. The 17th-century **Wachsenburg** is the best preserved after its restoration as a hotel and restaurant; it is worth a visit for the view from its perch above Holzhausen village. Continue for 5 km (3 miles) on the road to reach Thuringia's oldest castle, the **Mühlberg** *(Mar–Oct: open daily)*, a ruin located above its sleepy village. A further 2 km (1 mile) drive northwards towards Wandersleben leads to the ruined **Burg Gleichen**, which still retains its impressive defensive walls.

🚗 *From Mühlberg, continue to Gotha via Wechmar and Schwabhausen. Turn right on to the B247 and follow signs to Gotha and brown signs to Schloss Friedenstein.*

In Goethe's Footsteps

While JW Goethe admired Ilmenau town, it was the local countryside that inspired his artistic and scientific work. Many visitors come solely to walk "auf Goethes Spuren" (in Goethe's footsteps) on the Goethewanderweg. The appeal of this 20-km (13-mile) hike to Stützerbach is its scenic variety. Marked by Goethe's "g" monogram, the trail begins in Ilmenau's Markt and passes cliffs and caves before it ascends into high country. Goethe museums lie en route – the cabin in which he wrote *Wanderers Nachtlied* on Kickelhahn Hill and the ducal hunting lodge Jagdhaus Gabelbach *(closed Mon)*, which has exhibits on his science studies. The Ilmenau tourist office *(www. rennsteig-bus.de)*, in the Amtshaus, stocks maps of the walk.

🔟 Schloss Friedenstein

Thuringia; 99867

The dynastic residence of the House of Saxe-Coburg *(closed Mon; www.stiftungfriedenstein.de)* – better known in Britain as the House of Windsor – holds interest for everyone. Works by Cranach the Elder and a sumptuous oil painting of 15th-century suitors, *Gotha Lovers*, star in an art gallery. The floors above have fabulously stuccoed period rooms, museums of antiquities and regional culture, and the perfectly preserved court theatre, Eckhof-Theater. One of the oldest stages in Europe, it hosts a drama festival in July and August.

🚗 *Continue on Stieler Strasse, across the B247, to take the B7 to Erfurt. At the B7/B4 junction, turn left on to Heinrichstrasse towards the Dom. Park in Domplatz's underground car park.*

🔟 Erfurt

Thuringia; 99084

Bursting with history and university life, Erfurt is a splendid little city and the capital of the Thuringian state. It is also the oldest settlement in the region, with its earliest historical records dating from AD 729. Ascend the sweeping steps from Domplatz to the **Dom St Marien**. This cathedral has a low-lit High Gothic choir, with original choir stalls, 14th- and 15th-century stained-glass windows and Wolfram, a Romanesque bronze candelabra (c. 1160) shaped like a man. The adjacent five-nave **Severikirche** has more Gothic furnishings and the sarcophagus of St Severus. The high street off Domplatz, Marktstrasse, leads to Fischmarkt, surrounded by Renaissance patricians' houses. The "merchant's bridge", **Krämerbrücke**, spans the Gera river and has picture-postcard views.

🚗 *Return to the B4/B7 junction to take the B7 to Weimar. Follow signs to Zentrum and park at the Goethehaus car park on Ackerwand.*

Above left Well-restored Wachsenberg, Drei Gleichen **Above right** Sculptures around the ornate entrance to the Dom in Erfurt **Below** Pretty buildings lining Fischmarkt, Erfurt

VISITING ERFURT

Parking
Parking is available in the underground car park in Domplatz and in a car park beside the cathedral on Domstrasse.

Tourist Information
Benediktsplatz 1, 99084; 0361 664 00; www.erfurt-tourist-info.de

EAT AND DRINK IN ERFURT

Schildchen *inexpensive*
Hidden away in a pretty riverside backwater, this rustic *Gaststätte* (restaurant) specializes in well-priced versions of local classics such as goulash with red cabbage and *Klösse* (dumplings). *Schildgasse 3–4, 99084; 0361 540 22 90; closed Sun*

Zum Goldenen Schwan *moderate*
Hearty fare such as *Rostbrätel* (roast pork with onions) and home-brewed beers are served in this traditional inn. *Michealisstrasse 9, 99084; 0361 262 37 42; Jan–Feb: closed Sat & Sun*

Eat and Drink: inexpensive, under €20; moderate, €20–€40; expensive, over €40

Top Modest façade of the Schillerhaus in Weimar **Above** Town hall and cafés on the Markt in Weimar

VISITING WEIMAR

Parking
Parking is available at the Goethehaus car park on Ackerwand.

Tourist Information
Markt 10, 99423; 03643 74 50;
www.weimar.de

WHERE TO STAY IN WEIMAR

Amalienhof *moderate*
This is a good-value, medium-sized hotel near Goethe's house, most of whose spacious rooms feature Neo-Classical style furnishings.
Amalienstrasse 2, 99423; 03643 54 90;
www.amalienhof-weimar.de

Elephant *expensive*
A rendezvous for artists, poets, intellectuals and statesmen since the 16th century, Elephant is a superbly sited and elegant Art Deco hotel.
Markt 19, 99423; 03643 80 20;
www.luxurycollection.com/elephant

Russischer Hof *expensive*
Sumptuously decorated, Russischer Hof was once the haunt of the composers Franz Liszt and Robert Schumann. The hotel's suites are similarly grand and its standard accommodation is very comfortable.
Goetheplatz 2, 99423; 03643 77 40;
www.russischerhof-weimar.de

⑫ Weimar

Thuringia; 99423

For outsiders, Weimar is synonymous with the Weimar Republic government of Germany in the 1920s. At home, however, the erstwhile court-town is lauded as a cradle of German culture, a former home to poets, artists, composers and philosophers, a wellspring of the German Enlightenment and the birthplace of Bauhaus design.

A 90-minute walking tour

Walk to Ackerwand from the car park and turn right into the pedestrianized Frauenplan to reach **Goethes Wohnhaus** ① *(closed Mon)* on the corner of Seifengasse. Goethe occupied this Baroque house for 50 years as an adviser to the Saxe-Weimar court. Displays in its rooms include sculpture and art acquired during his Italian travels and a piano on which composer Felix Mendelssohn showcased work-in-progress after dinner. An adjacent museum *(closed Mon)* details court life in contemporary Weimar. Walk down to the end of Seifengasse to see the **Platz der Demokratie** ②. Surrounded by ducal Baroque palaces, this square helps visitors gauge the former glory of Weimar. The centrepiece of the square is an equestrian statue of Goethe's aesthete employer, Duke Carl August. To the right of the square is the **Grünes Schloss** ③ *(closed Mon; limited number of tickets)* home to one of Europe's finest Rococo libraries,

established by the duke's wife, Duchess Anna Amalia. Walk west across the square to reach the **Markt** ④, which has a Renaissance fountain; houses, including that of the great German painter Lucas Cranach the Elder; and the Neo-Gothic town hall. Walk across the Markt and turn left into Frauentorstrasse and then right into Schillerstrasse, named after the dramatist Friedrich von Schiller. At No. 12 is **Schillerhaus** ⑤ *(closed Mon)*, a relatively modest residence compared to that of Schiller's friend, Goethe. Schillerstrasse arcs into **Theaterplatz** ⑥, which has a famous statue of Goethe and Schiller by sculptor Ernst Rietschel and the theatre in which the German National Assembly ratified the liberal Weimar Republic in 1919. Opposite is the **Wittumspalais** ⑦ *(closed Tue)*, where at a round table, the duchess hosted soirées attended by Weimar's intellectual luminaries. Its Neo-Classical interiors are the town's finest. Next door is the museum of Bauhaus design. Zeughof threads

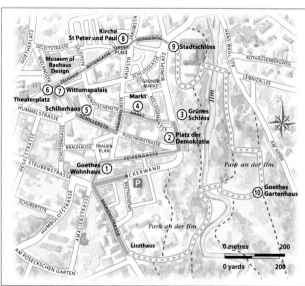

Left Approach to the Baroque Schloss Belvedere near Weimar **Below** Goethes Gartenhaus, the summerhouse given as a gift to Goethe, Weimar

EAT AND DRINK IN WEIMAR

Crêperie du Palais *inexpensive*
Gallettes (savoury crêpes), crêpes and Breton cider are served in this cozy sidestreet French café near Herderplatz. *Am Palais 1, 99423; 03643 40 15 81; closed Mon*

Anna Amalia *expensive*
The Italian cuisine of master-chef Marcello Fabbri is hailed as the culinary highlight of Thuringia. Tables are available on the garden terrace in summer. *Markt 9, 99423; 03643 80 20; closed Jan & Feb, Mar–Apr & Oct–Dec: closed Sat & Sun, May–Sep: closed Mon*

Zum Weissen Schwan *expensive*
Regional fare such as *Sauerbraten* (marinated beef) with *Klösse* (dumplings) plus Goethe's favourite dish, boiled beef in green herb sauce, is served in the writer's local inn. *Frauentorstrasse 23, 99423; 03643 90 87 51; closed Sun & Mon*

between the two and joins Rittergasse to emerge at Herderplatz, on which is the **Kirche St Peter und Paul** ⑧. The church's sumptuous triptych was painted by Cranach. This painting serves as an introduction to the art in the **Stadtschloss** ⑨ *(closed Mon)* at the end of Vorwerksgasse, which runs behind the church. Rebuilt in Neo-Classical style on Goethe's advice, this palace houses the Saxe-Weimar dynasty's gallery, including Cranach's wedding portraits of Johann Friedrich and his bride. On leaving the palace from the southern side, emerge at its original Renaissance gateway and tower. Walk behind the palace and cross the Ilm to reach a broad park. Follow signs to the **Goethes Gartenhaus** ⑩ *(closed Tue)* beside the Ilm. This summerhouse was given to Goethe for drawing up the plans for Weimar. Cross the river on a footbridge to the left of the house, and turn right. Beyond a folly, on

Statue of Duke Carl August, Theaterplatz

Marienstrasse, lies Liszthaus *(Apr–mid-Oct: open Tue–Sun; mid-Oct–end Mar: open Sat & Sun)*, home of the Romantic composer Franz Liszt. Turn right into Ackerwand to return to the car park.

🚗 *Turn left on to Marienstrasse and continue on it to reach the Schloss Belvedere.*

⑬ Schloss Belvedere
Thuringia; 99425
The summer palace of Duke Carl August, the Baroque Schloss Belvedere has a cheery canary-yellow colour scheme. Some of its outbuildings have been modernized as a music school, but the rooms in the main residence *(Apr–Oct: closed Mon)* have been restored as a historical backdrop for displays of porcelain, glass and furniture. Learn about the lovely gardens in the west pavilion before exploring the 43 ha (106 acres) of greenery, landscaped into the naturalistic English style of the late 1700s.

DAY TRIP OPTIONS
Meiningen is an ideal base for exploring the Thuringian Forest, while Weimar makes an excellent base for most sights along this drive.

Outdoor pursuits
Explore Meiningen ⑤ before driving to the half-timbered houses in Schmalkalden ④, leaving time for the palace chapel before setting off to ski or hike in Oberhof ⑥, and to work up an appetite for lunch in Arnstadt ⑧. Visitors can then either

stroll its streets or drive to Ilmenau ⑦ for a walk on the Goethewanderweg.

Follow the B19 to Schmalkalden, then retrace the route to Meiningen and take the B62 and Heinrich-Ehrhardt-Strasse to Oberhof. Follow the route to Arnstadt, and then retrace the route to Ilmenau.

Classics and culture
In Weimar ⑫, tour Goethe's house before travelling back in time with Erfurt's ⑪ Krämerbrücke and cathedral, both medieval

showpieces of the state's capital city. Next, browse the art in Schloss Friedenstein ⑩, then return east past Drei Gleichen ⑨ to Arnstadt ⑧. Drivers can then travel back to Weimar to spend time in Schloss Belvedere's ⑬ gardens.

Follow the B7 to Erfurt, then continue on it to Schloss Friedenstein. Follow the tour in reverse order to Arnstadt and then retrace the entire route back to Weimar to reach Schloss Belvedere.

Eat and Drink: inexpensive, under €20; moderate, €20–€40; expensive, over €40

On the Trail of the Sun King

Zwickau to Bautzen

Highlights

- **Local folk crafts**
  Explore the historic mining towns in the Erzgebirge and buy beautiful wooden toys and traditional Christmas decorations

- **Baroque Dresden**
  Tour the rebuilt grand palaces and impressive churches that spread the fame of the "Florence of the Elbe"

- **Riverside beauty**
  Cruise down the Elbe on a vintage paddlesteamer, stopping off along the way at pretty spa villages

- **Magical scenery**
  Visit the Bastei to see the fantastical gorges and plateaus of Saxon Switzerland

Fürstenzug, a frieze made of Meissen china tiles, Dresden

On the Trail of the Sun King

Saxony (Sachsen) promotes itself as the "state of the arts" and its brooding castles, Gothic hall churches and opulent palaces are fine representatives of centuries of artistic brilliance. This is a state as rich in landscapes as it is in culture. There is a real sense of transition on this route, as it emerges from the Erzgebirge, an upland whose old towns are full of mining history, folk crafts and charm, to follow the trail of Augustus the Strong, an 18th-century Saxon Sun King who erected some of the most sensational Baroque architecture around his capital, Dresden. The mood changes again as the route travels east along the Elbe into Saxon Switzerland, a realm full of fantastical rock plateaus and mystery.

ACTIVITIES

Shop for traditional wooden toys in the towns of the Erzgebirge

Sample Saxon wines in an old town *Weinstube* in Meissen

Stroll through elegant Baroque gardens at Schloss Moritzburg and Gross Sedlitz

Hike in the beautiful forests from Festung Königstein

Take a historic paddlesteamer from Dresden, then walk through the Bastei

Go ghost-hunting in the cellars of Burg Stolpen

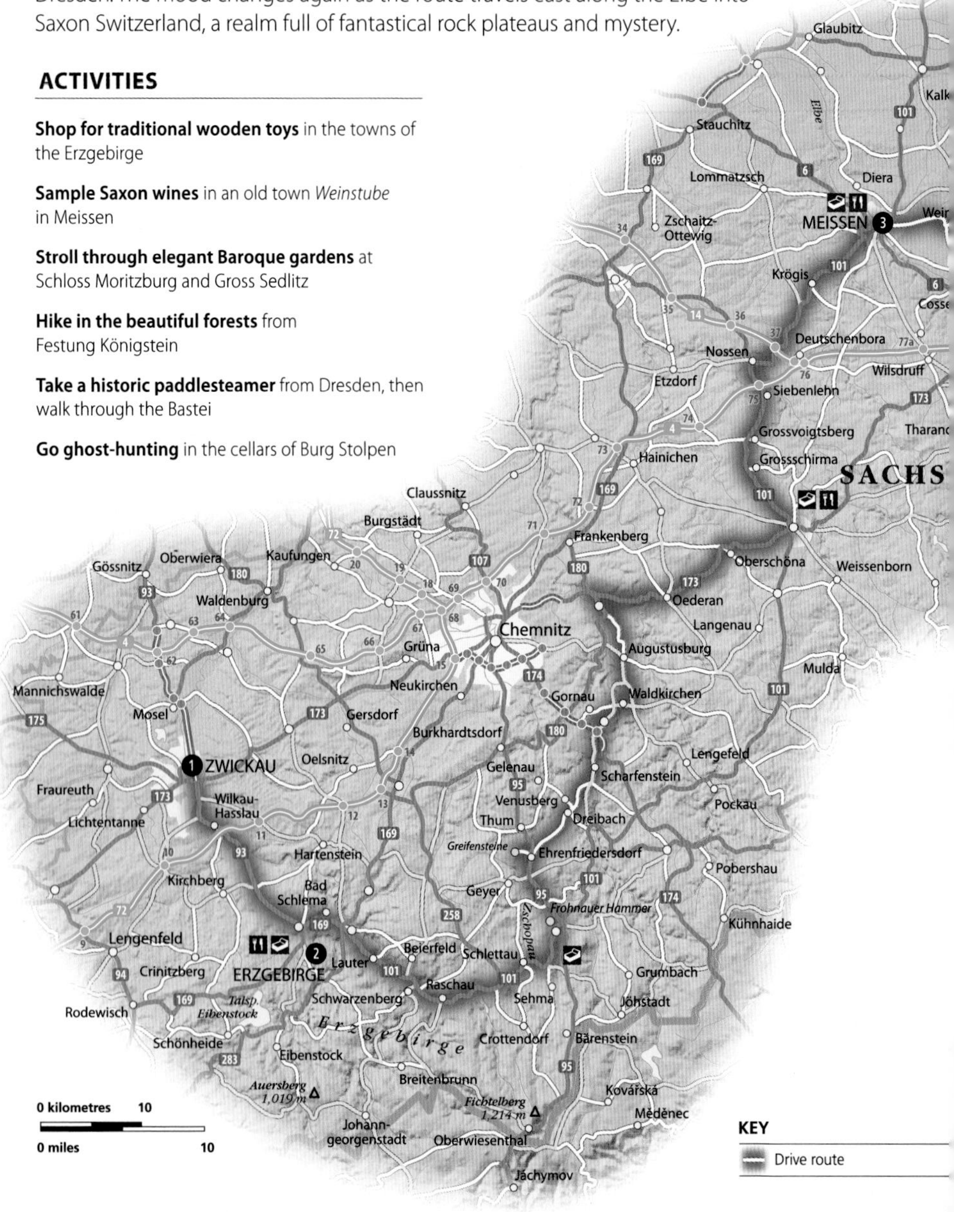

KEY

Drive route

0 kilometres 10

0 miles 10

PLAN YOUR DRIVE

Start/finish: Zwickau to Bautzen.

Number of days: 5–6 days, with at least a day each in Dresden and around Saxon Switzerland.

Distance: 284 km (177 miles).

Road conditions: There are good, well-signposted roads throughout the region.

When to go: The best time to visit the region is between late June and September, when small town festivals are in full swing, gardens are in bloom, steamboats ply the Elbe and the hiking season is on. However, Dresden is busy at this time. Christmas markets are charming in December.

Opening times: Shops open from 9am to 6pm Monday to Friday. Most museums and monuments are closed on Mondays.

Main market days: Zwickau: Thu & Fri; Erzgebirge: Wed–Fri (Schneeberg); Tue & Fri, Apr–Oct (Annaberg-Buchholz); Thu (Freiburg); **Meissen:** Mon–Wed & Fri; **Dresden:** Fri; **Pirna:** Wed & Sat; **Bautzen:** Tue, Thu & Sat.

Shopping: Wooden toys and traditional Christmas decorations are available in stores throughout the Erzgebirge, while wines and porcelain can be purchased around Meissen.

Major festivals: Erzgebirge: Bergstadtfest (mining festival), last Sun in Jun; Schneeberg (Bergstreittag Miners' Parade), 22 Jul; Weihnachtsmarkt (Christmas markets), first three weeks of Advent; **Dresden:** Dixieland Festival, early May; Musikfestspiele (classical music festival) mid-May–early Jun; **Bautzen:** Sorbischer Ostereiermarkt (Easter egg market), five weeks before Easter; Osterreiten (Sorb Easter Sunday parade), Easter Sun.

Above Meadows on the way to Bad Schandau, *see p122* **Below** Cobbled street in the old town, Meissen, *see p118*

DAY TRIP OPTIONS

With Dresden as a base day trips can be made to the **Baroque palaces** and **beautiful gardens** in Schloss Pillnitz, while Bad Schandau provides access to the brooding **castles** and the **small village-resorts** on the Elbe. For full details, *see p123*.

Right Rock formations along the Sächsische Silberstrasse

VISITING ZWICKAU

Tourist Information
*Hauptstrasse 6, 08056; 0375 271 32 40;
open Mon–Sat*

SHOPPING IN ERZGEBIRGE

Try **Zentrum Erzgebirgische
Volkskunst** *(Frauenmarkt 2, 08289
Schneeberg; 03772 289 45; www.bauer-
volkskunst.de)* and **Erzgebirgische
Volkskunst** *(Weingasse 6, 09599
Freiberg; 03731 21 29 02)* for lace and
wooden decorations.

WHERE TO STAY IN
ERZGEBIRGE

Büttner *moderate*
A pocket of relaxed country charm on
the main square of Schneeberg, Büttner
has 12 rooms; all are enjoyably snug
and some feature old beams.
*Markt 3, 08289 Schneeberg; 03772 35 30;
www.hotel-buettner.de*

Silberhof *moderate*
Although dated in decor, the Silberhof
is comfortable and provides spacious
and bright accommodation.
*Silberhofstrasse 1, 09599 Freiberg;
03731 268 80; www.hotel-silberhof.de*

Wilder Mann *moderate*
Housed in a 16th-century building,
this smart, traditional hotel has rich
wood furnishings.
*Markt 13, 09456 Annaberg-Buchholz;
03733 114 40; www.hotel-
wildermann.de*

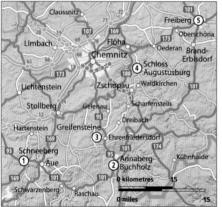

❶ Zwickau
Saxony; 08056

Music and motor cars have made
Zwickau famous. In 1810, Romantic
composer Robert Schumann was born
in **Hauptmarkt** *(closed Mon)*, in the old
town, a block across from the **Dom St
Marien**. This church's richly decorated
Gothic altar was made by the tutor of
the Renaissance master-artist Albrecht
Dürer. In more recent history, Zwickau
was renowned for the cars produced

by the Horch factory – Audis,
Daimlers and Trabants, the 500 cc
steel and plastic workhorses of Eastern
Bloc transport. Some of these models
are superbly displayed in the **August
Horch Museum** *(closed Mon)* to the
north of the centre.

🚗 *From the Zentrum car park, turn
right on to the B173/Dr-Friedrichs-Ring,
a one-way system. At the T-junction,
turn left towards Schneeberg on the
B93. Park on the Markt.*

❷ Erzgebirge
Saxony; 08289, 09456, 09427, 09573 & 09599

Rich deposits of silver, tin, copper and cobalt earned the uplands along the
Czech border the name "Ore Mountains". When these reserves waned, the
miners turned to folk crafts, so this route along the Sächsische Silberstrasse
(Saxon Silver Route) offers both historical romance and an opportunity to
buy beautiful handicrafts such as wooden toys and lace.

① Schneeberg
An enormous Markt boxed in by
Baroque townhouses and signs
declaring *Glück auf* – the traditional
"good luck" salutation of miners – are
reminders of the
wealthy past of this
silver-mining town.
Another testament
to Schneeberg's
former status is
St Wolfgangkirche
at the top of the
Markt, a late-Gothic
hall church whose
altarpiece is by the
Renaissance artist
Lucas Cranach the
Elder (1472–1553).
The **Museum für
bergmännische
Volkskunst** *(closed
Mon)* beneath the

church contains examples of the
miners' folk crafts.

🚗 *Retrace the route to B93, then take
the B169 to Aue. Take the B101 past
Schwarzenberg and Raschau to
Annaberg-Buchholz. Turn left on to
the Sehmatalstrasse at the sharp right
bend before the viaduct and park at
Frohnauer Hammer car park.*

② Annaberg-Buchholz
One of the major attractions in this
hilltop town is the **Frohnauer
Hammer** *(tours daily)*. Visitors will
probably hear this mechanical
marvel before seeing it. Inside a
shingle-roofed building, a 17th-
century contraption harnesses
energy from a stream to power three
hammers that weigh up to 250 kg
(551 lb) each. It is the last forge of its
kind in Europe and until 1904 it
produced iron and copper products,

samples of which are on display in an exhibition room above. Drive back to the B101, go beneath the viaduct and then turn left at the roundabout. Around a tight bend, turn right into the Altstadt and park at the Markt. In Annaberg-Buchholz's old town, grand townhouses suggest a place of some importance. The richest silver seams in the area funded both its main square and **St Annenkirche**, whose bold exterior belies a beautiful interior. Notoriously superstitious, miners hoped their lavish outlay would find favour with St Anne, the profession's patron saint. Prayers were said just before a shift in a contemporary shaft, now accessed via a mining museum *(open daily)* opposite the church door.
🚗 *Continue north on the B101 and turn left on to the B95 towards Chemnitz. Turn left in central Ehrenfriedersdorf towards Greifensteine for the entrance.*

③ **Greifensteine**
Around 300 million years ago, magma bubbling up through fissures in the Earth's crust wore away the surrounding sandstone to leave these strange granite outcrops, which appear unexpectedly in a pine forest like fortifications of a fantastic castle. Walk around their bases before ascending a walkway for a panoramic view. Long mined as a quarry by locals, the rocks are put to better use today as a natural amphitheatre for musicals and opera in summer *(www.greifensteine.com)*.
🚗 *Back in Ehrenfriedersdorf, turn left at the T-junction and then right towards Dreibach and Scharfenstein to Zschopau. Drive through the town centre to Waldkirchen and turn left to Augustusburg; park below the Schloss.*

④ **Schloss Augustusburg**
Several sights in one courtyard castle make this 16th-century royal hunting lodge *(open daily)* a family favourite. Visitors can buy a combination ticket to access a trio of museums: former banqueting chambers whose displays on hunting are upstaged by murals of gambolling hares; displays of vintage motorbikes; and the fairy-tale carriages of Saxony's rulers in the old stables. Also of interest are the historic rooms of the **Lindenhaus** *(tours daily)* and a dungeon full of grisly torture instruments. Displays of falconry staged by the drawbridge offer a glimpse of the castle's past *(open daily)*.
🚗 *Continue north, following signs to Flöha and join the B180 then the B173 to Freiburg. Follow signs to Zentrum and park on Schlossplatz.*

⑤ **Freiberg**
Historic and postcard-pretty, old Freiberg is a delight. Having emerged from World War II unscathed, the main square, **Obermarkt**, crowded by narrow 17th-century merchants' houses, is a slice of bygone Germany. The town's name literally means "Free Mountain", as the wealth from silver-mining was all tax free. Silver also funded Freiberg's architectural treasure, the late-Gothic **Dom St Marien** *(tours daily)*, which has a sculpture of a miner gesturing up to its Tulip Pulpit (1505). A town and mining museum, **Stadt-und Bergbaumuseum** *(closed Mon)*, stands opposite the cathedral.
🚗 *Turn right from Schlossplatz and then right again on to Leipziger Strasse to find the B101 to Nossen then Meissen. Park beside the river at Zentrum.*

Above Pretty pastel-hued houses, Augustusburg village **Centre left** Sculptures on the walls of Dom St Marien, Zwickau **Below** Schloss Augustburg, on its wooded perch above the town

EAT AND DRINK IN ERZGEBIRGE

Ratskeller *moderate*
With its panelled dining room and dishes such as Erzgebirge trout pan-fried in butter, this local institution is a bastion of traditional dining.
Obermarkt 16, 09599 Freiberg; 03731 221 51

Ratskeller Schneeburg *moderate*
As the name suggests, this restaurant is situated beneath the old town hall. It is good for both formal dining and casual outdoor eating. The menu offers several deer dishes as well as a variety of pork options.
Markt 1, 08289 Schneeberg; 03772 224 84; www.ratskeller-schneeberg.de

Right Aerial view of the charming town of Meissen **Below** Frauenkirche's ornate cupola, Dresden

VISITING DRESDEN

Parking
Ample parking is available on Schiessgasse and in Neumarkt.

Tourist Information
Schössergasse 23, 01067;
0351 50 16 01 60; www.dresden.de

WHERE TO STAY

MEISSEN

Fuchshöhl *inexpensive*
Personality abounds in this homely pension in a half-timbered house, whose artist-owner cherishes a relaxed atmosphere and charmingly mismatched furnishings.
Hohlweg 7 (top of Burgstrasse), 01662;
0351 888 85 34; www.fuchshoehl.de

Goldener Löwe *moderate*
The decor in this small, pleasant hotel just off the Markt is reminiscent of Baroque grandeur.
Heinrichsplatz 6, 01662; 03521 411 10;
www.welcome-hotels.com

DRESDEN

Bülow Palais and Residenz *expensive*
Formerly the Baroque palace of Augustus the Strong's master-architect, this Relais & Chateaux hotel is all old-world opulence and faultless service.
Königstrasse 14, 01097; 0351 800 30;
www.buelow-residenz.de

Taschenbergpalais Kempinski
expensive
Housed in the palace where Augustus the Strong installed his mistress, this hotel affords five-star luxury. "Kurfürsten" deluxe rooms offer the best views of the Residenzschloss or Zwinger.
Taschenberg 3, 01067; 0351 491 20;
www.kempinski-dresden.de

❸ Meissen
Saxony; 01662
Although famous for porcelain, Meissen is also worth visiting for its cobbled lanes. In the town's Domplatz, a High Gothic cathedral with a ducal chapel and an altarpiece by Lucas Cranach the Elder adjoins the 16th-century **Albrechtsburg** *(open daily)*. In 1710, Augustus the Strong converted the palace into the first porcelain factory outside East Asia. Meissen china is now manufactured at a factory *(tours daily)* 1.5 km (1 mile) south of the centre, where there is an exhibition centre and a shop *(open daily)*.
🚗 *Turn right beneath Albrechtsburg to cross the river on the B101. Follow signs to Moritzburg; park at the palace.*

❹ Schloss Moritzburg
Saxony; 01468
Unimpressed by a small hunting lodge he had inherited, Augustus the Strong ordered his court architect Matthäus Daniel Pöppelmann to build him a Baroque pleasure palace. The finest craftsmen in Saxony were hired to create the decadent interiors *(Apr–Oct: tours daily; Nov–mid-Jan & Feb–Mar: tours Tue–Sun)*. Highlights include a banqueting hall with hunting trophies and the royal four-poster bed with iridescent feather tapestries.
🚗 *Follow signs to Dresden and to Innere Altstadt, crossing the Elbe on Carolabrücke. Go over Rathenauplatz on to St Petersburger Strasse and turn right for the car park.*

❺ Dresden
Saxony; 01067
So devastating was an Allied air raid in February 1945 that, for most, the name of Saxony's capital is synonymous with destruction. In fact, Dresden is better understood in terms of its resurrection. After decades of Communist neglect, the old town's Baroque monuments are being rebuilt and the "Florence of the Elbe" is regaining its former glory.

A one-hour walking tour
From the car park on Schiessgasse, walk up Landhausstrasse to reach the epicentre of Dresden's rejuvenation, the Neumarkt, and the symbol of its revival, the **Frauenkirche** ①. After it was rebuilt, thousands gathered to celebrate the reconsecration of this Baroque church in October 2005. Original fire-blackened blocks stand out in its new sandstone. The crucifix in its interior was forged by a Coventry silversmith whose father flew in the Allied raid – a poignant symbol of reconciliation. A rear entrance provides access up the bell-like cupola *(open daily)* for views over the cafés of the Neumarkt. Turn right on to Salzgasse and visit the Museum Festung Dresden *(open daily)* to explore casements and cannon rooms. Visitors can admire sculpture and art from the 19th century in the Albertinum *(closed Mon)*, reopened in 2010, or art exhibitions in the Staatliche Kunstsammlungen, its interior still raw from bomb damage, or simply stroll on the **Brühlscher Terrasse** ②, the handsome riverfront belvedere that was revered as the

Where to Stay: inexpensive, under €70; moderate, €70–€150; expensive, over €150

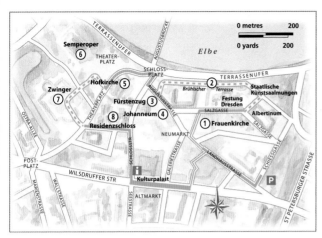

Above Baroque Zwinger, the showpiece of Dresden **Below** Field of flowering crops along the road to Dresden

EAT AND DRINK

MEISSEN

Zum Löwen *moderate*
Pasta, meat, fish and some vegetarian dishes feature on the menu at this hotel restaurant. For a large appetite, try the Argentinian steak. The wine bar next door is good for an aperitif.
Heinrichsplatz 6, 01662; 03521 411 10

Vincenz Richter *expensive*
This restaurant, housed in a snug 16th-century tavern, has been run by over four generations of the Richter family, who also sell their own wines.
An der Frauenkirche 12, 01662; 03521 45 32 85; closed Sun dinner & Mon

DRESDEN

Alte Meister *moderate*
Modern international dishes such as grilled fish with potato and saffron risotto are served in this stylish café-restaurant at the back of the Zwinger.
Theaterplatz 1a, 01067; 0351 481 04 26

Sophienkeller *moderate*
Waitresses in period costume serve hearty fare such as roast suckling pig in this restaurant in the stone cellars opposite the Zwinger.
Taschenburg 3, 01067; 0351 49 72 60; www.sophienkeller-dresden.de

Villandry *moderate*
A relaxed locals' restaurant and bar specializing in Mediterranean cuisine.
Jordanstrase 8, 01099; 0351 899 67 24; closed Sun

"balcony of Europe" in Dresden's heyday. Ascend a staircase, to the left, to access the Brühlscher Terrasse atop the town's fortifications

Continue down the terrace, towards the tiered spire of the Hofkirche and the Schlossplatz, beside the State Parliament. First, though, turn left on to Augustusstrasse for the **Fürstenzug** ③, a 102-m (335-ft) long frieze, made of 24,000 Meissen china tiles, which depicts eight centuries of Saxon rulers in a medieval pageant. Behind this is the Renaissance courtyard of the royal stables, the **Johanneum** ④, which houses a transport museum *(closed Mon)*. Return to the Schlossplatz. The Italian-designed Catholic **Hofkirche** ⑤ was Augustus's bid to appease the Pope, who had begun to suspect that the elector's conversion to Catholicism was just a ruse to claim the Polish crown. Take a look at its all-German interior, furnished with a Rococo pulpit by court sculptor Balthasar Permoser. Then walk round to Theaterplatz and the prestigious **Semperoper** ⑥, which replicates the opera house where composer Richard Wagner premiered works such as *Tannhäuser*. The showpiece of Dresden is the Baroque palace, **Zwinger** ⑦, next door. Ascend via its outstanding Wallpavillon gateway to walk the balustrade. It has three museums *(closed Mon)*: the Gemäldegalerie Alte Meister,

Rüstkammer and Porzellansammlung. Exit via the Glockenspielpavillon, named for its carillon of porcelain bells, and pass the former palace guard-house, now a ticket booking centre, to reach the **Residenzschloss** ⑧ *(open Wed–Mon)*, the colossal electors' palace. Augustus's treasury (Grünes Gewölbe) within has many bejewelled gold and porcelain trinkets. Ascend the tower *(late Mar–Oct: open Wed–Mon)* for a view over the skyline. Exit left from the palace to see the antithesis of such decadence, the Kulturpalast, now the tourist office, an example of stark Communist architecture. Walk alongside it to return to Neumarkt to relax in its cafés and then take Landhausstrasse back to the car park.

Sculpture on a dome in Dresden

🚗 *Follow signs for Pillnitz along the south bank of the river, across a bridge and then along the north bank for about 6 km (4 miles). Parking is available at the Schloss on the left.*

Eat and Drink: inexpensive, under €20; moderate, €20–€40; expensive, over €40

Above left Wall and tower of the Festung Königstein **Above right** Spire of the Stadtkirche St Marien towering over rooftops, Pirna **Below** Gross Sedlitz, on the outskirts of Pirna

CRUISING THE ELBE

River cruisers ply the Elbe three times a day, stopping at various destinations along the river. At Königstein, **Kanu Aktiv Tours** (035021 59 99 60; www. kanu-aktiv-tours.de) rents canoes and kayaks. The modern cruisers of **Sächsische Dampfschiffahrt** (www.saechsische-dampfschiffahrt. de) depart regularly on stately cruises up the Elbe to Bad Schandau via all the destinations included in this tour.

WHERE TO STAY IN PIRNA

Deutsches Haus *moderate*
Old-fashioned furnishings meet modern, friendly service in this small hotel installed in a Renaissance courtyard residence. It makes a fine base for visiting Dresden and Saxon Switzerland and has a good restaurant. *Niedere Burgstrasse 1, 01796; 03501 468 80; www.romantikhotel-pirna.de*

⑥ Schloss Pillnitz
Saxony; 01326
A drive along the Elbe offers views of the 19th-century villas and palaces on the river's northern bank. The inspiration for these buildings was Schloss Pillnitz, an extraordinary ensemble begun in 1720 to host the summer-time revels of Augustus the Strong. Architect Pöppelmann reflected the ruler's admiration for autocratic Oriental emperors in the chinoiserie of the facing wings, one of which contains a crafts museum *(Apr–Oct: open Tue–Sun; Nov–Mar: open Sat & Sun)*. Learn about the complex's creation in the **Neues Palace** *(Apr–Oct: closed Mon; Nov–Mar: open Sat–Sun)*, then explore the gardens *(open daily)* to find a large palm house and the Triton Gondola in which Augustus' son cruised the Elbe.

🚗 *Continue on north bank road to reach the main road and the B172 to Pirna-Zentrum. In the town centre, turn right following signs to Gross Sedlitz and park at Barockgarten.*

⑦ Gross Sedlitz
Saxony; 01809
Fountains and flowerbeds, parterre patterns and statues of antique deities make this the most grandiose of Augustus's pleasure gardens. A synthesis of late-Baroque Italian and French styles, its symmetry reflects the Age of Reason (the 17th century flourishing of philosophical thought). It opens onto an immaculate green where Augustus the Strong played bowls, then sweeps down to a lower terrace, a radiant green divided by channels and backed by the rhythmic arches of an orangery full of fragrant Tuscan orange trees.

🚗 *Return to Pirna and drive over the B172 into the Zentrum. Park beside the river in the car park P6, or on Markt beyond the viaduct.*

Wines of Saxony
The northern slopes of the Elbe are sufficiently sun-drenched to allow viticulture. Müller-Thurgau (also called Rivaner), fresh and characterful, is the most popular variety of grape cultivated here, followed by Riesling and Weissburgunder (Pinot Blanc). This region's white wines are generally medium-dry and sprightly, while reds such as Traminer and Blau Spätburgunder tend to be aromatic. Although locally produced wines can be tasted in a *Weinstube* in Meissen, aficionados should visit the acclaimed Schloss Wackerbarth estate *(open daily; www.schloss-wackerbarth.de)* in Radebul, near Dresden.

Left Breathtaking view from Festung Königstein **Below** Cannon on the fortified walls of Festung Königstein

8 Pirna
Saxony; 01796

A chequerboard of Baroque streets shaded in dusty pastels, the town of Pirna is centred on the cobbled **Markt**, seemingly unchanged since it was painted by the Italian artist Canaletto in 1754; a copy of the painting is in the tourist office at No. 7. Carved portals still front handsome merchants' mansions, the town hall continues to be the town's centre-piece, even though its Renaissance looks suffered during 19th-century renovations, and **Schloss Sonnenstein** remains on a hill above. The town's church, **Stadtkirche St Marien** *(open daily)*, is worth visiting for its vaulted roof and a Renaissance pulpit adorned with coquettish cherubs.

🚌 *Return to the B172, going left towards Bad Schandau. After 12 km (8 miles) turn right to reach Festung Königstein; tourist trains ascend to the fortress from the car park.*

9 Festung Königstein
Saxony; 01824

This mountain fortress *(open daily)* looks so impregnable that no attempt has been made to conquer it in over 600 years. The stronghold is 240 m (787 ft) above the Elbe with unscal-able 42-m (138-ft) tall walls. Visitors can peer down a 152-m (499-ft) deep well dug by Augustus the Strong and tour the prison where he imprisoned an alchemist to force him to create gold from base metals. These experiments resulted in the creation of his "white gold" – porcelain. If inspired by the

views, visitors can drive 2 km (1 mile) east to Königstein village for walks to the **Lilienstein** (435 m/1,427 ft) or **Pfaffenstein** (415 m/1,362 ft) plateaus; maps are available at the fortress's ticket office *(035021 646 07; www.festung-koenigstein.de)* and the village information centre.

🚌 *Take the B172 and cross the river to reach Bad Schandau. Park by the river.*

Augustus the Strong

Frederick Augustus (1670–1733) was nicknamed "Augustus the Strong" either because of his physical strength or his rumoured 370 ille-gitimate children. Impressed by France's Palace of Versailles, Augustus styled himself as a Saxon Sun King and began to transform his capital to mirror his own magnificence. His admiration for omnipotent Oriental rulers also made him covet Asian porcelain. His alchemist, Johann Friedrich Böttger, cracked the secret of "white gold" while incarcerated in Festung Königstein.

Eat and Drink: inexpensive, under €20; moderate, €20–€40; expensive, over €40

Above left Ruins of Burg Stolpen on a basalt ridge **Above right** Kirnitzschtalbahn tram running through Bad Schandau **Below** Verdant scenery around the Bastei

HIKING AROUND BAD SCHANDAU

Tourist Information
Markt 12, 01814; 03502 29 00 30;
www.bad-schandau.de

WHERE TO STAY

BAD SCHANDAU

Elbresidenz moderate
Five townhouses have been conjoined to create a smart five-star retreat with tastefully and stylishly decorated rooms; the best have views of the Elbe. Guests can have relaxing massages in the spa.
Markt 1, 01814; 03502 291 90;
www.elbresidenz-bad-schandau.de

AROUND BASTEI

Luk moderate
Set amid gardens in a village and with just five rooms, this is a charming home-away-from-home. Luk offers excellent value for money.
Basteiweg 12, 01848 Rathewalde
(5 km/3 miles north of Bastei); 035975 800 13; www.luk-landhotel.de

BAUTZEN

Goldener Adler moderate
Rather dated furnishings do not detract from the appeal of the spacious rooms of this hotel, housed in a grand townhouse in a central location. Guests should visit the romantic wine cellar.
Hauptmarkt 4, 02625; 03591 486 60;
www.goldeneradler.de

⑩ Bad Schandau
Saxony; 01814
Spa waters have attracted visitors to this gentle riverside resort for over a century. Take the **Personenaufzug** (open daily), the 50-m (164-ft) iron lift built in 1904, to a spectacular viewing platform. It is advisable to carry walking boots – an hour's walk east leads to another viewpoint at **Schrammsteineaussicht**, which offers sweeping views of the area's most fissured plateau. For another walk, take the **Kirnitzschtalbahn** (open daily), the historic tram from the Kurpark, for a rickety ride up a wooded valley. Alight at Lichtenhainer Wasserfall to walk to the waterfall and a rock arch called Kuhstall, or cowshed.

🚗 **Return towards the bridge but turn right before it towards Bastei via Porschdorf, then a left turn at the main road towards Lohmen. If the**

inner car park is full, park by the turn-off and use the shuttle bus.

⑪ Bastei
Saxony; 01847
The astonishing sandstone formations at Bastei were created millions of years ago by water erosion. Popular with 19th-century Romantics, the area was featured in the fantasy film The Chronicles of Narnia: the Lion, the Witch and the Wardrobe. A footbridge connects the pinnacles that jut high above pinewoods and leads to the remains of a 13th-century fortress, the Bastei (open daily), from where there are panoramic views over the river to Festung Königstein. Arrive early before it gets crowded; there are postcard views from the path ascending to the left, before the bridge. Return to the main road to drive 3 km (1 mile) east to Hohnstein village, in an idyllic setting beneath a castle that is now a youth hostel.

🚗 **Retrace the route towards Lohmen, and then turn right to Stolpen (left after Rathewalde if driving from Bastei). Park on Marktplatz.**

⑫ Burg Stolpen
Saxony; 01833
A picturebook-pretty Marktplatz offers no hint of Stolpen's sombre history. Countess von Cosel (1680–1765), once wooed passionately by Augustus the Strong as a mistress and mother to three of his children, was imprisoned in the lofty 17th-century stronghold of Burg Stolpen (open daily) for 49 years.

Courtiers, fearing her influence over the besotted ruler, had plotted to have the 36-year-old black-eyed beauty incarcerated in what was already a decaying castle. She died here at the age of 84. Indeed, some say that the countess still roams the castle – her ghost is said to haunt a dark cellar.

🚗 *Follow the one-way road from Marktplatz to the T-junction, turn left towards Dresden then right after 4 km (2 miles) on to the B6 to Bautzen. Park in the multi-storey car park on Lauengraben, 300 m (329 yards) across the river.*

⓭ Bautzen
Saxony; 02625

The view of tightly packed medieval defence towers and spires seen on the drive across the Spree river is the finest introduction possible to the cultural capital of the Slavic Sorbs, Germany's only indigenous minority. Known mainly for its top-security jail for political prisoners during the German Democratic Republic era, today Bautzen enchants visitors with its beautifully reconstructed old town. The winding streets with their

original houses, the city walls, the curiously crooked Reichenturm tower and the Baroque town hall in the town square, all form a very attractive complex. Take a riverside path past fortifications to see Slavic folk crafts and costumes in the **Sorbisches Museum** *(open daily)*, located beside the late-Gothic Schloss Ortenburg. The **Dom St Petri's** interior is curious – its nave bends to gain extra space on the square, and is divided and used by both Catholics and Protestants. A cathedral treasury *(open Mon–Fri)* is located behind in the Baroque Bishopric.

EAT AND DRINK

BAD SCHANDAU
Elbterrasse *moderate*
Housed in the Elbresidenz hotel, this restaurant offers the best summer terrace in the area, as well as classic Saxon cooking with dishes such as *Sauerbraten* (marinated pot roast).
Markt 1, 01814; 035022 91 90

AROUND BASTEI
Landgasthaus zum Schwarzbachtal *expensive*
The rustic ambience of this restaurant belies the quality of the food that chef Barbara Siebert prepares from the freshest ingredients. Expect handwritten menus of modern German and regional dishes.
Niederdorfstrasse 3, 01848 Lohsdorf-Hohnstein (10 km/6 miles east of Bastei); 035975 803 45; www.schwarz bachtal.de; closed Thu, Jan & Feb

BAUTZEN
Mönchshof *moderate*
Wine in earthenware jugs, waiters in sackcloth and meaty recipes from 1560 make this medieval-themed inn very popular.
Burglehn 1, 02625; 03591 49 01 41; www.moenchshof.de

Wjelbik *moderate*
Traditional specialities such as ox fillet with horseradish sauce are served in this Sorbian restaurant behind the Dom.
Kornstrasse 7, 02625; 03591 420 60; Nov–Mar: closed Sun dinner & Mon

DAY TRIP OPTIONS

Drivers can base themselves in Dresden to follow the cultural trail left by Augustus the Strong, or choose Bad Schandau to explore the great outdoors of Saxon Switzerland.

Grace and grandeur
In Dresden ❺, visit the Zwinger and treasury, then drive to Schloss Pillnitz ❻ and Augustus' beautiful garden, Gross Sedlitz ❼ – the ideal

way to work up an appetite for lunch in Pirna ❽. Walk it off with a tour of the monarch's hunting lodge, Schloss Moritzburg ❹, then go west to Meissen ❸ to end the day with a taste of local wines in a *Weinstube*.

Follow the driving instructions to Pirna. Return to the dual-carriageway and continue north to Radeburg, across the A4 and then follow signs to Moritzburg. Follow instructions in reverse to Meissen.

Mountains and valleys
From Bad Schandau ❿, drive to the Bastei ⓫ with a packed picnic to enjoy breathtaking views of this landscape. Drive to Burg Stolpen ⓬ then head south to Pirna ❽ for lunch and window-shopping along the cobbled lanes of its Baroque grid.

Follow the driving instructions to Stolpen, return via the road to Lohmen then continue to Pirna.

In the Land of the Brothers Grimm

Wiesbaden to Steinau an der Strasse

Highlights

- **Nineteenth-century opulence**
  Explore Wiesbaden, with its grand opera house and hotels that evoke the imperial swagger of the Kaiser's day

- **Chocolate-box charm**
  Visit the pretty half-timbered towns in Hesse, from ancient Limburg an der Lahn to quaint Steinau an der Strasse

- **Impressive palace and gardens**
  Admire Kassel's Wilhelmshöhe, a magnificent palace with a landscaped 18th-century park

- **Cultural extravaganza**
  Marvel at Hesse's contribution to world culture, from Goethe and Heidegger to the Brothers Grimm

Latticed façades of half-timbered houses on a cobbled street, Bad Wildungen

In the Land of the Brothers Grimm

The hilly, wooded landscape of Hesse (Hessen) is dotted with perfectly preserved medieval towns and crowned with castles of fairy-tale charm. If at times this most quintessentially German of regions seems like a storybook brought to life, that is no surprise, since it nurtured the careers of the Brothers Grimm and of Germany's greatest writer, JW Goethe. These literary giants have left their mark on Hesse, but so have the Landgraves and churchmen who held sway over it. Lovers of architecture will be enchanted by the area's many quaint small towns, those interested in art will take to the Baroque glories of Kassel or Fulda and for those who wish to unwind, the region's lazy waterways and spa towns offer plenty of opportunities for relaxation.

Above Carolingian burial chapel of Michaelskirche, Fulda, *see p135*

KEY

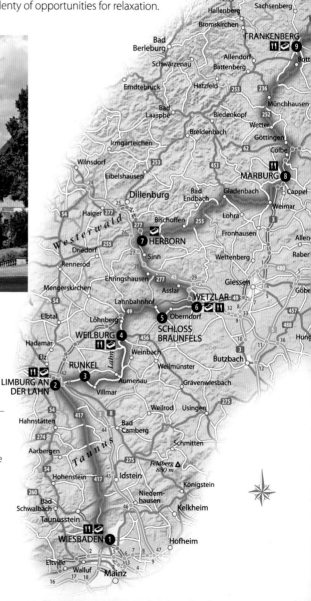

Drive route

ACTIVITIES

Pamper yourself with a day at one of Hesse's elegant spas

Take a walk on one of the long-distance footpaths that crisscross the region

Explore the Fulda and Lahn rivers by canoe

Cycle through the gentle valleys of the Fulda and Lahn rivers

Climb up the steep steps to the great cascade at the Schlosspark Wilhelmshöhe

PLAN YOUR DRIVE

Start/finish: Wiesbaden to Steinau an der Strasse.

Number of days: 5–6 days, allowing half a day to explore Limburg an der Lahn.

Distance: 425 km (287 miles).

Road conditions: The roads are mostly well surfaced. Signposting is intermittently poor around Marburg and Frakenberg.

When to go: The best time to visit this region is between Easter and October.

Opening times: In larger cities, shops are open from around 9am to 6pm. Museums are generally open from 9am to 6pm but may be closed on Mondays.

Main market days: Wiesbaden: Wed & Sat; Limburg an der Lahn: Wed & Sat; **Marburg:** Wed & Sat.

Shopping: Anything from vintage couture to Art Deco glass can be purchased in Wiesbaden.

Major festivals: Wiesbaden: Maifestspiele (theatre festival), May; **Bad Hersfeld:** Festspiele (theatre festival), Jun–Aug.

DAY TRIP OPTIONS

Start from Limburg an der Lahn or Wetzlar to discover the **Lahn Valley** and Melsungen. Bad Wildungen makes a good base from which to explore the **Waldecker Land**. For full details, *see p135*.

Below Tranquil country landscape near Limburg an der Lahn, *see pp128–9*

Above Country road leading to Limburg an der Lahn

① Wiesbaden
Hesse; 65183

The opulent 19th-century architecture of Hesse's leafy capital recalls its heyday as Kaiser Wilhelm II's favourite watering hole. The focal point here is the colonnaded bowling green, fringed by the Neo-Classical **Kurhaus**, the **Casino** (open daily), and the imposing Neo-Baroque **Hessiches Staatstheater**, or Hessian State Theatre, which has an extravagant Neo-Rococo foyer. The best of Wiesbaden's spa facilities is the **Kaiser Friedrich Therme** (open daily; Langgasse 38-40; 0611 31 70 60). Opened in 1913 on the site of a hot spring, it has retained its original Jugendstil (Art Nouveau) interior.

🚗 *Leave Wiesbaden along Taunusstrasse and Nerotal, following the road uphill to reach the B417 to Limburg an der Lahn.*

Shopping in Wiesbaden
Wiesbaden's elegance extends to its shops, from the designer boutiques along Wilhelmstrasse to the antique shops and fine-art galleries of Taunusstrasse, where visitors can buy anything from vintage couture or antiquarian books to Art Deco glass. In keeping with the city's refined, "old money" ambience, established and independent firms prevail.

② Limburg an der Lahn
Hesse; 65549

There is a powerful sense of antiquity to be discovered in the exceptionally well-preserved centre of Limburg an der Lahn. In this lovely city, tall half-timbered houses built between the 13th and 16th centuries lean across narrow, meandering lanes and are overshadowed in turn by the seven-towered St Georg's Dom. This cathedral was built in the 13th century on a dramatic site high above the Lahn river and is visible from miles around.

A two-hour walking tour
Exit the car park and walk up Grabenstrasse and right along Konrad-Kurzbold Strasse on to the **Alte Lahnbrücke** ①, a medieval stone bridge over the Lahn. It dates from 1315–54 and is crowned by an early 14th-century watch tower. The bridge, damaged towards the end of World War II, was restored and widened between 1946 and 1947.

There is a wonderful view of the Dom high above the river on a crag, with the ancient Altstadt huddled at its base. Return across the bridge, bearing slightly left up **Brückengasse** ② to reach the Altstadt. The 18th-century house at No. 2 was once an office belonging to the postal service of the aristocratic Thurn and Taxis Dynasty. Continue uphill into Rütsche, lined with tall, gabled half-timbered houses.

VISITING LIMBURG AN DER LAHN

Parking
The Alstadtparkhaus is on the corner of Grabenstrasse and Sackgasse.

Tourist Information
Hospitalstrasse 2, 65549; 06431 20 32 22; www.limburg.de; Apr–Oct: open Mon–Sat; Nov–Mar: open Mon–Fri

WHERE TO STAY

WIESBADEN

Nassauer Hof *expensive*
Kings, princes and the Russian novelist Fyodor Dostoevsky are among the illustrious past guests of Wiesbaden's grandest hotel. Rooms are furnished in a crisp but conservative style. The hotel also has a Michelin-starred fine dining restaurant called Ente.
Kaiser-Friedrich-Platz 3-4, 65183; 0611 13 30; www.nassauer-hof.de

LIMBURG AN DER LAHN

Dom Hotel *moderate*
This long-established hotel occupies a central site close to the Altstadt. Rooms are tastefully decorated in contemporary style with en suite bath or shower, wireless Internet and TV.
Grabenstrasse 57, 65549; 06431 90 10; www.domhotellimburg.de

Nassauer Hof *moderate*
A comfortable three-star hotel right on Limburg's Alte Lahnbrücke, Nassauer Hof was destroyed during World War II but reconstructed in 1991. There is a good restaurant and a pretty terrace overlooking the Lahn river.
Brückengasse 1, 65549; 06431 99 60; www.hotel-nassauerhof-limburg.de

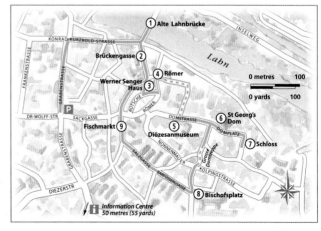

Where to Stay: inexpensive, under €70; moderate, €70–€150; expensive, over €150

The **Werner Senger Haus** ③ at No. 5, built in the 13th century, is one of the oldest in Limburg. With a lofty, beamed hall on the ground floor, typical of the Altstadt's houses, it is now a hotel and restaurant. Turn left into **Römer** ④, dominated by a beautifully restored 13th-century Gothic Hallenhaus. Archaeological excavation at the site of this hall house has unearthed the remains of a Jewish ritual bath or mikvah. Turn right at the end of Römer and take the steps up to Domstrasse. Cross the road to reach **Diözesanmuseum** ⑤ (mid-Mar–mid-Nov: closed Mon). The museum's collection of ecclesiastical treasures includes the Staurothek, a 10th-century Byzantine cross reliquary. Leaving the museum, turn right up Domstrasse on to the Domplatz to visit the magnificent red-and-white bulk of **St Georg's Dom** ⑥. The cathedral was built in the early 13th century with the wealth accrued by Limburg's merchants in the Crusades. Its architecture is a blend of Rhenish Romanesque and early French Gothic. The interior has some early medieval frescoes.

Return to the Domplatz and walk along the southern walls of the cathedral to reach the **Schloss** ⑦. Though built on a superb defensive site high above the river, it is hard to imagine anything less forbidding than the castle's picturesque collection of stone and half-timbered buildings grouped around a central courtyard. Return to Domplatz, turning left down the atmospheric Grosse Domtreppe, the great cathedral steps, to reach **Bischofsplatz** ⑧. On the right, tall half-timbered houses lean at giddy

Sculpture in Limburg an der Lahn's old town

angles and on the left is the Stadtkirche or parish church, built around 1300. From Bischofsplatz follow Barfüssergasse and Salzgasse through the bustling heart of the Altstadt, stopping to admire the antiques and gift shops on the way to **Fischmarkt** ⑨. This contains the most impressive concentration of beautiful early-medieval houses in Limburg, including the Altes Rathaus, with its fine beamed hall and lovely spiral staircase. The old town hall now houses the municipal art collection (open during exhibitions only). Turn into Sackgasse to reach the car park on the corner with Grabenstrasse.

🚗 **Leave the city on Eschhöfer Weg, following signs to Runkel.**

③ Runkel
Hesse; 65594

The Lahn Valley narrows and becomes steeper at Runkel, where the mighty **Burg** (Easter–Oct: closed Mon) overlooks a 15th-century stone bridge. The older, upper fortress was left a ruin by Austrian troops during the Thirty Years' War, while the 13th-century Unterburg, the lower castle, contains a museum and is the seat of the Wied family. On the opposite bank of the river stands another castle, **Burg Schadeck**. Known as the "swallows nest", it was built as a result of a dispute within Runkel's founding family.

🚗 **Leave Runkel on Borngasse following signs to Villmar and Aumenau. At Aumenau, turn left on to Elkerhäuser Strasse, then follow route to Weilburg. Use the Parkdeck Rathaus close to the tourist office to park.**

EAT AND DRINK

WIESBADEN

Ente *expensive*
The Nassauer Hof's gourmet restaurant oozes class, from the understated elegance of its ocean liner-like decor to the 1,800-bottle wine cellar and the creative menu, which offers the likes of Scottish scallops with corn crème brûlée, green asparagus and coconut jelly. *Kaiser-Friedrich-Platz 3-4, 65183; 0611 13 30; www.nassauer-hof.de; closed Sun & Mon*

Kaefer's *expensive*
There is a club-like atmosphere at this elegant bistro in the Kurhaus. The menu blends German, French and other international influences and includes plenty of seafood. *Kurhausplatz 1, 65189; 0611 53 62 00; www.kurhaus-gastronomie.de*

Other options
Wiesbaden's traditional high temple of cake and coffee is **Café Maldaner** (Marktstrasse 34, 65183; 0611 30 52 14), founded in 1859. Head to **Fritz Kunder** (Wilhelmstrasse 12, 65183; 0611 44 13 59), to sample *Wiesbadener Ananastörtchen* (refined bitter chocolate with a pineapple jelly filling).

LIMBURG AN DER LAHN

Der kleine Prins *moderate*
A cosy restaurant in the Nassauer Hof hotel, Der kleine Prins serves a seasonal menu of creative German dishes and a selection of fine wines. Eat outside on the terrace in summer. *Brückengasse 1, 65549; 06431 99 60; www.hotel-nassauerhof-limburg.de*

Above left Landscaped garden, Schloss Weilburg **Above right** Landgrafenschloss, perched above the town of Marburg

VISITING WETZLAR

Parking
There is limited on-street parking on the Domplatz. Parking is available in the Dom Garage car park, the entrance to which is on the square.

Tourist Information
Domplatz 8, 35573; 06441 99 77 50; www.wetzlar.de; open Mon–Sat

WHERE TO STAY

WEILBURG

Schlosshotel Weilburg *moderate*
Housed in the Baroque stable block of the Schloss, this four-star hotel has individually decorated rooms with en suite bath or shower, TV and minibar. *Langgasse 25, 35781; 06471 509 00; www.schlosshotel-weilburg.de*

WETZLAR

Bürgerhof *moderate*
This hotel occupies an 18th-century house and has en suite rooms with cable TV and wireless Internet. *Konrad Adenauer Promenade 20, 35578; 06441 90 30; www.buergerhof-wetzlar.com*

HERBORN

Hohe Schule *moderate*
The 16th-century buildings of Hohe Schule, or high school, are the setting for this hotel with just nine rooms. *Schulhofstrasse 5, 35745; 02772 927 90; www.hohe-schule.de*

FRANKENBERG

Die Sonne *expensive*
Located in the former Stadtweinhaus, Die Sonne has air-conditioned rooms with TVs and wireless Internet. *Marktplatz 2-4, 35066; 06451 75 00; www.sonne-frankenberg.de*

4 Weilburg
Hesse; 35781
Tucked into a loop of the Lahn so tight that just one gate guards the entrance to its compact Altstadt, Weilburg is dominated by its sprawling **Schloss** *(closed Mon)*. The castle's surviving Renaissance core was expanded in the 18th century to create a suitably palatial Residenz, or seat, for the counts of Nassau-Weilburg. The lovely complex stretches 400 m (438 yards) along the hillside above the river, and there is a sunny Baroque garden *(open daily)* complete with an orangery and a café.

🚗 *Cross the Steinerne Brücke below Weilburg's old town, then turn left and follow Bahnhofstrasse and Löhnberger Weg to Löhnberg. At Löhnberg, follow signs to Wetzlar, then join the B49 to Lahnbahnhof. From here, take Mühlengrund to the town of Braunfels.*

5 Schloss Braunfels
Hesse; 35619
With its impressive forest of towers rising high above the half-timbered town of Braunfels huddling at its gate, **Schloss Braunfels** *(tours Apr–Oct: open daily; Nov–Mar: open Sat, Sun & holidays)* looks every inch the romantic medieval fortress, though it owes its present fairy-tale appearance to a 19th-century Neo-Gothic rebuild. The seat of the Counts of Solms since the 13th century, it remains in the hands of the Solms-Braunfels family.

🚗 *Leave Braunfels along Wetzlarer Strasse. After crossing Oberndorf, take Braunfelser Strasse to Wetzlar.*

Goethe in Wetzlar
Wetzlar was the seat of the highest civil court of the Holy Roman Empire. This was the reason the young lawyer Goethe travelled here in the summer of 1772. During his brief stay, Goethe formed an unrequited attachment to Charlotte Buff, who was already engaged. This unhappy romance formed the basis for *The Sorrows of Young Werther*, the novel that brought him international fame. Charlotte's family home is now a museum, the Lottehaus *(closed Mon)*.

6 Wetzlar
Hesse; 35573
Rising steeply from the banks of the Lahn, Wetzlar's hilly **Altstadt**, or old town, with its sloping squares and lanes graced by attractive half-timbered houses, requires leisured exploration. The main focus here is the peculiar-looking **Dom** *(open daily)*, in which parts of the original Romanesque Stiftskirche coexist with incomplete sections of the grander 13th-century Gothic hall church intended to replace it. Both Catholic and Protestant congregations use the church.

🚗 *Leave Wetzlar along Hermannsteiner Strasse. Follow signs to Dillenburg/B277 until Herborn.*

7 Herborn
Hesse; 35745
Nestling beneath its 13th-century castle, Herborn has a beautifully preserved historic core. The stubby 16th-century **Rathaus** seems half fortress, and there is an impressive parade of five-storey houses along

Where to Stay: inexpensive, under €70; moderate, €70–€150; expensive, over €150

Hauptstrasse, half-timbered or shingle-hung, with gables facing the street. Also worth a visit is the 17th-century tannery and the neighbouring hangman's house in Schmaler Weg. Herborn's now defunct **Hohe Schule** was once an educational institution of international repute; the upper floors now house a museum *(closed Mon & Thu)* with displays relating to archaeology, war and weaponry in the region.

🚗 *Leave Herborn along Bahnhofstrasse, following signs for Marburg to reach the B277, then follow the B255 signposted to Marburg.*

Above Intricate Gothic entrance to the Elisabethkirche, Marburg

8 Marburg
Hesse; 35037
Marburg is home to the world's oldest Protestant university, Philipps Universität, and with its arty cinemas,

cheap cafés and student bars, the hilly, attractive **Oberstadt**, or upper town, has a classic university town atmosphere. Crowning the heights above it is the impressive **Landgrafenschloss**, former home of the Hessian Landgraves and now a museum *(closed Mon)*. In the Unterstadt, or lower town, the **Elisabethkirche** *(open daily)* is Germany's oldest purely Gothic hall church, dedicated to Elisabeth of Thuringia.

🚗 *Take the B3 as far as Cölbe, then take the B62 signposted Münchhausen/Bottendorf then on to B252 via Münchhausen to reach the town of Frankenberg.*

9 Frankenberg
Hesse; 35066
An attractive base from which to discover the unspoiled wooded hills of the Waldecker Land *(www.waldecker-land.de)*, Frankenberg has a half-timbered old town, the **Altstadt**, tumbling downhill from its ten-towered early 16th-century **Rathaus**. The town hall's busy outline includes eight oriel windows and an eight-sided stair tower dating from 1535. Neustadt – the present-day town centre at the foot of the hill – was once a separate municipality with its own, much more modest Rathaus.

🚗 *Leave Frankenberg along Hainstrasse, then follow the B253 to Bad Wildungen. There is paid on-street parking in the Altstadt.*

Above Half-timbered houses in Wetzlar
Below Boats moored along Marburg canal

VISITING MARBURG

Parking
The Parkhaus Oberstadt is close to the tourist information office and convenient for the lift up to Oberstadt.

Tourist Information
Pilgrimstein 26, 35037; 06421 991 20; www.marburg.de; open Mon–Sat

EAT AND DRINK

WEILBURG

Alte Reitschule *expensive*
Fresh produce is used at the Schlosshotel's restaurant. Specialities include roast wild boar in sour cherry sauce with *Spätzle* (Swabian noodles). *Langgasse 25, 35781; 06471 509 00; www.schlosshotel-weilburg.de*

WETZLAR

Der Postreiter *moderate*
Trout is a speciality of the Bürgerhof's cosy restaurant. Vegetarian choices include *Maultaschen* (Swabian ravioli). *Konrad Adenauer Promenade 20, 35578; 06441 90 30; www.buergerhof-wetzlar.com; open daily*

MARBURG

A Casa Nostra *inexpensive*
Hearty Italian food is served here, including a selection of pastas and pizzas. Local dishes such as *Schnitzel* (pork fillet) are also on the menu. *Steinweg 44, 35037; 06421 628 38; www.acasanostra.de*

FRANKENBERG

Restaurant Philipp Soldan *expensive*
This restaurant serves haute cuisine with French and Mediterranean touches. Its à la carte menu varies every month according to seasonal produce. *Marktplatz 2-4, 35066; 06451 75 00; www.sonne-frankenberg.de*

Eat and Drink: inexpensive, under €20; moderate, €20–€40; expensive, over €40

Above View of Fritzlar from St Petri Dom
Below left Stunning view of Edersee Below
right Old fortress of Schloss Waldeck

ACTIVITIES ON EDERSEE

Windsurfing
*Seestrasse/Bringhäuser Bucht, 34549
Edertal; 0562 325 82*

Sailing
*Randstrasse 3, 34549 Edertal-Edersee;
0562 349 01; www.sun-fun.de*

WHERE TO STAY

WALDECK

Schlosshotel Waldeck *expensive*
This four-star hotel with 42 en suite
rooms is equipped with a minibar,
safe and modern multimedia systems.
*Schloss Waldeck 1, 34513;
0562 358 90; www.schloss-hotel-
waldeck.de*

KASSEL

Schlosshotel Bad Wilhelmshöhe
moderate
This four-star hotel has two categories
of rooms, both offering wireless Internet,
flat screen TV and en suite bath.
*Schlosspark 8, 34131; 0561 308 80;
www.schlosshotel-kassel.de*

⑩ Bad Wildungen
Hesse; 34537

The town's half-timbered Altstadt
crowns a hilltop overlooking its
spacious 19th-century spa quarter.
The 14th-century Lutheran
Stadtkirche *(open daily)* blends
Hessian and Westphalian influences
and contains a beautiful winged altar
by the medieval artist Conrad von
Soest (1394–1422). North of the old
town is the Baroque **Schloss
Friedrichstein**, which houses a
museum *(closed Mon)* of Hessian
military history and hunting.

🚗 *Leave Bad Wildungen following
brown signs for Edertalsperre on
B485. Turn left for Affoldern then
follow Randstrasse to reach the right
bank of the Eder Dam.*

⑪ Edersee
Hesse; 34549

One of Germany's largest reservoirs,
the 27-km (17-mile) long Edersee
enjoys a scenic position amid the
wooded hills of the Naturpark

Kellerwald-Edersee. It is known for
outdoor activities such as angling,
sailing, waterskiing, hiking, mountain
biking and Nordic walking; other
pastimes include cruises on the lake
(personenschifffahrt.edersee.com).
The dam here is famed as one of
the targets of the 1943 Dambuster
raids, though it was swiftly repaired
and looks as solid today as when it
was completed in 1914.

🚗 *Continue beside the reservoir on
the Randstrasse, turning right on to
Abelauf/Seestrasse to reach Waldeck.*

Above Hochzeitshaus, the most impressive
half-timbered house in Fritzlar

⑫ Waldeck
Hesse; 34513

Although it is little more than a couple
of streets lined with half-timbered
houses, Waldeck attracts many visitors
thanks to the town's scenic position
high above the Edersee. Its castle,
Schloss Waldeck *(closed Mon)*, was

Where to Stay: inexpensive, under €70; moderate, €70–€150; expensive, over €150

Far left Grand façade of Schloss Wilhelmshöhe, Kassel **Left** Karlsaue garden and orangery, Kassel **Below** Majestic Herkules-Oktagon, Kassel

once the seat of the counts of Waldeck. The views over the lake from its battlements are breathtaking.

🚗 *Leave Waldeck via Bahnhofstrasse. Turn right on to the B485 towards Bad Wildungen, before turning left at the roundabout on to the Lieschensruh through Bergheim to Fritzlar. Parking is available outside the town walls.*

⑬ Fritzlar
Hesse; 34560

The beautiful town of Fritzlar has preserved its original, nearly complete ring of medieval walls with watchtowers and bastions. Snug behind these lofty walls, Fritzlar has over 450 half-timbered houses from various periods, the grandest of which is the Renaissance Hochzeitshaus or wedding house. Built between 1580 and 1590, it now houses the **Regionalmuseum** *(closed Mon)*. In the 8th century, the Anglo-Saxon apostle St Boniface had the holy oak of the Germanic god Donar cut down to build a chapel here. This was later replaced by the **St Petri Dom** *(open daily)*, built in a handsome blend of the Romanesque and Gothic styles. The church's interior is rich in historic treasures. Adjacent to the church is a lovely 14th-century cloister and the **Domschatz** or cathedral treasury *(open daily)*; tickets for the Domschatz also allow a visit to the beautiful Romanesque crypt.

🚗 *Leave Fritzlar along Kasseler Strasse, following the yellow signs for Kassel and Gudensberg, avoiding the A49 Autobahn. At Gudensberg, take Besser Strasse past Besse,*

following signs to Kassel and Kassel-Wilhelmshöhe, then to Zentrum.

⑭ Kassel
Hesse; 34117

Ravishing garden landscapes are the legacy of Kassel's 18th-century heyday. The most impressive of these is the Neo-Classical **Schlosspark Wilhelmshöhe**, dominated by the **Herkules-Oktagon**, a hilltop folly from which the **Wasserkünste** cascade flows downhill to power a 52-m (170-ft) high fountain *(May–Oct: open Wed, Sat, Sun & holidays)*. The castle houses the **Gemäldegalerie Alte Meister** *(closed Mon)* a picture gallery whose collection of Old Masters is particularly strong on Flemish and Dutch artists.

🚗 *Take the B3/Frankfurter Strasse, briefly joining the A49 towards Frankfurt and Hannover before exiting for Kassel-Waldau signposted Melsungen. Then turn right on to the B83 for Melsungen.*

VISITING KASSEL

Parking
Street parking is available in front of the Hessisches Landesmuseum, a short walk from the tourist information office.

Tourist Information
Wilhelmsstrasse 23, 34117; 0561 70 77 07; www.kassel-tourist.de; open Mon–Sat

EAT AND DRINK IN KASSEL

Schlosshotel Bad Wilhelmshöhe
moderate
The chef and his team delight with their regional and international dishes at this restaurant. Every month there is a different culinary highlight. *Schlosspark 8, 34131; 0561 308 80; www.schlosshotel-kassel.de; open daily*

Kaskadenwirtschaft Grischäfer
expensive
A strategically located restaurant and café at the foot of the Wasserkünste, Kaskadenwirtschaft Grischäfer has a wide terrace and a prettily furnished, formal interior. It serves a broad menu, from coffee and cake to rustic regional fare and refined international cooking. *Schlosspark 22 am Kaskadenteich, 34131; 0561 288 77 44; www.kaskaden-wirtschaft.de; closed Mon*

Right Quaint town of Steinau an der Strasse
Below View of the monastery ruins from the tower of the town church, Bad Hersfeld

VISITING FULDA

Parking
Paid on-street parking is available close to the tourist information office. Drivers can also use the underground car park on Heertorplatz.

Tourist Information
Bonifatiusplatz 1, 36037; 0661 102 18 14; www.tourismus-fulda.de; open daily

Canoeing on Lahn and Fulda rivers
Canoes can be hired with **Kanu Lahn-Dill** *(Garbenheimer Strasse 21, 35578 Wetzlar; 06445 601 99 70).*

Cycle Hire
For cycle hire contact **FMG Weilburg** *(Mauerstrasse 6/8, 35781 Weilburg; 06471 13 30).*

WHERE TO STAY

MELSUNGEN

Centrinum *moderate*
This smart hotel in Melsungen's Altstadt offers a blend of historic half-timbered architecture and glossy modernity. There are just 12 tastefully decorated rooms as well as an apartment. *Rosenstrasse 1, 34212; 05661 92 60 60; www.centrinum.de*

BAD HERSFELD

Zum Stern *moderate–expensive*
A traditional four-star hotel with original beams, stripped stonework and warm wood panelling as well as more contemporary touches. Each of the 45 en suite rooms is unique; those in the annexe are furnished in farmhouse style. *Linggplatz 11, 36251; 06621 18 90; www.zumsternhersfeld.de*

FULDA

Hotel Zum Ritter *moderate*
With a boutique hotel ambience, the 150-year-old Zum Ritter is in a quiet sidestreet a few minutes' walk from Fulda's principal sights. The hotel has just 33 rooms. *Kanalstrasse 18-20, 36037; 0661 25 08 00; www.hotel-ritter.de*

Goldener Karpfen *expensive*
This long-established four-star hotel in Fulda's attractive old town has an excellent restaurant. The rooms vary from slick minimalism to more traditional styles, complete with antiques. All rooms have free wireless Internet. *Simpliziusbrunnen 1, 36037; 0661 868 00; www.hotel-goldener-karpfen.de*

⑮ Melsungen
Hesse; 34212
A 16th-century stone bridge crosses the Fulda at the little spa town of Melsungen. The town has a beautiful **Altstadt**, in which, with the exceptions of the stone-built **Landgrafenschloss** and late-Gothic parish church, almost all buildings are half-timbered. Pride of place on the central market square goes to the dignified 16th-century **Rathaus**.
🚗 *Continue along the B83 to reach Rotenburg an der Fulda.*

⑯ Rotenburg an der Fulda
Hesse; 36199
Pretty, half-timbered Rotenburg an der Fulda straddles the Fulda river and is dominated by the Landgrave's castle, the **Schloss Rotenburg**, which is now a college of law and finance. The town preserves poignant reminders of small-town Jewish life in Germany before the Holocaust, including the former Jewish school at No. 19 Brotgasse as well as the half-timbered building on the riverside that housed the **mikvah**, or ritual bath, which is now a small museum *(06623 24 82; May–Oct: open on the first Sun or by appointment).*
🚗 *Continue on the B83 to Bebra, then take the B27 to Bad Hersfeld.*

⑰ Bad Hersfeld
Hesse; 36251
The austere ruins of Bad Hersfeld's **Benediktinerabtei** *(mid-Mar–Apr & mid-Sep–Oct: open Tue, Wed & Fri–Sun)* provide a memorable setting for the spa town's summer theatre festival, the Festspiele. The museum *(closed Mon)*, located next to the abbey, has exhibits on the history of the town and the region. Bad Hersfeld also has a splendid twin-gabled **Rathaus** in the Weser Renaissance style as well as many fine half-timbered houses.
🚗 *Leave Bad Hersfeld along the B27/ Frankfurter Strasse and follow this road to Fulda.*

 Fulda

Hesse; 36037

Fulda was once an independent prince-bishopric, and its 18th-century **Barockviertel**, or Baroque Quarter, retains the air of a capital city. Its grand, twin-towered **Dom** was designed by Bavarian architect Johann Dientzen-hofer. The cathedral holds the tomb of St Boniface, the Anglo-Saxon apostle of the Germans. The neighbouring **Dommuseum** *(closed Mon)* displays Boniface's ghoulish skull reliquary. The **Stadtschloss** *(open daily, guided tours only)*, former residence of Fulda's bishops, has a cabinet of mirrors.

→ *Leave Fulda's Aldstadt along the B254/Frankfurter Strasse, joining the B27 to the B40. This runs parallel to the Autobahn as far as Flieden; thereafter, the road has been declassified and is no longer signposted as a trunk road, but continues via Schlüchtern to Steinau an der Strasse.*

 Steinau an der Strasse

Hesse; 36396

The childhood home of the Brothers Grimm certainly looks the part, with a stern-looking castle presiding over

a quaint, half-timbered **Altstadt**, untouched by time. The Renaissance **Amtshaus** in which the family lived is one of the most impressive houses in the town; it is now a museum, the **Brüder Grimm-Haus** *(open daily)*. The Amtshaus's former barn now hosts the **Museum Steinau** *(open daily)*, a well-laid-out local history museum.

The Brothers Grimm

Born in Hanau, near Frankfurt, in 1785 and 1786, Jacob and Wilhelm Grimm achieved fame thanks to their collection and popularization of traditional folk tales, nurturing the image of a make-believe Germany that has much in common with their Hessian homeland. They grew up in Steinau an der Strasse and studied law at Marburg University before working as lib-rarians at the elector's court in Kassel. However, political disfavour forced them to move to Göttingen and they finally settled in Berlin. Though best known for stories such as *Hansel and Gretel*, *Rumpelstiltskin* and *Snow White*, the brothers were serious academics who also wrote a German dictionary together.

Above Stately façade of the Stadtschloss in Fulda

Left Baroque Dom housing the tomb of St Boniface, Fulda

EAT AND DRINK

MELSUNGEN

Rathaus Café *inexpensive*
The Rathaus Cafe is known for dishing up excellent German staples.
Am Markt 22, 34212; 05661 60 25

Ratskeller *moderate*
Located in Melsungen's marketplace, the Ratskeller serves wholesome, home-made fare.
Am Markt 1, 34212; 05661 928 96 89

BAD HERSFELD

L'Etable *expensive*
Zum Stern's gourmet restaurant features creative modern European cooking, with everything from savoury or sweet tapas to a trio of *foie gras* ser-ved roasted, poached and as ice cream.
Linggplatz 11, 36251; 06621 18 90; www.zumsternhersfeld.de; closed Mon & Tue

FULDA

Restaurant zum Ritter *moderate*
Seasonal produce sets the tone at Zum Ritter's traditional dining room, where there is a big selection of *Schnitzels* (pork fillet) and steaks.
Kanalstrasse 18-20, 36037; 0661 25 08 00; www.hotel-ritter.de

Goldener Karpfen *expensive*
This restaurant's menu changes seasonally and it serves dishes such as crispy pork cheeks and Thai asparagus followed by rack of lamb under herb crust, celery mash, rosemary sauce and potatoes.
Simpliziusbrunnen 1, 36037; 0661 868 00; www.hotel-goldener-karpfen.de

DAY TRIP OPTIONS

This region can also be enjoyed as a series of day trips with either Limburg an der Lahn or Bad Wildungen as a base.

Castles and historic towns
Explore Limburg an der Lahn ❷ before driving to the two castles near Runkel ❸. Stop by the castle in Weilburg ❹ and the medieval

Schloss Braunfels ❺ before heading to see Wetzlar's ❻ hilly Altstadt.

Follow signs from Limburg an der Lahn to Runkel and then to Weilburg. Then follow the route through Schloss Braunfels to Wetzlar.

Unspoiled natural beauty
With Bad Wildungen ❿ as a base, drive to the Edersee and take a boat

cruise on the lake ⓫, one of Germany's largest reservoirs, then visit Schloss Waldeck ⓬, perched high above the Edersee. Continue to Fritzlar ⓭ with its half-timbered houses.

Follow the route from Bad Wildungen to Edersee and then to Schloss Waldeck. Then take Bahnhofstrasse, turn right on to the B485 and follow signs to Fritzlar.

Eat and Drink: inexpensive, under €20; moderate, €20–€40; expensive, over €40

Roman Ruins and Fine Wines

Remagen to Trier

Highlights

- **Thrilling motorsport**
  Get an adrenaline rush at the Nürburgring, where rural tranquillity and vehicles hurtling at breakneck speeds combine to provide a unique experience

- **Fantasy castles**
  Explore the Mosel Valley's fairy-tale castles, which are every bit as impressive as those on the Rhine

- **World-class wine**
  Sample some of Germany's best wines, particularly the Mosel vintages

- **Historic ruins**
  Visit some of Europe's greatest Roman ruins – from an isolated country house to Trier's magnificent sites

Vine-covered slopes along the route to Bernkastel-Kues

Roman Ruins and Fine Wines

The Ahr and Mosel, tributaries of the Rhine, carve their way through the Eifel uplands, creating deep and twisted valleys. Despite being in the middle of western Europe, these valleys remain among Germany's rural backwaters and the attractions along these major rivers offer a quieter version of those on the romantic Rhine. Both valleys offer the classic German mix of atmospheric medieval castles, such as the magnificent Burg Eltz, and pretty half-timbered towns surrounded by steep vineyards that produce wonderful full-bodied wines. The drive visits the Nürburgring, the famous Formula One race car track, and finishes at the venerable city of Trier, the region's southern gateway, with its major collection of interesting Roman ruins.

Above Boats cruising along the Mosel at Bernkastel-Kues, *see p142*

```
0 kilometres        10
0 miles             10
```

ACTIVITIES

Enjoy the thrill of motor-racing on the hallowed asphalt of the Nürburgring

Explore Burg Eltz, tucked away in a quiet valley beside the Mosel

Sample some of Germany's finest wines in the quintessential wine town of Bernkastel-Kues

Tour Trier to get a glimpse of Roman culture among the most spectacular remains north of the Alps

Cruise the Mosel by boat or enjoy a hike on vineyard paths with views of the winding river

KEY

⬢ Drive route

PLAN YOUR DRIVE

Start/finish: Remagen to Trier.

Number of days: 3–4 days, allowing half a day to explore Trier.

Distance: 261 km (162 miles).

Road conditions: Roads are paved and in good condition; most are relatively minor and twist along the Ahr Valley and over the Hunsrück mountains.

When to go: It is possible to tour the area all year round but the drive is particularly good during the wine festivals (late summer–early autumn).

Opening times: Most attractions open daily, while shops are open from 9am to 5pm, Monday to Friday, but close early on Saturdays. Most shops and services are closed on Sundays. Restaurants generally close around 10pm.

Main market days: Trier: Mon–Sat.

Shopping: Pick up local wines, particularly those of small vineyards that are not widely exported.

Major festivals: Bernkastel-Kues: Weinfest (wine festival), first weekend, Sep; Trier: Mosel Musikfestival (Moselle music festival), Jul–Sep; Weinfest (wine festival), late Aug; Trierer Weihnachtsmarkt (Christmas market), late Nov–late Dec.

DAY TRIP OPTIONS

Families should not miss a visit to the Nürburgring, where they can enjoy **motor-racing** before a relaxing stop at Burg Eltz. **Wine lovers** can explore one of Germany's best **wine-producing regions**, which can also be toured on **river cruises**. For full details, see p143.

Below Viewpoint near the attractive town of Cochem, see p141

Above Vineyards near Altenahr

WHERE TO STAY

AROUND RÖMERVILLA

Hohenzollern *moderate*
A short walk from the Römervilla leads to this smart hotel with fine views.
Am Silberberg 50, 53474 Ahrweiler (west of Römervilla); 02641 97 30; www.hotelhohenzollern.com

ALTENAHR

Gasthaus Assenmacher *moderate*
Housed above a restaurant, this family-run hotel has simple and bright rooms.
Brückenstrasse 12, 53505; 02643 18 48; www.gasthaus-assenmacher.de

AROUND NÜRBURGRING

Motorsporthotel *moderate*
Located close to the main grandstand, this hotel offers stylish rooms and is a hub for motorsports enthusiasts.
Hauptstrasse 34, 53520 Nürburg (north of Nürburgring); 02691 920 00; www.motorsporthotel.de

COCHEM

Alte Thorschenke *moderate*
This central guesthouse dates back to 1332. Many of the rooms are in the hotel's modern wing.
Brückenstrasse 3, 56812; 02671 70 59; www.castle-thorschenke.com

Below left Ahrweiler's quaint medieval town centre **Below right** Ruins of Burg Are on a craggy hill, Altenahr

❶ Remagen
Rhineland-Palatinate; 53424
The Ahr river flows into the Rhine just south of Remagen, but the town is better known for its pivotal position in World War II. It was here that American forces captured a bridge across the Rhine, in an act that was celebrated as a strategic victory. Located in the former bridgehead on the Rhine's left bank, the **Friedensmuseum Brücke von Remagen** or bridge museum *(early-Mar–early-Nov: open daily)*, details the history of the bridge and its conquest.

🚗 *From the cul-de-sac road beside the museum, turn left down Goethestrasse then right down Südallee to take the B9 towards Koblenz. Turn right on the B266 to Ahrweiler. Get on to the B267, and follow signs to the Römervilla car park.*

> **The Bridge at Remagen**
> The capture of the Ludendorff Bridge at Remagen by American forces in March 1945 has been seen as a turning point in World War II, since this was the last remaining bridge over the Rhine. President Eisenhower declared the bridge "worth its weight in gold" and Hitler had the officers in charge of the bridge shot. Yet there were further crossings over the Rhine, and 10 days later, the bridge collapsed. Its symbolic significance has grown over time, partly due to the 1969 film *The Bridge at Remagen*.

❷ Römervilla
Rhineland-Palatinate; 53475
In 1980, road constructions at the base of vineyards just north of Ahrweiler chanced upon the foundations of an ancient building. Closer examination revealed this to be part of a 3rd-century Roman country mansion, now protected by the **Museum Römervilla** *(Apr–mid-Nov: closed Mon)* where the building's foundations can be seen. Evidence suggests that the place, preserved under a 5th-century landslide, was inhabited from at least as early as the middle of the 1st century. After exploring the museum, walk down Am Silberberg and turn left along Walporzheimer Strasse for a stroll into the heart of the charming half-timbered centre of Ahrweiler.

🚗 *Turn left out of the car park, then right on the B267. Pass through a tunnel into Altenahr and park in the adjacent car park on the left.*

❸ Altenahr
Rhineland-Palatinate; 53502
Surrounded by vineyards and wooded crags, the town of Altenahr is wrapped around a couple of bends of the Ahr river. Take a ten-minute walk uphill via the street opposite the car park, Rossberg, to the ruined 11th-century **Burg Are**. From the top of this fortification, the chairlift *(Easter–Oct: open daily)* further up the valley is clearly visible. It provides access to higher points and the **Rotweinwanderweg**, *(www.rotweinwanderweg.de)* a signposted red wine walking trail that can be followed for a pleasant hour or two of hiking *(tourist office: Altenburger Strasse 1a; www.altenahr-ahr.de; closed Sat & Sun)* around Altenahr. The chairlift also leads to a summer toboggan run.

🚗 *Turn left on to the B257 and follow it past Breidscheid to turn left in the direction of Nürburgring. Turn right on the B258 to the car parks beside the Nürburgring grandstand.*

Where to Stay: inexpensive, under €70; moderate, €70–€150; expensive, over €150

Left Impressive Burg Eltz perched on a hilltop **Below** Nürburgring, the Famous Formula One race track

EAT AND DRINK

AROUND RÖMERVILLA

Ambiente *moderate*
This is an ideal restaurant for those who enjoy Mediterranean dishes, ranging from pasta to fish.
Telegrafenstrasse 10, 53474 Bad Neuenahr-Ahrweiler; 02641 205 961

Eifelstube *moderate*
Quality traditional German food such as venison in elderberry sauce with *Spätzle* (Swabian noodles) is served here.
Ahrhutstrasse 26, 53474 Ahrweiler (west of Römervilla); 02641 348 50; www.eifelstube-ahrweiler.de

ALTENAHR

Gasthaus Assenmacher *expensive*
A gourmet restaurant serving seasonal specialities such as veal with pigeon breast, lemon confit and pistachio oil.
Brückenstrasse 12, 53505; 02643 18 48; www.gasthaus-assenmacher.de

AROUND BURG ELTZ

Schloss-Hotel Petry *expensive*
Housed in a castle, this restaurant serves specialities such as ox medallions with *foie gras* on asparagus risotto.
St-Castor-Str 80, 56253 Treis-Karden (south of Burg Eltz); 02672 93 40

COCHEM

Alte Thorschenke *moderate*
Traditional German food is served in this atmospheric restaurant.
Brückenstrasse 3, 56812; 02671 70 59; www.castle-thorschenke.com

④ Nürburgring

Rhineland-Palatinate; 53520
Dubbed by British motor-racing driver Jackie Stewart as "Green Hell", the Nürburgring is revered as one of the world's most difficult and treacherous motor-racing circuits. Completed in 1927, its 73 curves have claimed dozens of lives. By the 1970s, the course was deemed too dangerous for top-class racing but in 1984 Formula One returned to a safer loop. The track is regularly used for motorsports and novelty events, such as old-timer races, but at other times it is possible to drive the course in one's own vehicle. There are no speed limits on some sections, though passing on the right is prohibited. To experience speeds of up to 320 kph (199 mph), book a seat in the **BMW Ring-Taxi** *(book in advance: 02691 302 9777; www.bmw-motorsport.com/en/fascination/bmw-ring-taxi.html; children must be taller than 150 cm/5 ft)*. Otherwise, visit the visitor centre **Ring Werk** *(open daily; call ahead: 02691 302 6607)* with its many high-tech racing simulators, films and exhibits, which will keep children busy for hours.

🚗 *Return to the B258 and continue on it. Turn right onto the B262 to Naunheim. From here, turn right again onto a minor road signed Burg Eltz to reach the castle car park.*

⑤ Burg Eltz

Rhineland-Palatinate; 56294
Tucked in a hidden valley, Burg Eltz *(late Mar–Oct: open daily; 02672 950 500)* is one of Germany's most attractive castles. The construction of its cluster of archetypal turrets on a perfect knuckle of rock began in the 12th century and, though plenty of additions followed, it has never been destroyed or rebuilt. It survived a 2-year siege and was saved during the French campaigns of 1689 by having a member of the von Eltz family in the French Army. The interiors are preserved as they were in medieval times. The treasury displays valuables of gold and silver, while the armoury boasts many lethal-looking weapons.

Coat of Arms, Burg Eltz

🚗 *Return to Münstermaifeld and turn right to Hatzenport. Then turn right on to the B416 along the Mosel, which becomes the B49. In Cochem, use the car park beneath the Mosel bridge.*

⑥ Cochem

Rhineland-Palatinate; 56812
Half-timbered Cochem is striking, but can sometimes be overrun by visitors. From the town, a 15-minute signposted walk leads up to the town's main landmark, the **Reichsburg** *(mid-Mar–Nov: open daily)*. A turreted medieval-style castle built in 1877, albeit on 11th-century foundations, its antique-filled interior can be explored. Take the chairlift, **Cochemer Sesselbahn**, *(mid-Mar–mid-Nov: open daily)* to the summit of Pinnerkreuz hill. Located along Endertstrasse, the main road through the town, the chairlift offers great valley views as well as a chance to walk downhill between vineyards back into town.

🚗 *Continue eastwards on the B49, which becomes the B53, to follow the Mosel. At Traben-Trarbach follow signs to Bernkastel-Kues, taking the B50 and the B53 to park beside the Mosel bridge.*

Right Steep vineyards near the twin-town of Bernkastel-Kues

VISITING TRIER

Parking
The multi-storey car park is just off Simeonstiftsplatz, near the Porta Nigra.

Tourist Information
Simeonstrasse 60, 54290; 0651 97 80 80; www.tourist-information-trier.de; open daily

WHERE TO STAY

BERNKASTEL-KUES

Doctor Weinstuben *moderate*
This half-timbered guesthouse with renovated rooms has a sauna.
Hebegasse 5, 54470; 06531 966 50

Gasthaus Burkhard *moderate*
A pleasant guesthouse with modern rooms as well as an excellent restaurant.
Burgstrasse 1, 54470; 06531 23 80; www.gasthaus-burkard.de

TRIER

Villa Hügel *moderate*
This highly recommended Art Nouveau villa offers cheerful rooms.
Bernhardstrasse 14, 54295; 0651 93 71 00; www.hotel-villa-huegel.de

Weinhaus Becker *expensive*
Located in a wine-producing suburb, this is a stylish pension with sleek rooms.
Olewiger Strasse 206, 54295; 0651 93 80 80; www.weinhaus-becker.de

⑦ Bernkastel-Kues
Rhineland-Palatinate; 54470

On a serpentine bend in the river, among woods and vineyards, the twin-towns of Bernkastel-Kues have the perfect Mosel setting. They have many amazingly crooked houses, some of which house wine taverns, specializing in the local *Bernkasteler Doctor*. Bernkastel clusters behind the **Pfarrkirche St Michael**, once part of the town's defences. The **Marktplatz** is surrounded by half-timbered houses. Before settling down to wine-tasting, explore **Burg Landshut** *(www.bernkastel.de)*, a 13th-century castle ruin with views of rolling hillsides. From the Marktplatz, follow Mandatstrasse to a 3-km (2-mile) hiking trail to the castle, or take the hourly shuttle bus *(Apr–Oct: open daily)* from the riverfront tourist office.

🚗 *Turn right out of the car park on to the B53. In Trier, turn left on to Kaiser-Wilhelm-Brücke and then right on to Martinsufer to Friedrich-Ebert-Allee to Nordallee. Turn right at Simeonstiftsplatz to park on the left.*

⑧ Trier
Rhineland-Palatinate; 54290

Founded in 15 BC, Trier boasts northern Europe's greatest collection of Roman remains. It became the capital of the Western Roman Empire in the 3rd century. Today, the town's wine culture, combined with its proximity to Luxemburg provides a cosmopolitan feel.

A two-hour walking tour

An alley from the Simeonstiftsplatz car park leads to the colossal 2nd-century **Porta Nigra** ① *(open daily)*, the last of Trier's four city gates. Named for its blackening, which had already occurred by the Middle Ages, it is remarkable for its ingenious design – the structure is supported by just a few iron rods. It was inhabited by a Greek hermit, Simeon, after 1028. Turned into a church after his death and sanctification, it was dissolved along with the adjoining monastery by Napoleon in 1802. South of the gate, Simeonstrasse leads to the **Hauptmarkt** ②, the hub of the old town where the sculpted fountain Petrusbrunnen lies encircled by grand houses including the vivid red Baroque Rotes Haus and the 15th-century Steipe, once a banqueting hall now housing Germany's oldest pharmacy, the Löwenapotheke.

Where to Stay: inexpensive, under €70; moderate, €70–€150; expensive, over €150

A block east of the Hauptmarkt lies Trier's Romanesque **Dom St Peter** ③ *(open daily)*. Technically the oldest church in Germany, it was once a basilica but since the late 3rd century, it has been a bishops' seat. The current building originated in the 11th century and contains a robe believed to have been worn by Christ at his crucifixion, though this has not been scientifically authenticated. Housed in the extravagant Baroque Heilumskammer, the robe has not been on display since 1996.

North of the church, the Bischöfliches Dom und Museum am Dom *(closed Mon)* is famed for an early 4th-century Roman fresco removed from the palace that once stood where the Dom does today. Turn left then right for a walk down Liebfrauenstrasse to the **Konstantinbasilika** ④ *(Nov–Mar: closed Mon, Apr–Oct: open daily)*. It originally provided a throne hall for Emperor Constantine in the 4th century but later became a Protestant church for the prince-electors who resided in the Baroque **Rokoko-Palais** ⑤ next door. The formal gardens beside the palace lead to the **Rheinisches Landesmuseum** ⑥

(closed Mon), a Roman archaeology museum with many beautifully presented treasures, including coins and mosaics. A walk south through the pretty gardens leads to the **Kaiserthermen** ⑦ *(open daily)*, once the largest baths in the Roman world. Their foundations remain intact, making it easy to visualize the scale of this 4th-century complex. The scale also impresses at Trier's **Amphitheater** ⑧ *(open daily)*, a signposted ten-minute walk southeast along Olewiger Strasse from the underpass at the southeast corner of Kaiserthermen. This 20,000-capacity arena was built for gladiatorial and animal fights around AD 100, making it Trier's oldest Roman structure.

Return to the Kaiserthermen, turn right along Weberbach, left down Wechselstrasse, right again on Neustrasse, then left on Viehmarktstrasse to arrive at the Viehmarktplatz. The glassy cube in the centre protects the **Viehmarktthermen** ⑨ *(closed Mon)*, the smallest and oldest of Trier's Roman baths. From the opposite side of Viehmarktplatz, turn right down Stresemanstrasse, then left down Brückenstrasse to **Karl-Marx-Haus** ⑩ *(open daily)* where this political philosopher was born and grew up in the 19th century. Now a museum, it focuses on Marxian philosophy. From here, turn left and walk along Fleischstrasse to the Hauptmarkt. Return via Simeonstrasse to Porta Nigra and turn left along the alley to the Simeonstiftsplatz car park.

Sculpture, Trier's Electoral Palace

Left Porta Nigra, Roman gateway into Trier
Below Entrance to Kaiserthermen, Trier

CRUISING THE MOSEL

For cruising the Mosel by boat, visitors can opt for the **Mosel-Schiffs-Touristik** *(06531 82 22; www.moselpersonenschifffahrt.de)*, which operates out of Bernkastel-Kues, while **Personen-Schifffahrt Gebrüder Kolb** *(02673 15 15; www.moselfahrplan.de)* sails from Trier.

EAT AND DRINK IN TRIER

Weinstube Kesselstatt *moderate*
Enjoy regional dishes and wines in one of the prettiest settings in Trier.
Liebfrauenstrasse 10, 54290; 0651 411 78

Zum Domstein *moderate*
Dishes with a regional twist, as well as some inspired by old Roman recipes, are served here.
Hauptmarkt 5, 54290; 0651 744 90; www.domstein.de

Other options
Many restaurants in Trier have lively wine bars in the basement. One such is the **Ratskeller zur Steipe** *moderate (Hauptmarkt 14, 54290; 0651 750 52)*, which serves local and Russian dishes.

DAY TRIP OPTIONS
Trier is a good base along this drive. Visitors can also consider staying in atmospheric Bernkastel-Kues. This tour can be covered along the A1 motorway on a two-day trip from both these places.

Fantastic thrills
Unmissable for those travelling with children, the Nürburgring ④ offers

plenty of motor-racing excitement and has an excellent visitor centre. Then head to the fantasy castle, Burg Eltz ⑤.

From Trier, follow signs to Koblenz and drive north to the end of the A1. Follow signs to Nürburgring.

Enchanting Mosel Valley
From Burg Eltz ⑤, drive to Cochem ⑥, then drive back along the Mosel

river to visit Bernkastel-Kues ⑦. Wine lovers should consider heading straight to the twin-town via a cruise from Trier ⑧ to sample the wines without having to drive later.

From Trier, follow signs to Koblenz but leave the A1 at exit 123 to take the signed route to Bad Bertrich, then head to Cochem.

Eat and Drink: inexpensive, under €20; moderate, €20–€40; expensive, over €40

The Romantic Rhine

Koblenz to Mainz

Highlights

- **Castle hopping**
  Explore the Rhine's many fairy-tale castles, such as Rheinfels, Pfalzgrafenstein and Rheinstein

- **Rhine wine**
  Cozy up in a half-timbered inn at Bacharach and sample the famous Rhineland wines

- **History in print**
  Admire some of the world's earliest printed books in the town of Mainz, where Gutenberg invented the process

- **Craggy cliffs**
  Appreciate cascading vineyards and sweeping views of the Rhine Gorge, a spectacular stretch of Germany's most celebrated river

Imposing Burg Rheinstein overlooking the Rhine

The Romantic Rhine

Slicing through the Taunus and Hunsrück hills, Germany's mighty Rhine river has sculpted a craggy and dramatic gorge classified by UNESCO as a World Heritage Site. Here, near-perfect wine-growing conditions and the lucrative tolls on passing river traffic gave rise to a multitude of wealthy castles during the Middle Ages. Many of these were destroyed in the 17th century and then rebuilt in the 18th and 19th centuries during the Romantic movement, which celebrated the valley as a source of Germanic identity. This tour visits many of these grand fortresses and explores the sleepy and traditional towns of Marksburg and Bacharach, where half-timbered houses have survived alongside Roman fortifications. Scores of local wines await discovery all along the way.

ACTIVITIES

Cruise the most scenic stretches of the Rhine at Koblenz aboard a pleasure boat

Taste flinty Rieslings, dry reds and sparkling wines on a wine-tasting tour at Boppard

Ascend the chairlift to the Vierseenblick at Boppard for extraordinary views of the Rhine

Explore the labyrinthine fortifications of the mighty Burg Rheinfels

Hike steep twisting paths to the Loreley Rock for views of the most treacherous part of the Rhine

Learn to print at the Druckladen workshop in Mainz, home of the printing press inventor Johannes Gutenberg

Below The Rhine flowing past lush green forested hills in the Rhineland-Palatinate

Above left Pretty town centre of Bacharach, *see p152* **Above right** Pfalzgrafenstein, a toll castle built on an island in the Rhine, *see p152*

KEY

Drive route

0 kilometres   5

0 miles   5

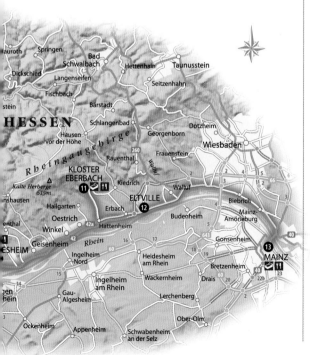

PLAN YOUR DRIVE

Start/finish: Koblenz to Mainz.

Number of days: 3–4 days, allowing a day to explore Koblenz, Mainz and the major castles along the route.

Distance: 116 km (72 miles).

Road conditions: Well paved and signposted alongside the Rhine.

When to go: A good drive year round, this route is particularly attractive in August and September when wine festivals abound.

Opening times: Most attractions open daily; shops are open between 9am and 5pm, Monday to Friday, but close early on Saturdays. Shops and services are closed on Sundays. Most restaurants close their kitchens by 10pm.

Main market days: Boppard: Fri; Mainz: Tue, Fri & Sat.

Shopping: Pick up local wines, such as Rieslings, in Bacharach or Rüdesheim. In Mainz, browse the hand-printed posters, cards and flyers of the Druckladen for gifts or souvenirs.

Major festivals: Koblenz: Rhein in Flammen (Rhine in flames – a fireworks spectacular), late Aug; **Boppard:** Weinfestwochenende Boppard (weekend wine festival), early Oct; **Loreley:** Rhein in Flammen, late Sep; **Oberwesel:** Weinmarkt Oberwesel (wine market), late Sep; **Rüdesheim:** Rhein in Flammen, early Jul; Rüdesheimer Weinfest (wine festival), late Aug; **Mainz:** Mainzer Fastnacht (carnival), mid-Feb; Mainzer Johannisnacht (midsummer night), late Jun.

DAY TRIP OPTIONS

Wine lovers will appreciate not having to drive after a visit to Bacharach for **wine-tasting**. Visitors can explore both banks of the Rhine separately, avoiding the use of car ferries. The highlights on both banks are the chairlift-assisted **walks** and **castles**. On the **right bank**, the walk leads from Rüdesheim to Assmannshausen after a visit to the **Marksburg**. On the **left bank**, the chairlift climbs to **hikes** around Vierseenblick before a visit to **Burg Rheinstein**. For full details, *see p155*.

Above Restaurant Terrasse along the Rhine, Koblenz

BOATING ON THE RHINE

Several boats chug up and down the Rhine, allowing one to enjoy the scenery as well as sample wines. The largest company, **Köln-Düsseldorfer** *(0221 208 83 18; www.k-d.com)*, has five sailings daily from Koblenz.

VISITING KOBLENZ

Parking
The most convenient car park, the Schloss Tiefgarage, is in the corner of Stresemannstrasse and Neustadt, just northeast of the Kurfürstliches Schloss.

Tourist Information
Rathaus, Jesuitenplatz 2, 56068; 0261 13 09 20; www.koblenz-touristik.de

WHERE TO STAY

KOBLENZ

Diehl's Hotel *moderate*
This riverside hotel has pastel-coloured rooms, complete with claw foot bathtubs. Facilities include a pool and sauna. *Rheinsteigufer 1, 56077; 0261 19 70 70; www.diehls-hotel.de*

Kleiner Riesen *moderate*
Housed in a modern building, this guesthouse has elegant rooms. A continental breakfast buffet is served too. *Kaiserin-Augusta-Anlagen 10, 56068; 0261 30 34 60; www.hotel-kleinerriesen.de*

AROUND MARKSBURG

Zum Weissen Schwanen *moderate*
This family-owned country hotel has interesting themed rooms. Two of them are inspired by the work of 19th-century Austrian artist Friedensreich Hundertwasser, who stayed here. *Brunnenstrasse 4, Braubach, 56338 (2 km/1 mile north of Marksburg); 0262 798 20; www.zum-weissen-schwanen.de*

❶ Koblenz
Rhineland-Palatinate; 56001

Located at the confluence of the Rhine and Mosel, Koblenz marks the northern end of the Rhine Gorge. Built in 9 BC as a Roman settlement, the city was repeatedly fought over for many centuries because of its strategic riverside location. Following its comprehensive destruction during World War II, it was rebuilt in a mix of old and new. Its pedestrianized centre has many pavement cafés and is surveyed from across the Rhine by the grandiose Ehrenbreitstein citadel.

A 90-minute walking tour

From the car park at the Kurfürstliches Schloss turn left down Stresemannstrasse to the Rhine, then left, following the river to its confluence with the Mosel. Known as the **Deutsches Eck ❶**, or "German corner", the headland is presided over by a giant equestrian statue of Emperor Wilhelm I. Behind it, the Deutschherrenhaus was once the 13th-century headquarters of the Teutonic Knights, but the building is now home to the Ludwig Museum *(closed Mon)*, displaying modern and contemporary art. Walking west along the thin strip of parkland from the Deutsches Eck, the picturesque old town, Altstadt, comes into view. To the right is the arresting castle **Alte Burg ❷** on the banks of the Mosel. The first fortress here was built in the Middle Ages by

Madonna and Child, Liebfrauenkirche

the von Arken family, but in 1277, it was taken over by the archbishop of Koblenz, who sought to protect himself from the city's citizens, who were seeking independence. The fortress now houses the town archives. Walk through the archway just to the right, up a flight of stairs and left on Burgstrasse for the short walk to the **Florinsmarkt ❸**. One of several focal points in the Altstadt, the Romanesque-Gothic church of Florinskirche *(Jun–Aug: open daily)* is known, above all, for the Augenroller, a figure that rolls its eyes and sticks out its tongue every half hour from its perch below the clock. The square is also home to the Mittelrhein-Museum *(closed Mon)*, a regional history museum with some 19th-century paintings. Also of interest are the works of 18th-century Rococo painter Januarius Zick, who lived in Koblenz. From the Florinsmarkt, head south

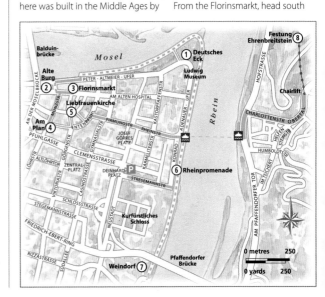

Left Medieval Marksburg, Braubach
Below Deutsches Eck, the spur between
the Mosel and the Rhine

EAT AND DRINK

KOBLENZ

Weindorf *inexpensive*
This "wine village", set around a mock
village square beside the Rhine promenade, is a fun place to sample local
wines and traditional German food.
*Julius-Wegeler Strasse 2, 56068; 0261
13 37 19; www.weindorf-koblenz.de;
Jan–Feb: closed Mon–Thu*

Augusta *moderate*
Located on the Rhine, this restaurant
uses local produce and serves wines
from nearby vineyards. The lunch
specials include regional dishes.
*Rheinstrasse 2a, 56068; 0261 91 44
68 22; www.augusta-koblenz.de*

Weinhaus Hubertus *moderate*
This traditional wine tavern in the heart
of the old town offers an excellent selection of local wines and a seasonal menu.
Sample the *Zander* (local perch) and seasonal dishes such as the autumnal rack
of lamb flavoured with pumpkin seeds.
*Florinsmarkt 6, 56068; 0261 311 77;
www.weinhaus-hubertus.de*

Schiller's Restaurant *expensive*
Housed in Hotel Stein, this restaurant
offers three-course seafood menus and
four-course menus of world cuisines.
*Mayener Strasse 126, 56070;
0261 963 530*

AROUND MARKSBURG

Zum Weissen Schwanen *moderate*
The hotel Zum Weissen Schwanen has
an excellent restaurant for local fish
and lamb dishes in particular.
*Brunnenstrasse 4, Braubach, 56338
(2 km/1 mile north of Marksburg);
0262 798 20*

on Münzstrasse, which becomes
Löhrstrasse before intersecting
with **Am Plan** ④, Koblenz's most
famous street corner. Here, the
17th-century buildings on each
corner, Vier Türme, are celebrated
for their ornate façades. Am Plan
once served as a butcher's market,
the city's main execution site and
the venue for medieval tournaments.
An alley off its left side leads to the
Liebfrauenkirche ⑤, Koblenz's
main church. Despite its Baroque
onion domes and Gothic choir and
chancel, the church is Romanesque
in origin. With the church to the
right, follow Braugasse east, turn
left onto Entenpfuhl and then right
along Firmungstrasse to head back
to the Rhine. Alongside the river,
the **Rheinpromenade** ⑥, a pleasant
promenade, stretches south and
is worth strolling down as far as
the quaint wine village **Weindorf** ⑦.
Back near the junction of Rheinstrasse,
a passenger ferry *(Easter–mid-Nov:
open daily)* crosses to the right bank
of the Rhine. From here, turn left then
right down the Charlottenstrasse
and Obertal to the chairlift *(Easter–
Oct: open daily)* up to the **Festung
Ehrenbreitstein** ⑧ *(open daily)*,
which has a commanding position
over the city. First built in AD 1000,
the fortress was extended by the
archbishop of Trier who lived here
between 1648 and 1768 until its
destruction by Napoleonic troops
in 1801. Today's version, a Prussian
rebuild from 1832, houses the
Landesmuseum *(mid-Mar–mid-Nov:
open daily)*. The state museum looks
at local trade, including car manufac-
ture in a tribute to Audi, which was
founded nearby. Return to the

Rheinpromenade, turn right onto
Stresemannstrasse to the car park.
🚗 **From the Kurfürstliches Schloss
turn left and get on to B49. Turn right
on to B42 in the direction of Lahnstein.
Follow signs to the Marksburg car park.**

② Marksburg
Rhineland-Palatinate; 56338
The huddle of towers and turrets
high above the delightful half-
timbered town of Braubach belongs
to the Marksburg *(open daily)*. Built
in 1117, it is one of the Rhine's most
impressive castles, and is particularly
remarkable for being the only
medieval castle in the region never
to have been destroyed. It is easy to
imagine lively banquets in its Gothic
grand hall, while its armoury and
array of torture instruments recall
a more gory past.
🚗 **Return to B42 and turn left. Take
the Kamp-Bornhofen-Boppard ferry
across the Rhine, then in Boppard,
turn left along Rheinallee for car park.**

Eat and Drink: inexpensive under €20; moderate €20–€40; expensive over €40

Above The Rhine meandering between forested hillsides **Below** Sculpture of the mythical siren beside the Rhine, Loreley

WHERE TO STAY

BOPPARD

Weinhaus Heilig Grab *moderate*
This 200-year-old historic wine tavern in the town centre has been converted into a hotel with a few basic rooms and a lovely garden.
Zelkesgasse 12, 56154; 06742 23 71; www.heiliggrab.de

AROUND BURG RHEINFELS

Berghotel auf der Loreley *moderate*
A modern hotel with small, basic rooms enjoying a great setting at the tip of the Loreley Rock. The Loreley visitors' centre is a short walk away.
Auf der Loreley, Sankt Goarshausen, 56436 (2 km/1 mile west of Burg Rheinfels); 06771 809 20; www.berghotel-loreley.de

OBERWESEL

Burghotel Auf Schönburg *expensive*
An unusual opportunity to stay in a castle overlooking the Rhine. A castle has stood here since the 10th century, though this is a 1914 rebuild of the one burned down by French troops in 1689. Rooms have a glamorous, turn-of-the-20th-century feel.
Auf Schönburg, 55430; 06744 939 30; www.burghotel-schoenburg.de; closed in Feb

❸ Boppard

Rhineland-Palatinate; 56154
Just two horseshoe bends upstream from Braubach and on the opposite bank of the Rhine, the atmospheric town of Boppard gathers around a riverfront promenade. Located beside the ferry terminal, the **Alte Burg** is the most impressive building on the waterfront. Built as a stronghold and tollhouse in 1340, it now houses the **Museum der Stadt Boppard** *(Apr–Oct: closed Mon)*, which celebrates local cabinet-maker Michael Thonet (1796–1871), who invented bent-wood furniture. By soaking layered strips of wood veneer in hot glue and then bending them into shape in metal moulds, he created elegantly curved furniture that became hugely popular in the mid-19th century.

A block southeast lies Boppard's marketplace and the tourist office *(May–Sep: closed Sun; Oct–Apr: open Mon–Fri)*, which organizes wine tastings *(open Apr–Oct; www.boppard-tourismus.de)* at local vineyards. Just beyond, crossing Oberstrasse, the town's main shopping street, a short walk down Kirchgasse leads to the **Römer-Kastell**, where four of Boppard's 4th-century Roman watchtowers are preserved.

Back on Oberstrasse, a few minutes' walk west leads to the Karmeliterstrasse and its church, **Karmelitenkirche**. Local farmers place the

season's first ripe grapes in a niche outside the church, beside the Traubenmadonna, or Grape Madonna, to gain her blessing. At the northern end of Boppard – a 20-minute walk along the promenade – a chairlift *(Apr–Oct: open daily)* ascends to a fine lookout known as the **Vierseenblick**, or Four Lakes View, because the four sections of the Rhine visible from here look unconnected. Several hiking trails fan out from here, and bus No. 34 takes an easy one-hour route back into Boppard.

🚗 *Turn right from the car park and right again to turn left onto Mainzer Strasse and on to B9 to Sankt Goar, then follow signs up Schlossberg to the Burg Rheinfels car park.*

❹ Burg Rheinfels

Rhineland-Palatinate; 56329
The Rhine's largest castle, **Burg Rheinfels** *(mid-Mar–mid Nov: open daily; mid-Nov–mid-Mar: open Sat & Sun;)* is a maze of sprawling passages, trenches and tunnels and ruined battlements (a torch is handy for exploration). Equally incredible is the fact that the castle was once five times its present size and mighty enough to survive a 14-month siege by 9,000 troops in 1255 and repel an army of 28,000 in 1692. It would never be taken by force, for in 1794 it was handed over without a shot to the

French Revolutionary Army who soon set about demolishing the citadel.

🚗 *Return to Sankt Goar, turn right down B9 and park at the Sankt Goar-Sankt Goarshausen ferry terminal. Leave the car here and board the ferry across the Rhine as a foot passenger if intending to walk or take the shuttle bus up the Loreley, since the tour returns this way.*

⑤ Loreley
Rhineland-Palatinate; 56346

The giant rock outcrop on the opposite side of the Rhine from Sankt Goar, and above Sankt Goarshausen, is known as the Loreley. Vistors can either hike, drive or take a shuttle bus *(Apr–Oct: hourly)* from the ferry terminal to the summit for breathtaking views. The visitors' centre *(Mar–mid-Nov: open daily; Besucherzentrum Loreley; www. loreley-touristik.de)* has an English-language exhibition on the region's past and natural history.

The Legend of Loreley
The name Loreley is thought to originate from the old German and Celtic words for "lure" and "rock" and the legend of a lady who threw herself into the Rhine near St Goarshausen in despair over a faithless lover. On dying, she transformed herself into a bewitching siren and sat on the rock singing alluring songs. Distracted sailors would then fall foul of the undercurrents and rocky riverbed beneath the giant cliff that marks the narrowest point on the Rhine between Switzerland and the North Sea.

🚗 *Return to Sankt Goar on the ferry and turn left on to B9. In Oberwesel, park on riverfront.*

⑥ Oberwesel
Rhineland-Palatinate; 55430

Located on the left bank of the Rhine, the charming wine town of Oberwesel boasts a well-preserved 3-km (2-mile) long medieval wall around the old town that makes for a good walk. The local history museum in the central **Kulturhaus** *(Apr–Oct: open daily)* has a good collection of 19th-century engravings of the sort that helped romanticize the Rhine and photographs of the local ladies who have been crowned *Weinhexe* – the good "wine witch" who protects the wine harvest – every April since the 1940s, following a local tradition.

🚗 *Continue on the B9 to the Kaub-Langscheid ferry. Leave the car and cross the Rhine on ferry as a foot passenger and take the passenger boat to Burg Pfalzgrafenstein.*

Above left Remains of a Roman military camp, Boppard **Above right** Marktplatz and Romanesque Severuskirche, Boppard **Below** Outer walls of the formidable Burg Rheinfels

EAT AND DRINK

AROUND BURG RHEINFELS

Berghotel auf der Loreley *moderate*
This restaurant in the Burghhotel auf der Loreley serves traditional German food.
Auf der Loreley, Sankt Goarhausen, 56436 (2 km/1 mile west of Burg Rheinfels); 06771 809 20;
www.berghotel-loreley.de

Loreley Weinstuben *moderate*
A snug place with fresh fish and an excellent *Reslingschnitzel* (veal in wine).
Bahnhofstrasse 16, Sankt Goarhausen, 56346 (2 km/1 mile west of Burg Rheinfels); 06771 70 68

Zum Goldenen Löwen *moderate*
The Zum Goldenen Löwen serves top-notch German cuisine. Specialities include *Braten vom Spanferkal* (roasted suckling pig).
Heerstrasse 82, Sankt Goar, 56329 (south of Burg Rheinfels); 06741 16 74;
www.goldener-loewe-stgoar.de

Schlossrestaurant *expensive*
An elegant restaurant in Hotel Schloss Rheinfels offering game from the nearby Hünsrück highlands. Try the pork tenderloin with mushroom sauce on fine vegetables and tagliatelle.
Schlossberg 47, Sankt Goar, 56329 (south of Burg Rheinfels); 0641 80 20

OBERWESEL

Hotel Römerkrug *moderate*
A range of German favourites, from pork medallions and steak in wild mushroom sauce to local fish such as *Zander* (local perch), is served here.
Marktplatz 1, 55430; 06744 70 91; closed Wed, Sat & Sun in winter

Burghotel Auf Schönburg *expensive*
This restaurant serves regional recipes made from fresh, seasonal ingredients.
Auf Schönburg, 55430; 06744 939 30

Eat and Drink: inexpensive, under €20; moderate, €20–€40; expensive, over €40

Right Burg Stahleck towering over the town of Bacharach **Below** Canons facing the Rhine Valley, Burg Rheinstein

WHERE TO STAY

BACHARACH

Burg Stahleck/Jugendherberge Bacharach *inexpensive*
The budget alternative to Auf Schönburg in Oberwesel, Burg Stahleck is a 12th-century castle that once served as the seat of the Count-Palatinate of the Rhine and is now a stunning youth hostel. One does not need to be a member to stay, and most of the basic rooms are en suite and sleep between one and six people.
Bacharach, 55422; 06743 12 66; www.diejugendherbergen.de

Rhein Hotel *moderate*
This family-run half-timbered hotel beside the town walls has spotless, plain and compact rooms.
Langstrasse 50, 55422; 06743 12 43; www.rhein-hotel-bacharach.de

RÜDESHEIM

Burghotel Rheingauner *moderate*
This modest guesthouse in a quiet neighbourhood, just west of the town centre, has bright, cheerful rooms with fashionably dated 1970s decor.
Oberstrasse 7, 65385; 06722 23 94; www.rheinromantikhotel.de

Central Hotel *moderate*
A smart family-run place in the centre of Rüdesheim with bright, immaculate rooms and bathrooms and an excellent buffet breakfast.
Kirchstrasse 6, 65385; 06722 91 20; www.centralhotel.net

⑦ Burg Pfalzgrafenstein
Rhineland-Palatinate; 56349

One of the most beautifully situated castles in Europe, the mighty fortress of Burg Pfalzgrafenstein *(Jan, Feb & Nov: open Sat & Sun; Mar–Oct: open Tue–Sun; closed Dec)* stands in the middle of the Rhine river. With its unusual island perch, the castle was built to levy tolls on Rhine shipping. Constructed in 1325 by Ludwig the Bavarian, the castle's gun bastions and its present shape are the result of Baroque refurbishments in the 17th and 18th centuries.

🚗 *Exit the ferry terminal car park and turn left on to the B9. In Bacharach, park in the riverside car park.*

⑧ Bacharach
Rhineland-Palatinate; 55422

The pretty town of Bacharach has a unique complex of historic buildings, with fortified town walls, the church of St Peter, the ruins of the Gothic chapel of St Werner, and **Burg Stahleck** – the 12th-century castle towering over the town. Once the seat of the Count-Palatinate of the Rhine, today it is an impressive youth hostel.

A gate in the town wall, opposite Bacharach's main car park, provides access to its 14th-century fortifications, with views of the huddle of half-timbered buildings. Among these is the celebrated old house, **Altes Haus** on Oberstrasse 61, which is so wonky that it seems to lean in all directions at once. This building and many others house wine taverns, which serve up local wines such as Hahnenhof Riesling.

🚗 *Turn right out of the Bacharach car park on to the B9. Park at the signed car park beside the B9 in Trechtingshausen.*

⑨ Burg Rheinstein
Rhineland-Palatinate; 55413

The compact castle of **Burg Rheinstein** *(mid-Mar–mid-Nov: open daily; mid-Nov–mid-Mar: open Sat & Sun)* sits in a spectacular location 82 m (270 ft) above the Rhine. After falling into ruin, the 13th-century castle was acquired by Prince Friedrich Ludwig of Prussia and given a complete makeover in 1820. This helped begin a Romantic architectural trend, which swept down the Rhine and across Germany and saw many medieval ruins rebuilt as castles in an age in which fortifications no longer served a practical purpose. Here, the resulting twee pastel-coloured interior rooms seem out of place in a castle, but convey a good sense of the early 19th-century tastes.

🚗 *Continue south on the B9, turn left over a bridge into Fruchtmarkt, then Vorstadt and Espenschiedstrasse/Mainzer Strasse. Follow ferry signs left down Hafenstrasse. Take the ferry across the Rhine. Turn right to Rüdesheim then left down Burgstrasse to the roadside car park opposite the Rheingauer Weinmuseum.*

⑩ Rüdesheim
Hesse; 65385

Enjoying a picturesque location on the banks of the Rhine, Rüdesheim has a long history going back to Roman times. The town is famous for its main street, the Drosselgasse,

Where to Stay: inexpensive under €70; moderate €70–€150; expensive over €150

Left Panoramic view of the Rhine from Burg Rheinstein **Below left** Quirky Altes Haus, Bacharach **Below right** Picturesque Burg Pfalzgrafenstein along the Rhine

which is lined with countless wine bars and shops. There are also the remains of three castles: the Boosenburg, the Vorderburg and the 12th-century Bromserburg, which houses a wine museum. The **Rheingauer Weinmuseum Brömserburg** *(Mar–Oct: open daily)* has a wide array of wine-making items from Roman times, particularly aged wine presses, but also antique amphorae, wine coolers and goblets. Walking up Burgstrasse from the museum and turning right along Oberstrasse leads to the centre of Rüdesheim and Drosselgasse, the tourist hub where strings of souvenir shops peddle their wares. The top of the lane is close to the chairlift *(Mar–Nov: open daily)* to viewpoints above, while around its base are many lanes lined with wine taverns offering samples of the celebrated local Riesling.

Rüdesheim also has several historic mansions, including the half-timbered **Brömserhof** (1559), with a collection of musical instruments, and the early 16th-century Klunkhardshof.

Above the town towers the **Niederwalddenkmal**, a huge 38-m (125-ft) statue of Germania, built to commemorate German unity and the foundation of the German Reich in the wake of the country's victory in the Franco-Prussian War of 1870–71.

🚗 *Return to the B42 in the direction of Wiesbaden/Eltville to Hattenheim. Turn left at Schlossergasse, left on to Hauptstrasse, then right on to Eberbacher Strasse to signs for Kloster Eberbach car park.*

Walk to Assmannshausen

Taking the chairlift from the centre of Rüdesheim allows for an excellent two-hour hike to Assmannshausen, from where it is possible to get a boat or bus back to Rüdesheim; the boat is included in the price of a "Ringtrip". The chairlift climbs to the impressive Niederwalddenkmal, after which the hiking trail passes through a series of fine Rhine viewpoints before descending past vineyards into Assmannshausen.

EAT AND DRINK

BACHARACH

Zum Grünen Baum *moderate*
For a good wine tavern experience, try Zum Grünen Baum, which offers a well-priced 15-wine sampler.
Oberstrasse 63, 55422; 06743 12 08

The Stüber Restaurant *expensive*
This excellent restaurant in the Rhein Hotel is particularly good for its *Rieslingbraten* – a pot roast marinated for three days in Riesling and mustard – served with *Spätzle* (Swabian noodles).
Langstrasse 50, 55422; 06743 12 43; www.rhein-hotel-bacharach.de

RÜDESHEIM

Breuer's *moderate*
Despite its location on the tourist strip, Breuer's is a stylish rustic restaurant specializing in classic regional cuisine such as venison *Schnitzel* (pork fillet) in herb sauce or monkfish in lemon sauce.
Drosselgasse, 65385; 06722 905 00; www.ruedesheimer-schloss.com

Eat and Drink: inexpensive, under €20; moderate, €20–€40; expensive, over €40

Above Pretty rose garden in the town of Eltville **Below left** Café in the grounds of Kloster Eberbach **Below right** Gutenberg-Museum, a tribute to Mainz's most famous resident, Johannes Gutenberg

WHERE TO STAY

KLOSTER EBERBACH

Gästehaus Kloster Eberbach
moderate
This hotel offers simple rooms in one of the outlying monastery buildings. It is set in peaceful wooded surroundings and serves a sumptuous buffet breakfast.
Eltville, 65346; 06723 99 30;
www.klostereberbach.com

MAINZ

Hotel Schwan *moderate*
The elegant Hotel Schwan, housed in a 16th-century town building, has spacious rooms with Baroque touches.
Liebfrauenplatz 7, 55116; 06131 14 49 20; www.mainz-hotel-schwan.de

⑪ Kloster Eberbach
Hesse; 65346
The monastery of Kloster Eberbach *(open daily)* is best known as the Romanesque setting for the medieval murder mystery film *The Name of the Rose* (1986). Its most impressive feature is its austere basilica. Here, a steep staircase in the north transept climbs to the dormitory where monks slept on pallet-like beds. The walk around the cloisters to the lay refectory passes massive wine presses built of timbers sturdy enough for galleons; its shop has excellent wines.

🚗 *From the car park, head south to the T-junction, turn left towards Erbach and follow signs to Eltville. On arriving in the town, turn right and park at the Schwimmbad, then walk down to the riverfront and turn left towards the town centre.*

⑫ Eltville
Hesse; 65343
The oldest town in the region, Eltville is gathered around a cozy nest of lanes, but it is best known for its many rose beds, whose perfume thickens the summer air. Many rose bushes line the Rhine promenade and grow in the moat of the adjacent 14th-century castle, the **Burg** *(gardens and courtyard: open daily)*, which was laid to waste by fierce Swedes during the Thirty Years' War (1618–48). Stirred up by the Counter-Reformation, this war between the Protestant Union and Catholic League raged across Europe. Only the four-storey residential tower of the Burg survived and climbing it *(Apr–mid-Oct: open Fri–Sun)* provides a glimpse of a stained-glass window celebrating Johannes Gutenberg, as well as fine views of the town's waterfront.

🚗 *Turn right out of the car park, following Wallufer Strasse, turn right again at the next junction. Head south to Mainz-Amöneburg. Take the B40 then the Theodor-Heuss-Brücke bridge over the Rhine into Mainz, then take the first left to a handy riverside car park.*

⑬ Mainz
Rhineland-Palatinate; 55001
As capital of Rhineland-Palatinate, and with good transport links to Frankfurt, large and cosmopolitan Mainz *(see p165)* has none of the sleepy atmosphere of the rest of the Rhineland. Originally a strategic settlement at the confluence of the Main and Rhine, by the 8th century it was the main religious centre north of the Alps. Its importance was enhanced by Johannes Gutenberg (c. 1400–68), who invented the printing press here in the 15th century.

Like Koblenz, Mainz suffered massive bombardment during World War II, though a large section of its half-timbered old town including the cathedral, survived or was rebuilt to create an attractive town with many tempting traditional wine bars.

Mainz's majestic six-towered late-Romanesque **Kaiserdom** *(open daily)* is of 12th-century origin and unusual for sharing its exterior walls with adjoining houses. Inside, the highlight of the spartan cathedral is the Dommuseum and the adjacent

Left Lovely view of the domed Christuskirche, Mainz **Below** Wine cellars, Kloster Eberbach

Gewölbehallen *(open daily)*, which stores its treasures. These include sparkling reliquaries, intricate 15th- and 16th-century tapestries, a 13th-century rood screen by the Master of Naumburg, which vividly depicts Sin and Salvation, and some Rococo choir stalls.

Celebrating Mainz's most famous son, Johannes Gutenberg, the **Gutenberg-Museum** *(closed Mon)* on Liebfrauenplatz shows a reconstruction of his workshop from 1450 and has a rare copy of his first major work: the 42-line Bible, from 1455, which was named after the number of lines on each page. The museum also puts Gutenberg's invention in context with a look at Asian printing techniques and the hand copying of manuscripts, which he effectively turned into a dying art. For a hands-on experience, visit the nearby printing shop **Druckladen** *(closed Sun)*, where visitors can hand-set type (aprons are provided) to produce posters, cards and flyers. Enthusiastic staff offer guidance to those trying their hand at printing.

Invention of the Printing Press

In the early 15th-century, goldsmith Johannes Gutenberg experimented with several technologies that led to the invention of the printing press. These included the development of movable metal type and moulds, oil-based inks and the mechanical printing press, for which he initially adapted wine presses. The results changed the world forever as information could spread more quickly. This gave more power to the masses and helped to spread the Protestant Reformation.

EAT AND DRINK

KLOSTER EBERBACH

Klosterschänke *moderate*
This restaurant at Kloster Eberbach serves plenty of uncomplicated hearty dishes such as pork ragout with potato dumplings and some lovely wines from the estate to wash them down with.
Kloster Eberbach, Eltville, 65346; 06723 99 30; www.klostereberbach. com

MAINZ

Heiliggeist *inexpensive–moderate*
The main menu at this restaurant offers an eclectic mix of German, Asian and Italian-style dishes. It is especially known for its *croustarte*, a crispy pizza-like dish which is a little different from the traditional German *Flammkuchen*.
Mailandgasse 11, 55116; 06131 22 57 57

Haus des Deutschen Weines *moderate*
Visit this restaurant for the sheer number of choices and the reasonably priced, good-quality German food. If you don't want a full meal, try the traditional accompaniment *Spundekäse* (a cheese, onion and cream dip with crusty bread).
Gutenbergplatz 3–5, 55116; 06131 22 13 00

Hotel Schwan *moderate*
Traditional wine bars or *Weinstuben* abound in Mainz, but this cozy place is the oldest in the region and worth seeking out.
Liebfrauenplatz 7, 55116; 06131 14 49 20; www.mainz-hotel-schwan.de

---

DAY TRIP OPTIONS

All the stops on this route can be visited on day trips. Koblenz in particular is a good base for boat trips.

Medieval castles and monasteries

Drive along the banks of the Rhine, stopping at the Marksburg **2**, the Rhine's most attractive castle and the unusual islet-based Burg Pfalzgrafenstein **7** before arriving at the bustling

town of Rüdesheim **10** on the banks of the Rhine. Take its chairlift over the pretty vineyards to the excellent and downhill two-hour walk to Assmannshausen, with sweeping Rhine Valley views along the way. End the day with a sumptuous meal at the peaceful and atmospheric Kloster Eberbach **11**.

Take the B42 along the right bank of the Rhine.

Mighty fortifications

Explore Boppard **3**, with its remaining Roman walls then ride the chairlift up to the Vierseenblick. Next, wander around the splendid medieval town fortifications of Oberwesel **6** and those of the quaint wine town of Bacharach **8** before a visit to the Gothic fantasy castle of Burg Rheinstein **9**.

Take the B9 along the left bank of the Rhine.

Eat and Drink: inexpensive, under €20; moderate, €20–€40; expensive, over €40

The German Wine Route

Deutsches Weintor to Speyer

Highlights

- **Vintage wines**
  Sample the wines of Pfalz and Rheinhessen, from crisp Rieslings to Auslese and *barrique*-aged Pinot Noir

- **Gourmet delights**
  Enjoy the region's restaurants, where regional specialities such as *Saumagen* meet European sophistication

- **Rural idyll**
  Admire Pfalz's rustic beauty, from castle-topped hills to the half-timbered villages of Leinsweiler and St Martin

- **Religion and culture**
  Visit the ancient Jewish cemeteries and cathedrals at Oppenheim, which bear witness to its cultural and historical legacy

Panoramic view of vineyards from Villa Ludwigshöhe, Edenkoben

The German Wine Route

Set in gently rolling countryside between Pfälzer Wald's wooded hills and the Rhine, with the French Alsace to the south, the wine-growing regions of Pfalz and Rheinhessen are Germany's largest. This area has much in common with its southern neighbour, Alsace – from its architecture to the dialects spoken. They also share a history of alternating periods of French and German control. The drive follows an established and well-signposted wine route past picturesque vineyards, beautiful villages, chic hotels and top-quality restaurants. A gourmet experience is guaranteed. Visitors can look foward to tasting the different types of wine made by the numerous small vineyards scattered throughout the region. Other highlights include the ancient and historic cathedral cities of Mainz, Worms and Speyer.

Above Vineyards along the way to Nierstein, *see p165*

ACTIVITIES

Sample the wines on an oenophile's tour of the region's superb wineries

Take a hike in the unspoiled Naturpark Pfälzer Wald in St Martin

Scare yourself in the ossuary at Oppenheim and then tour the underground passages

Hike to the impressive ruins of Wachtenburg for spectacular views over the Rhine Valley

Acquire a taste for *Saumagen*, Pfalz's most famous regional speciality

Above Busy street, Neustadt an der Weinstrasse, *see p163*

0 kilometres   10

0 miles   10

KEY

Drive route

Below View of the rocky outcrop from Burg Trifels, Annweiler, *see p161*

PLAN YOUR DRIVE

Start/finish: Deutsches Weintor to Speyer.

Number of days: 5 days, allowing half a day to explore Oppenheim.

Distance: 260 km (162 miles).

Road conditions: The region has well paved minor roads with gentle gradients. The Deutsche Weinstrasse is well signposted; look for the grape symbol.

When to go: The tourist season begins with the Mandelblütenfest in March and continues until the end of October. Some attractions close for winter.

Opening times: Most attractions open daily, while shops are open 9am to 5pm Monday to Friday, but close early on Saturdays. Shops and services are closed on Sundays. Most restaurants close their kitchens by 10pm.

Major festivals: Neustadt an der Weinstrasse: Deutsches Weinlesefest (wine festival), Oct; **Gimmeldingen:** Mandelblütenfest (almond blossom festival), Mar/Apr; **Bad Dürkheim:** Wurstmarkt (sausage festival), Sep; **Mainz:** Mainzer Fastnacht (pre-Lent carnival), Feb; **Worms:** Nibelungen Festspiele (theatre festival), Jul; Backfischfest (folk and wine festival), late Aug/early Sep.

DAY TRIP OPTIONS

Lovers of **fine food** and **wine** will find the Weinstrasse at its most chic between Edenkoben and Freinsheim and enjoy the drive from Mainz to Worms, which is famous for **wine-growing villages**. For the lost-in-time charm of **sleepy villages** and **hilltop castles**, a drive from Bad Bergzabern to Burg Trifels is particularly magical. For full details, *see p167*.

Right Schloss of the Counts Palatine of Zweibrücken, Bad Bergzabern **Centre right** Imposing Burg Trifels, Annweiler **Below** Sweeping view of Annweiler from Burg Trifels

WHERE TO STAY

AROUND BAD BERGZABERN

Zum Lam *moderate*
Located just off the Deutsche Weinstrasse, between Bad Bergzabern and Klingenmunster, this hotel is housed in an 18th-century half-timbered inn. It offers rustic but comfortable en suite rooms as well as a decent restaurant serving Pfalz specialities.
Winzergasse 37, 76889 Gleiszellen-Gleishorbach (5 km/3 miles from Bad Bergzabern); 06343 93 92 12; www.zum-lam.de

LEINSWEILER

Hotel Rebmann *moderate*
This three-star hotel-cum-restaurant, in the centre of Leinsweiler, has refurbished en suite rooms with pale maple furnishings.
Weinstrasse 8, 76829; 06345 954 00; www.hotel-rebmann.de

Leinsweiler Hof *moderate*
A four-star hotel in the countryside near Leinsweiler offering sweeping views over the surrounding vineyards. The elegant decor boasts modern and rustic touches. Facilities include a spa and an outdoor pool.
Weinstrasse, 76829; 06345 40 90; www.leinsweilerhof.de

ANNWEILER

Scharfeneck *moderate*
Offering good value, this refurbished, centrally located, non-smoking hotel has prettily furnished en suite single and double rooms and one spacious and stylish apartment.
Altenstrasse 17, 76855; 06346 83 92; www.hotel-scharfeneck.de

① Deutsches Weintor
Rhineland-Palatinate; 76889
Marking the start of the 85-km (53-mile) Deutsche Weinstrasse (German Wine Route) since 1936, the Deutsches Weintor or German Wine Gate *(Jan & Feb: closed Mon–Wed)*, located in the town of Schweigen-Rechtenbach, is a monumental sandstone gatehouse on the French border just north of the Alsatian town of Wissembourg. Visitors can taste and buy Pfalz wines here and there is a restaurant serving regional fare.
🚗 *Leave Schweigen-Rechtenbach on the B38 north, then turn left at the Deutsche Weinstrasse symbol to Bad Bergzabern and left on to Kettengasse to park.*

② Bad Bergzabern
Rhineland-Palatinate; 76887
With its leafy spa quarter and a quaint historic centre focused on the **Schloss** of the Counts Palatine of Zweibrücken, Bad Bergzabern is the capital of the southern Weinstrasse. The ornate Renaissance **Gasthaus Zum Engel** (Angel's Inn) near the Schloss houses a local history museum *(Apr–Dec: open Tue–Sun)*. In the late 1930s, Bad Bergzabern formed part of the fortifications

known as the **Westwall**; a bunker on Kurfürstenstrasse *(Apr–Oct: open Sun)* now houses a museum.
🚗 *Leave Bad Bergzabern along the B48/Weinstrasse north to Burg Landeck. Park at the Burg.*

③ Burg Landeck
Rhineland-Palatinate; 76889
There is a fairy-tale quality to the village of **Klingenmünster**, nestling beneath forested hills and dominated by the ruined fortress of Burg Landeck *(open daily)*, which towers 300 m (984 ft) above it. Built in the 13th century to defend a Benedictine abbey, it was destroyed by French troops in 1680 during the War of the Palatine Succession. It now houses a small museum and provides superb views.
🚗 *Return to the B48 north, turn left and then right, following signs to Slevogthof, to reach Leinsweiler.*

④ Leinsweiler
Rhineland-Palatinate; 76829
The arcaded town hall, the **Rathaus** of 1619, is the focus of this pretty, half-timbered village. Leinsweiler was the summer home of the German Impressionist painter Max Slevogt,

who died in 1932 and is buried here. Lansweiler is also home to a corkscrew museum, **Korkenzieher Museum** *(Sonnenberg 7–9, 76829; open 4–6pm Mon–Wed)*, which features a variety of interesting corkscrews.

🚗 *Continue to Birkweiler, take the slip road up to the B10, turning left for Annweiler. Take care as this is a dangerous junction. Park near the town hall and tourist information office.*

Wine Country
Vineyards dominate the picture-perfect landscape of the Pfalz and Rheinhessen region. Many local wine growers have a room set aside to sample and buy wines from the vineyard itself. However, German wineries tend to be family-run affairs, so it is wise to call before visiting. Dry white wines predominate – Rieslings are often excellent. Red wines made with the Spätburgunder (Pinot Noir) grape are also gaining popularity. The region also produces Sekt (sparkling wines) and small quantities of *Tresterbrand*, the German equivalent of the spirit, grappa.

5 Annweiler
Rhineland-Palatinate; 76855
A former Free City of the Holy Roman Empire, Annweiler lies on the Queich river, which was once harnessed to provide power for the town's tanneries. The **Gerberviertel** (tannery district) is particularly picturesque, with its watermill and half-timbered houses, three of which house the local history museum, the **Museum Unterm Trifels** *(Mid-Mar–Nov: closed Mon; Nov–mid-Mar: open Sat & Sun)*.

🚗 *Leave the town of Annweiler along Altenstrasse, turning left on to Trifelsstrasse and follow signs to Burg Trifels. Park below the Burg.*

6 Burg Trifels
Rhineland-Palatinate; 76855
Perched on a narrow crag 300 m (984 ft) above Annweiler, Burg Trifels *(Jan–Nov: open daily)* is reached after a beautiful looping ascent through the forest. First mentioned in the 11th century, the castle was where the Salian emperors kept the imperial regalia of the Holy Roman Empire; Richard the Lionheart was briefly a prisoner here in 1193. The ruined castle was extensively restored between 1938 and 1942. Visitors can also explore two more castle ruins – Scharfenberg and Anebos – which crown neighbouring crags.

🚗 *Return to Annweiler on Trifelsstrasse, leaving Annweiler on Landauerstrasse. Rejoin the B10 and then turn onto Weinstrasse to reach the village of Siebeldingen.*

Above View of the surrounding countryside from Burg Landeck, Klingenmünster
Below Dense forest near Burg Trifels

EAT AND DRINK

DEUTSCHES WEINTOR

Deutsches Weintor Restaurant *moderate*
Elegantly modern, the restaurant at the Deutsches Weintor serves creative dishes based on regional and seasonal ingredients accompanied by red and white Pfalz wines.
Weinstrasse 4, 76889 Schweigen-Rechtenbach; 06342 922 78 88; www.weintor.de; open daily

AROUND BURG LANDECK

Café Rosinchen *inexpensive*
In a pretty, half-timbered house on Klingenmünster's main street, Café Rosinchen serves home-made cakes, soups and Alsatian-style *Flammkuchen* (pizzas).
Weinstrasse 39, 76889 Klingenmünster (1 km/half a mile from Burg Landeck); 06349 33 93; closed Mon

LEINSWEILER

Leinsweiler Hof *expensive*
This restaurant provides lovely views across the countryside of the southern Weinstrasse. The menu emphasises regional and seasonal produce and includes refined versions of local specialities such as *Saumagen*.
Weinstrasse, 76829; 06345 40 90; www.leinsweilerhof.de

ANNWEILER

S'Reiwerle *inexpensive*
Housed in a lovely half-timbered house in the centre of Annweiler, this traditional *Weinstube* (wine bar) and restaurant serves dishes such as *Saumagen* or lamb sausages with savoy cabbage.
Flitschberg 7, 76855; 06346 92 93 62; www.reiwerle.de; closed Tue eve

Eat and Drink: inexpensive, under €20; moderate, €20–€40; expensive, over €40

Left Deidesheim town centre **Right** Vineyards around Villa Ludwigshöhe, Edenkoben **Below** Ruins of Wachtenburg in the town of Wachenheim

VISITING NEUSTADT AN DER WEINSTRASSE

Parking
The car park in the Hetzelgalerie shopping centre is convenient for reaching the tourist information office.

Tourist Information
Hetzelplatz 1, 67433; 06321 926 80; www.neustadt.eu; Apr–Oct: open Mon–Sat; Nov–Mar: open Mon–Fri

WHERE TO STAY

EDENKOBEN

Pfälzer Hof *moderate*
This well-established hotel offers a cosy atmosphere and beautiful views of the surrounding landscape. It also boasts a fine restaurant.
Weinstrasse 85, 67480; 06323 938 910; www.pfaelzerhof-edenkoben.de

MAIKAMMER

Gasthaus zum Winzer *moderate*
This hotel, in a Baroque former *Weingut* (winery), has five non-smoking, Mediterranean-style double rooms with hypoallergenic furnishings. It also has an excellent restaurant and offers free wireless Internet access.
Weinstrasse Süd 8, 67487; 06321 54 10; www.gasthaus-zum-winzer.de

ST MARTIN

St Martiner Castell *moderate*
A hotel-cum-restaurant situated in the old part of St Martin offering single, double or three-bedded rooms, all with en suite baths and some with balconies.
Maikammerer Strasse 2, 67487; 06323 95 10; www.hotelcastell.de; closed late Jan–late Feb

GIMMELDINGEN

Weingut Mugler *moderate*
The Weingut Mugler has two stylish, modern guest rooms. Diners can sample Mugler's wines along with the regional fare at their Kutscherhaus restaurant across the street.
Peter-Koch-Strasse 50, 67435; 06321 660 62; www.weingut-mugler.de

DEIDESHEIM

Deidesheimer Hof *expensive*
Dating from the 18th century, this inn is set in one of the Weinstrasse's most chic villages. The rooms and spacious suites are comfortable and tastefully furnished.
Am Marktplatz, 67146; 06326 968 70; www.deidesheimerhof.de

⑦ Siebeldingen
Rhineland-Palatinate; 76833

The village of Siebeldingen lies on the Queich river, which once formed France's northeast military frontier. Among the village's wine growers, the **Ökonomierat Rebholz** *(open Mon–Fri; www.oekonomierat-rebholz.de)* is the most distinguished, producing *Grosses Gewächs* wines – the German equivalent of the French premier cru.

🚗 *Follow the Deutsche Weinstrasse beyond Frankweiler and continue via Burrweiler to Hainfeld. Watch out for the sharp left turn in Hainfeld. Villa Ludwigshöhe is west of Edenkoben along Villastrasse.*

⑧ Edenkoben
Rhineland-Palatinate; 67480

Edenkoben was Bavarian territory from 1816 until 1945. On the outskirts of the town, Bavarian King Ludwig I built his residence, **Villa Ludwigshöhe** *(Jan–Nov: closed Mon)*, which was designed by Friedrich Wilhelm von Gärtner in the style of a Roman villa. It was built between 1846 and 1852 on an idyllic site between woods and vineyards and contains a gallery devoted to the German Impressionist painter Max Slevogt. It is also the venue for chamber music concerts *(www.villamusica.de)*.

🚗 *From the villa, return to Deutsche Weinstrasse, continuing north through Edenkoben to Maikammer.*

⑨ Maikammer
Rhineland-Palatinate; 67487

With seemingly every second building a *Weingut* (winery), Maikammer is a Weinstrasse village *par excellence*. Grandiose 19th-century premises line the route from the village to its railway station; one of the finest buildings is home to **Weingut August Ziegler** *(open Mon–Sat; www.august-ziegler.de)*, which has thrice been declared German Winemaker of the Year. Alongside Riesling and Pinot Noir, the estate also produces varieties of wine quite unusual for Germany, including Shiraz and Sauvignon Blanc.

🚗 *St Martin is signposted from Maikammer along the minor road.*

⑩ St Martin

Rhineland-Palatinate; 67487

With a beautiful setting on the fringes of the **Naturpark Pfälzer Wald** (www. pfaelzerwald.de), a biosphere reserve, St Martin is among the loveliest villages in the region. With plenty of surviving half-timbered cottages and noblemen's houses, it is also the starting point for a number of hiking trails into the Naturpark Pfälzer Wald; one popular route ascends to the summit of the 673-m (2,208-ft) **Kalmit**, the highest hill in the district.

🚗 *Return to Maikammer and turn north towards Hambach. At Hambach turn left up Schlossstrasse to the Hambacher Schloss; the route is one-way. Continue on it, following signs to Hauptbahnhof (station) to Neustadt.*

⑪ Neustadt an der Weinstrasse

Rhineland-Palatinate; 67433

Neustadt is the most important urban centre on the Deutsche Weinstrasse, with a traffic-free historic core centred on the **Marktplatz** and its Gothic **Stiftskirche** and Baroque town hall, the **Rathaus**. The town's most famous sight is the **Hambacher Schloss** (open daily), a hilltop castle to the south, famous for the Hambacher Fest of 1832, during which a patriotic crowd hoisted the black-red-gold colours of German unity in one of the founding acts of German democracy.

🚗 *Leave Neustadt an der Weinstrasse along Karl-Helffenrich-Strasse, turn right on to Maximilianstrasse, taking Gimmeldinger Strasse, the middle of three roads, to reach Gimmeldingen. The village centre is a one-way system.*

⑫ Gimmeldingen

Rhineland-Palatinate; 67435

The pretty wine growing village of Gimmeldingen lies on the edge of the Naturpark Pfälzer Wald and is the starting point for several hiking trails. The village is famous for its almond blossom, celebrated with an annual spring festival, the Mandelblütenfest.

🚗 *Continue along Meerspinnstrasse to reach Deidesheim.*

⑬ Deidesheim

Rhineland-Palatinate; 67146

Designer jewellery jostles for attention next to a butcher selling the local delicacy, *Saumagen*, on Deidesheim's

Marktplatz. The juxtaposition of rustic authenticity and metropolitan chic makes this one of the most intriguing villages on the Weinstrasse. The Rathaus houses the **Museum für Weinkulture** (museum of viticulture) (open Wed–Sun; Jan & Feb: closed). Local wine growers include **Reichsrat von Buhl** (open daily), a renowned producer of Sekt (sparkling wine).

🚗 *Continue on the minor road along the B271 signposted to Wachenheim.*

⑭ Wachenheim

Rhineland-Palatinate; 67157

The impressive ruins of the 12th-century castle of **Wachtenburg** dominate Wachenheim. Constructed under the authority of Konrad von Hohenstaufen, half-brother of Emperor Frederick Barbarossa (1122–90), it was besieged in the 15th century, damaged in the Peasants' War of 1524–25 and finally blown up by French troops in 1689. Known as the "Balcony of the Pfalz" for the superb views it offers over the Rhine Valley, the castle ruins are a popular destination for hikers and are floodlit to spectacular effect at night.

🚗 *Continue on the minor road to Bad Dürkheim. Follow signs to Kurpark.*

Above Café tables on the main square of Siebeldingen **Below** Decorative sign outside a winery, Maikammer

---

EAT AND DRINK

MAIKAMMER

Gasthaus zum Winzer *expensive*
This Baroque former winery enjoys an attractive courtyard. The menu features modern European dishes. *Weinstrasse Süd 8, 67487; 06321 54 10; www.gasthaus-zum-winzer.de; open Wed–Sun*

ST MARTIN

St Martiner Castell *moderate*
A handsome old hotel-cum-restaurant with a menu that blends local and international influences. *Maikammerer Strasse 2, 67487; 06323 95 10; www.hotelcastell.de; closed Tue & late-Jan–late-Feb*

GIMMELDINGEN

Netts *expensive*
Housed in a restored late Baroque village house, this modern restaurant and wine bar offers creative fare with outstanding wines. *Meerspinstrasse 46, 67435; 06321 601 75; www.nettsrestaurant.de; open Wed–Sun*

DEIDESHEIM

Turm Stübl *moderate*
Regional specialities and French dishes are served at this wine bar. *Turmstrasse 3, 67146; 06326 98 10 81; www.turmstuebel.de; closed Mon*

Schwarzer Hahn *expensive*
The Deidesheimer Hof's Michelin-starred restaurant blends French, German and Mediterranean influences to impressive effect. The hotel also has a more traditional restaurant. *Am Marktplatz, 67146; 06326 968 70; www.deidesheimerhof.de; open Tue–Sat; closed Jan, Jul*

Eat and Drink: inexpensive, under €20; moderate, €20–€40; expensive, over €40

Above left Ruins of Kloster Limburg, Bad
Dürkheim **Above right** Vineyards around
Nierstein **Below left** Village centre, Nackenheim
Below right Wine cellar in Bockenheim

WHERE TO STAY

BAD DÜRKHEIM

Hotel Annaberg *moderate*
Surrounded by vineyards, this
four-star hotel enjoys an idyllic location
and has a delightful restaurant.
*Annabergstrasse 1, 67098; 06322
940 00; www.hotel-annaberg.com*

FREINSHEIM

Luther *moderate*
Rooms at this celebrated hotel range
in style from contemporary to rustic.
All are en suite and are equipped with
LCD televisions and wireless Internet.
*Hauptstrasse 29, 67251; 06353 934 80;
www.luther-freinsheim.de; closed Jan*

Freinsheimer Hof
moderate–expensive
A beautifully restored winery in the
old town, this hotel has just four pretty
rooms off an open verandah overlooking the lovely central courtyard.
*Breite Strasse 7, 67251; 06353 50 804 10;
www.restaurant-freinsheimer-hof.de*

NACKENHEIM

St Gereon *moderate*
This lovely hotel and restaurant in a
half-timbered house is in the village
centre. It offers ten en suite double
rooms, three suites and one single,
decorated in simple, country style.
*Carl-Zuckmayer-Platz 3, 55299; 06135
70 45 90; www.landhotel-st-gereon.com*

AROUND NIERSTEIN

Jordan's Untermühle *moderate*
The rooms are simple but attractive
at this rustic half-timbered hotel on
the edge of Köngernheim, between
Westhofen and Mainz. It has an
outstanding restaurant.
*Ausserhalb 1, 55278 Köngernheim
(west of Nierstein); 06737 710 00;
www.jordans-untermuehle.de*

⑮ Bad Dürkheim
Rhineland-Palatinate; 67098
The pleasant spa town of Bad
Dürkheim has a neat, traffic-free
core fringing the **Kurpark**, a grassy
park where the 33-m (108-ft) long
Gradierwerk – a giant outdoor
saline air purifier – is one of the
largest of its kind in Germany. Dating
from 1847, it is the sole survivor of
five similar structures in the town.
To the west of the town centre, on
Luitpoldweg, are the ruins of the
Romanesque Benedictine abbey
of **Kloster Limburg** *(open daily)*.
🚗 *Leave Bad Dürkheim along the
B271 to Ungstein, then take the minor
road signposted to Freinsheim.*

⑯ Freinsheim
Rhineland-Palatinate; 67251
Snug behind its surviving medieval
walls, Freinsheim is a historic gem
with a perfectly preserved old
town focused on the diminutive
yet dignified 18th-century **Rathaus**.
Visitors can enjoy a walk around the
inner circuit of the town's walls and
discover houses built into them in
a picturesque fashion. A gastronomic
hotspot, Freinsheim also boasts a
number of interesting restaurants.
🚗 *Return to Ungstein, then turn
right along the B271 to Bockenheim.*

Saumagen
Saumagen – stuffed pig's stomach
is the Pfalz's great regional speciality.
Like the Scottish dish haggis, it
delights some and intimidates
others; as with haggis, the stuffing
is consumed, not the stomach itself.
In the case of *Saumagen*, the filling
is prepared with a mixture of potatoes, carrots and pork, flavoured with
marjoram and often served sliced
and seared.

⑰ Bockenheim
Rhineland-Palatinate; 67278
Situated beside a lake, the village
of Bockenheim is supposedly
built in the style of a Roman fort.
The Deutsche Weinstrasse ends
at Bockenheim, where the **Haus
der Deutschen Weinstrasse**, or
House of the German Wine Route,
acts as the northern counterpart

to the **Deutsches Weintor** at the southern end of the route. The building spans the road and contains a restaurant and tourist information office.

🚗 *Continue along the B271 Weinstrasse to Flörsheim, turning right towards Westhofen.*

⑱ Westhofen

Rhineland-Palatinate; 67593
Enjoying a pretty setting, the vineyards surrounding the village of Westhofen are dotted with stone huts. These are characteristic of Rheinhessen's wine-growing country, and were originally built by vineyard workers to provide shelter during bad weather. **Weingut Wittmann** *(Mainzer Strasse 19; 06244 90 50 36; www. weingutwittmann.de; open Mon–Sat, by appointment)* produces top-notch dry Rieslings using organic methods.

🚗 *Leave Westhofen along Mainzer Strasse, signposted to Mainz.*

⑲ Mainz

Rhineland-Palatinate; 55116
The capital of Rheinland-Pfalz, Mainz *(see pp154–55)* is dominated by the late Romanesque **Kaiserdom** *(open daily)*. The magnificence of this imperial cathedral reflects the importance of the Prince-Bishops of Mainz, who were Electors of the Holy Roman Empire. The cathedral was burned down the day before its consecration in 1009 and again in 1081. It was rebuilt in the first quarter of the 12th century. Mainz was also the birthplace of printing pioneer Johannes Gutenberg. Exhibits in the **Gutenberg-Museum** *(closed Mon)* include a priceless Gutenberg Bible printed in Mainz in 1455.

🚗 *Leave Mainz along Rheinstrasse, following signs to Laubenheim. At Laubenheim continue through Bodenheim to Nackenheim.*

⑳ Nackenheim

Rhineland-Palatinate; 55299
Nackenheim is closely associated with the German playwright Carl Zuckmayer, who was born here in 1896. Nestled between vine-covered slopes and the Rhine, the village has a long history of producing wine. The long-established **Weingut Gunderloch** *(Carl-Gunderloch-Platz 1,*

06135 23 41; www.gunderloch.de; open Mon–Sat) produces traditional sweet wines of exceptional quality and some fine dry Rieslings.

🚗 *Leave Nackenheim on the Wormser Strasse, which joins the B9. Continue on the B9 to Nierstein, then turn left on to Pestalozzistrasse to the car park.*

㉑ Nierstein

Rhineland-Palatinate; 55283
Shuttered, half-timbered houses and *Strausswirtschaften* – temporary wine taverns run by the wine growers – characterize Nierstein. The village is famed for its Riesling and is focused on its central Marktplatz. Visitors can go on a signposted 14-km (8-miles) walk, the **Drei Türme Wanderweg** or Three Towers Walk *(www.nierstein.de)*, which heads up into the vineyards of the **Roter Hang** above the village for views over the Rhine and the surrounding countryside.

🚗 *Continue south on the B9 to Oppenheim, then turn right on to Mainzstrasse and follow signs to Zentral Park-Platz to park.*

Discovering German Wines

Wine labels reveal much about the style and quality of German wine. Dry wines are labelled *Trocken*, semidry or slightly sweet wines are *Halbtrocken* and sweet wines are *Lieblich*. *Kabinett* refers to a wine made with fully-ripened grapes; *Spätlese* means wine made from late-picked grapes, while *Auslese, Beerenauslese, Eiswein* and *Trockenbeerenauslese* are made with grapes picked progressively later, producing intense flavour and longevity. Many, though not all, quality wines display the symbol of the VDP *(Verband Deutscher Prädikatswein)*, whose members include many of the nation's top wine growers.

Above left Outdoor café, Nierstein **Above right** Village gate of Nackenheim

VISITING MAINZ

Parking
The Karstadt multi-storey car park in Weissliliengasse is convenient for visiting the Kaiserdom and Gutenberg-Museum.

Tourist Information
Brückenturm am Rathaus, 55116; 06131 28 62 10; www.tourist.mainz.de; open daily; closed on public hols

EAT AND DRINK

FREINSHEIM

Freinsheimer Hof *expensive*
Terracotta tiles and a vaulted ceiling provide a Mediterranean setting for this restaurant's sophisticated cooking.
Breite Strasse 7, 67251; 06353 50 804 10; www.restaurant-freinsheimer-hof.de; closed Wed, Thu

Luther *expensive*
This renowned restaurant, named for chef-proprietor Dieter Luther, offers creative *haute cuisine* that uses seasonal produce in its constantly changing menu.
Hauptstrasse 29, 67251; 06353 93 480; www.luther-freinsheim.de; open Mon–Sat; closed Jan

NACKENHEIM

St Gereon *moderate*
Beautifully scrubbed stonework and timber beams create a country setting for this restaurant's European menu. There are several vegetarian options and a great selection of wines.
Carl-Zuckmayer-Platz 3, 55299; 06135 70 45 90; www.landhotel-st-gereon.com

AROUND NIERSTEIN

Jordan's Untermühle *moderate*
An award-winning restaurant in Köngernheim, Jordan's Untermühle offers a good selection of wines.
Ausserhalb 1, 55278 Köngernheim (west of Nierstein); 06737 710 00; www.jordans-untermuehle.de

Eat and Drink: inexpensive, under €20; moderate, €20–€40; expensive, over €40

Right Red sandstone Katharinenkirche, Oppenheim **Far right** Old city walls in the town of Worms **Below** Outdoor cafés in front of the Kaiserdom, Speyer

WHERE TO STAY

OPPENHEIM

Hotel Merian *moderate*
A 17th-century house has been transformed into this stylish hotel in the centre of town, with 11 double rooms and one single room.
Wormser Strasse 2, 55276; 06133 949 40; www.merianhotel.de

Hotel Zwo *moderate*
The 13 modern, stylish rooms in this boutique hotel have well-equipped bathrooms and wireless Internet.
Friedrich-Ebert-Strasse 84, 55276; 06133 949 40; www.hotelzwo-oppenheim.de

SPEYER

Domhof *moderate*
This ivy-clad hotel is very close to Speyer's cathedral, with 49 single and double rooms furnished in conservative style. It also has its own microbrewery.
Bauhof 3, 67346; 06232 132 90; www.domhof.de

㉒ Oppenheim

Rhineland-Palatinate; 55276

A ruined castle and a magnificent Gothic church are powerful reminders of Oppenheim's medieval heyday. Raised to the status of a Free City of the Holy Roman Empire in 1225, it lost its independence in the following century and was levelled by French troops during the War of the Palatine Succession (1688–97). This wine-growing village, on a pretty, sunny site overlooking the Rhine, also has an intriguing underground labyrinth to explore.

A one-hour walking tour

Park at the Zentralparkplatz, on the western edge of the Altstadt, before heading uphill along Gaustrasse and Burgstrasse. At the top of Burgstrasse ascend the Schlangenweg path to reach **Landskron** ①, a ruined imperial castle. At the far end of the castle, metal steps lead into a vineyard. Take the path through it, beyond the gate in the town wall at the far end. Cross the road to the Landskronhalle. The Burgrestaurant Landskrone here is a good place for a snack. Follow the road downhill to the **Ruprechtsturm** ②, a mock-medieval folly built in 1903 on the site of a medieval tower destroyed during the French occupation. Continue downhill to Geschlechterbrunnen, a Renaissance well dating from 1546, and the arched entrance to the churchyard beyond it. Go through this,

Winery sign, Oppenheim

turning right to reach the **Michaelskapelle** ③, a 13th-century Gothic chapel. In the basement is the macabre Beinhaus (ossuary), where the bones of 20,000 citizens of Oppenheim who died between 1400 and 1750 lie neatly stacked. Further along the north wall is the Lapidarium, with gargoyles and Gothic carvings. Continue around the outside of the **Katharinenkirche** ④ *(open daily)*, a Protestant parish church, to enter on the south side. Construction began in 1225 in the Romanesque style, but most of what exists today is Gothic, including the 14th-century Rose of Oppenheim window. From the south side of the churchyard, go down the steps to Merianstrasse to the **Oppenheimer Stadtmuseum** ⑤ *(open daily)*, with displays on local history, and the tourist information office

(www.stadt-oppenheim.de), which organizes tours of the Oppenheimer Kellerlabyrinth (tours Sat, Sun & public hols), an extensive subterranean network of cellars and passageways. Merianstrasse leads onto the central **Marktplatz** ⑥, dominated by the 17th-century Rathaus. Cross the square to reach the Catholic church of St Bartholomäus, once part of a now-vanished Franciscan monastery. Follow Kirchstrasse to Wormserstrasse to the **Deutsches Weinbaumuseum** ⑦ (Apr–Oct: closed Mon), with exhibits on Germany's winemaking history. Walk back up Wormserstrasse and turn left into Rathofstrasse, following the street around to the **Rathofkapelle** ⑧, a tiny chapel which is now a restaurant. Beyond it, a plaque commemorates Oppenheim's Jewish community on the site of a synagogue destroyed on "Kristallnacht" in an anti-Jew attack in 1938 in Nazi Germany. At the end of the Rathofstrasse, turn left into Krämerstrasse, which ends at the Gautor, a surviving gate of the town walls, built in 1566. Exit through the gate to return to the car park.

🚗 *Leave Oppenheim along the B9/ Rheinstrasse to Guntersblum, turn right and continue through Alsheim and Osthofen to Worms.*

㉓ Worms

Rhineland-Palatinate; 67547
One of Germany's oldest cities, Worms is closely associated with Protestant reformer Martin Luther and the Legend of the Nibelungen from Germanic mythology. It boasts a magnificent 12th-century cathedral, the **Dom St Peter** (open daily) and an ancient Jewish cemetery, **Heiliger Sand** (open daily), where the oldest gravestone dates from 1076.

🚗 *Follow Ludwigstrasse to the B9, then follow signs for Speyer. At Speyer follow signs for Zentrum along the B39.*

Above Oppenheim's Marktplatz, lined with tall buildings

㉔ Speyer

Rhineland-Palatinate; 67346
The smallest of Pfalz's three great cathedral cities is also the most perfectly preserved, with a broad main street, Maximilianstrasse, which runs west from the **Kaiserdom** (open daily). One of the finest surviving examples of Romanesque architecture in Europe, the imperial cathedral is a UNESCO World Heritage Site.

Above Heiliger Sand, an ancient Jewish cemetery in Worms

Jews of the Rhineland

Jewish culture was established in the region in the 10th century with settlements in Speyer, Worms and Mainz. The cities had a major influence on the development of Ashkenazi Jewish culture, since it was here in the early Middle Ages that the Yiddish language emerged as an offshoot of the Middle High German.

VISITING WORMS

Parking
The Parkhaus Am Dom is a two-minute walk from the Dom, Rathaus and Marktplatz.

Tourist Information
Am Neumarkt 14, 67547; 06241 853 73 06; www.worms-de; Apr–Oct: open daily; Nov–Mar: open Mon–Fri

EAT AND DRINK

OPPENHEIM

Ristorante Il Camino moderate
Mediterranean dishes prepared with seasonal produce are a speciality here. For a lighter meal try a focaccia with tasty toppings.
Friedrich-Ebert-Strasse 20, 55276; 06133 577 8633

Restaurant Völker expensive
This restaurant was once home to Paul Wallot, architect of the Reichstag in Berlin. Excellent wines are available here.
Krämerstrasse 7, 55276; 06133 22 69; www.restaurant-voelker.de; open Wed–Sun

SPEYER

Ratskeller moderate
Brick-vaulted cellar-restaurant beneath Speyer's 18th-century town hall.
Maximilianstrasse 12, 67346; 06232 786 12; closed Sun dinner & Mon

Zum Alten Engel moderate
Cozy cellar-restaurant that is an adherent of the Slow Food movement.
Mühlturmstrasse 5, 67346; 06232 709 14; www.zumaltenengel.de; open Mon–Sat dinner; open Sun in winter

---

DAY TRIP OPTIONS
The route can be broken down into day trips for those with less time or a special interest to follow.

Wine country
Food and wine lovers should head to Edenkoben ⑧ and stop at the restaurants and wineries along the route to

Freinsheim ⑯. Oenophiles can take the drive from Mainz ⑲ to Worms ㉓ through some of the most popular wine-growing villages.

Follow the driving instructions from Edenkoben to Freinsheim, then follow the route to Mainz. From Mainz follow instructions to Worms.

Castles and villages
Those interested in art and architecture can explore fairy-tale castles and charming half-timbered villages along the route from Bad Bergzabern ❷ to Burg Trifels ⑥.

Follow the driving instructions from Bad Bergzabern to Burg Trifels.

Eat and Drink: inexpensive, under €20; moderate, €20–€40; expensive, over €40

Franconia of the Prince-Bishops

Bayreuth to Aschaffenburg

Highlights

- **Spiritual Franconia**
  Visit Franconia's palaces and churches, where spiritual and temporal power meet divine inspiration

- **Crags and caves**
  Experience the strange, intriguing geology of the Fränkische Schweiz, both above and below the ground

- **Riverside landscape**
  Explore the Main's varied landscapes, from castle-topped hillsides to the vineyards of the Mainschleife

- **Delectable tipple**
  Sample the delicious, distinctive beers of Bavaria's traditional independent brewers

View of Marienburg fortress from the city of Würzburg

Franconia of the Prince-Bishops

For many centuries, Franconia's Prince-Bishops held both spiritual and political power in this region. Drawn from the ranks of the nobility, they left a lasting cultural legacy in this fascinating corner of northern Bavaria (Bayern), which ranges from Bamberg's well-preserved historic core to the splendid Baroque and Gothic masterpieces throughout the region. Amidst the palaces and churches are traditional *Weinstuben* and old pubs where one can enjoy Franconia's distinctive food, wine and beer. Away from the cities, the smaller towns and villages often have a rustic, lost-in-time charm. This drive takes visitors through lovely landscapes ranging from the valley of the meandering Main river to the startling geology of Fränkische Schweiz and the unspoiled rural idyll of Naturpark Steigerwald.

KEY

 Drive route

0 kilometres 20

0 miles 20

Below Eighteenth-century Residenz, set in a magnificent park, Würzburg, *see p178*

ACTIVITIES

Test the waters with a relaxing day at Bayreuth's Lohengrin Therme spa

Raise your glass to Franconia's smoked beers and distinctive dry wines

Feel the rush on Pottenstein's snow-free summer toboggan run

Take a hike through Naturpark Steigerwald or among the Mainschleife's vineyards

Shop at the designer outlets in Wertheim village

Above Half-timbered houses and the Martinskirche on the Rathaus, Forchheim, *see p173*

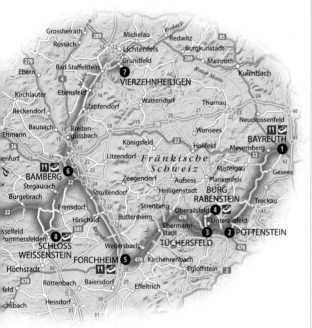

PLAN YOUR DRIVE

Start/finish: Bayreuth to Aschaffenburg.

Number of days: 5 days, allowing a day to explore Bamberg.

Distance: 440 km (273 miles).

Road conditions: Roads are generally well paved and signposted and have gentle inclines. Snow and ice can be a problem in winter.

When to go: The region is at its best from May to October, when the weather is most agreeable. In some smaller villages, hotels and museums are closed in January or February.

Opening times: Shops are generally open from 9am to 8pm, while sights of interest are open from 9am to 6pm.

Main market days: Bamberg: Mon–Sat; **Würzburg:** Mon–Sat; Fri & Sat (farmer's market); **Aschaffenburg:** Wed & Sat (farmer's market).

Shopping: Souvenirs from the region include Rauchbier, the smoky local beer from Bamberg, and Franconian wines from Würzburg and Volkach.

Major festivals: Bayreuth: Bayreutner Festspiele (Wagner festival), Jul–Aug; **Bamberg:** Sandkerwa (folk festival), Aug; **Dettelbach:** Altstadt (wine festival), Jun; **Würzburg:** Kiliani Volksfest (procession in traditional costumes and funfair), Jul; Weinparade am Dom (wine festival), Aug/Sep; **Klingenber:** Clingenburg Festspiele (open-air operas, plays and musicals), every summer; **Aschaffenburg:** Kulturtage (culture days), Jun/Jul.

DAY TRIP OPTIONS

The **castles**, **caves** and outdoor activities of Fränkische Schweiz will appeal to **families**, while **art** and **architecture buffs** will find much to admire between Vierzehnheiligen, Bamberg and Würzburg. **Epicureans** will relish the **wines** and the **food** in the villages of the Mainschleife. For full details, *see p179.*

Below Pompejanum villa, on the banks of the Main, Aschaffenburg, *see p179*

Right View of the countryside near Bayreuth **Below left** Entrance to the Markgräfliches Opernhaus, Bayreuth **Below right** Decorative signpost in Tüchersfeld

VISITING BAYREUTH

Parking
There is a signposted public underground car park (Parkhaus Rathaus) beneath the Rathaus (town hall).

Tourist Information
Opernstrasse 22, 95444; 0921 88 588; www.bayreuth.de; Sep–Apr: open Mon–Sat; May–Oct: open daily

WHERE TO STAY

BAYREUTH

Lohmühle *moderate*
Housed in two fine gabled houses on the site of a former tannery, close to the centre of Bayreuth, this hotel has 21 simple but comfortably furnished en suite rooms as well as a restaurant. *Badstrasse 37, 95444; 0921 530 60; www.hotel-lohmuehle.de; prices are higher during the Festspiele*

Goldener Anker *expensive*
This old and rather grand family-run hotel has 35 individually styled rooms that are traditionally furnished. The in-house restaurant has preserved its original 1920s Art Deco interior. *Opernstrasse 6, 95444; 0921 787 77 40; www.anker-bayreuth.de*

BURG RABENSTEIN

Burg Rabenstein *expensive*
There are just 22 individually styled rooms and suites in this historic castle, varying in style from prettily rustic to plush; some include beds with tapestries and canopies. *Rabenstein 33, 95491; 0920 29 70 04 40; www.burg-rabenstein.de*

FORCHHEIM

Hotel am Kronengarten *inexpensive*
A small and pleasant modern hotel on the edge of Forchheim's historic old town offering comfortable rooms, some of which are singles and triples. *Bamberger Strasse 6a, 91301; 09191 725 00; www.hotel-am-kronengarten.de*

❶ Bayreuth
Bavaria; 95444
The city of Bayreuth came into its own in the early 18th century, when it was transformed into a fine stone-built capital for Margravine Wilhelmine (1709–58), sister of Frederick the Great of Prussia. Her residence, the **Neues Schloss** *(Apr–Sep: open daily; Oct–Mar: closed Mon)*, was built by Joseph Saint-Pierre. The elongated three-storey palace combines Classical lines with a rustic ground floor.

Another highlight of the city is the magnificent Baroque opera house, the ornate **Markgräfliches Opernhaus** *(partially closed for renovation until 2018)*. Built in the 1740s, it has an interior designed by Giuseppe Galli Bibiena, who came from a famous Bolognese family of theatre architects, and his son Carlo. The city is associated with composer Richard Wagner (1813–83),

who took up residence here in 1872. His home, **Villa Wahnfried** *(open daily)*, is on the northeastern side of Neues Schloss and is now a museum. In the villa's garden are the tombs of Wagner and his wife, Cosima, the daughter of Franz Liszt. Each summer Bayreuth hosts the Wagner festival, the **Bayreuther Festspiele**, held in the Festspielhaus, the imposing but spartan theatre built between 1872 and 1875 to a design by Gottfried Semper.

Visitors to Bayreuth can also take a cure at the **Lohengrin Therme** *(www.lohengrin-therme.de)*, a thermal spa.

🚗 *Follow signs to Fränkische Schweiz/ Hollfeld, Erlanger Strasse, later signed as B22, then turn left on to the road signposted Pottenstein.*

❷ Pottenstein
Bavaria; 91278
Four valleys meet at Pottenstein, yet the village feels almost walled in by the high crags surrounding it. One such rock is topped by the region's oldest castle, **Burg Pottenstein** *(Easter: open daily; Apr: open Sat & Sun; May–Oct: closed Mon)*; below ground are the **Teufelshöhle Caves** *(Easter– Oct: open daily; Nov–Easter: open Sun)*. Besides visiting these sights, visitors can also enjoy the snow-free summer toboggan run *(www.sommerrodel bahnen-pottenstein.de)* here.

🚗 *Head west from Pottenstein along the B470/Forchheimer Strasse to reach the village of Tüchersfeld.*

❸ Tüchersfeld
Bavaria; 91278

Looking as though its houses have been dropped at random among rocky pinnacles, tiny Tüchersfeld is even more improbably scenic than its bigger neighbour, Pottenstein. The village is home to the **Fränkische Schweiz Museum** *(Apr–Oct: closed Mon; Nov–Mar: open Sun)*, which has peasant costumes, furniture, arts and crafts and an 18th-century synagogue alongside displays on the region's geology and archaeology.

🚗 *At the end of Tüchersfeld turn left to Unterailsfeld. In Unterailsfeld, turn right on to Oberailsfeld Strasse to Oberailsfeld. Take Burgenstrasse driving through the village of Oberailsfeld; follow brown signs signposted to Burg Rabenstein.*

❹ Burg Rabenstein
Bavaria; 95491

Perched on a dramatic crag overlooking the Ailsbach Valley and with its oldest parts dating from the 12th century, the castle of Rabenstein *(guided tours: Apr–Oct: Tue–Sun; Nov–Mar: Sat & Sun)* looks every inch the impregnable medieval fortress, though much of it was ruined during the Thirty Years' War (1618–48). There are regular interesting **falconry displays** *(Apr–Oct: Tue–Sun)* here. The **Sophienhöhle Caves** *(guided tours: Apr–Oct: Tue–Sun)*, among the most beautiful showcaves in Germany, are just a ten-minute walk away.

Pillar with sculptures in Forchheim

🚗 *Take the B470 and follow it westwards to Forchheim. Parking is available in the car park on Pradeplatz.*

Crags, Castles and Caves

The Franconian Switzerland (Fränkische Schweiz) has long been one of Germany's most popular regions for its startling, craggy natural beauty and dramatic castles and pretty villages, as well as for the opportunities it offers for outdoor activities, from cycling and hiking to rock climbing and canoeing. The region's limestone geology ensures the natural wonders continue underground in the form of strikingly beautiful cave systems, some of which can be visited.

❺ Forchheim
Bavaria; 91301

With a historic core centred on the tall, onion-domed tower of **Martinskirche** and a 15th-century half-timbered **Rathaus**, this lively small town, with timber-framed houses, is well worth exploring. It was the second seat of the Bamberg Prince-Bishops in the Middle Ages. Their palace, the **Kaiserpfalz**, has precious late-Gothic frescoes and is now the **Pfalzmuseum** *(May–Oct: closed Mon, Nov–Apr: open Wed, Thu & Sun)*, with sections devoted to local history, archaeology and folk costume.

🚗 *Leave Forchheim along Bamberger Strasse, following yellow signs for Bamberg. This joins the B22. At Bamberg, follow signs to Zentrum to reach the car park.*

EAT AND DRINK

BAYREUTH

Lohmühle *moderate*
Regional produce forms the basis for the excellent Franconian cooking in this rustic restaurant.
Badstrasse 37, 95444; 0921 530 60; www.hotel-lohmuehle.de; opening hours change during the Festspiele, closed Jan–Apr: Sun dinner; Sep–Oct: Mon–Fri dinner

Restaurant 1927 *expensive*
The Goldener Anker hotel's restaurant offers refined Franconian cooking, with a few Mediterranean influences, matched with fine German and French wines.
Opernstrasse 6, 95444; 0921 787 77 40; www.anker-bayreuth.de; open Wed–Sun dinner only, daily during the Festspiele

FORCHHEIM

Kammerersmühle *moderate*
A late-Renaissance watermill is the setting for this *Weinstube* and restaurant, which serves Franconian and international dishes with wines from Franconia.
Wiesenstrasse 10, 91301; 09191 70 45 55; www.kammerers-muehle-forchheim.de; open Mon–Sat

Other options
Forchheim has a number of tiny breweries, some of which operate traditional *Brauereigaststätten* – rustic old pubs in which to sample the brew – such as **Eichhorn** *(Bamberger Strasse 9; 09191 64 768)* and **Hebendanz** *(Sattlertorstrasse 14, 09191 607 47)*.

Above left Canoeists on the banks of the Püttlach river, near Tüchersfeld
Below Pottenstein's main street

Above Impressive façade of the Neue Residenz, Bamberg

VISITING BAMBERG

Parking
The City-Altstadttiefgarage, an underground car park, is located near the tourist office.

Tourist Information
Geyerswörthstrasse 3, 96047; 0951 297 62 00; www.bamberg.info; open daily; closed Easter Fri, Halloween, Christmas, New Year

WHERE TO STAY IN BAMBERG

Messerschmitt *moderate*
Family owned since 1832, this beautiful hotel is a mix of traditional and modern, set in the house that belonged to the parents of the famous aviation pioneer, Willy Messerschmitt. The hotel also has a renowned restaurant.
Lange Strasse 41, 96047; 0951 29 78 00; www.hotel-messerschmitt.de

St Nepomuk *moderate*
This stylish hotel offers views of the Altes Rathaus. It has 23 rooms, a suite and two restaurants and a bar.
Obere Mühlbrücke 9, 96047; 0951 984 20; www.hotel-nepomuk.de

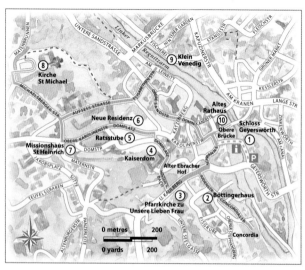

⑥ Bamberg
Bavaria; 96047

For centuries the seat of an independent Prince-Bishopric within the Holy Roman Empire, Bamberg has survived the turmoil of Germany's history unscathed, with an exceptionally well-preserved historic core that was added to UNESCO's list of World Heritage Sites in 1993. The city centre is divided into three parts by the Main-Danube canal and the Regnitz river, but most of the major sights are in the hilly Bergstadt to the west of the river, dominated by a splendid four-spired cathedral. This walk explores the Bergstadt and the riverside areas of Bamberg.

A two-hour walking tour
From the car park, walk to the tourist office, where visitors can pick up the key to the tower of **Schloss Geyerswörth** ① *(open Mon–Fri)*, which lies across the road from the office. There are fine views over Bamberg from the top of this 16th-century Prince-Bishop's residence. Afterwards, cross the river by the wooden footbridge. Then turn left into Schranne, right into Balthasargässchen then left again to reach Judenstrasse, a street of historic townhouses, including the **Böttingerhaus** ②, built for the privy councillor Ignaz Tobias Böttinger between 1707 and 1713. Take the left fork into Concordiastrasse to reach another of Böttinger's residences, Concordia, which dates from 1722. Return to Judenstrasse. Thirsty walkers can

Traditional biscuits, Bamberg

stop at Klosterbräu *(open daily)* on the right, which was once the Prince-Bishops' brewery.

At the end of Judenstrasse, turn left to head up Untere Kaulberg to reach the 14th-century **Pfarrkirche zu Unsere Lieben Frau** ③. The parish church of Our Dear Lady has a lovely tabernacle in the ambulatory and Tintoretto's *Assumption* just by the door. Cross the busy road in front of the church, descending the steps signposted Dom to reach Hinterer Bach. Follow this curving cobbled lane uphill, admiring the 17th-century Alter Ebracher Hof on the climb up. At the top is Domplatz, Bamberg's showpiece square. On the left is the 13th-century **Kaiserdom** ④ *(open daily)*, a cathedral filled with artistic treasures such as the Bamberger Reiter, an equestrian likeness of a medieval knight. The cathedral cloisters house the Diözesanmuseum *(closed Mon)*, with a remarkable collection of 11th-century clerical vestments. Beyond the Dom, on the left, is the elaborate Renaissance façade of the **Ratsstube** ⑤, a part of the Alte Hofhaltung, a rambling complex that once housed the Prince-Bishops' household. The Ratsstube houses the Historisches Museum *(May–Nov: closed Mon; Dec–Apr: temporary exhibitions only)*, with displays relating to Bamberg's history. Return to Domplatz and cross the road to reach the **Neue Residenz** ⑥ *(open daily)*, whose Baroque façade zigzags across the north side of the square. Work started on it in 1613, but the palace attained its current magnificence under Prince-Bishop Lothar von Schönborn between 1697 and 1703. The palace is the work of Leonhard Dientzenhofer, from the

Bavarian Dynasty, whose architectural influence reached as far as Prague. A guided tour goes through the richly decorated state rooms but visitors are free to admire the German medieval and Baroque paintings in the palace gallery at leisure. Don't miss the lovely rose garden behind the palace, with its pretty Baroque café *(open summer)* and excellent views over the old city.

Leave Domplatz along Obere Karolinenstrasse. On the corner of Domstrasse stands the **Missionshaus St Heinrich** ⑦, an elegant mansion that was once the Bamberg residence of Bayreuth's Margraves. Turn right down Michaelsberger Strasse, following the street uphill to the former Benedictine monastery of **Kirche St Michael** ⑧, whose church *(open daily)* was rebuilt in the late-Gothic style after a fire in 1610. The Baroque monastery buildings contain a brewery museum, the Fränkisches Brauereimuseum *(open Wed–Sun)*. On leaving the museum, stop by the garden behind the monastery. Next, return to the Aufsess Strasse, which becomes Elisabethen Strasse to reach the river. On the opposite bank is a picturesque huddle of fishermen's cottages known as **Klein Venedig** ⑨, or Little Venice. Turn back up Elisabethen Strasse and left into Obere Sandstrasse, which leads to Dominkanerstrasse. Bear right into Herrenstrasse then left to the Obere Brücke, a bridge that passes through the **Altes Rathaus** ⑩, set on a mid-river island. The old town hall houses the Sammlung Ludwig *(closed Mon)* collection of Strasbourg and Meissen porcelain. Retrace the route, turn left on to Geyersworthplatz and then left again on to the wooden footbridge to the car park.

🚗 *Leave the town of Bamberg along the B4/Hallstädter Strasse. At Breitengüssbach, follow signs to Bad Staffelstein via Zapfendorf and Ebensfeld to Grundfeld. At Grundfeld, follow the road signposted to Vierzehnheiligen.*

Bishops and Empire

Formed from the eastern part of Charlemagne's empire in the 9th century and dissolved in 1806, the Holy Roman Empire was a loose alliance of states under the aegis of an emperor chosen by *Kurfürsten* (electors), though in practice the Habsburgs dominated. Bamberg and Würzburg were independent Prince-Bishoprics of the empire in which the bishops wielded temporal and spiritual power. Aschaffenburg was the second seat of the archbishops of Mainz, since the city dominated the largest of their territories.

⑦ Vierzehnheiligen
Bavaria; 96231

A worthwhile excursion from Bamberg, Vierzehnheiligen is best known for its splendid pilgrimage church, **Basilika Vierzehnheiligen** *(open daily)*, a masterpiece of southern German Baroque and Rococo styles. Designed by the Franconian architect Balthasar Neumann, it was built between 1743 and 1772 at the site where a shepherd had a vision of a crying child accompanied by the Holy Helpers – the Vierzehnheiligen – or 14 saints of intercession of the church's name.

🚗 *Return to Bamberg and take Unterer Kaulberg and Würzburger Strasse. Follow the yellow signs for Würzburg to reach the B22 and then signs to Pommersfelden and Schloss Weissenstein.*

Above left Riverside view of Bamberg and Kirche St Michael **Above right** Visitors strolling along Obere Brücke, Bamberg **Below** Pretty Altes Rathaus, set on a mid-river island, Bamberg

EAT AND DRINK IN BAMBERG

Brudermühle *moderate*
Wild boar, venison, carp and trout are among the specialities on the menu of this atmospheric riverside restaurant. *Schranne 1, 96049; 0951 95 52 20; www.brudermuehle.de*

Messerschmitt *expensive*
Regional produce, including goose liver, duck and venison, features on the menu of the Messerschmitt's fine dining room. *Lange Strasse 41, 96047; 0951 29 78 00; www.hotel-messerschmitt.de; Jan–Mar: closed Sun*

Other options
The best-known local beer in Bamberg is the Rauchbier. A few of *Brauereigaststätten* (brewery-owned restaurants) worth visiting are **Greifenklau** *(Laurenziplatz 20, 0951 532 19)*, **Spezial** *(Obere Königstrasse 10, 0951 243 04)* and **Schlenkerla** *(Dominkanerstrasse 6)*.

CYCLING IN VOLKACH

Pick up maps of the Mainschleife for cycling routes from the tourist office in the town hall *(Rathaus, Marktplatz 1, 97332; 09381 401 12).*

WHERE TO STAY

SCHLOSS WEISSENSTEIN

Schlosshotel Pommersfelden *moderate*
Located in Schloss Weissenstein's elegant Baroque stable block and brewery directly opposite the main façade of the palace, this hotel has simply furnished but comfortable rooms. *Schloss 1, 96178; 0954 86 80; www.schlosshotel-pommersfelden.de*

EBRACH

Klosterbräu Landidyll *moderate*
Housed in the 18th-century guesthouse of the former Cistercian abbey of Ebrach, this hotel has simple but comfortable rooms appropriate to its monastic setting. *Marktplatz 4, 96157; 09553 180; www.Landidyll.com*

PRICHSENSTADT

Alte Schmiede *inexpensive*
This ancient half-timbered inn faces a lovely fountain in the heart of Prichsenstadt's old town. The rooms are rustic in style with lots of wood, and there is a restaurant serving traditional Franconian fare. *Karlsplatz 7, 96157; 09383 972 213; www.alte-schmiede-prichsenstadt.de*

VOLKACH

Zur Schwane *expensive*
A lovely old hotel and restaurant with wooden ceilings and cozy, individually styled rooms furnished with antiques. It also has its own winery in a stylish, ultra-modern property on the outskirts of Volkach. *Hauptstrasse 12, 97332; 09381 806 60; www.schwane.de*

Above Main street of Prichsenstadt, lined with pretty houses **Below** Grand façade of Schloss Weissenstein

⑧ Schloss Weissenstein
Bavaria; 96178

The Prince-Bishops of both Bamberg and Würzburg were members of the Schönborn Dynasty, and the familiy's wealth and power are reflected in the splendour of their family seat, **Schloss Weissenstein** *(Apr–Oct: open daily).* The design was a collaboration between the Bamberg court architect Johann Dientzenhofer and the celebrated Viennese Baroque master Johann Lukas von Hildebrandt. The palace was completed in 1718 and is notable for the ceremonial *Treppenhaus* (staircase) and its collection of Old Masters.

Sign for a walking circuit, Prichsenstadt

🚗 **Return to the B22, following signs for Steppach and Burgebrach, and continue along it to Ebrach.**

⑨ Ebrach
Bavaria; 96157

Ebrach sits at the heart of the idyllic forested **Naturpark Steigerwald** *(www.steigerwald.org),* offering scope for relaxing country walks. The village is dominated by the buildings of a former Cistercian abbey. The cathedral-like **Klosterkirche** *(mid-Apr–Oct: open daily)* is an important work of the early Gothic period and has a beautiful rose window; the Baroque abbey buildings now house a prison, but the splendid *Treppenhaus* and **Kaisersaal** (imperial hall) can still be visited *(Apr–Oct: open daily).* Ebrach is an ideal base for exploring Naturpark Steigerwald,

the unspoiled upland landscape which is notable for its biodiversity.

🚗 **Continue west along the B22 to Neuses am Sand, where there is a signposted left turn that leads to Prichsenstadt.**

⑩ Prichsenstadt
Bavaria; 97357

With a well-preserved set of defensive walls and towers rising above vineyards to shelter an intact historic core, tiny Prichsenstadt is a gem, its appearance to this day reflecting the urban forms of the Middle Ages. The town has a nightwatchman who conducts guided tours *(Sat & Sun)* that can be booked from all hotels. Wine aside, Prichsenstadt is also known for its asparagus and strawberries.

🚗 **Leave Prichsenstadt on the road signposted to Volkach from the west gate of the old town.**

⑪ Volkach
Bavaria; 97332

With two lofty 13th-century town gates, a fine 16th-century Rathaus and numerous *Winzer* (wine growers), Volkach is the attractive "capital" of the Mainschleife. Historic houses here include the splendid Baroque **Schelfenhaus** and Renaissance **Echterhof**. A short walk from the town is the late-Gothic pilgrimage church of **Maria im Weingarten** *(Mar–Nov: open daily).* Idyllically situated amid vineyards to the

northwest of Volkach, this church has a *Madonna* by the Würzburg sculptor Tilman Riemenschneider.

🚗 *Follow Brückenstrasse to reach the bridge over the Main, then turn left after the bridge, on to Escherndorfer Strasse to reach the village of Dettelbach.*

⑫ Dettelbach
Bavaria; 97337
Dettelbach is another handsome village behind intact defensive walls. Tucked between the medieval **Rathaus** and the eccentric-looking parish church is **KuK** *(open daily)*, a modern cultural centre where visitors can sample local wines and learn about Dettelbach's religious tradition. The pilgrimage church of **Maria im Sand** lies east of the village centre. Visitors should not leave Dettelbach without sampling the delicious local *Muskazinen* – hard-baked biscuits similar to Italian *biscotti*.

🚗 *Follow the road leading southwards along the Main to Kitzingen. In Kitzingen, follow signs for Ochsenfurt, then after the railway bridge for Sulzfeld and Marktbreit.*

⑬ Sulzfeld am Main
Bavaria; 97320
The picturesque wine-growing village of Sulzfeld boasts a remarkably complete medieval town wall dating from the 15th and 16th centuries. With 21 towers, it creates a convincing impression of a child's toy fort brought

magically to life. The village's other main claim to fame is as the birthplace of the *Meterbratwurst* – a giant sausage sold by length (half-metre or metre).

🚗 *Take the An der Staatsstrasse, which becomes Sulzfelder Strasse to Segnitz, where a signposted left turn brings drivers to the bridge to Marktbreit.*

The Mainschleife
The Mainschleife is a loop-like meander of the Main river east of Würzburg at a point where the landscape has a particularly gentle beauty, framed by low, vine-covered hillsides and dotted with attractive small villages. The popular local explanation for the Main river's eccentric course at this point is that it is here the river feels most at home. One excellent way to enjoy the area's beauty is by bicycle *(Fahrradverleih "Gazelle", Am Bach 1; 09381 71 57 31)* on the annual car-free Sunday in early May.

Above Late-medieval Rathaus in Dettelbach
Below Meandering Mainschleife-Main river east of Würzburg

EAT AND DRINK

EBRACH
Restaurant Mönchsstube *moderate*
Prize-winning interpretations of traditional Franconian cuisine are served in the abbey's 18th-century guesthouse. The large beer garden is a good place to try the Klosterbier brewed for the hotel in Bamberg.
Marktplatz 4, 96157; 09553 180; www. Landidyll.com; open from 7am daily

PRICHSENSTADT
Zum Goldenen Adler *moderate*
Fish, game and lighter fare, including vegetarian options, grace the menu of this pleasant restaurant in Prichsenstadt's tiny old town. The food is accompanied by Silvaner, Müller-Thurgau and Weissburgunder wines from Prichsenstadt's own winemakers.
Karlsplatz 10, 97357; 09383 60 31; www.adler-prichsenstadt.de; open from 11am daily; closed Feb & summer: Wed; winter: Wed & Thu

VOLKACH
Zur Schwane *moderate-expensive*
In keeping with the theme of the hotel to which it belongs, this restaurant provides a romantic ambience in its wood-panelled dining room. Some of the dishes served are for two people, such as lamb rack with hazelnut-flavoured vegetables and couscous. The chef focuses on French cuisine.
Hauptstrasse 12, 97332; closed Mon lunch

DETTELBACH
Café Kehl *inexpensive*
One of the nicest places to try Dettelbach's famous fat-free biscuits and the *Muskazinen,* the Café Kehl is a snug and rustic café that serves good coffee and cakes.
Eichgasse 5, 97337; 09324 9/3 00

Eat and Drink: inexpensive, under €20; moderate, €20–€40; expensive, over €40

Right Outdoor café outside tall, half-timbered houses, Ochsenfurt **Below** Vineyards near the small town of Markbreit

VISITING WÜRZBURG

Parking
The 600-space Marktgarage underground car park, beneath the Marktplatz, is near the tourist information office.

Tourist Information
Falkenhaus, Marktplatz 9, 97070; 0931 37 23 98; www.wuerzburg.de; Jan–Mar: open Mon–Sat; Apr–Dec: open Mon–Sat; May–Oct: open daily

WHERE TO STAY

MARKTBREIT

Zum Löwen *moderate*
Located close to the Rathaus, the rooms at this splendid half-timbered inn vary in style from rustic to elegant.
Marktstrasse 8, 97340; 09332 505 40; www.zum-hotel-loewen.de

OCHSENFURT

Gasthof zum Bären *moderate*
This traditional hotel and restaurant at the entrance to Ochsenfurt's old town has 24 refurbished rooms, each with an en suite bathroom and TV.
Hauptstrasse 74, 97199; 09331 86 60; www.hotel-baeren-ochsenfurt.de

WÜRZBURG

Zur Stadt Mainz *moderate*
Housed above a wonderfully traditional restaurant, this family-run hotel has 15 comfortable rooms with en suite bathrooms and TV.
Semmelstrasse 39, 97070; 0931 531 55; www.hotel-stadtmainz.de

Hotel Rebstock *expensive*
With a wonderful Rococo façade and a history that goes back to 1408, this hotel has individually designed rooms in a tasteful, contemporary style. The restaurant is one of Würzburg's best.
Neubaustrasse 7, 97070; 0931 309 30; www.rebstock.com

ASCHAFFENBURG

Wilder Mann *moderate*
On the edge of the old town, this is a historic four-star hotel that has 74 en suite rooms. The 600-year-old, half-timbered Goldener Karpfen opposite is run by the same group.
Löherstrasse 51, 63739; 06021 30 20; www.hotels-wilder-mann.de

⑭ Marktbreit

Bavaria; 97340
Marktbreit was once a significant centre for trade between the Main and the Danube. With a splendid gabled Renaissance **Rathaus** of chateau-like proportions and a number of imposing merchants' houses, this town has an architectural heritage that outshines its relatively modest present-day importance. It was the birthplace of the psychiatrist and neuropathologist Alois Alzheimer (1864–1915), after whom the degenerative brain disease is named.
🚗 *Take Ochsenfurter Strasse, following signs for Stadtmitte (city centre) to Ochsenfurt's old town.*

⑮ Ochsenfurt

Bavaria; 97199
Though its outskirts are somewhat disfigured by the sugar works for which it is known, Ochsenfurt preserves a wonderful historic **Altstadt** (old town) behind high medieval walls. The focal point is the 16th-century **Rathaus**, with a clock upon which miniature figures perform each

hour. The 14th–15th-century **Stadtpfarrkirche St Andreas,** St Andreas's church, contains a statue of St Nicholas by sculptor Tilman Riemenschneider (1460–1531), while alongside the wall is the **Palatium**, the seat of the Würzburg cathedral chapter between 1334 and 1810.
🚗 *Cross the Main on the B13 and continue to Würzburg.*

⑯ Würzburg

Bavaria; 97070
One of Franconia's finest historic cities, Würzburg rose from the ashes after being destroyed in World War II. It was the home of sculptor Tilman Riemenschneider and his wood-carvings can be seen at the **Mainfränkisches Museum** *(closed Mon)* in the **Marienberg** fortress above the city. The 18th-century **Residenz** *(open daily)* is Bavaria's most enchanting Baroque palace, designed by the German architect Balthasar Neumann and the Viennese archi-tect Johann Lukas von Hildebrandt for Prince-Bishop Johann Philipp Franz von Schönborn.
🚗 *Take the B8, following signs to Marktheidenfeld. At Marktheidenfeld,*

Sculpture in Würzburg's magnificent Residenz

Franconian Wine

Würzburg's traditional *Weinstuben* (wine bars) are excellent places to try Franconia's dry white wines, which are as distinctive as the stubby *Bocksbeutel* in which they are bottled. The climate encourages the use of earlier-ripening grape varieties, with Silvaner being the best known; Müller-Thurgau, also known as Rivaner, and Bacchus are also popular as well. Red wines are grown in the western part of the region, close to Aschaffenburg.

Above left Spectacular fresco in the Residenz, Würzburg **Above right** Imposing fortress of Marienberg, Würzburg

take the signposted left turn to Wertheim. Turn right on the road signposted to Wertheim. Parking is available along the riverside.

⑰ Wertheim
Baden-Württemberg; 97877
Wertheim has a pretty **Altstadt** on a wedge of land at the confluence of the Tauber and Main rivers. The town is overlooked by **Burg Wertheim** (open daily), a castle that has been a ruin since the Thirty Years' War. Today, Wertheim is known above all for its shops, in particular at Wertheim Village (open Mon–Sat), a shopping centre just east of town.

🚗 **Continue along the south bank of the Main to reach Miltenberg.**

⑱ Miltenberg am Main
Bavaria; 63897
Miltenberg am Main stands on a tight bend in the Main river and until 1803, was part of the territories of the Mainz Prince-Bishops. The focal point of the Altstadt here is the **Marktplatz** (marketplace), fringed by half-timbered houses and with a Renaissance fountain, the **Marktbrunnen**, which dates from 1583. The statue in the centre depicts Justice.

🚗 **Cross the Main and then follow Brückenstrasse to reach Klingenberg.**

⑲ Klingenberg
Bavaria; 63911
Klingenberg lies at the foot of steep slopes on the **Fränkische Rotwein Wanderweg**, a footpath through the red wine country of Lower Franconia (Unterfranken). In summer, the ruin of the castle of **Clingenburg** high above the village is the venue for the Clingenburg Festspiele (www.clingenburg-festspiele.de). The festival features open-air operas and plays.

🚗 **Follow the road to Aschaffenburg.**

⑳ Aschaffenburg
Bavaria; 63739
Aschaffenburg is dominated by the Renaissance **Schloss Johannisburg** (closed Mon), built for the Mainz Prince-Bishops between 1605 and 1614. Inside, visitors can see the princely apartments and admire a selection of Old Masters as well as the world's largest collection of cork architectural models. Overlooking the Main nearby is the **Pompejanum** (Apr–mid-Oct: closed Mon), a re-creation of a Roman villa built for the Bavarian King Ludwig I between 1840 and 1848.

VISITING ASCHAFFENBURG

Parking
The underground car park at Stadthalle is near the tourist information office.

Tourist Information
Schlossplatz 1, 63739; 06021 39 58 00; www.info-aschaffenburg.de; Apr–Sep: open daily; Oct–Mar: closed Sun

EAT AND DRINK

MARKTBREIT

Zum Löwen moderate
Seasonal produce from the region is the mainstay of this traditional dining room. Marktstrasse 8, 97340; 09332 505 40; www.zum-hotel-loewen.de; closed for two weeks in Feb

WÜRZBURG

Zum Stachel expensive
Regional and organic produce are on the menu in this historic Weinstube. Gressengasse 1, 97070; 0931 527 70; www.weinhaus-stachel.de; closed Sun & Mon

ASCHAFFENBURG

Restaurant Schlossweinstube moderate
This atmospheric vaulted Weinstube serves Franconian specialities. Schlossplatz 4, 63739; 06021 124 40; www.schlossweinstuben.de; closed Mon

---

DAY TRIP OPTIONS
Bayreuth and Bamberg make great bases for day trips around the region.

Architectural wonders
In Bamberg ⑥, admire the frescoes on the old town hall and the Baroque architecture on a visit to Vierzehnheiligen ⑦, and its magnificent pilgrimage church designed by Balthasar Neumann. Then head for Schloss Weissenstein ⑧, the

ancestral home of the Schönborn family, who provided the region with many of its Prince-Bishops.

Head north to Vierzehnheiligen on the B4, returning to Bamberg to take the B22 towards Pommersfelden.

Wine and dine
Discover the scenic wine-growing country around Würzburg ⑯ with a day trip to the Mainschleife. Start at

Prichsenstadt ⑩ before lunch and a winery visit at Volkach ⑪, then continue south to Dettelbach ⑫ to sample the delicious Muskazinen biscuits. Return to Würzburg for a leisurely dinner in one of the city's old traditional restaurants.

Head east to Prichsenstadt along the A3, continuing to Volkach, then south along the Main to Dettelbach. Return to Würzburg on the B22 and B8.

Eat and Drink: inexpensive, under €20; moderate, €20–€40; expensive, over €40

Jurassic Crags and Feudal Fiefdoms

Ingolstadt to Landshut

Highlights

- **Jurassic park**
  Discover Naturpark Altmühltal's dramatic limestone crags and Jurassic fossils

- **Divine inspiration**
  Enjoy the rich artistic legacy of the region's complex religious history

- **The Donaudurchbruch**
  Visit the lovely wooded stretch of the Danube, where the pretty landscape is punctuated with architectural delights

- **Beer culture**
  Look out for the region's distinctive hop-growing frames before sampling the excellent local beers

Limestone crags along the scenic route to Solnhofen

Jurassic Crags and Feudal Fiefdoms

Jurassic geology adds drama to the gentle landscapes of Bavaria's Naturpark Altmühltal, one of Germany's largest nature reserves. Castle-topped crags stand sentinel over the valley of the placid Altmühl river that flows east to join the Main-Donau canal and the Danube. Along the way, there are small towns of great historic and architectural interest, while the Danube has produced a landscape of extraordinary loveliness in the narrow gorge known as the Donaudurchbruch. Gourmets will enjoy the hearty regional fare served in rustic surroundings, while the Hallertau district to the south of Ingolstadt and Kelheim is the world's largest hop-growing region, supplying not only Munich's internationally renowned brands but also local brewers, whose beers are worth sampling.

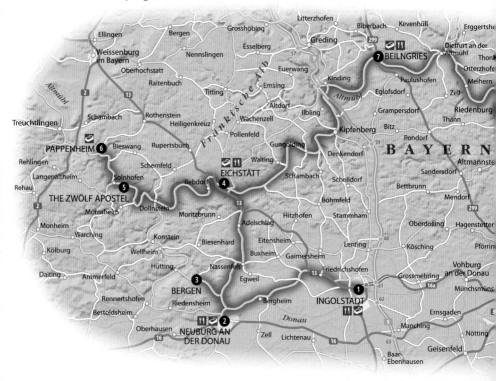

ACTIVITIES

Admire Eichstätt's varied handicrafts, from ceramics and soap to jewellery

Take a hike on the Altmühltal Panoramaweg path at Solnhofen

Hire a canoe and paddle down the slow-flowing Altmühl river

Cruise the Danube on a boat trip through the Donaudurchbruch gorge near the Befreiungshalle

Take a tour of the breweries at Kelheim or Weltenburg to soak up the local culture

Above View of the Willibaldsburg in Eichstätt, *see p186* **Below left** Cafés outside the old town hall, Ingolstadt, *see p184*

PLAN YOUR DRIVE

Start/finish: Ingolstadt to Landshut.

Number of days: 3 days, allowing half a day to explore Neuburg an der Donau.

Distance: 292 km (181 miles).

Road conditions: Roads have gentle inclines and are well signposted; snow and ice can be a problem in winter.

When to go: May to October is the best time to enjoy the scenery, while Christmas markets and snow ensure a magical atmosphere in December.

Opening times: Most attractions are open daily. Shops are open from 9am to 6pm, Monday to Friday, and close early on Saturdays.

Main market days: Ingolstadt, Neuburg an der Donau, Eichstätt: Wed, Sat; Landshut: Fri.

Major festivals: Beilngries: Bayerische Zwiebelmarkt (Bavarian onion market), biennial, Oct; Neuburg an der Donau: Schlossfest (castle festival), biennial, Jun–Jul, next in 2015; Landshut: Landshuter Hochzeit (Landshut wedding), every four years in Jun & Jul, next in 2017.

DAY TRIP OPTIONS

Art and architecture buffs will enjoy the historic **cathedrals**, **castles** and **museums** of Neuburg an der Donau and Eichstätt while **families** can hunt for **fossils** in Eichstätt and Solnhofen. **Lovers of scenic grandeur** will appreciate the remarkable landscape of Eichstätt. For full details, *see p189*.

Below Brewer's dray, Kelheim, *see p188*

0 kilometres 10

0 miles 10

KEY

Drive route

Above left Imposing Neues Schloss in Ingolstadt Above right Baroque interior of Kirche Maria de Victoria, Ingolstadt

VISITING INGOLSTADT

Parking
Ample parking is available beneath the Stadttheater, along the northern Danube embankment.

Tourist Information
Rathausplatz 2, 85049; 0841 305 30 30; www. ingolstadt–tourismus.de; Apr–Oct: open daily; Nov–Mar: closed Sun & public hols

VISITING NEUBURG AN DER DONAU

Parking
There is parking along Luitpoldstrasse as well as in the underground Tiefgarage Schrannenplatz along Weinstrasse.

Tourist Information
Ottheinrichplatz A118, 86633; 08431 552 40; www.neuburg-donau.de; Good Friday–Oct: open daily; Nov–Good Friday: open Mon–Fri

WHERE TO STAY

INGOLSTADT

Altstadthotel Ingolstadt *moderate*
Comfortable rooms, a sauna and a hot tub feature at this hotel. Of the 41 rooms, the larger ones facing the courtyard are recommended.
Gymnasiumstrasse 9, 85049; 0841 88 690; www.altstadthotel-ingolstadt.de

NEUBURG AN DER DONAU
Gasthaus Zur Blauen Traube
inexpensive
This historic inn dates from 1701 and has a restaurant that serves traditional Bavarian fare.
Amalienstrasse A49, 86633; 08431 83 92; www.zur-blauen-traube.de

Hotel-Gasthof Bergbauer *moderate*
A few minutes' walk from the Obere Altstadt district, this hotel has modern decor as well as a restaurant.
Fünfzehnerstrasse 11, 86633; 08431 61 68 90; www.hotel-gasthof-bergbauer.de

① Ingolstadt
Bavaria; 85049
Located on the Danube, bustling Ingolstadt was once a formidable fortress and, in the Middle Ages, capital of the Duchy of Bayern-Ingolstadt. The town houses many important historic buildings, including the whitewashed Gothic **Neues Schloss** *(closed Mon)*, home to Germany's oldest military museum; the brick-built

Liebfrauenmünster *(open daily)*, the largest late-Gothic hall church in Bavaria, with seven storeys of attics in its roof; and the Baroque church, **Kirche Maria de Victoria**, a masterpiece by the renowned Asam brothers of Munich.

🚗 *Leaving Ingolstadt, follow the B13/Neuburgerstrasse west, bearing left 8 km (5 miles) west of the town to Neuburg an der Donau.*

② Neuburg an der Donau
Bavaria; 86633
With a splendid Renaissance Schloss overlooking the Danube and a compact, beautiful old town, this historic Residenzstadt, or feudal seat, has architectural glories that outstrip its modest present-day status. From 1505, it was the capital of the independent principality of Pfalz-Neuburg for 300 years. Be sure to sample the Schrobenhausen asparagus, grown in the late spring in the countryside to the south.

A two-hour walking tour
Park the car on Luitpoldstrasse at the foot of the Obere Altstadt (upper town), and ascend the broad stone steps to pick up a free map from the tourist office on Ottheinrichplatz. Turn right at the **Stadttheater** ①, a former ducal grain warehouse,

following Residenzstrasse to reach the main portal of **Schloss Neuburg** ②. This magnificent Renaissance palace was built between 1530 and 1545 for Ottheinrich, the first Count Palatinate of Neuburg. Following a makeover, it became one of the earliest Baroque palaces in Germany.

Where to Stay: inexpensive, under €70; moderate, €70–€150; expensive, over €150

Visit the **Schlosskapelle** ③ *(open daily)*, a little further to the right, before entering the palace. The first purpose-built Protestant church in Bavaria, it is decorated with frescoes. The arcaded inner courtyard, or *Schlosshof*, boasts faded murals depicting scenes from the Old Testament. Created by Hans Schroer sometime after 1555, the murals remained long buried beneath a coat of paint and were only rediscovered in the 1960s. The palace houses the Schlossmuseum *(closed Mon)*, whose varied exhibits include the Bavarian state collection of Flemish Baroque painting, with works by Rubens and Jacob Jordaens. Inside the Schloss, the grandest room is the Renaissance Rittersaal, or Knights' Hall, in the north wing, with a heavy wooden ceiling and stout stone columns. Return to the palace entrance and stop for refreshments at the **Vivat** ④, a wine bar opposite, then ascend the gentle slope of Amalienstrasse, which is lined with town-houses from the 16th–18th centuries. Halfway along Amalienstrasse is Karlsplatz, around which Neuburg's principal civic buildings are ranged. These include the late-Renaissance Hofkirche Unsere Liebe Frau (Court Church of Our Dear Lady), the **Rathaus** ⑤ or town hall – a Renaissance palazzo built by Josef Heintz and Alexander Pasqualini between 1603 and 1609 – and the Rococo **Provinzialbibliothek** ⑥ or provincial library *(May–Oct: guided tours on Wed; 8431 91 06)*. Dating from 1731, it has a Baroque hall on its upper floor. The neighbouring **Weveldhaus** ⑦ is a fine example of a nobleman's town-house. Built in 1517 and raised by one storey in 1713, it has graceful stucco ceilings and houses the Stadtmuseum *(Mar–Dec: closed Mon)* with well-presented displays on the town's history. Continue along Amalienstrasse to reach the **Obere Tor** ⑧, a Renaissance gateway whose terracotta-coloured gable marks the western exit from the Obere Altstadt. Decorated with Neuburg's heraldic crest, it depicts Ottheinrich and his brother, Philipp. Pass through the gate to

Column in Karlsplatz, Neuburg an der Donau

Wolfgang-Wilhelm-Platz and the Hützeldörr, the southern portion of the garden. Return to the Obere Tor, pass through the gate and turn right into **Herrenstrasse** ⑨, which has some historic houses. It leads to the Luitpoldstrasse car park via Landschaftsstrasse.

🚗 *From Luitpoldstrasse head north over Elisenbrucke, following signs for Eichstätt. After a few kilometres, turn left at the signpost for Bergen.*

Reformation and Counter-Reformation

Neuburg's pragmatic rulers straddled the religious divisions of 16th- and 17th-century Germany. Ottheinrich condemned Lutheranism in 1522 but converted in 1542; a later Count Palatinate, Wolfgang Wilhelm (1578–1653), converted back to Catholicism to inherit his mother's estate.

❸ Bergen
Bavaria; 86633

Nestled in the rolling countryside between the Danube and Altmühl, this sleepy village is worth a detour to see the pilgrimage church of **Heilig Kreuz**, whose elegant white-and-gold Baroque interior by the Eichstätt court architect Giovanni Domenico Barbieri dates from 1756. Be sure to visit the Romanesque crypt; water from the well in the north aisle was once believed to have healing properties.

🚗 *Return to the T-junction, then turn left and head to Nassenfels. Take Eichstätter Strasse, pass Adelschlag to get on to the B13, following signs to Eichstätt.*

Above Schloss overlooking the Danube, Neuburg an der Donau **Below** Arcaded courtyard of Schloss Neuburg, Neuburg an der Donau

EAT AND DRINK

INGOLSTADT

Gaststätte Daniel *inexpensive*
Ingolstadt's oldest restaurant, dating back to 1471, provides an atmospheric setting for traditional Bavarian cooking and Herrnbräu beers.
Roseneckstrasse 1, 85049; 0841 352 72; closed Mon

Kuchlbauer Biermuseum *inexpensive*
Rustic beams and masses of brewing paraphernalia ensure that this "beer museum" lives up to its name. Try the ox marinated in strong beer with a mug of the delicious, dark Kuchlbauer Vollbier Dunkel.
Schäffbräustrasse 11a, 85049; 0841 355 12; www.biermuseum-ingolstadt.de; closed Mon

NEUBURG AN DER DONAU

Neuwirt *moderate*
Seasonal produce, including Schrobenhausen asparagus, potatoes and game, feature on the menu of this restaurant, which serves local beers.
Färberstrasse 88, 86633; 08431 20 78; www.neuwirt-neuburg.de; open till midnight; closed Tue

Eat and Drink: inexpensive, under €20; moderate, €20–€40; expensive, over €40

Right View of the Altmühl Valley from Willibaldsburg, Eichstätt **Centre right** Bishop's palace in the Residenzplatz, Eichstätt **Below** Limestone crags, Altmühl Valley

VISITING EICHSTÄTT

Parking
On quiet days, it is relatively easy to find on-street parking in the town centre. Drivers can also use the Altstadt car park on Ostenstrasse.

Tourist Information
Domplatz 8, 85072; 08421 600 13 00; www.eichstaett.info; Apr–Oct: open daily; Nov–Mar: open Mon–Fri

WHERE TO STAY

EICHSTÄTT

Waldgasthof Geländer *inexpensive*
Situated in a tranquil forest clearing just north of Eichstätt, this three-star hotel offers comfortable modern rooms and excellent regional cuisine in its award-winning restaurant.
B13, Eichstätt-Weissenburg 85132; 08421 93 77 70; www.waldgasthof-gelaender.de

PAPPENHEIM

Zum Goldenen Hirschen *inexpensive*
Tucked behind the gabled Renaissance façade of this 16th-century former brewery, are 14 atmospheric and tastefully renovated rooms and suites.
Marktplatz 4, 91788; 0914 34 34; www.gasthof-zum-goldenen-hirschen.de

BEILNGRIES

Der Millipp *moderate*
This stylish, half-timbered, 16th-century hotel in the historic town of Beilngries has plenty of spacious rooms.
Hauptstrasse 9, 92339; 08461 12 03; www.der.millipp.de

④ Eichstätt
Bavaria; 85072
The university town of Eichstätt, an independent Catholic bishopric for centuries, retains the feel of a miniature capital city. The **Dom** is remarkable for its Gothic Pappenheim altar, but Baroque architecture transformed the town after the Thirty Years' War. This is most apparent in the **Residenzplatz**, which is dominated by the bishops' palace. High above the town, the castle of **Willibaldsburg** houses the **Jura Museum** (closed Mon), with Jurassic-era fossils from the surrounding district.

Explore Eichstatt's dinosaur trails by picking up a map from the tourist office to follow the Fossilienpfad or fossil path, which leads to the fossil quarry of Blumenberg. Afterwards, ask at the tourist office for information about visiting the town's artist's studios and crafts workshops.

🚗 *Take the B13/ Weissenburger Strasse, turn left on to Rebdorfer Strasse after the bridge at the signpost for Solnhofen. Follow the road along*

the Altmühl Valley to the Zwölf Apostel. Continue past it to the car park just before Solnhofen village.

⑤ The Zwölf Apostel
Bavaria; 91807
The dolomite outcrops known as the Zwölf Apostel (Twelve Apostles) at Solnhofen are among the most impressive of the Altmühl Valley's Jurassic landforms. Easily reached along the Panoramaweg footpath from the car park west of the cliffs, this site is a nature reserve. The 200-km (124-mile) Altmühltal Panoramaweg hiking trail (NATOUR; Gänswirtshaus 12; www.natour-altmuehltal.de) is a relaxing way of discovering the valley's unique scenery. The area southwest of Solnhofen has yielded many of the region's most outstanding fossils, while to the east, at **Dollnstein**, canoes can be hired on the Altmühl river (www.kanuvermietung-altmuehltal.de).

🚗 *Continue north to Pappenheim.*

Fascinating Geology
Solnhofen's fossils were formed in a salty lagoon on the edge of the sea. The animals that died in the lagoon were well preserved due to the lack of oxygen in the water. Among the specimens found are those of the earliest known bird, archaeopteryx.

Where to Stay: inexpensive, under €70; moderate, €70–€150; expensive, over €150

6 Pappenheim

Bavaria; 91788

With its picturesque setting and historic architecture, Pappenheim is one of the most attractive small towns in the region. Impressive 18th- and 19th-century houses line the main street, Deisingerstrasse, where the merchant's house at No. 16 has an inscription giving the date of its construction as the year 5608, according to the Jewish calendar. In the Middle Ages, Pappenheim was the seat of the Holy Roman Empire's field marshal, but today there is nothing warlike about this sleepy, ruritanian town. It is dominated by a romantic ruined **castle** *(open daily)* that hosts one of the region's most atmospheric Christmas markets. Pappenheim also boasts two stately piles – the festive-looking Renaissance **Altes Schloss**, or old palace, and the Neo-Classical new palace, or **Neues Schloss**, built between 1819 and 1820 by Bavarian court architect, Leo von Klenze.

🚗 *Return to Eichstätt via Solnhofen, and enter the town on the B13. Turn left at the roundabout following signs for Kinding and Beilngries.*

Romans and Bavarians

The Limes – the frontier between the Roman Empire and the Germanic tribes – passed through the Altmühl region. A museum *(Apr–Oct: open daily; Nov–Mar: open Sat & Sun)* at Kipfenberg Castle, between Eichstätt and Beilngries, tells both sides of the story.

7 Beilngries

Bavaria; 92339

Children and adults alike will be charmed by the magical old toys and dolls at Beilngries's **Spielzeug and Figuren Museum** *(Apr–Oct: open Mon–Sat pm & Sun; Nov–Mar: open Wed, Sat & Sun pm)*. Take a stroll around the picturesque **Innerer Graben** street in the old town, which reveals the toy-town dimensions of the medieval fortifications, complete with nine of the original twelve 15th-century towers. The town also has a number of characterful old inns, making it a good base for exploring this part of the Altmühl Valley.

🚗 *Take the Kelheimer Strasse/B299 then turn left following signs for Dietfurt/Kelheim. Continue beyond Dietfurt along the the north bank of the Main-Donau canal to Prunn. At Prunn, turn left to get on to a minor road, which ascends to the castle car park.*

Left Tall Romanesque tower, a remnant of Beilngries's medieval fortifications **Below left** Willibaldsburg, perched on a hill above Eichstätt **Below right** Tomb of St Willibald at the Willibaldsburg in Eichstätt

EAT AND DRINK

EICHSTÄTT

Gasthof Krone *inexpensive*
Altmühl Valley lamb is the speciality of this snug, welcoming *Gasthof* (inn) opposite Eichstätt's cathedral. The emphasis here is on local and seasonal produce.
Domplatz 3, 85072; 08421 44 06; www.krone-eichstaett.de; closed Wed; beer garden in summer

BEILNGRIES

Der Millipp *moderate*
Regional produce dominates the menu of this historic old guesthouse and butcher's shop in the old town of Beilngries. The setting is simple but elegant, with pretty, rustic furniture, wood and pale colours. In summer, there is also a beer garden.
Hauptstrasse 9, 92339; 08461 12 03; www.der.millipp.de

Eat and Drink: inexpensive, under €20; moderate, €20–€40; expensive, over €40

Right Gabled burghers' houses in the centre of Landshut **Below left** Paintings on a shop's façade in Landshut **Below right** View of the Danube and the Befreiungshalle

DANUBE BOAT CRUISES

Several boat cruises through the Donaudurchburch between Kelheim and Kloster Weltenburg are available daily from late March to the end of October. During the peak season, from late April to mid-October, there is at least one boat every 45 minutes in both directions, with greater frequency on weekends. *www.schiffahrt-kelheim.de*

WHERE TO STAY

AROUND BEFREIUNGSHALLE

Weisses Lamm *moderate*
A traditional small town inn next to one of Kelheim's town gates, the Weisses Lamm has comfortable rooms. Its welcoming restaurant serves good regional dishes and Weltenburg beer.
Ludwigstrasse 12, 93309 Kelheim (east of Befreiungshalle); 09441 200 90; www.weisses-lamm-kelheim.de

LANDSHUT

Goldene Sonne *moderate*
This smart and comfortable family-run hotel, housed in a gabled house with beams and attics, has views over the old town and the Burg Trausnitz. The hotel's restaurant serves Bavarian and Italian cuisine.
Neustadt 530, 84028; 0871 925 30; www.goldenesonne.de

⑧ Burg Prunn
Bavaria; 93339

Its gravity-defying site atop a crag makes the medieval castle of Prunn (*mid-March–Oct: open daily, Nov–mid-March: closed Mon; guided tours only*) perhaps the most photogenic of the Altmühltal's fortresses. In the Middle Ages, under the Frauenberg knights of Haag, it was an important cultural centre; fragments of frescoes survive from this period. Later, the castle passed to the Jesuits, who crafted the rich stuccowork in its chapel. The views from the castle, up the Altmühl Valley along the Main-Donau canal, are spectacular. Opposite the castle gates is a restaurant and café, the Burgschenke Schloss Prunn, serving snacks and cakes as well as full meals.

🚗 *From the car park, return to Prunn village, turn left and then continue to Kelheim. At Kelheim turn right over the bridge along Alleestrasse towards the town centre. Turn right again up Hienheimer Strasse to reach the Befreiungshalle, which is signposted.*

⑨ Befreiungshalle
Bavaria; 93309

High above the modest town of Kelheim lies the vast Neo-Classical Befreiungshalle, or Liberation Hall (*open daily*), which guards the entrance to the Donaudurchbruch gorge. It was commissioned by the Bavarian King Ludwig I to commemorate victory over Napoleon's armies in the wars of 1813–15. The circular, domed interior has 34 winged angels of victory. Stairs lead to a viewing platform that has superb views over Kelheim and the gorge. Next, take a tour of the **Schneider Weisse** brewery in Kelheim (*guided tours: May–Oct: Tue & Thur, Nov–Apr: Tue; 09441 70 50; www.schneider-weisse.de*) followed by a boat cruise (*May–Oct: daily; www.schiffahrt-kelheim.de*) through the gorge to Kloster Weltenburg.

🚗 *Return to Kelheim, turn right along Alleestrasse and right again at the fork to reach the bridge across the Danube; on the south side, take the road to Weltenburg. Park in the riverside car park or in Kelheim and take the boat.*

Where to Stay: inexpensive, under €70; moderate, €70–€150; expensive, over €150

Left Picturesque Kloster Weltenburg on the Danube near Kelheim

Hop-growing

The Hallertau district between Kelheim and Landshut is the world's largest hop-growing region. Hops are climbing plants and the distinctive posts and wires of hop fields enable the plant to grow high. Flowers from the female plant are used in the brewing process.

⑩ Kloster Weltenburg

Bavaria; 93309

With a sumptuous Baroque chapel designed by the Asam brothers and excellent beer courtesy of the world's oldest abbey brewery *(tours Apr–Oct: open Sat & Sun)*, the Benedictine Abbey of Weltenburg is well worth a visit. However, its beautiful setting on a tight bend of the Danube at the western end of the Donaudurchbruch is undoubtedly the highlight here. The most popular way to arrive is on a boat trip *(late Mar–Oct)* through the wooded gorge from Kelheim.

🚗 *Return to Kelheim, following Regensburger Strasse on the south bank of the Danube to the B16, before taking the road via Rohr in Niederbayern to Alzhausen. Here, the road continues via Rottenburg an der Laaber to Landshut.*

⑪ Landshut

Bavaria; 84028

The broad main streets of Landshut's handsome old town are lined with fine gabled houses overlooked by the slender 130-m (427-ft) high brick tower of the Gothic **St Martinskirche** *(closed Mon–Fri)*. The **Stadtresidenz** *(closed Mon, guided tours)*, or town palace, has a lovely inner courtyard in Italian Renaissance style. Looming over the town is **Burg Trausnitz** *(open daily)*, the ancestral castle of Bavaria's royal family, the Wittelsbachs.

Above Pretty staircase in Burg Trausnitz, Landshut

VISITING LANDSHUT

Parking
The well-signposted car park beneath the City Centre mall is convenient for the old town's main sights.

Tourist Information
Altstadt 315, 84028; 0871 92 20 50; www.landshut.de; Mar–Oct, Nov–Feb: closed Sun

BREWERIES

Sample the local brew at the Schneider-Weisse brewery's **Weisses Brauhaus** *(Emil-Ott-Strasse 3; 09441 70 50; www.weisses-brauhaus-kelheim.de)* in Kelheim or at Kloster Weltenburg's **Klosterschenke** *(Asamstrasse 32, Weltenburg; 09441 675 70; www. klosterschenke-weltenburg.de)*, where the malty Barock Dunkel is a speciality.

EAT AND DRINK

AROUND BEFREIUNGSHALLE

Gasthof Berzl *inexpensive*
A traditional, family-run inn next to the Altmühl gate, this place offers excellent meat and home-made sausages. *Hafnergasse 2, 93309 Kelheim (east of Befreiungshalle); 09441 14 25; www.gasthof-berzl-kelheim.de*

LANDSHUT

Restaurant Stegfellner *moderate*
Tucked above a Gothic vaulted shop, this restaurant serves Bavarian cuisine. *Altstadt 71, 84028; 0871 319 11 33; closed Sun*

Other options
Coffee with cake is a German ritual and can be enjoyed at **Café-Conditorei Belstner** *(Altstadt 295, 84028; 0871 221 90; www.cafe-belstner.de)*

DAY TRIP OPTIONS

Ingolstadt and Eichstätt are good bases for day trips.

Art and architecture

Explore Ingolstadt's ❶ historic old town, then head to Neuburg an der Donau ❷ to admire the impressive castles of the Counts Palatinate before continuing via the pilgrimage church at Bergen to the delightful cathedral city of Eichstätt ❹.

Head west from Ingolstadt on the B13. From Neuburg an der Donau, follow signs for Eichstätt and Bergen. From Bergen, follow signs to Eichstätt on the B13. Return to Ingolstadt on the B13.

Photographer's treat

Follow the fascinating dinosaur trail in and around Eichstätt ❹ before heading to inspect the spectacular Jurassic fossils at Eichstätt's Jura Museum in the attractive castle of Willibaldsburg. Next, head to Solnhofen to admire the impressive limestone crags, the Zwölf Apostel ❺.

Head west towards Solnhofen along the Altmühl Valley to reach Solnhofen, returning by the same route.

Eat and Drink: inexpensive, under €20; moderate, €20–€40; expensive, over €40

The Northern Romantic Road

Würzburg to Donauwörth

Highlights

- **Old-world charm**
  Experience the world of knights and princes, from Würzburg's Residenz to Schloss Harburg

- **Local wines**
  Taste the local Taubertal and Franconian wines in one of Würzburg's traditional *Weinstuben*

- **Medieval time travel**
  Be enchanted by the medieval towns of Rothenburg ob der Tauber, Dinkelsbühl and Nördlingen

- **Exquisite scenery**
  Enjoy the magnificent countryside, from vine-clad slopes to wooded hills and the extraordinary landscape of the Ries crater

View of the pretty hilltop town of Rothenburg ob der Tauber

The Northern Romantic Road

The northern section of Germany's most celebrated travel route is characterized by its breathtaking landscape. Rolling countryside provides a picturesque setting for small historic towns strung out along the rivers Tauber and Wörnitz. This tour passes through the medieval townscapes of Rothenburg ob der Tauber and Dinkelsbühl. Further south, Nördlingen combines spectacular beauty with its curious setting in the Ries crater. This is by no means an unknown corner of Germany, but its popularity has not dimmed its charm: hotels are characterful, regional cooking is hearty, and there are crisp Baden or Franken wines from vineyards to enjoy along the way.

Above Cycle path beside the main road to Nördlingen, *see p198*

KEY

Drive route

ACTIVITIES

Take a hike past vineyards, castles and churches on the long-distance footpath that follows the "Romantic Road"

Sample the wines of the Tauber Valley, where a cycle route runs along the vineyard trail on the boundary between Bavaria and Baden Württemberg

Encounter wildlife at Bad Mergentheim's Wildpark, where the attractions include deer, lynx, brown bears and a pack of wolves

Discover Rothenburg ob der Tauber on an English-language evening walk with the town's night watchman

Take a walk along the signposted footpaths of the Geopark Ries for a close view of the meteorite crater

Below Courtyard and well, Schloss Harburg, *see p199*

Above Resplendent Schlossgarten, Weikersheim, *see p195*

PLAN YOUR DRIVE

Start/finish: Würzburg to Donauwörth.

Number of days: 3–4 days, allowing half a day to explore Rothenburg ob der Tauber.

Distance: 215 km (134 miles).

Road conditions: The route is marked with brown "Romantische Strasse" signposts. Roads are generally well paved, with gentle inclines. However, some stretches in the Tauber Valley are narrow.

When to go: May to October is a good time to drive along this scenic route. Lively Christmas markets are an added attraction in December.

Opening times: Most attractions are open daily, while shops are open from 9am to 6pm, Monday to Friday, and close early on Saturdays.

Major festivals: Rothenburg ob der Tauber: Meistertrunk (historical re-enactment), May; **Feuchtwangen:** Kreuzgangspiele (theatre festival), end May–Aug; **Dinkelsbühl:** Kinderzeche (children's and folklore festival), Jul; **Nördlingen:** Historisches Stadtmauerfest (town walls festival), every three years in Sep, next in 2016; **Donauwörth:** Schwäbischwerder Kindertag (children's historical procession), Jul.

DAY TRIP OPTIONS

The northern section of this wine producing country will be of special interest to **wine lovers**, while history-lovers will enjoy a visit to the **historic towns** of Rothenburg ob der Tauber and Nördlingen. For **family fun**, the valley of the Wörnitz river offers plenty of opportunities for **angling**, **kayaking** and **boat trips**. For full details, *see p199*.

Above left View from Türmer's Tower, Tauberbischofsheim **Above right** Rose garden in bloom, Schloss Weikersheim **Below right** Festung Marienberg, overlooking the Main river, Würzburg **Below far right** Elegant façade of Deutschordensschloss, Bad Mergentheim

VISITING WÜRZBURG

Parking
The 600-space Marktgarage underground car park is located beneath the Marktplatz and is a convenient spot for visiting the tourist information office.

Tourist Information
Falkenhaus, Marktplatz 9, 97070; 0931 37 23 98; www.wuerzburg.de; Apr–Dec: closed Sun; May–Oct: open daily; Jan–Mar: closed Sun

WHERE TO STAY

WÜRZBURG

Schlosshotel Steinburg *expensive*
This four-star country house hotel has 52 individually styled rooms. Facilities include an indoor pool and a sauna.
Auf dem Steinberg, 97080; 0931 970 20; www.steinburg.com

TAUBERBISCHOFSHEIM

Badischer Hof *moderate*
Located in the town centre, this three-star hotel has well-equipped en suite rooms, complete with wireless Internet, TV and, in some cases, a balcony.
Sonnenplatz, 97941; 09341 98 80; www.hotelbadischerhof.de

BAD MERGENTHEIM

Hotel Alte Münze *moderate*
The three-star Alte Münze offers 30 simple, modern rooms, including singles and doubles and three suites.
Münzgasse 12, 97980; 07931 56 60; www.hotelaltemuenze.de

WEIKERSHEIM

Laurentius *moderate*
This small hotel, with varying views over vineyards and the Schloss, has just 13 wine-themed rooms. All have a shower, flat screen TV and Internet.
Marktplatz 5, 97990; 07934 910 80; www.hotel-laurentius.de

1 Würzburg
Bavaria; 97070
The capital of Franconia's wine country, Würzburg became an independent prince-bishopric between 1168 and 1803. Occupying a picturesque position on the banks of the Main river, the town boasts many impressive churches. Of these, the most notable is the Romanesque **Dom St Kilian** *(open daily)*, which was built between 1045 and 1188. Towering above the town, the mighty castle, **Festung Marienberg**, is also worth a visit. One of the later Baroque additions to the fortress, the former arsenal now houses the **Mainfränkisches Museum** with a valuable collection of medieval art treasures *(closed Mon)*. However, Würzburg's greatest attraction is the Baroque **Residenz** *(open daily)*, a palace of the prince-bishops, now a UNESCO World Heritage Site. Built between 1720 and 1744, the centre-piece of the palace is the sumptuous emperor's chamber, the **Kaisersaal**.

🚗 *Take the Röntgenring, cross the Main river then bear left on the B27 as far as the A3, beyond which the Romantische Strasse continues to the town of Tauberbischofsheim. Park at the back of the Rathaus on Ringstrasse.*

2 Tauberbischofsheim
Baden-Württemberg; 97941
Formerly part of the territories of the Mainz archbishops, Tauberbischofs-heim has an Altstadt, or old town, focused on its **Marktplatz**. The market square is fringed by half-timbered houses and dominated by the Neo-Gothic town hall, or **Rathaus**. On the square is the Baroque house, the Reh-Hof (1702) and the old **Sternapotheke** (1670), or Star Pharmacy, in a house once occupied by Georg Michael Franck, grandfather of the Romantic poets Clemens and Bettina Brentano. The town's main symbol is the Türmersturm or Türmer's Tower, part of the **Schloss Kurmainz**. Dating from 1250, the castle now houses the **Tauberfränkisches Landschafts-museum** *(Palm Sun–Oct: open Tue–Sun; closed Nov–Palm Sun)*, whose collections include local *Tracht* (peasant costumes) and handicrafts.

🚗 *Take Würzburger Strasse, before turning right on to Mergentheimer Strasse. This becomes the B27 and then, after the A81, the B290.*

❸ Bad Mergentheim

Baden-Württemberg; 97980

Lying in a charming spot on the Tauber river, Bad Mergentheim was home to the Teutonic Knights from 1527 to 1809. First built in the 12th–13th centuries, the **Deutschordensschloss** dominates this leafy little spa town. The castle houses a **museum** *(closed Mon)* with staterooms and displays relating to the Knight's history. Just south of the town, **Pfarrkirche** *(closed Mon)*, the parish church at Stuppach, contains a masterpiece, the *Stuppacher Madonna* (1519), by German Renaissance painter Matthias Grünewald. Around 2 km (1 mile) from the town is the **Wildpark Bad Mergentheim** *(07931 413 44; www. geopark-ries.de)*, which is spread over 35 ha (86 acres), and features more than 75 species in a natural setting.

🚗 *Head east along the B19/ Igersheimer Strasse. From Igersheim, turn right. Follow signs to Weikersheim.*

❹ Weikersheim

Baden-Württemberg; 97990

Weikersheim's neat central square acts as a picturesque frame for **Schloss Weikersheim** *(open daily)*, transformed in the 16th century, on the orders of Count Wolfgang II of Hohenlohe, into one of Germany's most beautiful Renaissance palaces. The highlight of the interior is the **Rittersaal**, or knight's hall, a vast banqueting hall with a magnificent fireplace and painted ceiling. The Baroque palace garden, **Schlossgarten**, is graced by many fountains and more than 50 statues.

🚗 *Continue along the Tauber Valley. Follow signs to Rottingen taking the same road to Bieberehren, then drive south to Creglingen. Herrgottskirche is south of the junction with Rothenburger Strasse; there is parking on the side of the road.*

The Teutonic Knights

Formed at the end of the 12th century to protect pilgrims in the Holy Land, the Order of the Teutonic Knights of St Mary's Hospital in Jerusalem turned its attention to Europe after the Crusades. In the 13th century, it took Christianity and the German language to the Baltic, creating the German colony of East Prussia. After the Order's Grand Master, Albert of Brandenburg, converted to Lutheranism in 1525, its seat moved from Königsberg to Bad Mergentheim. The Order's distinctive black cross has become famous as the model for the Iron Cross, Germany's decoration for gallantry.

---

❺ Creglingen

Baden-Württemberg; 97993

Upstream from Weikersheim, on the Bavarian border, is the small town of Creglingen. Just south of its half-timbered centre is the **Herrgottskirche** *(Feb–Mar & Nov–Dec: closed Mon; Apr–Oct: open daily; closed Jan)*. This pilgrimage church shelters a masterpiece by sculptor Tilman Riemenschneider. Carved between 1493 and 1510, the **Marienaltar** was so aligned that the central figure of Mary is lit up through the chapel's rose window on the Feast of the Assumption on 25 August.

🚗 *Return to Creglingen, turning right on to the Romantische Strasse towards Rothenburg ob der Tauber.*

Centre left Stunning Marienaltar with Mary as the central figure, Crelingen
Below Pretty rural landscape, Creglingen

HIKING NEAR THE ROMANTISCHE STRASSE

A long-distance hiking trail runs parallel to the Romantic Road, threading through meadows and forests. Visitors can contact the nearest local tourist office *(www.romantischestrasse.de)* for more information.

EAT AND DRINK

WÜRZBURG

Ratskeller *moderate*
The menu at this lovely, atmospheric restaurant is a mix of steaks, salads and hearty regional fare, such as liver dumpling soup or Franconian bratwurst, all accompanied by delicious local wines.
Langgasse 1, 97070; 0931 130 21; www.wuerzburger-ratskeller.de

TAUBERBISCHOFSHEIM

Badischer Hof *moderate*
Regional cooking using seasonal ingredients typifies the menu at the Badischer Hof, where dishes such as roast stuffed pork with bread dumplings or trout with potatoes are accompanied by wines from the surrounding district.
Sonnenplatz, 97941; 09341 98 80; www.hotelbadischerhof.de

WEIKERSHEIM

Restaurant im Gewölbe *expensive*
A stone-vaulted cellar is the setting for Jürgen Koch's gourmet cooking, which fuses international sophistication with regional ingredients in dishes such as smoked trout fillet on verjuice foam.
Marktplatz 5, 97990; 07934 910 80; www.hotel-laurentius.de; closed Mon & Tue

Eat and Drink: inexpensive, under €20; moderate, €20–€40; expensive, over €40

Above Galgentor, an old execution place, Rothenburg ob der Tauber

VISITING ROTHENBURG OB DER TAUBER

Parking
There are paid car parks at the northern and southern ends of the old town, outside the town walls.

Tourist Information
Marktplatz 2, 91541; 09861 40 48 00; www.rothenburg.de

WHERE TO STAY

ROTHENBURG OB DER TAUBER

Gasthof Goldener Greifen *moderate*
This family-run inn offers simple but charming accommodation. Rooms are well equipped.
Obere Schmiedgasse 5, 91541; 09861 22 81; www.gasthof-greifen-rothenburg.de

Burg Hotel *expensive*
A delightful hotel with lovely views over the Tauber Valley. There are 15 individually decorated rooms and suites, with en suite bathrooms.
Klostergasse 1–3, 91541; 09861 948 90; www.burghotel.eu

Eisenhut *expensive*
Located in the heart of the Altstadt, this old hotel occupies four 16th-century patrician houses. Some of its 78 individually styled rooms have four poster beds. All have satellite TV, wireless Internet and en suite bath or shower.
Herrngasse 3–7, 91541; 09861 70 50; www.eisenhut.com

SCHILLINGSFÜRST

Die Post *moderate*
The Die Post offers superb views over the valley. The in-house distillery produces Obstwasser, the fruity schnapps of the region.
Rothenburger Strasse 1, 91583; 09868 95 00; www.flairhotel-diepost.de

❻ Rothenburg ob der Tauber
Bavaria; 91541

Without the catastrophe of the Thirty Years' War (1618–48), Rothenburg ob der Tauber might have been very different, for the loss of population and vitality that followed the conflict helped preserve its medieval and Renaissance townscape. Once a Free City of the Holy Roman Empire, Rothenburg is now no more than a minor country town, but its exceptional architectural heritage and scenic position above the lovely Tauber Valley ensure that this perfect little time capsule is one of Germany's most beloved attractions.

A two-hour walking tour

Park outside the old town, Altstadt, on Bezoldweg and head to the **Klingentor** ①, one of several lofty gates that punctuate Rothenburg's well-preserved medieval defences. Built around 1400, the Klingentor also served as a water tower. Within the bastion is the late 15th-century fortified church of St Wolfgang, built into the town walls. Continue into the Altstadt, heading south along Klingengasse, with the Gothic bulk of the Lutheran parish church of **St Jakobs Kirche** ② *(open daily)* ahead. The interior is worth visiting for the Heilig Blut Altar, or holy blood altar, by the Würzburg-based master-sculptor Tilman Riemenschneider. The altar's detailed portrayal of the Last Supper ranks as one of Riemenschneider's finest woodcarvings. Leave the church and turn left along Kirchplatz, to carry on

Eagle crest from the Rathaus

to the 12th-century **Weisser Turm** ③. Part of the original inner town wall, the "White Tower" is the highest point in the Altstadt. Next to it, the half-timbered Judentanzhaus, or Jewish dance hall, is a reminder of the town's importance as a centre of Jewish culture in the Middle Ages. The street leading east from Weisser Turm is known as Galgengasse, or Gallows' Lane, as it once led to the Galgentor, the town's gallows. Turn right down Pfarrgasse, then left into Rödergasse, looking right to admire the picturesque huddle of buildings around the Markusturm and Röderbogen, a town gate and former prison built around 1200. Walk to the end of Rödergasse to the **Röderturm** ④ *(Mar–Nov & Christmas Market: open daily)*, the only one of the town gates that can be climbed for views over the town. It contains an exhibition on the bombing of Rothenburg

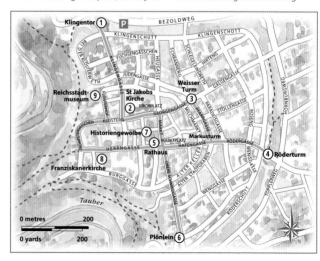

during World War II, of which barely a trace now remains. Head back to Markusturm, through the Markt, to see the splendid **Rathaus** ⑤ rising above. The town hall consists of two structures: the Renaissance building in front of the Markt dates from the late 16th century, while the Gothic structure behind it is much older. To the right, the gabled Ratstrinkstube, or City Councillors'Tavern, is graced by a 17th-century clock. Mechanical figures emerge on the hour to depict the story of the Meistertrunk, the drinking bet that spared the city during the Thirty Years'War. Return to the Markt, heading downhill along Schmiedgasse to **Plönlein** ⑥, a

The Meistertrunk Legend

Protestant Rothenburg sided with the Swedes during the Thirty Years' War, but was occupied by Catholic troops under General Tilly in 1631. According to a legend, Tilly agreed to spare the town from destruction if a councillor could down a 3.25 litre (5 pints) tankard of wine in one draught; former mayor Georg Nusch did so and Rothenburg was saved. This tale forms the basis for the Meistertrunk Festival, a re-enactment of the mythical story, which takes place at Whitsun.

charming little fork in the road, one of the most photographed spots in Rothenburg. Return to the Markt, turning left into Herrngasse, which boasts the town's most imposing patrician houses. A vaulted passageway leads through the Rathaus to the historic vaults, or **Historiengewölbe** ⑦ (Jan–Feb: closed; Mar–Dec: open daily), where Rothenburg's travails during the Thirty Years'War are brought to life. Continue down Herrngasse to **Franziskanerkirche** ⑧ (Jan–mid-Feb: closed; mid-Feb–Dec: open daily), which contains another Riemenschneider altar. Turn right into Trompetergässchen, and then left into Klosterhof to reach the **Reichsstadtmuseum** ⑨ (open daily). Housed in a former convent, the imperial city museum's collections include the Rothenburg Passion paintings from the Franziskanerkirche and a section on the town's Jewish history.

🚗 *Head south on Nördlinger Strasse on to Rothenburger Strasse to Insingen. Turn left to Diebach for Schillingsfürst.*

⑦ Schillingsfürst

Bavaria; 91583
Lording over the countryside from the highest outcrop of the Frankenhöhe hills, the Baroque palace of **Schloss Schillingsfürst** (Apr–Oct: open daily) is still the seat of the princes of Hohenlohe-Schillingsfürst. While its history dates back to the 11th century, the present building was built in the 18th century to designs by Darmstadt court architect Louis Rémy de la Fosse. Highlights include the Empfangssalon, or reception room, hung with Gobelin tapestries.

🚗 *Take the Frankenheimerstrasse. From Feuchtwanger Strasse turn right on to a minor road. Turn left to Wornitz. Follow signs to B25/Feuchtwangen.*

Above left View of the medieval town of Rothenburg ob der Tauber **Above right** Stately Rathaus, Rothenburg ob der Tauber **Below** Retable depicting The Stigmatization of St Francis, Franziskanerkirche

GUIDED TOURS

Wine Tours
Wine has been grown in the Tauber Valley since the 11th century with Silvaner and Müller-Thurgau as the main grape varieties. Local tourist offices have a list of wineries that can be visited by making an appointment.

Night Walk
Listen to the story of this medieval town on a guided walk with the night watchman of Rothenburg ob der Tauber. www.nightwatchman.de

EAT AND DRINK

ROTHENBURG OB DER TAUBER

Eisenhut expensive
The Eisenhut hotel's dining room serves Franconian and international fare in comfortable surroundings. It uses regional and seasonal produce to create dishes such as game terrine with frisée and cranberry vinaigrette or vol-au-vent filled with veal and mushroom ragout.
Herrngasse 3–7, 91541; 09861 70 50; www.eisenhut.com

Reichsküchenmeister expensive
This snug, traditional restaurant serves refined German cooking such as carp fillet in white wine sauce or Schnitzel (venison fillet in breadcrumbs).
Kirchplatz 8, 91541; 09861 97 00; www.reichskuechenmeister.com; closed Mon, Tue

SCHILLINGSFÜRST

Schlosscafe Schillingsfurst moderate
A stone-walled restaurant that serves Franconian specialities, notably desserts like Schneeballen (snowballs).
Am Wall 10, 91583; 09868 74 06; www.schlosscafe-schillingsfuerst.de

Right Patchwork of fields and forested hills near Harburg **Below** Schloss Harburg, on a rocky hill overlooking the Wörnitz Valley, Harburg

WHERE TO STAY

FEUCHTWANGEN

Greifen-Post *moderate*
This lovely hotel occupies a pair of 14th- and 15th-century buildings on Feuchtwangen's marketplace. Facilities include a library, indoor pool, sauna and steam bath.
Marktplatz 8, 91555; 09852 68 00; www.hotel-greifen.de

DINKELSBÜHL

Deutsches Haus *moderate*
This 15th-century inn exudes character, from its lively, decorated wooden ceilings to the individually styled rooms with modern comforts, including wireless Internet.
Weinmarkt 3, 91550; 09851 60 58; www.deutsches-haus.net; closed Jan & Feb

NÖRDLINGEN

Kaiserhof Hotel Sonne *moderate*
With a central location, this traditional hotel has peasant-style furniture in some rooms, all of which have bath or shower, TV and Internet. Past guests include four Holy Roman emperors and the writer J W von Goethe.
Marktplatz 3, 86720; 09081 50 67; www.kaiserhof-hotel-sonne.de

HARBURG

Fürstliche Burgschenke *moderate*
A hotel-restaurant with a rustic feel, located within the precincts of Harburg's castle, this has seven simple but pretty double rooms with en suite shower.
Burgstrasse 1, 86655; 09080 15 04; www.burgschenkeharburg.de

DONAUWÖRTH

Goldener Hirsch *moderate*
The Goldener Hirsch offers comfortable en suite rooms. Its restaurant serves Swabian specialities.
Reichsstrasse 44, 86609; 0906 31 24; www.goldener-hirsch-donauwoerth.de

⑧ Feuchtwangen
Bavaria; 91555

This city originated in the 9th century as a Benedictine abbey, which was dissolved during the Reformation. Feuchtwangen's attractive Altstadt (old town) is dominated by two churches; the larger of the two, **Stiftskirche**, is the former abbey church. Nestling alongside is a 12th-century **cloister**, the setting for the annual summer Kreuzgangspiele Theatre Festival. Feuchtwangen's **Fränkisches Museum** *(Jan & Feb: closed; Apr–Dec: open Wed–Sun)* is one of southern Germany's best folk art museums.

🚗 **Leave Feuchtwangen on the B25/ Dinkelsbühler Strasse to Dinkelsbühl.**

⑨ Dinkelsbühl
Bavaria; 91550

Though its peaceful setting on the Wörnitz river lacks the scenic splendour of Rothenburg ob der Tauber, Dinkelsbühl is one of the best-preserved medieval urban complexes in Germany, with lofty walls and towers encircling the Altstadt. At its heart is the soaring **Münster St Georg**, the town's 14th-century Gothic parish church. Its tower offers a fine view of the town. Opposite, on **Weinmarkt**, is a parade of tall, gabled houses as grand as any in Germany.

🚗 *Continue south along the B25. Pass Wallerstein and continue on the B25, which becomes the B29 to Nördlingen. Obtain a Parkscheibe (parking disc) from the tourist office car park for 1–5 hours for free. Park for free on car parks outside Altstadt near the gates.*

Above Colourful gabled houses in the old town centre in Dinkelsbühl

⑩ Nördlingen
Bavaria; 86720

This town stands at the centre of the Geopark Ries *(www.geopark-ries.de)*, in the Ries Basin, a huge crater over 100 m (110 yards) deep, formed millions of years ago by a meteor strike. With intact medieval walls encircling a well-preserved Altstadt, Nördlingen has its share of grandiose architecture. The late-Gothic **St Georgskirche** or Church of St George is a triple-nave hall church with round pillars and network vaults. It is possible to climb the 90-m (295-ft) high church tower, known as the **Daniel** *(open daily)*, for a bird's-eye view of the distant rim of the Ries Crater. Visit the **Rieskrater**

Where to Stay: inexpensive, under €70; moderate, €70–€150; expensive, over €150

Far Left Portcullis over the gateway, Schloss Harburg **Left** Row of traditional buildings along Reichstrasse, Donauwörth **Below** Pretty houses in the town of Nördlingen

Museum *(closed Mon)* to learn more about the meteorite strike that created the Ries.

🚗 *Continue along the B25 to Harburg.*

⑪ Harburg
Bavaria; 86655
Diminutive Harburg nestles on the banks of the Wörnitz river, which can be crossed on a restored 18th-century stone bridge that is worth a stroll for the views of the **Burg Harburg** *(mid-Mar–Oct: closed Mon)* of the princes of Oettingen-Wallerstein. One of the best preserved medieval castles in Germany, it sprawls along the hilltop, dominating the town below. The 18th-century **synagogue** in Egelstrasse is a reminder that a quarter of Harburg's population was once Jewish.

🚗 *Continue south along the B25 to Donauwörth. The Am Münster underground car park is well signposted.*

⑫ Donauwörth
Bavaria; 86609
Donauwörth underwent careful restoration after terrible destruction in 1945. Its main street, Reichsstrasse, is lined with patrician houses that hint at the town's former importance as a Free City of the Holy Roman Empire. The abbey church of **Heilig Kreuz** is a florid example of southern German Baroque, while the wooden-galleried

Invalidenkaserne was originally built as barracks. From Reichsstrasse, a bridge leads through the **Rieder Tor** across a branch of the Wörnitz river onto the island of Ried. From here, visitors can get fine views of the town's medieval fortifications.

The Ries Crater

Around 15 million years ago, a meteorite 1 km (1,093 yards) in diameter slammed into what is now northern Bavaria at a speed of about 70,000 kph (43,496 mph). The impact had the force of 250 Hiroshima atomic bombs and left behind a crater 25 km (16 miles) in diameter, nown as the Ries. When viewed from a suitable vantage point – such as the top of the Daniel in Nördlingen – the rim of the crater is still clearly visible.

EAT AND DRINK

FEUCHTWANGEN

Greifenstube *expensive*
This restaurant offers regional cooking with creative touches such as duck liver parfait in a *Baumkuchen* (layered cake) crust or fillet of young pork wrapped in savoy cabbage. There is a limited choice of vegetarian dishes.
Marktplatz 8, 91555; 09852 68 00; www.hotel-greifen.de; closed Mon

DINKELSBÜHL

Deutsches Haus *moderate*
Local produce is to the fore at the 15th-century Deutsches Haus, where the rustic dining room offers an atmospheric setting for typical regional and Mediterranean dishes.
Weinmarkt 3, 91550; 09851 60 58; www.deutsches-haus.net; closed Jan & Feb

Goldene Rose *expensive*
This 500-year-old inn once hosted Queen Victoria and now offers a choice of dining options. At its gourmet restaurant, Ollmann's, there is an international gloss to the six-course degustation menu, while its more rustic dining room serves dishes such as medallions of veal on morel cream sauce with browned Swabian noodles.
Marktplatz 4, 91550; 09851 577 50; www.hotel-goldene-rose.com

NÖRDLINGEN

Restaurant Joachim Kaiser im Meyers Keller *expensive*
Located on the southern outskirts of Nördlingen, this Michelin-starred restaurant offers a choice of menus: a cosmopolitan degustation menu or a regional menu, which emphasises the culinary tradition of the Ries region.
Marienhöhe 8, 86720; 09081 44 93; www.meyerskeller.de; closed Mon & Tue

---

DAY TRIP OPTIONS
This beautiful region can be explored in a series of day trips.

Medieval Würzburg
In Würzburg ❶, tour the Residenz before heading to the delightful towns of Tauberbischofsheim ❷ and Bad Mergentheim ❸ to visit the local wineries.

Take the B27 as far as the A3, beyond which the Romantische Strasse continues to Tauberbischofsheim. Take the B27, then the A81 and the B290 to Bad Mergentheim.

Charming towns
Explore the perfectly preserved town of Rothenburg ob der Tauber ❻ before stopping to tour the Schloss

at Schillingfürst ❼. Head to Dinkelsbühl ❾ and stroll around its medieval fortifications. Stop at Nördlingen ❿ to see the Ries crater.

Take Rothenburger Strasse to Schillingsfurst, take the B25 and continue on it to Dinkelsbühl. Continue on the same road, which becomes the B29 to Nördlingen.

Eat and Drink: inexpensive, under €20; moderate, €20–€40; expensive, over €40

The Southern Romantic Road

Augsburg to Füssen

Highlights

- **Wealthy Augsburg**
  Admire the art and architecture paid for by Augsburg's bankers, from exquisite gold and silver work to the world's first social housing complex

- **Baroque and Rococo grandeur**
  Wonder at the architectural opulence, from Landsberg am Lech to Wieskirche, a UNESCO World Heritage Site

- **Hiking landscape**
  Enjoy a wealth of activities, from walking in Pfaffenwinkel to mountain hikes around Hohenschwangau

- **Romantic fantasy**
  Explore "Mad" King Ludwig's medieval castle of Neuschwanstein

Opulent façade of the Historisches Rathaus in Landsberg am Lech

The Southern Romantic Road

The southern section of Germany's most famous tourist route begins at splendid Augsburg. The city's creative and architectural splendour was funded by its bankers, making it one of Europe's richest and most important cities at the height of the German Renaissance. Further south, a dream-like artistic vision prevails in the heavenly creations of Baroque and Rococo church builders and in the Wagnerian fantasies of "Mad" King Ludwig at Schloss Neuschwanstein, Germany's best-loved castle. Overshadowing everything is the majestic grandeur of the Alps, visible on a clear day even from Augsburg. Swabian cuisine hints at Italy's proximity, with ravioli-like *Maultaschen* and gnocchi-like *Spätzle* or *Kasspätzen* featuring on menus, although beer remains the drink of choice.

Above Lush, grassy slopes beside the road between Wildsteig and Rottenbuch, *see p206*

KEY

 Drive route

ACTIVITIES

Go on a mountain hike or opt for a ramble in the lovely walking country of Pfaffenwinkel in Schongau

Slide downhill on the popular 760-m (2,493-ft) summer toboggan run at Schwangau

Take off on a hang-gliding or paragliding course on the Tegelberg at Schwangau

Experience high-altitude scenic thrills on the Buchenberg or Tegelberg cable cars

Enjoy classical music in an Alpine setting at Schloss Neuschwanstein's Schlosskonzerte, held every September

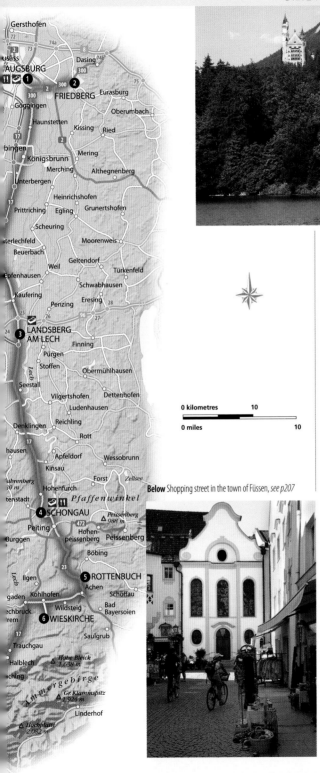

Above Neo-Gothic Schloss Hohenschwangau, Hohenschwangau, *see p207*

PLAN YOUR DRIVE

Start/finish: Augsburg to Füssen.

Number of days: 3 days, allowing a day to explore Augsburg.

Distance: 140 km (87 miles).

Road conditions: Roads are well surfaced and signposted with brown "Romantische Strasse" signs. Traffic can be heavy in the urban sections in and around Augsburg, where drivers should also watch out for trams.

When to go: This drive is best from May to October. There are a limited number of winter sports available in the Alpine south during winter.

Opening times: Museums often close on Mondays, while the royal castles at Hohenschwangau are open daily. Shops are closed on Sundays.

Major festivals: Augsburg: Plärrer (folk festival and funfair), Easter and late summer; Landsberg am Lech: Ruethenfest (children's folk festival), every four years, next 3rd week Jul 2015.

DAY TRIP OPTIONS

Lovers of historic towns will enjoy Augsburg and Landsberg am Lech in the north, while for an unrivalled combination of **scenic grandeur** and **architectural fantasy**, the Romantic Road is at its **prettiest** in the south, between Schöngau and the **royal castles** at Hohenschwangau. For full details, *see p207.*

Below Shopping street in the town of Füssen, *see p207*

Parking
The Annahof underground car park
is signposted off Fuggerstrasse and is
close to the tourist information office.

Tourist Information
*Rathausplatz 1, 86150; 0821 50 20 70;
www.augsburg-tourismus.de; Apr–Oct:
open daily; Nov–Mar: closed Sun*

WHERE TO STAY IN AUGSBURG

Hotel am Rathaus *moderate*
Tucked in a discreet lane near
Augsburg's Rathaus, this hotel has 31
rooms, each equipped with cable TV.
*Am I Iinteren Perlachberg 1, 86150;
0821 34 64 90; www.hotel-am-
rathaus-augsburg.de*

Steigenberger Hotel Drei Mohren
expensive
Augsburg's top address since the
17th century, this hotel is part of
the Steigenberger chain today. Its
rooms and suites are contemporary
and tasteful.
*Maximilianstrasse 40, 86150; 0821 503
60; www.augsburg.steigenberger.de*

Above right Fuggerei, the world's oldest
social housing complex, Augsburg

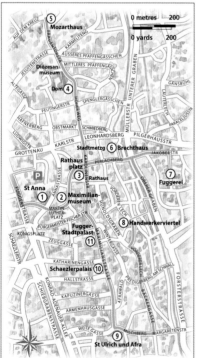

❶ Augsburg
Bavaria; 86150
Founded by the Romans, Augsburg reached its zenith during
the Renaissance. An important banking centre during this period,
the city attained renown all across Europe for its artists and craftsmen,
above all in England, where the Augsburg painter Hans Holbein the
Younger (1498–1543) became King Henry VIII's court painter. The
city also played a key role in the Reformation and its past glories
are reflected in the impressive architecture of its city centre.

A two-hour walking tour
Park in the Annahof underground car
park and walk through the courtyard
to the church of **St Anna** ① *(open daily)*,
which contains the Renaissance burial
chapel of the wealthy Fugger family.
There is also an exhibition
on Martin Luther, who
stayed here in 1518
during his meetings with
papal legate Cardinal
Cajetan following the
publication of his famous
95 Theses. Exit the church
and head down Martin-
Luther-Platz then bear left
to **Maximilianmuseum** ②
(closed Mon). Housed in a
16th-century merchant's
house, the museum con-
tains works by Augsburg's
famed gold and silver-
smiths and by the Dutch
sculptor Adriaen de Vries
(1556–1626), who was
responsible for several of
the city's splendid foun-
tains. From the museum,
Phillippine-Welser-Strasse
leads into **Rathausplatz**
③, the city's market
square. It is dominated by
the façade of the Rathaus,
one of Germany's finest
town halls and one of the
most important secular
Renaissance buildings

north of the Alps. Built from 1615–20,
it was designed by Elias Holl. Badly
burned during World War II, it has
since been carefully restored. Inside,
Goldener Saal, or Golden Hall *(open
daily)*, is a masterpiece of the restorer's
art, complete with a gilded walnut
ceiling. Head northwards up
Karolinenstrasse, cross Leonhardsberg
to the northern Altstadt, or old town,
and Augsburg's **Dom** ④, a blend of
the Romanesque and Gothic styles
with 12th-century stained-glass
windows and altar panels by Hans
Holbein the Elder, father of the
celebrated portraitist. On the
northern side of the cathedral is the
Diözesanmuseum *(closed Mon)*,
whose treasures include the cathedral's remarkable 11th-century bronze
doors, illustrated with scenes from
the Old Testament. North along
Frauentorstrasse is the **Mozarthaus** ⑤
at No. 20 *(closed Mon)*, where Mozart's
father Leopold was born in 1719, and
which now houses an interesting exhibition. Return to Rathausplatz and
turn left down Perlachberg, past Elias
Holl's gabled butcher's guild house,
the Stadtmetzg, and left again into
Auf dem Rain where the **Brechthaus**
⑥ *(closed Mon)*, birthplace of the playwright Bertolt Brecht, is now a
museum. Head back to the main road,
and turn left along Jakoberstrasse to
the **Fuggerei** ⑦ *(open daily)*. Founded
by Jakob Fugger the Rich in 1521, this

The Fuggers

In three generations, the Fugger family went from being weavers to bankers to the mighty Habsburgs. The greatest of the dynasty was Jakob Fugger the Rich, the wealthiest businessman of his day, who funded Charles V's ascent to the throne of the Holy Roman Empire. His town palace in Augsburg hosted the meeting between Martin Luther and Cardinal Cajetan and is to this day home to the Fugger Privatbank. However, his most famous memorial is the Fuggerei, the world's first social housing complex.

group of almshouses is thought to be the world's oldest social housing complex. One of the apartments is preserved in its original condition as a museum.

Head back to the city centre along Jakobstrasse and turn left into Oberer Graben, on the far side of which is the artisans' quarter, or **Handwerkerviertel** ⑧, a charming district of winding lanes. It was in one of the houses in this district, at Vorderer Lech, that Hans Holbein the Younger was born; the house was destroyed in World War II. In its place stands the Kunstverein Augsburg *(closed Mon)*, which hosts temporary exhibitions of modern art. Continue along Vorderer Lech into Bäckergasse; at the end, turn right up Milchberg to **St Ulrich und Afra** ⑨, a late-Gothic church which dominates the southern part of the Altstadt. Begun in 1474, it was not completed until 1603 and contains the tombs of St Ulrich, St Afra and St Simpert. North from here stretches Maximilianstrasse, lined with mansions and cafés.

Among the grandest mansions is the **Schaezlerpalais** ⑩, built in 1765 as the town palace of the banker Liebert von Liebenhofen and now a museum of German Baroque art *(closed Mon)*. The former palace's Rococo ballroom is the venue for concerts during the summer. In front of the Schaezlerpalais stands the Herkulesbrunnen, or Hercules Fountain, one of the three Renaissance fountains by Adriaen de Vries, completed around 1600. Go north along Maximilianstrasse, past the Fugger City Palace, or **Fugger-Stadtpalast** ⑪, to see the fountains, Merkurbrunnen and Augustusbrunnen, which stand in front of the Rathaus. Continue on the same road to the car park.

Detail on the balustrade, Fugger Chapel

🚗 *Take the B2/Friedberger Strasse to Friedberg. Paid parking is next to the Rathaus.*

② Friedberg

Bavaria; 86316

Founded by King Ludwig II in 1264, Friedberg is an impressive sight, snug behind well-preserved town walls. The town's hilltop Altstadt is rather over-restored, but there is a fine 17th-century **Rathaus** designed in the style of architect Elias Holl. Just beyond the fortifications is the **Wittelsbacher Schloss**, rebuilt in 1559 in Renaissance style, which is now a museum *(closed Mon & hols)*. Its collections include beautiful watches and faïence, or tin-glazed pottery, for which Friedberg was known in the 18th century.

🚗 *Return along Augsburger Strasse and take the B300/Haunstetter Strasse south from the city. This joins the B17 to Landsberg am Lech where there is limited parking on the main square.*

Above Magnificent coffered ceiling of the Goldener Saal, Rathaus, Augsburg **Below left** Baroque Rathaus, Friedberg **Below right** Gardens at the rear of the Fuggerei, Augsburg

EAT AND DRINK IN AUGSBURG

August *expensive*
This gourmet restaurant holds two Michelin stars. Try the Breton cannelloni with black curry and *Trompettes de mort* (black chanterelle mushrooms). Booking in advance is advisable. *Frauentorstrasse 27, 86152; 0821 352 79; closed Mon, Tue & Sun*

Die Ecke *expensive*
Situated down a flight of steps at the side of the Rathaus, this gourmet restaurant is an Augsburg favourite, serving refined German cuisine with wines from France, Italy and Germany. *Elias-Holl-Platz 2, 86152; 0821 51 06 00; www.restaurantdieecke.de*

Other options
König von Flandern *(Karolinenstrasse 12, 86152; 0821 15 80 50)*, a microbrewery, serves excellent beers and regional food. Also worth trying is the **Fuggerei Stube** *(Jakoberstrasse 26, 86152; 0821 308 70)*. The cheapest meals in town are at the stand-up stalls in the **Stadtmarkt** off Annastrasse – a lunchtime favourite with locals.

Above Old town walls, Schongau **Below left** View of the green countryside along the road to Rottenbuch **Below right** Cafés lining a cobbled street in Füssen

WHERE TO STAY

LANDSBERG AM LECH

Hotel Goggl *moderate*
Dating back to 1667, this hotel close to the main square offers clean rooms.
Hubert von Herkomerstrasse 19-20, 86899; 08191 32 40; www.hotelgoggl.de

SCHONGAU

Hotel Gasthof Blaue Traube *moderate*
This inn on Schongau's main street offers simple but attractive rooms.
Münzstrasse 10, 86956; 08861 903 29; www.hotel-blaue-traube.de

HOHENSCHWANGAU

Schlosshotel Lisl and Jägerhaus
moderate–expensive
This hotel consists of a main building and an annexe, the Villa Jägerhaus. Rooms in both are comfortable.
Neuschwanstein 1–3, 87645; 08362 88 70; www.lisl.de

FÜSSEN

Hotel Sonne *moderate*
The four-star Hotel Sonne has 50 rooms decorated in different styles.
Prinzregentenplatz 1, 87629; 08362 90 80; www.hotel-sonne.de

Hotel Kurcafé *expensive*
A long-established hotel with well-equipped doubles and deluxe rooms.
Prinzregentenplatz, 87629; 08362 93 01 80; www.kurcafe.com

③ Landsberg am Lech
Bavaria; 86899

With a sloping main square dominated by the historic town hall, the **Historisches Rathaus**, Landsberg am Lech has a well-preserved historic core. The façade of the town hall is richly ornamental, with stuccowork from 1719–21 by Dominikus Zimmermann, who, with his brother Johann Baptist, was also responsible for the Wieskirche. The town also has many gate towers, most notably the Gothic 15th-century 36-m (118-ft) high **Bayertor**, located at the top of the steep, pretty Alte Bergstrasse.

🚗 *Take the Katharinenstrasse, turn left on to the B17 and continue to Schongau, where there is on-street parking in the Altstadt.*

Hitler in Landsberg am Lech
For all its timeless beauty, Landsberg am Lech's chief historical claim to fame is as the place where Hitler wrote *Mein Kampf*. At his trial, following the disastrous coup attempt in Munich in 1923, the future dictator was given a lenient sentence despite charges of high treason. The case, far from being a humiliation, proved to be something of a propaganda platform and Hitler used the months of confinement to complete his notorious political manifesto.

④ Schongau
Bavaria; 86956

Perched above the Lech river in the district known as the **Pfaffenwinkel** (priests' corner), this former minor seat of the Wittelsbach Dynasty has an almost complete set of medieval town walls, which look particularly impressive when floodlit at night. The **Ballenhaus** in the centre of the old town is a former warehouse with a stepped gable, dating from 1420.

🚗 *Cross the Lech river to Peiting on the Peitinger Strasse and head south along the B23 to Rottenbuch. Parking is available in front of the church, follow signs to Ortsmitte.*

⑤ Rottenbuch
Bavaria; 82401

Rottenbuch's former Augustinian monastery complex was secularized in 1803 although its appearance remains unaffected. The village's focus is the convent church of **Marlä Geburt**, which has an opulent interior in the Rococo style, with stuccowork dating from the mid-18th century.

🚗 *Continue south on the B23. Beyond Achen, turn right on to Steingadener Strasse to Wildsteig. After Wildsteig, take the signposted turning to Wies/Wieskirche. There is paid parking at the side of the road, close to the church.*

⑥ Wieskirche
Bavaria; 86989

Located 5 km (3 miles) from Steingaden is the meadow church of **Wieskirche** *(open daily)*. Completed in 1754 at the spot where a farmer's wife had seen tears flow from the eyes of an abandoned statue of Christ, the church was the work of Dominikus Zimmermann. The building is a masterpiece of 18th-century southern German architecture.

🚗 *Return to the signposted turning. Continue to Steingaden, bearing left on to the B17. Follow brown signs, Königsschlösser, to the castles at Hohenschwangau. There are paid car parks at the base of the village. Ascend to Schloss Neuschwanstein by shuttle bus, horse and cart or on foot.*

"Mad" King Ludwig II

Bavaria's famous monarch Ludwig II, has become a revered figure since his drowning in the Starnberger See in 1886. Coming to the throne as a youth on the eve of Bavaria's defeat and incorporation into the Prussian-led German Empire, he was denied real power; instead, he lived out his absolutist fantasies in extravagant building projects that threatened to bankrupt the public purse. As a result he was forced to step down shortly before his untimely – and some still say suspicious – death, a few weeks before his 41st birthday.

⑦ Hohenschwangau

Bavaria; 87645

Germany's most famous castle sits in dreamy splendour on a forested crag above Hohenschwangau. **Schloss Neuschwanstein** *(open daily)* was built for Ludwig II between 1869 and 1884. Schlosskonzerte, or classical music concerts *(www.schlosskonzerte-neuschwanstein.de)*, are held here every September. The Neo-Gothic **Schloss Hohenschwangau** *(open daily)* in the valley below is where Ludwig spent much of his childhood. Enjoy a summer toboggan run *(www.tegelbergbahn.de)* or a cable car ride to the top of the the Tegelberg summit *(www.tegelbergbahn.de)* for spectacular views.

🚗 *Exit Hohenschwangau and take the Parkstrasse and turn left on to the B17 for Füssen. Park in one of the underground car parks close to the tourist office and the Altstadt.*

⑧ Füssen

Bavaria; 87629

The Romantic Road ends at Füssen in an enchanting landscape of lakes and mountains. The Altstadt is dominated by the late-Gothic **Hohes Schloss**, former summer palace of Augsburg's bishops, which houses two art galleries *(Apr–Oct: closed Mon; Nov–Mar: open Fri–Sun pm)*. The former Benedictine monastery of **Kloster St Mang** *(Apr–Oct: closed Mon; Nov–Mar: open Fri–Sun pm)* has a series of Baroque staterooms, while the **Heilig Geist Spitalkirche**, or Church of the Holy Ghost, has a pretty painted façade.

An Operatic Fantasy

Conceived by theatre designer Christian Jank, Neuschwanstein is the ultimate fantasy castle, inspired by the castles of the Age of Chivalry, notably the Wartburg in Thuringia. Ludwig II was the patron of the composer Richard Wagner, whose operas provided inspiration for the decor. The Sängersaal, or Singers' Hall, is modelled on the hall at Wartburg – the scene of the singer's contest in Wagner's opera *Tannhäuser*.

Above left Picturesque Schloss Hohenschwangau, Hohenschwangau **Above right** Landsberg am Lech from across the Lech river

HIKING IN THE PFAFFENWINKEL

The Pfaffenwinkel has three major hiking trails – the Konig-Ludwig-Weg, Lech-Hohenweg and the Pralatenweg – crisscrossing the district. There are also 28 self-guided hikes that range from easy strolls to mountain hikes. *www.pfaffen-winkel.de*

EAT AND DRINK

SCHONGAU

Gasthaus zum Lindauer *moderate*
The pine-panelled rustic interior is an appropriate setting for the Bavarian fare at the Gasthaus zum Lindauer. Enjoy fresh trout or pike-perch or venison goulash with Williams pear. *Löwenstrasse 1, 86956; 08864 81 42; www.zum-lindauer.de; closed Mon*

FÜSSEN

Gasthaus zum Schwanen *moderate*
Housed in a beautiful old gabled house close to Kloster Mang, this restaurant serves *Schnitzel* (pork fillet) alongside regional specialities from Swabia and the Allgäu, including *Maultaschen* (Swabian ravioli) and *Kasspätzen* (cheese-topped noodles) with roast onion and salad. *Am Brotmarkt 4, 87629; 08362 61 74; www.schwanen-fuessen.de; closed Mon & Tue*

DAY TRIP OPTIONS

Augsburg is a good base for exploring the northern section of the route, while Schongau and Füssen are excellent for discovering the southern part.

Historic towns
Explore historic Augsburg ❶ before heading to Friedberg ❷ to admire the exhibits in Wittelsbacher Schloss.

Stop at Landsberg am Lech ❸ to visit its Baroque town hall.

Head east to Friedberg along the B2, then south along the B300/B17 to Landsberg am Lech .

Scenic and architectural paradise
Stroll through Schongau's ❹ old town then head to

Hohenschwangau ❼ to explore its royal castles, which stand amid superb Alpine scenery.

Head south to Rottenbuch on the B23. At Achen, the Steingadner Strasse branches off to Wildsteig. Look out for brown signs to the Wieskirche. Bear left at Steingaden on to the B17 and follow signs to the castles.

Eat and Drink: inexpensive, under €20; moderate, €20–€40; expensive, over €40

Mountain Roads and Vineyards

Baden-Baden to Durbach

Highlights

- **Rejuvenating spas**
  Escape to the thermal baths in Baden-Baden, celebrated for their healing qualities

- **Fine wines**
  Taste and buy the wines produced in the region immediately south of Baden-Baden

- **Spectacular valley**
  Cruise through the Kinzig Valley on the Schwarzwaldhochstrasse, which is dotted with attractive villages and large traditional farmhouses

- **Amusement park**
  Delight the kids at Europa-Park, Germany's biggest theme park

Terraced vineyards rising above the scenic Schwarzwaldhochstrasse

Mountain Roads and Vineyards

The town of Baden-Baden, with its classy spas and air of 19th-century grandeur, defines the northern Black Forest, which is less wild and more accessible than the south. This tour follows the Schwarzwaldhochstrasse (Black Forest High Road), which rolls along the western edge of the mountain range, revealing fine views over the Rhine Valley. The road then leads to the eastern end of the Kinzig Valley, at the heart of the Black Forest, where pockets of traditional life have survived in small logging and farming villages. Of particular interest here is the brewery town of Alpirsbach and the half-timbered village of Schiltach. The tour finally takes drivers to the Badische Weinstrasse, a scenic road that meanders through an area known for its vineyards and wineries.

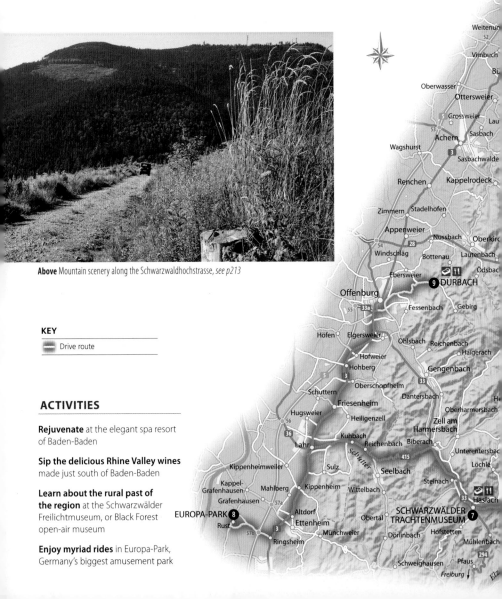

Above Mountain scenery along the Schwarzwaldhochstrasse, *see p213*

KEY

Drive route

ACTIVITIES

Rejuvenate at the elegant spa resort of Baden-Baden

Sip the delicious Rhine Valley wines made just south of Baden-Baden

Learn about the rural past of the region at the Schwarzwälder Freilichtmuseum, or Black Forest open-air museum

Enjoy myriad rides in Europa-Park, Germany's biggest amusement park

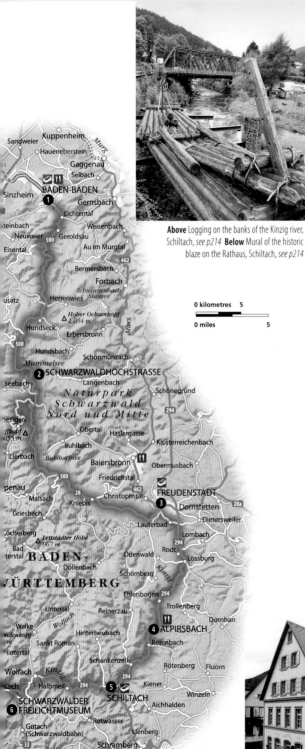

Above Logging on the banks of the Kinzig river, Schiltach, *see p214* Below Mural of the historic blaze on the Rathaus, Schiltach, *see p214*

0 kilometres 5

0 miles 5

PLAN YOUR DRIVE

Start/finish: Baden-Baden to Durbach.

Number of days: 3 days, allowing half a day in Baden-Baden.

Distance: 220 km (137 miles).

Road conditions: Roads are well paved but often steep and twisting, though driving is not particularly difficult. In winter, snow can cover higher portions of the drive.

When to go: This drive is possible throughout the year, although the higher points may be blocked by snow between December and March.

Opening times: Most attractions open daily. Shops open from 9am to 5pm on weekdays; and close early on Saturdays and remain closed on Sundays. Restaurants generally close at 10pm.

Main market days: Freudenstadt: Sat.

Shopping: The boutiques of Baden-Baden sport an array of luxury goods, while the vineyards and wine-sellers along the Badische Weinstrasse offer an excellent selection of local vintages.

Major festivals: Baden-Baden: Frühjahrsmeeting (spring meeting), May; Grosse Woche (great week), Aug.

DAY TRIP OPTIONS

Visitors interested in traditional rural life can follow the tour through the Gutach Valley where the **open-air museum** is a highlight, while **families** can head to Europa-Park where there are many attractions to fill the day. **Wine lovers** can take a relaxed tour of the Badische Weinstrasse and Durbach, where lovely walks pass through **vineyards**. For full details, *see p215*.

Above Interior of the grand Trinkhalle, Baden-Baden

① Baden-Baden

Baden-Württemberg; 76530

Founded as a Roman bathing spot, and a particular favourite of the Roman Emperor Caracalla (188–217 BC), Baden-Baden has an idyllic location in the midst of gentle wooded hills. In 1810, the Baden Margraves built Neo-Classical thermal baths around the springs here, to serve an early 19th-century fashion for bathing. Its importance has faded since, yet something of these halcyon days continues to live on in the elegant villas, grand hotels, spas and manicured gardens.

A 90-minute walking tour

From the car park entrance turn left to cross the park and the Oos river on a small footbridge. Then turn right along Lichtentaler Allee, which becomes Kaiserallee. This leads to a large building in the greenery on the left known as the **Trinkhalle** ① (open daily), the grandest of a series of 19th-century buildings and follies built alongside the Oos as social centres. It now houses the tourist information office. Turning right out of the Trinkhalle, a path leads through parkland to the Neo-Classical **Kurhaus** ② (open daily), the main venue for cultural

Façade of the Neo-Renaissance Trinkhalle

and social events in Baden-Baden, which includes a famous casino. Visits to the interior are possible on 20-minute tours held every 30 minutes. Outside the Kurhaus a bandstand marks the start of Kurgarten, an avenue of chestnut trees lined with expensive boutiques. A right turn at the bottom of this leads back to **Lichtentaler Allee** ③, a 3-km (2-mile) long promenade. Down this avenue is the Kunsthalle (closed Mon), home to international contemporary art. Walk along the promenade to Bertholdstrasse, which is on the left behind the Stadtmuseum, and turn right on to the footpath on the near-side of the river. Over the next footbridge lie the thick beech hedges of the **Gönneranlage** ④. These are ornamental gardens where over 400 varieties of rose thrive. Exiting the gardens from the opposite side, take the left turn that leads down Ludwig-Wilhelm-Strasse to the car park at Augustaplatz. From here, turn left then right down Lichtentaler Strasse to the square on Sophienstrasse. Gernsbacher Strasse, which is across the square leads into the old town, the **Altstadt** ⑤. This was reduced to ashes in 1689 during the Palatinate War of Succession; rebuilding it took a century. Follow Gernsbacher Strasse and turn left into an alley at Sonnenplatz. This leads to the marketplace,

VISITING BADEN-BADEN

Parking
Baden-Baden has a dozen central car parks of which several are underground. One such is the Augustaplatz car park.

Tourist Information
Kaiserallee 3, 76530; 07221 27 52 00; www.baden-baden.de; open daily

WHERE TO STAY

BADEN-BADEN

Heliopark Bad Hotel Zum Hirsch
moderate
This historic old town hotel's fine public rooms include a splendid ballroom. Thermal spring water flows from the taps of its antique-furnished rooms.
Hirschstrasse 1, 76530; 07221 93 90; www.bad-bad.de/hirsch-baden-baden/index.htm

Brenner's Park Hotel expensive
The best address in Baden-Baden, this hotel exudes 19th-century elegance. Its own park and an excellent modern spa and gym complex make it one of the finest hotels in the world.
Schillerstrasse 4-6, 76530; 07221 90 00; www.brenners.com

FREUDENSTADT

Bären moderate
A friendly and traditional three-star choice a block east of the Marktplatz, this hotel has rooms that have a comfortably dated, vaguely 1950s feel. Some rooms have balconies and the hotel provides Internet access.
Lange Strasse 33, 72250; 07441 27 29; www.hotel-baeren-freudenstadt.de

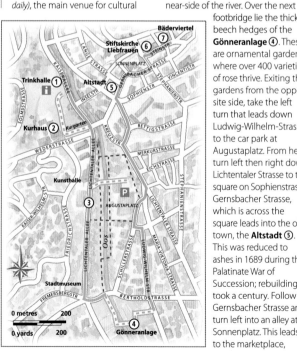

where villas surround the **Stiftskirche Liebfrauen** ⑥. This church's landmark spire summarizes its architectural history, with a Romanesque square tower forming the base for an octagonal Gothic cap that carries Baroque cupolas. Behind the church, occasional wisps of steam drifting over the cobbled street announce the presence of the **Bäderviertel** ⑦ at the base of some stone steps. The baths quarter was established by the Romans and its ruins can still be seen at the Römische Badruinen *(mid-March–mid-Nov: open daily)*. The ruins lie in the basement of the spa Friedrichsbad *(open daily)*, which looks like a minor palace with its green copper cupolas and colonnades. Return to Lichtentaler Strasse and Augustaplatz to reach the car park.

🚗 *Turn left out of the car park, right on to Lichentaler Strasse, which becomes Hauptstrasse. Turn right when this road meets the B500, which becomes the Schwarzwaldhochstrasse. Park at the roadside car park at Mummelsee.*

② Schwarzwaldhochstrasse
Baden-Württemberg; 77889

The Schwarzwaldhochstrasse, or Black Forest High Road (B500), climbs from Baden-Baden through meadows and valleys to the pine-covered hills that pave the way to Freudenstadt. Various viewpoints and belvederes along the route provide views to the rolling hills and vineyards of the upper Rhine Valley and beyond to the French Vosges Mountains. Visitors should allow time for several short hikes *(www.schwarzwaldhochstrasse.eu)* including the 2-km (1-mile) loop around the Mummelsee. Continue down the B500 and then turn right into the road signposted to Allerheiligen.

A 20-minute hike starts at the Gothic ruin of the Allerheiligen monastery and leads to an attractive waterfall.

🚗 *From Allerheiligen return to the B500 and continue south, then left on to the B28. In Freudenstadt, turn left on to the B462 to reach the car park.*

③ Freudenstadt
Baden-Württemberg; 72250

Built on a high plateau, Freudenstadt was commissioned by Duke Friedrich I in 1599. The town's giant marketplace is the biggest square in Germany. The most imposing buildings here are the town hall and **Stadtkirche**, an oddly L-shaped church designed to segregate men and women.

🚗 *Return to the B28, turn left down Lauterbadstrasse and then take the B294 towards Freiburg. In Alpirsbach, turn right into Alleenstrasse to park on the Krähenbadstrasse.*

The Who's Who of Baden-Baden

Though still a playground for the extremely rich, Baden-Baden had its heyday in the late 19th-century when the international elite flocked here to promenade and recuperate. Visiting luminaries included statesmen and monarchs such as Queen Victoria, Kaiser Wilhelm I and Otto von Bismarck, composers such as Pyotr Ilyitsch Tchaikovsky and Johannes Brahms and novelists such as Leo Tolstoy and Fyodor Dostoevsky.

Above Fountains in Freudenstadt's town centre **Below left** View of wooded hills and the town of Baden-Baden **Below right** Typical landscape, Scharzwalderhochstrasse

EAT AND DRINK

BADEN-BADEN

Café König *moderate*
This is the place to enjoy afternoon coffee and cake, in particular the exquisite *Schwarzwalder Kirschtorte* (black forest cherry gâteau).
Lichtentaler Strasse 12, 76530; 07221 235 73; closed dinner

Kurhaus Bistro *expensive*
A bistro attached to the Kurhaus, this restaurant serves dishes such as roast duck breast marinated with blackberry paste, fried green asparagus and wild rice risotto.
Kaiserallee 1, 76530; 07221 90 70

Le Jardin de France *expensive*
An elegant restaurant in a courtyard off Lichtentaler Strasse, this serves creative, modern French cuisine using ingredients such as pak choi and northern Iberian sausage.
Lichtentaler Strasse 13, 76530; 07221 300 78 60; Jan–Feb: open Wed–Sat, Mar–Dec: open Tue–Sat

AROUND FREUDENSTADT

Schwarzwaldstube *expensive*
With lovely views and countless international awards to its name, the Schwarzwaldstube is always full of gourmet surprises.
Tonbachstrasse 237, 72270 Baiersbronn (11 km/7 miles north of Freudenstadt); 07442 49 20; open Wed–Sun

Eat and Drink: inexpensive, under €20; moderate, €20–€40; expensive, over €40

Above left Farm mill in Vogtsbauernhof, Schwarzwälder Freilichtmuseum **Above right** Fountain outside a brewery, Alpirsbach **Below** View of the old square from the 16th-century Rathaus, Schiltach

WHERE TO STAY

SCHILTACH

Zum Weyssen Rössle *moderate*
A short walk from the marketplace, this traditional guesthouse features cheerful floral and modern rooms. It offers free wireless Internet as well as a good continental breakfast buffet.
Schenkenzeller Strasse 42, 77761; 07836 387; www.weysses-roessle.de

AROUND SCHWARZWÄLDER TRACHTENMUSEUM

Hotel Storchen *moderate*
The traditional half-timbered exterior of this guesthouse in Haslach suggests nothing of the eccentricities within. All its rooms are themed with concepts such as Oriental, aquatic, desert island and even a hot-air balloon.
Hauptstrasse 35, 77716 Haslach (east of Schwarzwälder Trachtenmuseum); 07832 97 97 97; www.hotel-storchen.de

DURBACH

Rebstock *moderate*
With lovely, individually decorated country-style or boutique rooms and suites, this family-run hotel has exquisite landscaped gardens that serve as a backdrop for its spa, which includes a sauna and steam room.
Halbgütle 30, 77770; 0781 48 20; www.rebstock-durbach.de

Hotel Ritter *expensive*
An upmarket, family-run boutique hotel, Ritter has tasteful decor and offers superb fitness and spa facilities.
Tal 1, 77770; 0781 932 30; www.ritter-durbach.de

Where to Stay: inexpensive, under €70; moderate, €70–€150; expensive, over €150

❹ Alpirsbach
Baden-Württemberg; 72271
Strung out along a tight valley, the town of Alpirsbach once basked in a medieval golden age that gave it the Romanesque Benedictine monastery **Kloster Alpirsbach** *(mid-Mar–Oct: open daily; Nov–mid-Mar: open Thu, Sat & Sun)*, whose church was built of regional red sandstone in the 11th century. The interior is largely empty, but worth a look for its powerful nave capitals, which illustrate the forces of good and evil. The cold Dormotorium and Calefectorium of the monks are visited by hour-long tours, which also give visitors background about life in the monastery. Other tours visit the adjacent brewery, the **Alpirsbacher Klosterbräu** *(tours Mon–Fri)*, which brews several fruity local beers.

🚗 **Return to the B294 from Krähenbadstrasse, turn right, following signs to Schiltach. Take the Schiltach-Ost entrance to the town,**

turn right at Hauptstrasse, then left on to Schramberger Strasse for on-street parking. Walk back to Hauptstrasse, turn left and take the alley on the right to the museum.

❺ Schiltach
Baden-Württemberg; 77761
The picture-postcard town of Schiltach was built on the banks of the Kinzig river, where a reconstructed lumber mill houses the **Schüttesäge-Museum** *(Apr–Oct: open daily; Nov–Dec: open Sat & Sun)*. The black and white photographs at this saw mill museum illustrate a bygone era when the town was the hub of a logging industry. A short walk along the river towards Hauptstrasse leads to a marketplace surrounded by half-timbered buildings, none of which date from before 1533, when a fire reduced the town to ashes. The **Rathaus** or town hall has murals of the blaze, including a depiction of the witch blamed for the fire.

🚗 **Continue on Schramberger Strasse and turn right on to the B294. Then turn right on to the B33 towards Villingen-Schwenningen. Park at the signed roadside parking beside the museum.**

❻ Schwarzwälder Freilichtmuseum
Baden-Württemberg; 77793
Close to the Gutach's confluence with the Kinzig is the Schwarzwälder Freilichtmuseum *(open daily)*, an open-air museum. The focus here is the **Vogtsbauernhof**, a 1570 farmhouse. Its roof is typical of the local building style. Arranged around the farm are 26 other traditional buildings, brought here from around the region to create a little village. Costumed guides and craft demonstrations help bring the place to life. Visitors can follow signs on the B33 from the museum to the **Sommerrodelbahn** *(Apr–Oct: open daily)*, a summer toboggan run.

🚗 **Return to the B33, turning left to Hofstetten. Turn right at Ringstrasse in Haslach. Follow signs to the museum and park in the car park beside it.**

Above left Sign for a restaurant serving wines from Baden-Baden **Above right** Vineyard in autumn, Durbach

⑦ Schwarzwälder Trachtenmuseum
Baden-Württemberg; 77716
Packed with a comprehensive collection of local costumes, this folk museum *(Apr–mid-Oct: closed Mon; mid-Oct–Dec & Feb–Mar: open Tue–Fri)* in the town of **Haslach** includes items such as the *Bollenhut*, a straw bonnet clustered with pompoms once worn by the unmarried women of the Gutach Valley. Look out for some of the costumes worn at carnival. Behind the museum, the old town of **Haslach** is worth exploring for the cluster of half-timbered houses funded by a silver-mining boom.
🚗 *Return to the B33. At Biberach get on to the B415 towards Lahr. Drive through Lahr, turning left on to the B3 and then right on to the road signposted to the Europa-Park.*

⑧ Europa-Park
Baden-Württemberg; 77977
The largest amusement park in Germany, Europa-Park *(late-Mar–Dec: open daily)* offers 50 rides, making it very popular with children. Its huge landscaped grounds are of interest

Euro Mouse at the Europa-Park

too; the size of 80 football fields, they contain several fun villages themed by European countries.
🚗 *Return along the B3 and head north through Lahr. In Offenburg take the Hauptstrasse and follow signs to Durbach. There are many places to park along the road through Durbach.*

⑨ Durbach
Baden-Württemberg; 77770
An important stop on the Badische Weinstrasse, Durbach is of particular interest to wine lovers for its shop, the **Durbacher Winzergenossenschaft** *(open daily)*. This wine cooperative offers a great selection of distinguished and well-priced local wines and is liberal with its samples. The shop is signposted and lies to the right of the main road in Durbach's centre. It faces the **Schloss Staufenberg**, which looms over the town from a vineyard-draped hill. The occupants of this 11th-century castle have been documented as producing wine since 1391. Visitors are not allowed inside the castle but can sample its wines in its earthy wine bar or outdoors on a terrace with spectacular views.

EAT AND DRINK

ALPIRSBACH
Zur Löwen-Post *moderate*
A traditional restaurant, Zur Löwen-Post also serves local innovations such as a salad garnished with roasted brewers malt and a beer-battered pork chop. A full selection of the local Alpirsbacher beers is available.
Marktplatz 12, 72275; 07444 955 95; closed Tue dinner; www.loewen-post.de

AROUND SCHWARZWÄLDER TRACHTENMUSEUM
Hotel Storchen *moderate*
The restaurant housed in this hotel serves traditional food. The menu spans simple inexpensive pizzas and pasta to venison stew with homemade *Spätzle* (Swabian noodles).
Hauptstrasse 35, 77716 Haslach (east of Schwarzwälder Trachtenmuseum); 07832 97 97 97; www.hotel-storchen.de

DURBACH
Hotel Ritter *expensive*
This hotel has an excellent restaurant that serves light regional nouvelle cuisine such as roasted lamb loin and braised lamb leg with artichokes and gnocchi. Simple meals are also served in the hotel's wine cellar.
Tal 1, 77770; 0781 932 30; www.ritter-durbach.de

DAY TRIP OPTIONS
Baden-Baden (on the A5 motorway) is a great base for day trips.

Past in the present
Spend the day at the interesting Schwarzwälder Freilichtmuseum ⑥ to get an insight into life on a farm in the 16th century.

From Baden-Baden follow the tour to the museum.

Themes and thrills
With more than enough attractions to fill a day, Europa-Park ⑧ near Rust is ideal for families.

Take the tour to the Schiltach and then to Rust. Follow signs to the park.

Wines and vineyards
Try a relaxed tour of the Badische Weinstrasse, following it from the spa town of Baden-Baden ① to

Durbach ⑨, where lovely walks through vineyards will enable visitors to appreciate the region. Also take a break and taste the local wines at Durbacher Winzergenossenschaft, the wine cooperative shop in Durbach.

Take the route to the B500 then turn in the direction of Karlsruhe, then turn left on to the B3 following signs to Durbach.

Eat and Drink: inexpensive, under €20; moderate, €20–€40; expensive, over €40

Cuckoo Clock Country

Freiburg to Schluchsee

Highlights

- **Sun-soaked city**
  Bask in the sunshine in Freiburg, one of the most attractive and sunny towns in Germany

- **Cuckoo clocks**
  Learn the history of the traditional Black Forest clock at the Deutsches Uhrenmuseum at Furtwangen, then choose a clock in Triberg

- **Serene lakes**
  Relax by boating or swimming in the tranquil Titisee or Schluchsee

- **International vistas**
  Climb Feldberg, the highest mountain of the southern Black Forest, for spectacular views of France and Switzerland

Shops with a fascinating display of cuckoo clocks, Triberg

Cuckoo Clock Country

Starting in the historic city of Freiburg, this drive leaves the broad Rhine Valley region and climbs up to the dense Black Forest on roads that twist through tiny villages and pass large, half-timbered farmsteads. The Black Forest is known as the land of cuckoo clocks and is famous for its Black Forest cherry gâteau. This tour takes drivers to the excellent clock museum in Furtwangen and to Triberg, where these timepieces can be bought as souvenirs. The wilder region to the southeast of Freiburg comes next and gathers around the Feldberg, which offers good hiking and, in winter, skiing. Neighbouring valleys contain the tranquil lakes of Titisee and Schluchsee and the spa town of St Blasien with its Baroque church.

KEY

  Drive route

Above Rolling hills en route from Todtnau to St Blasien, *see p223*

ACTIVITIES

Below Cuckoo-clock shop in Titisee, Black Forest, *see p222*

Trek to the Schlossberg or Rosskopf, near Freiburg, for spectacular views over the city as well as France

Pick a cuckoo clock as a souvenir from a selection of thousands in Triberg

Gorge on home-made Black Forest cherry gâteau in Triberg

Swim or go boating on the serene lakes of Titisee or Schluchsee

Take a chairlift or hike to the top of the Feldberg for wonderful views

Whiz down a summer toboggan run at Todtnau

Left Traditional cottage, Titisee region, *see p222*

Left Traditional cottage, Titisee region, *see p222*

Map labels:

33
Schonach im Schwarzwald
3 TRIBERG
Nussbach
Schönwald im Schwarzwald
Obertal
Brend △ 1,148 m
Stöcklewald 1,068 m △
Nonnenbach
Rohrbach im Schwarzwald
Katzensteig 500
Obersimonswald
Gütenbach
2 DEUTSCHES UHRENMUSEUM
Furtwangen
Sägendobel
Bregenbach
St Peter
Neukirch
Streichenbach
Sankt Märgen
Steinberg 1,141 m △
Eschbach
ckenberg
Neuhäusle
Glashütte
Waldau
Wagensteig
Hinterschollach
Unteribental
B A D E N
Turner
Langenordnach
Buchenbach
Dreieck
Bruckbach
Falkensteig
W Ü R T T E M B E R G
Breitnau 500
Siedelbach
Schwärzenbach
astler
Oedenbach
Hölzlebruck
Alpersbach
Neustadt
Hinterzarten 31
4 TITISEE 31
Windeck 1,209 m △
Titisee
317 Saig
eldberg 1,493 m △
Bruderhalde
315
FELDBERG Bärental
Lenzkirch
5
317 Falkau
Fahl
Neuglashütten
Raitenbuch
Altglashütten
Oberfischbach
Oberaha 500
Bildstein △ 1,142 m
Herzogenborn 1,415 m △
Aeule
Unterfischbach
Unteraha
Schluchsee
Hof
Menzenschwand
8 SCHLUCHSEE
Dorf
Habsberg △ 1,274 m
Faulenfürst
Innerlehen
Kaiserhaus
Muchenland
Seebrugg
lössling 309 m △
Oberlehen
Althütte 500
Hochkopf △ 1,263 m
Schönenbach
ST BLASIEN **7**
Staufen
Häusern
Urberg
Höchenschwand

0 kilometres 5
0 miles 5

PLAN YOUR DRIVE

Start/finish: Freiburg to Schluchsee.

Number of days: 2–3 days, allowing half a day to explore Freiburg.

Distance: 173 km (108 miles).

Road conditions: Roads are well paved but often steep and winding, though driving is not particularly difficult. In winter, snow can cover the higher portions of the drive; winter tyres are recommended.

When to go: This drive is best avoided in the winter months (December–March) when the top of the Feldberg is snowbound.

Opening times: Most attractions are open daily. Shops are usually open from 9am to 5pm from Monday to Friday, and close early on Saturdays. Many shops and services are closed on Sundays. Restaurants generally close around 10pm.

Main market days: Freiburg: daily.

Shopping: Cuckoo clocks and woodcarvings can be bought from Uhren-Park in Triberg.

Major festivals: Freiburg: Fasnet (pre-Lenten carnival), Sun & Mon before Shrove Tue; Frühlingsfest (spring festival), May; Zelt-Musik Festival (international tent music festival), late Jun/early Jul; Weintage (wine days), late Jul; Herbstfest (autumn festival), late Sep–early Oct; Triberg: Maifest (raising the Maypole), 1 May; Triberger Weihnachtszauber (fire and light show around Christmas), Dec; Titisee: Nacht in Weiss am Titisee (night in white), Jul; Feldberg: Sonnwendfeier (midsummer celebrations), 21 Jun.

DAY TRIP OPTIONS

Those interested in **history** can view the chronicles of the cuckoo clock by first visiting the **Deutsches Uhrenmuseum** in Furtwangen and then the cuckoo-clock capital of Triberg. **Adventure lovers** will enjoy exploring the **high mountains**, **waterfalls** and **lakes** south of Freiburg, including Germany's highest waterfalls in Triberg and the region's highest point, Feldberg. For full details, *see p223*.

Above Flowers displayed at the local market in Münsterplatz, Freiburg

VISITING FREIBURG

Parking
Of the half-dozen car parks in central Freiburg, the multi-storey one on Schlossbergring is the most central and convenient.

Tourist Information
Rathausplatz, 79098; 0761 388 18 80; www.freiburg.de; open daily

WHERE TO STAY

FREIBURG

Colombi *expensive*
The local *grande dame* of hotels, Colombi combines tradition with luxury and modern facilities such as a pool, steam baths, sauna and a gourmet restaurant.
Am Colombi Park, 79098; 0761 210 60; www.colombi.de

Zum Roten Bären *expensive*
Operating since 1120, this is the oldest hotel in Germany. It has scattered antiques to provide a historic atmosphere, but offers all modern amenities.
Oberlinden 12, 79098; 0761 38 78 70; www.roter-baeren.de

TRIBERG

Parkhotel Wehrle *expensive*
The most prestigious lodging in Triberg, this 17th-century house exudes old-fashioned charm in its individually decorated rooms with rustic frills, while the health centre with a pool and garden provides fine areas in which to relax.
Gartenstrasse 24, 78098; 07722 860 20; www.parkhotel-wehrle.de

❶ Freiburg

Baden-Württemberg; 79098
Blessed with the sunniest climate in Germany and wooded hills that rise above a picture-postcard old town, the Altstadt, Freiburg, or Freiburg im Breisgau, was founded in 1091. The old town fans out around a magnificent cathedral and has a series of quaint and historic squares with many tempting cafés and restaurants.

A 90-minute walking tour

From the Schlossbergring car park, turn left into Schoferstrasse, briefly right down Herrenstrasse and then left to reach the Gothic cathedral, the **Münster** ❶. Rising above this is a tower *(open daily)* with an openwork spire. On leaving the Münster by its main west entrance, enter the heart of a bustling daily market. To the left lies the bright-red **Historisches Kaufhaus** ❷ built in 1530 when Freiburg was ruled by the Habsburg Empire. The 1761 Baroque townhouse to its left is the **Wentzingerhaus** ❸, once the residence of sculptor Christian Wentzinger (1710–97) and now the Museum für Stadtgeschichte *(closed Mon)*, which offers an interesting insight into local history. To the right of the Wentzingerhaus is Buttergasse, which leads to **Schusterstrasse** ❹, one of Freiburg's best-preserved medieval streets. Turn left into this street and right into **Herrenstrasse** ❺, where pavement mosaics announce tradesmen and shops as they have

Wicker baskets, Freiburg market

done for centuries. Further down this street, turn right into Salzstrasse, looking out for the bronze tiles, **Stolpersteine** ❻, laid into the cobbled pavement outside No. 7 Salzstrasse. Literally translated as "stumbling blocks", these tiles commemorate the victims of Nazi persecution and are among 9,000 laid around Germany. Further down the street, a left turn down Annengässle and another left into Grünwälderstrasse leads to Augustinerplatz, where the **Augustinermuseum** ❼ *(closed Mon)* contains the extensive medieval art collection from a former monastery. A walk diagonally across the square leads down to the old tannery street, Gerberau. Continue to Kaiser-Joseph-Strasse, a main thoroughfare that leads to **Martinstor** ❽, a surviving town gate from 1202 that marks the beginning of the university quarter. Beyond, a left turn down Niemensstrasse leads to Universitätstrasse, where pavement cafés encourage lingering. A right

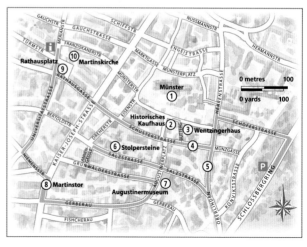

Where to Stay: inexpensive, under €70; moderate, €70–€150; expensive, over €150

Bächle

A curious feature of Freiburg is its *Bächle*, little streams that flow in pavement troughs through most streets. These streams originally provided water for animals, washing and for putting out fires, but today are largely decorative, though plenty of people use them to cool their feet on hot summer days.

turn down this street leads to **Rathausplatz ⑨**, where the Renaissance Neues Rathaus houses the tourist office. Towering beside this is the mid-14th-century **Martinskirche ⑩** *(open daily)*, a former Franciscan monastery church that was battered during World War II, but has since been rebuilt. Bear right out of Rathausplatz and follow Rathausgasse to cross Kaiser-Joseph-Strasse and follow the length of Schusterstrasse across the street. Turn left down Herrenstrasse, right down Schoferstrasse and right along Schlossbergring to reach the car park.

 Turn right on to Schlossbergring and left at Wallstrasse, which becomes Kartäuserstrasse. Follow signs to the town of St Peter then Sankt Märgen and Glashütte. Drive past Neukirch and turn left on to the B500 to Furtwangen. Turn right into Lindenstrasse to park.

❷ Deutsches Uhrenmuseum

Baden-Württemberg; 78113
Furtwangen's comprehensive Deutsches Uhrenmuseum *(open daily)* has a fascinating collection of 8,000 timepieces in myriad styles from almost every era. The display ranges from sundials and cuckoo clocks to mass-produced watches and clocks.

 Continue down Lindenstrasse, turn left on Gerwigstrasse, left at Marktplatz and then right on to the B500 to Triberg and park in the market square.

The Cuckoo Clock

It was in the 1730s that cuckoo clocks began to be made in the Black Forest area, with Triberg housing most of the early workshops. The quality of the craftsmanship quickly captured the imagination of the European market, as did the quirky designs, which included rooster clocks and moving automata of angry wives beating lazy husbands, as well as the traditional cuckoo popping out of a trapdoor.

❸ Triberg

Baden-Württemberg; 78098
The undisputed capital of cuckoo clocks, Triberg is also known for air so pure that it is now a health resort. The town centre, Marktplatz, is flanked by the Baroque **Wallfahrtskirche**. Uphill from here are two other attractions – a series of seven waterfalls and the **Schwarzwaldmuseum** *(Oct–Mar: closed Mon; Apr–Sep: open daily)*, with a large collection of clock-making apparatus. Continue on the B500, south of town, to reach **Uhren-Park** *(Schonachbach 27; open daily)*, a shop that claims to have the largest cuckoo clock in the world.

 Take the B500 to Furtwangen and further to the Titisee exit. Take Neustädter Strasse; park by the station.

Above left Painting on the exterior of a clock shop, Triberg **Above right** World's largest cuckoo clock, Triberg **Below** Forested slopes on the way to Titisee

HIKING AROUND FREIBURG

Freiburg is an excellent hub for hiking. An easy walk is the one up the Schlossberg or Castle Hill to the east of the old town, which links up with a good selection of further signposted trails. Recommended is the trail to the Rosskopf, the highest point in this cluster of hills, where a huge viewing tower provides superb views over the entire region. For hiking information and maps, contact the tourist information office in Freiburg. *www.freiburg-schwarzwald.de*

EAT AND DRINK

FREIBURG

Hausbrauerei Feierling *moderate*
A microbrewery with wood-and-copper interior decor and a lively beer garden, Hausbrauerei Feierling serves a range of pub food, including delicious giant *Schnitzel* (pork fillet).
Gerberau 46, 79098; 0761 24 34 80

Weinstube Oberkirch *moderate*
An excellent traditional restaurant with outdoor seating that serves large portions of regional food including poultry dishes, particularly pheasant.
Münsterplatz 22, 79098; 0761 202 68 68; closed Sun

Other options
The **Colombi** *expensive (Am Colombi Park, 79098; 0761 210 60)* has two restaurants – the rustic Hans-Thoma-Stube, with its veal and venison dishes, and the elegant Zirbelstube, which is rated among the best restaurants in Germany for its gourmet fare.

TRIBERG

Adler *inexpensive*
This is a café and hotel with some of the best cakes in the region – including a perfect *Schwarzwälder Kirschtorte* (Black Forest cherry gâteau).
Hauptstrasse 52, 78098; 07722 45 74

Right Rowing boats on Lake Schluchsee
Below left Church in the mountain town of
Todtnau **Below right** Visitors enjoying a day
out on Lake Schluchsee

BOATING AND CRUISING ON THE TITISEE

Bootsbetrieb Schweizer
Seerundweg 1, 79822; 07651 82 14;
www.bootsbetrieb-schweizer-titisee.de

WHERE TO STAY

TITISEE

Parkhotel Waldeck *moderate*
A traditional guesthouse with small,
simple rooms and spacious suites.
Parkstrasse 4–6, 79822; 07651 80 90;
www.parkhotelwaldeck.de

Treschers Schwarzwaldhotel
expensive
This hotel has superb facilities,
including a pool and sauna.
Seestrasse 10, 79822; 07651 805;
www.schwarzwaldhotel-trescher.de

FELDBERG

Haus Waldvogel *moderate*
This large Black Forest house has plush
modern rooms.
Köpfleweg 25, 79868; 07676 480;
www.cafe-waldvogel.de

ST BLASIEN

Hotel Klostermeisterhaus *moderate*
An early 19th-century villa behind the
Dom with elegant rooms.
Im Süssen Winkel 2, 79837; 07672 848

SCHLUCHSEE

Parkhotel Flora *expensive*
This charming four-star hotel boasts
lake views along with a pool and sauna.
Sonnhalde 22, 79859; 07656 974 20;
www.parkhotel-flora.de

④ Titisee
Baden-Württemberg; 79822
The lake resort of Titisee offers an
extensive network of well-marked
hiking trails, including an easy 6-km
(4-mile) loop around the lake past
several good swimming spots. A
strenuous alternative is climbing
the 1,200-m (4,000-ft) Hochfirst
Mountain. Maps are available at the
tourist office *(Strandbadstrasse 4, 79822;
07651 980 40)*. Several companies
also offer short lake cruises or rent
out rowing boats, both available on
the lakefront near the town centre.

🚗 *Turn right outside the car park to
follow Neustädter Strasse, then turn
right on to the B500 to join the B317.
Turn right following signs to Haus der
Natur to the large car park beside it.*

⑤ Feldberg
Baden-Württemberg; 79868
At 1,493 m (4,898 ft), Feldberg is the
highest point in the Black Forest. It
has a broad, well-rounded summit,
which rises above the tree line to offer
wonderful views of the region. With
much of the upper mountain being a
nature reserve, wildflowers flourish
here. The scattered presence of Black
Forest farmhouses and the occasional
Alpine hut add to the charm. There are
good hiking options available here.
The 12-km (8-mile) long Feldberg-
Steig is an excellent hiking loop
between five Alpine huts around the
upper reaches of the mountain for
experienced hikers, while others can
reach the summit on the Feldberg
chairlift *(May–Oct: open daily)*.

🚗 *Return to the B317 and continue on
it southwestwards towards Todtnau.
Turn left into Lindenstrasse to park at
the Hasenhorn chairlift car park.*

⑥ Todtnau
Baden-Württemberg; 79674
The quiet mountain town of
Todtnau bustles in winter as a gateway to the network of ski-lifts around
Feldberg. In summer, most visitors
travel up using the Hasenhorn chairlift *(May–Nov: open daily)* for the
summer toboggan run. This happens
on a thrilling 3-km (2-mile) long track
suitable for both children and adults.
Alternatively, explore a network
of hiking and mountain bike trails.
Maps are available at the tourist
office *(Meinard-Thoma-Strasse 21;
07671 96 96 95)*.

🚗 *Continue on the B317 and turn left
at Geschwend, following signs to St
Blasien. Take the signposted left turning
into the town. Continue on this till the
Hauptstrasse. Park on Hauptstrasse
across the river from the monastery.*

Left Scenic road between Todtnau and St Blasien **Below** Feldberg chairlift, which runs daily to the summit

BOAT TRIPS AROUND SCHLUCHSEE

Thomas Toth
Im Temprich 3, 79859; 07656 92 30; www.seerundfahrten.de

EAT AND DRINK

TITISEE

Treschers Schwarzwaldhotel *expensive*
An outstanding restaurant, particularly for fans of trout; the venison with cranberry sauce and wild herb salad is also exceptional.
Seestrasse 10, 79822; 07651 805

FELDBERG

Haus Sommerberg *expensive*
A hotel-cum-restaurant serving light, seasonal gourmet food. It specializes in fish. Try the crispy roast pike perch with saffron sauce, glazed peas and Bamberger potatoes.
Am Sommerberg 14, 79868; 07655 14 11; closed Mon

TODTNAU

Zum Hirschen *moderate*
This small guesthouse's restaurant serves seasonal regional cuisine – asparagus in spring, Chanterelle mushrooms in late summer and game in late autumn. All dishes are prepared by the chef-owner.
Kapellenstrasse 1, 79674; 07671 18 44; closed Tue

SCHLUCHSEE

Seehotel Hubertus *moderate*
Located in a lovely conservatory that boasts views of both Feldberg and the lake, this restaurant serves market-fresh produce and specializes in meat and game dishes.
Seebrugg 16, 79859; 07656 524

7 St Blasien
Baden-Württemberg; 79837

Nestled in a heavily forested valley, **Dom St Blasien** *(open daily)* dominates the skyline of St Blasien. This spa town can trace its roots to its 9th-century foundation as a Benedictine monastery. The Dom itself appeared almost a 1,000 years later. Commissioned by the powerful Prince-Abbot Martin Gerbert, this monastery was designed by French architect Michel d'Ixnard (1723–95), who used St Peter's Basilica in Rome as his model. Completed in 1783, it initiated a wave of monumental Neo-Classical architecture, which swept through Germany. The church has superb acoustics, which are best appreciated during the free classical music concerts *(Jun–early-Sep: open Tue & Sat)*.

🚗 *Return to the outskirts of the town and turn left on to the main road. At Häusern turn left on to the B500 to Schluchsee. On entering Schluchsee, park in the car park on the right.*

8 Schluchsee
Baden-Württemberg; 79859

A larger body of water than Titisee, and further off the beaten track,

Schluchsee is a calm and clean lake. There are many settlements on its eastern shore, the largest of which is also called Schluchsee. This town has a popular beach and a waterpark that is managed as Aqua Fun *(late-May–mid-Sep: open daily)*. Boat rides are possible with **Thomas Toth** *(May–late-Oct: open daily)*, which conducts trips around the lake with stops at various points. Since 1984, the Schluchseelauf, an 18-km (11-mile) run around the lake, has been held here.

DAY TRIP OPTIONS

To break up the drive into day trips, it is best to stay overnight in Freiburg, which is easily accessed from the B31.

On the trail of the cuckoo clock
After viewing the large collection of timepieces in Deutsches Uhrenmuseum ②, the clock museum in Furtwangen, travel on to Triberg ③. Here, visitors can browse through the numerous cuckoo-clock shops

that sit cheek-to-cheek, as well as explore the town's church, regional museum and waterfalls.

Follow the tour to Furtwangen, take the B500 to Triberg and then follow signs on the B500 and B31 to Freiburg.

Lakes and mountains
Nature lovers will be enthralled by the beautiful scenery around the lovely Titisee ④. From here, it is possible to

climb the Feldberg ⑤ and then visit Lake Schluchsee ⑧. Adventure enthusiasts can also make a stopover at the mountain town of Todtnau ⑥ and then head to St Blasien ⑦.

Follow the route to Titisee. Then follow signs on the B500 and B317 to Feldberg. Get onto the B317 to Todtnau. Pass Todtnau and come off the B317 at Geschwend and follow signs to St Blasien and then to Schluchsee.

Eat and Drink: inexpensive, under €20; moderate, €20–€40; expensive, over €40

DRIVE 22

Castles and Caves

Tübingen to Burg Hohenzollern

Highlights

- **Fairy-tale castles**
  Explore Schloss Lichtenstein and Burg Hohenzollern in their stunning cliff-top settings

- **Limestone caverns**
  Clamber down into the depths of limestone caves at Laichingen Tiefenhöhle

- **Sky-high spire**
  Marvel at Ulm's Münster, which has the tallest church spire in the world

- **Gregorian chanting**
  Relax at the Baroque Kloster Beuron, famous for its monastic singing

Neo-Gothic Burg Hohenzollern rising dramatically above the surrounding countryside

Castles and Caves

A vast plateau that stretches from Bavaria to the Black Forest, the Swabian Jura (Schwäbische Alb) has always been sparsely populated. Beech woods dominate the landscape, whose system of interconnected stalagmitic caves was carved from sedimentary limestone rocks. The dramatically steep escarpments and craggy outcrops offer ideal perches for an array of romantic castles. The limestone scenery also offers interesting hikes, particularly along the southeastern edge of the Jura, where the Danube begins its trans-European journey along a gorge lined with huge jagged cliffs. This stretch is particularly colourful in spring when wild flowers bloom and in autumn, when it glows in a magnificent blanket of golden foliage. The gateway cities of Tübingen and Ulm are both lively and atmospheric, with historic centres.

ACTIVITIES

Descend into the fascinating limestone caves at Laichingen

Take a hike to the many lovely viewpoints around the town of Blaubeuren

Climb the highest church spire in Ulm for views as far back as the Black Forest and the Alps

Hear the dulcet sounds of Gregorian chanting at Kloster Beuron

Explore a 1st-century Roman estate at Hechingen

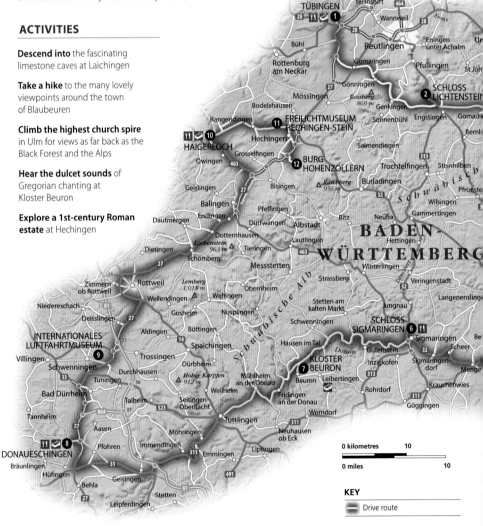

PLAN YOUR DRIVE

Start/finish: Tübingen to Burg Hohenzollern.

Number of days: 4–5 days, allowing half a day to explore Ulm.

Distance: 370 km (230 miles).

Road conditions: Though narrow and winding in places, all major and minor roads are well paved.

When to go: This route is generally accessible year round, though the Jura is sometimes snowbound in winter. Summer is the most enjoyable time to visit, particularly during one of Ulm's many festivals.

Opening times: Most attractions are open daily. Shops are open 9am to 5pm Monday to Friday and close early on Saturdays. Most shops and services are closed on Sundays. Restaurants generally close around 10pm.

Main market days: Tübingen: Mon, Wed & Fri; **Ulm:** Wed & Sat.

Shopping: Look out for delicious chocolates shaped like sparrows in the cafés in Ulm.

Major festivals: Ulm: Stadtfest (city festival), Jun; Bindertanz (coopers' dance), every four years in Jul, next in 2016; Donaufest (music and art festival), every two years in Jul, next in 2014; Schwörwoche (oath week), late Jul; **Donaueschingen:** Musiktage (music days), Oct.

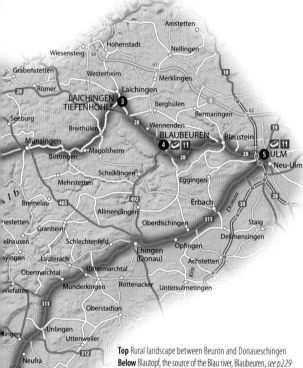

Top Rural landscape between Beuron and Donaueschingen
Below Blautopf, the source of the Blau river, Blaubeuren, *see p229*

DAY TRIP OPTIONS

Families should visit the **majestic castle** of Schloss Lichtenstein before exploring the **caves** at Laichingen and rounding the day off with an ascent of Ulm's Münster spire. **History enthusiasts** should make the Münster the highlight of a **walking tour in Ulm**, followed by a visit to the local galleries. Those interested in **castles** can combine sightseeing at Lichtenstein with tours of Sigmaringen and Burg Hohenzollern. For a more **scenic journey**, a walk around Blaubeuren is rewarding before following the Danube down to Beuron to hear **Gregorian chanting**. For full details, *see p233*.

Above Punting on the idyllic Neckar river, Tübingen Below Townhouses along the Neckar river, Tübingen

VISITING TÜBINGEN

Parking
The multi-storey Neckarparkhaus car park on Wöhrdstrasse is close to the tourist information office and only a short walk from the city centre.

Tourist Information
An der Neckarbrücke, 72072; 07071 913 60; www.tuebingen.de

WHERE TO STAY

TÜBINGEN

Hotel am Bad moderate
Located 2 km (1 mile) from the city centre, this good mid-range hotel beside the Neckar offers clean, simple rooms with facilities such as Wi-Fi.
Uferweg-Freibad 2, 72072; 07071 797 40; www.hotel-am-bad.de

Hotel am Schloss moderate
This half-timbered hotel with traditional charm, close to the Schloss, boasts fine views over the city.
Burgsteige 18, 72070; 07071 929 40; www.hotelamschloss.de

Hotel Krone moderate
A traditional-style riverside hotel by the Eberhardsbrücke with pleasant rooms that are furnished with the occasional antique.
Uhland Strasse 1, 72072; 07071 133 10; www.krone-tuebingen.de

BLAUBEUREN

Ochsen moderate
This traditional, half-timbered three-star guesthouse in the heart of the town has comfortable airy rooms and free wireless Internet.
Marktstrasse 4, 89143; 07344 96 98 90; www.ochsen-blaubeuren.de

Where to Stay: inexpensive under €70; moderate €70–€150; expensive over €150

① Tübingen
Baden-Württemberg; 72070
A charming medieval city, Tübingen first appeared in historical records in 1078 but only grew in status 400 years later when one of Germany's finest universities was established here. The **Eberhardsbrücke** over the Neckar river is a useful orientation point and the location of the tourist information office. The bridge overlooks the **Platanenallee**, a leafy boulevard on a narrow man-made island alongside which punts pass serenely in front of rows of pink-mustard- and cream-coloured houses. Crossing the bridge, a left turn on Neue Strasse leads to Holzmarkt, a square dominated by the late 15th-century Gothic **Stiftskirche St Georg** (open daily). Inside, magnificent star vaulting spreads across the nave and aisle roofs and the choir is dappled with beautiful stained-glass windows.

A climb up the church tower reveals fine views over the old town. On the opposite side of the Holzmarkt, Kirchgasse leads to Tübingen's **Markt**, whose fountain, Neptunbrunnen, has jolly cherubs depicting the seasons. Behind the fountain, the Gothic **Rathaus** is decorated with Neo-Renaissance frescoes of local heroes, painted to celebrate the university's 400th birthday. On the lower side of the marketplace, Marktgasse runs into a network of old streets of the former wine-growing neighbourhood. Back at the Markt, a walk uphill leads to Burgsteige where antique shops encourage lingering on the way to **Schloss Hohentübingen**. Expanded in the early 17th century, this 11th-century castle now serves various university departments and houses a history museum (open Wed–Sun).

🚗 From the multi-storey car park on Wöhrdstrasse, turn left and left again at Friedrichstrasse. Head south on B27, then turn for Gomaringen and follow Lichtensteinstrasse until signs for Genkingen. Here, look out for brown signs to Schloss Lichtenstein car park.

Tübingen's Scholars
Tübingen has attracted many fine scholars over the years, including theologian Philipp Melanchthon, philosopher Georg Wilhelm Friedrich Hegel, astronomer Johannes Keppler and psychiatrist Alois Alzheimer. The Romantic poet Friedrich Hölder spent the latter part of his life in the city, while Johann Wolfgang von Goethe published his first works here. More recently, Hermann Hesse worked as a bookbinder here before achieving literary fame.

② Schloss Lichtenstein

Baden-Württemberg; 72805

Perched at the top of a cliff on the edge of the Swabian Jura, the photogenic Schloss Lichtenstein *(Feb, Mar & Nov: open Sat & Sun; Apr–Oct: open daily)* overlooks the plains around Tübingen conveying a sense of being at the very periphery of a mountain range. The gabled and turreted castle dates back to the 1840s, when it was built according to the exaggerated literary descriptions of fairy-tale writer Wilhelm Hauff about an earlier castle that occupied this site. Bristling with horrific-looking weapons, the castle's most impressive feature, its armoury, is as vivid as any fairy tale.

🚗 *Return downhill from car park then turn left towards Riedlingen/ Reutlingen, then Münsingen. From here, follow B465 through the town and on towards Laichingen until signs for Tiefenhöhle.*

③ Laichingen Tiefenhöhle

Baden-Württemberg; 89146

This cave network *(open week before Easter–early-Nov: daily)* was discovered in 1892 by local sand digger Johann Georg Mack, who wondered where all his piles of sand were disappearing until he found a crack in the ground into which he lowered his son. The local community developed Laichingen Tiefenhöhle into an attraction in the 1930s, building walkways and fitting ladders. It is now possible to descend 55 m

(180 ft) into the caves without any special equipment. Visitors can wander the caverns at their own pace, which provides a sense of exploration. Warm clothing is required as the caves are at a constant temperature of 8° C (46° F).

🚗 *From Tiefenhöhle, turn left and follow signs for Blaubeuren via B28. Turn left at Marktstrasse, right at Bergstrasse, straight on to Weilerstrasse and then into Auf dem Graben where there is a car park.*

④ Blaubeuren

Baden-Württemberg; 89143

Blaubeuren is worth a stop simply to see the source of the Blau river, which joins the Danube in Ulm. The 20-m (65-ft) deep **Blautopf**, or "Blue Pot", is usually an incredible, clear, turquoise-coloured pool of water, although rain transforms this into green, then yellowy-brown. Beside it lies the **Hammerschmiede**, a mid-18th-century mill and smithy, which is at the trailhead of a number of hikes. Over the road, but accessed by entrances to the right, are the town's half-timbered former monastery workshops. Dating from 1510, these only saw 25 years of use before the Reformation disbanded the monastery, which had been founded here in 1085.

🚗 *Follow signs from centre of Blaubeuren to Ulm via B28. At Ulm follow signs for "Stadtmidt" over the bridge on to Wengengasse and turn right at Sedelhofgasse to the multi-storey car park, Parkhaus Sedelhof.*

Above Schloss Lichtenstein, immortalized in a novel by Wilhelm Hauff

HIKING AROUND BLAUBEUREN

The Blautopf is the trailhead of a number of hikes, including a circuit of Blaubeuren. Marked by an "A" on the trailhead map, this 6-km (4-mile) long trail circuits the valley to provide good views and takes around 90 minutes to complete. *www.stadt-blaubeuren.de*

EAT AND DRINK

TÜBINGEN

Neckarmüller *inexpensive*
A convivial riverside beer garden, attached to a microbrewery, with a fine selection of beers. The restaurant also serves good basic dishes, such as *Maultaschen* (Swabian ravioli). *Gartenstrasse 4, 72074; 07071 278 48*

Ratskeller *moderate*
Enjoy quality traditional fare served behind the Rathaus. Great for meat dishes, the restaurant is also known for its giant pancakes. *Haagasse 4, 72070; 07071 25 79 85*

Weinstube Forelle *expensive*
This traditional, old-world wine bar offers good food such as trout in almond butter and a range of game dishes. An excellent selection of local wines is also available. *Kronenstrasse 8, 72070; 07071 240 94; www.weinstubeforelle.de*

BLAUBEUREN

Ochsen *moderate*
This restaurant has a reputation for fine regional cuisine. The oxtail ragout is a speciality as is the seasonal asparagus. *Marktstrasse 4, 89143; 07344 96 98 90; www.ochsen-blaubeuren.de*

Below Limpid, aqua-coloured waters of Blautopf, Blaubeuren

Eat and Drink: inexpensive under €20; moderate €20–€40; expensive over €40

Above Weekly market in Münsterplatz, Ulm

VISITING ULM

Parking
The Parkhaus am Rathaus car park on Neue Strasse is very near the Münster.

Tourist Information
Münsterplatz 50, 89073; 0731 161 28 30; www.tourismus.ulm.de; Apr–Oct: open daily; Nov–Mar: open Mon–Sat

WHERE TO STAY

ULM

Hotel Bäumle *moderate*
A renovated building from 1413 with standard hotel rooms and free Internet.
Kohlgasse 6, 89073; 0731 622 87; www.hotel-baeumle.de

Hotel Schiefes Haus *moderate*
Famously crooked half-timbered house from 1443 with floors that are so uneven that the bed legs have to be of different lengths.
Schwörhausgasse 6, 89073; 0731 96 79 30; www.hotelschiefeshausulm.de

Münster Hotel *moderate*
The Münster Hotel provides en suite rooms with pretty views of the Münster.
Münsterplatz 14, 89073; 0731 641 62; www.muenster-hotel.de

Maritim Hotel *expensive*
With modern rooms, this is Ulm's best hotel. Facilities include bike hire.
Basteistrasse 50, 89073; 0731 92 30; www.maritim.de

AROUND KLOSTER BEURON

Burg Wildenstein *inexpensive*
This 11th-century stronghold on a cliff is now a youth hostel. The accommodation is ideal for family stays.
Jugendherberge Burg Wildenstein, 88637 Leibertingen (7 km/4 miles east of Kloster Beuron); 07466 411; www.jugendherberge-burg-wildenstein.de

⑤ Ulm
Baden-Württemberg; 89073

Lying on the Danube river, Ulm grew prosperous in the Middle Ages. Over time, corruption, wars and epidemics undermined the city's wealth. In 1944, its glorious historic core was destroyed during bombing raids. Fortunately, its giant Münster came out relatively unscathed. Today, a great deal of the city has been replaced by modern buildings.

A two-hour walking tour

From the Parkhaus am Rathaus car park, it is a very short walk up the Kramgasse to reach the vast sweep of **Münsterplatz** ①, which gives Ulm its focal point. The dimensions of the square are matched by the gigantic Gothic Münster *(open daily)*, which was begun in 1377. Designed for a standing congregation of 20,000, its plans included the world's tallest spire. However, it wasn't until 1890 that the spire reached its full height of 161 m (530 ft). The climb up its 768 steps offers fine views of the Black Forest and, on clearer days, the Alps. Inside, the eye is drawn upwards by the 42-m (138-ft) high nave and the pulpit. The elegant 26-m (85-ft) tabernacle is eye-catching, as is the vast 1471 fresco that covers the chancel arch. Turning left out of the Münster, cross Neue Strasse and turn right along Sattlergasse to arrive at Weinhof Square. The **Schwörhaus** ②, or oath house, is where Ulm residents gather

Flower market, outside the Münster

on *Schwörmontag* in the annual tradition of hearing their mayor pledge the 1397 city oath.

Back on Sattlergasse, a left turn leads to Weinberghof and down to the start of Fischergasse and the heart of the old fisherman's quarter, **Fischerviertel** ③, once home to medieval artisans. Look out for the pretzel carved in the door frame of a baker at Fischergasse 22, and the symbol of a boat-man at Fischergasse 18. An alley at the end of Fischergasse turns left to the quirky medieval **Schiefes Haus** ④, or crooked house, which leans precariously over a stream. Return to Fischergasse and turn left to a small square where stairs climb onto the 1480 riverside defence wall.

A walk further along reveals another crooked building: the 14th-century defensive tower of the **Metzgerturm** ⑤. Walking uphill beneath the Metzgerturm leads to the marketplace, where the glassy central library, Zentralbibliothek,

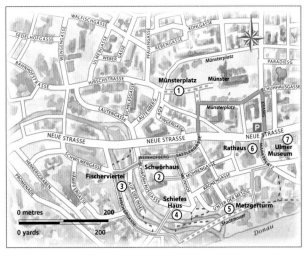

by architect Gottfried Böhm, lies opposite the Fischkastenbrunnen, or Fish Crate Fountain. Between the two, the 16th-century **Rathaus** ⑥ is decorated with lavish frescoes on its façade celebrating Ulm's medieval heyday. To the right of the Rathaus, the Kunsthalle Weishaupt *(open daily)*, a striking modern building over the square, displays Modern and Pop art by various artists including Andy Warhol, Paul Klee, Wassily Kandinsky and Pablo Picasso. The gallery is joined to the **Ulmer Museum** ⑦ *(closed Mon)*, the city's history museum, which is interesting for paintings of medieval Ulm. Walk back to the corner of Neue Strasse and Kramgasse to the Parkhaus am Rathaus car park.

🚗 *Take the B19 and turn left on to B311. Turn right on to B32 and left in Sigmaringen on to Fürst-Wilhelm-Strasse to the car park.*

The Tailor of Ulm
Dangling inside Ulm's Rathaus is a replica of the hang-glider of local tailor Albrecht Berblinger, who crash-landed this design into the Danube in 1811. Worn down by ceaseless jibes with his business in tatters, he died bankrupt in 1825. His design has since proved to be the world's first workable aircraft.

⑥ Schloss Sigmaringen
Baden-Württemberg; 72481
The stately Schloss Sigmaringen *(open daily)* dominates the skyline of the small regional town of Sigmaringen. First mentioned in 1077, the castle was brutally ransacked by Swedes in 1632 during the Thirty Years' War and destroyed by a huge domestic fire in 1893, leaving only two towers standing. Substantially redesigned in the eclectic style from 1899, the castle is still owned by a branch of the Hohenzollern family who unified Germany in the 19th century; a process helped by having this powerbase in the south. Its impressive armoury is a highlight of the castle tours.

🚗 *Return to B32 cross the bridge and turn left following signs to Beuron. At Beuron, turn left at signpost for Kloster Beuron for the car park.*

⑦ Kloster Beuron
Baden-Württemberg; 88631
Some of the most dramatic sections of the Upper Danube Valley lie around the village of Beuron. An enormous Baroque monastery, Kloster Beuron, was founded here in 1077 by Augustinians. Most of the buildings date from the late 17th century, and its church is relatively restrained by regional Baroque standards, though lively frescoes of the patron saints and legends of the foundation of the monastery decorate the naves. Of greatest interest is the glorious Gregorian chanting that accompanies all services *(daily)*. Beuron is also a good base for hiking trips, and a map at the car park details well-marked local options.

🚗 *Return to Beuron and turn left to Tuttlingen on to B311, which becomes B31. Turn left on to B27 signposted Donaueschingen, then right for Donaueschingen-Mitte, following signs for Schloss.*

Above View of Kloster Beuron in the Danube Valley **Below** Schloss Sigmaringen towering over town buildings

EAT AND DRINK

ULM

Allgäuer Hof *moderate*
Fine old-fashioned inn where almost everything is served on a sweet or savoury *Pfannkuchen* (crêpe).
Fischergasse 12, 89073; 0731 674 08; www.erstes-ulmer-pfannkuchen haus.de

Zur Forelle *moderate*
This snug 1626 Fischerviertel house, with a Napoleonic cannonball lodged in the wall, serves good regional food. Try the *Gaisburger Marsch* (a hearty beef, potato and *Spätzle* stew), or the house speciality, *Forelle* (trout). Physicist Albert Einstein and conductor Herbert von Karajan both dined here. Booking is required.
Fischergasse 25, 89073; 0731 639 24; www.zurforelle.com

Panorama *expensive*
The best of three restaurants in the Maritim hotel serves high-quality international and regional cuisine with lovely views over Ulm from the 16th floor.
Basteistrasse 50, 89073; 0731 923 17 39; www.maritim.de

Pflugmerzler *expensive*
A cozy restaurant featuring Swabian cuisine, including pasta specialities such as *Maultaschen* (Swabian ravioli) and *Spätzle* (Swabian noodles).
Pfluggasse 6, 89073; 0731 602 70 44; www.pflugmerzler.de; closed Sun

AROUND SCHLOSS SIGMARINGEN

Gasthaus Bären *moderate*
This hotel-restaurant serves traditional German food, Balkan dishes, game and, in the winter, fine Prague roast goose.
Burgstrasse 2, 72488 Sigmaringen (west of Schloss Sigmaringen); 07571 73 09 99; closed Mon

Above Lovely view of the town from castle grounds, Haigerloch **Below left** Orchestra fountain, Donaueschingen **Below right** Gateway to Schloss Haigerloch

WHERE TO STAY

DONAUESCHINGEN

Hotel Linde *moderate*
Traditional, central guesthouse above a good restaurant with standard rooms and free wireless Internet.
Karlstrasse 18, 78166; 0771 831 80; www.hotel-linde-donaueschingen.de

Zum Hirschen *moderate*
Family-run guesthouse whose spacious rooms have a contemporary elegance. All have access to wireless Internet.
Herdstrasse 5, 78166; 0771 898 55 80; www.hotel-zum-hirschen.de

Öschberghof *expensive*
This health and golf resort-hotel with boutique-style rooms offers a range of saunas and a large pool. The golf course is one of the best in the region.
Golfplatz 1, 78166; 0771 840; www.oeschberghof.com

HAIGERLOCH

Schloss Haigerloch *expensive*
Housed in a 16th-century castle, this lovely hotel offers brightly coloured rooms with all modern comforts.
Schlossstrasse 3, 72401; 07474 69 30; www.schloss-haigerloch.de

⑧ Donaueschingen
Baden-Württemberg; 78166
The longest river in Western Europe, the Danube begins in Donaueschingen, where its source is marked by a stone basin, Donauquelle. This lies on the fringes of the palace gardens of **Schloss Donaueschingen** *(Apr–Oct: open daily, guided tours only; 0771 22 96 75 60)*, an 18th-century Baroque palace that was extensively renovated in *belle époque* style at the end of the 19th century. Tours visit the luxurious rooms of the Fürstenberg family who once resided here. In 1283, this family also started the **Fürstenberg Brewery**, which can be visited on pre-booked tours *(Mon–Fri; 0771 862 06)*. To get there from the car park, turn right and then take the first right down Postplatz before walking left along Halden strasse to the brewery complex.

Logo, Fürstenberg beer

🚗 **Return to the B27 following signs to Villingen-Schwenningen then to Schwenningen Ost. At the first roundabout follow brown signs to Internationale Luftfahrtmuseum for the car park.**

Baden-Württemberg; 78056
The private collection of an avid pilot, Schwenningen's **Internationales Luftfahrtmuseum** *(closed Mon)* is the fruit of a lifetime spent collecting and reconstructing aeronautical memorabilia. Among the collection are rebuilt versions of early World War I planes of the kind that the Red Baron, the German flying ace, once flew. But most of the aircraft are Cold War-era oddities, bought upon their decommissioning and flown here from around Europe. Sadly, many were damaged by heavy hailstorms in 2002 and 2006, leaving smashed wings and broken windows.

🚗 **Return to B27 then turn on to B463 at Balingen and continue northwards, following signs for Haigerloch. Turn right to park in small multi-storey park in lower town centre.**

⑩ Haigerloch
Baden-Württemberg; 72394
Pretty Haigerloch is draped around a ridge and surrounded by lush greenery where lilacs blossom in spring. It is a quiet town, and very remote, which is why, during World War II, an old beer cellar at the base of a cliff here became a secret atomic research laboratory. Today, the **Atomkeller-Museum** *(May–Sep: open daily; Mar, Apr, Oct & Nov: open Sat & Sun)* commemorates this research. At the time, atomic science was still in its infancy but the threat of an atom bomb was taken so seriously by the occupying American forces that everything was methodically dismantled and destroyed, or shipped to the US. The whole site was to be blown up, but luckily, the priest from the 16th-century Gothic **Schlosskirche** *(open daily)*, perched on the cliff above, begged for mercy. An explosion in the cave would have destroyed not only the cave, but much of Haigerloch. Fortunately, the Americans changed their minds once they saw the church's ornate Rococo decor and the impressive 1609 altar. The Renaissance **Schloss Haigerloch**

(1580) beside the church is now an attractive hotel, restaurant and arts venue. On the opposite side of its courtyard, a short path leads along a cliff to a lookout with great views of the town. The steps up to the church and castle are found by turning right out of the Atomkeller and following the base of the cliff.

🚗 *From the car park turn left in the direction of Rangendingen and continue towards the signposted Freilichtmuseum car park.*

⑪ Freilichtmuseum Hechingen-Stein
Baden-Württemberg; 72379
A fascinating open-air museum, Freilichtmuseum Hechingen-Stein *(Apr–May & Oct: closed Mon; Jun–Sep: open daily)* preserves the ruins of a sizable Roman country estate, the result of a chance discovery during road construction. Between AD 1–3 this estate was of regional importance and a vital staging post for travellers passing through the area. Some key buildings have been reconstructed, while an ongoing archaeological excavation uncovers more foundations beyond the estate compound. Little is known about the estate – even its name is a mystery – but it was certainly destroyed by Germanic tribes as they pushed the Romans out of southern Germany.

🚗 *Exit the car park and take the first right down Römerstrasse. Continue towards the B27 junction and drive south until brown signs for Burg Hohenzollern lead to the castle.*

Turn right to car park at shuttle bus stop below Burg Hohenzollern.

⑫ Burg Hohenzollern
Baden-Württemberg; 72379
Sitting on an isolated crag in a broad valley, Burg Hohenzollern *(open daily)* is one of Germany's finest fairy-tale castles. Yet its medieval-looking battlements and towers are deceptive, since they were built between 1846 and 1867, albeit using the foundations of castles that have stood here since the 11th century. Only St-Michael-Kapelle, a chapel with ornate stained glass, survives in its original state. The castle still belongs to the Hohenzollern family, who reigned over a united Germany between 1871 and 1918, and the crown of German Emperor Wilhelm II is the pride of the castle treasury. Also among the family artifacts are several snuff boxes from the collection of Frederick the Great.

Above Soaring towers of the majestic Neo-Gothic Burg Hohenzollern

EAT AND DRINK

DONAUESCHINGEN

Hotel Linde *moderate*
A traditional restaurant serving a mix of fish, meat and vegetarian dishes. *Karlstrasse 18, 78166; 0771 831 80; www.hotel-linde-donaueschingen.de*

Other options
For simple pub food and a full range of beers, try the **Bräustüble** *(Postplatz 1)*, the inn of the Fürstenberg brewery. The **Öschberghof** *(Golfplatz 1, 78166; 0771 840)* is the best restaurant in town.

HAIGERLOCH

Schloss Haigerloch *expensive*
National and international dishes are offered at this classy restaurant. There is live piano music on Saturday nights. *Schlossstrasse 3, 72401 Haigerloch; 07474 69 30; closed Sun*

Other options
Best for traditional fare, **Gaststätte Schlössle** *(Hechinger Strasse 9; 07474 62 35)* also serves local beers.

DAY TRIP OPTIONS
With its pleasant atmosphere, Tübingen makes the best base along this drive. Local motorways, particularly the A81, help speed up the return part of day trips to the southern portion of the route.

Caves and historic Ulm
Visit Schloss Lichtenstein ② before heading to explore the caves at Laichingen ③. Tour Ulm ⑤ at a more relaxed pace with an ascent of the Münster spire and a visit to the art museum, Kunsthalle Weishaupt, as well as the Ulmer Museum.

Follow the tour to Ulm, but skip stop at Blaubeuren. Follow the B28 to A8 then to Ulm. Return via the A8 and B28.

Castle hopping
Treat yourself to three of Germany's finest castles – Schloss Lichtenstein ②, Schloss Sigmaringen ⑥ and Burg Hohenzollern ⑫ – in a day and enjoy scenic drives on minor roads across the Swabian Alb.

Follow the route to Schloss Lichtenstein and beyond to the B313, turn left to Gammertingen on to the B32. Turn left to Sigmaringen. Retrace the route,

follow the B32 to turn left on to the B463, and then left again to Burg Hohenzollern.

Scenic trail and chants
The walk around picturesque Blaubeuren ④ is a relaxed and scenic option. Next, follow the Danube to reach the imposing Kloster Beuron ⑦ to hear Gregorian chanting.

Follow the tour to Blaubeuren, take the B492, turn right at the B311 and right again on to the B32 via Sigmaringen to Beuron.

Eat and Drink: inexpensive under €20; moderate €20–€40; expensive over €40

Germany's Riviera

Konstanz to Lindau Island

Highlights

- **Tranquil islands**
  Take a day trip to the Bodensee
  Islands of Reichenau and Mainau,
  rich in history and flora

- **Prehistoric homes**
  Visit the Pfahlbauten, an open-air
  museum that has a reconstruction of
  how Bodensee man is believed to
  have lived 3,000 years ago

- **Zeppelins**
  Stop by the Zeppelin Museum in
  Friedrichshafen, which commemorates an important aeronautical
  achievement and is a hub for
  modern Zeppelin trips

- **Wines and vineyards**
  Sample local vintages from Germany's
  sunniest region at the wine bars and
  vineyards along the route

Grapevines against the backdrop of Lake
Konstanz, Pfahlbauten

Germany's Riviera

The giant Lake Constance (Bodensee) forms much of Germany's southwest border with Switzerland, which provides a spectacular Alpine backdrop. The lake's balmy, dry climate makes it perfect for lounging on beaches and for outdoor activities such as hiking, cycling on lakeside trails, swimming and boating. The cosmopolitan hub of Konstanz has boat services to many points on the lake. Rich soils and a near-tropical climate have enabled Mainau to maintain one of Germany's most elaborate landscaped gardens, while Reichenau has specialized in market-gardening. The towns that line Bodensee's northern shore include the attractive, medieval Meersburg, which boasts the oldest castle in Germany. To the east, Friedrichshafen, once the hub for Zeppelin flights around the world, has a fine museum devoted to the airships. Further east, just over the Bavarian border, Lindau Island awaits with its charming half-timbered old town.

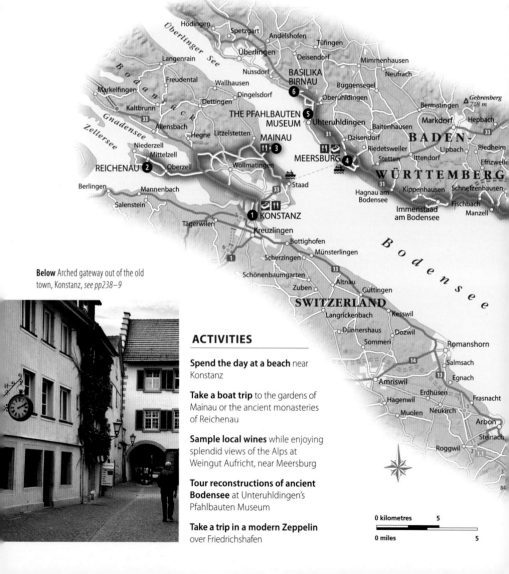

Below Arched gateway out of the old town, Konstanz, *see pp238–9*

ACTIVITIES

Spend the day at a beach near Konstanz

Take a boat trip to the gardens of Mainau or the ancient monasteries of Reichenau

Sample local wines while enjoying splendid views of the Alps at Weingut Aufricht, near Meersburg

Tour reconstructions of ancient Bodensee at Unteruhldingen's Pfahlbauten Museum

Take a trip in a modern Zeppelin over Friedrichshafen

Map labels:
Hödingen, Spetzgart, Andelshofen, Tüfingen, Überlingen, Deisendorf, Mimmenhausen, Langenrain, Überlinger See, Nussdorf, BASILIKA BIRNAU, Neufrach, Freudental, Wallhausen, Buggensegel, Markelfingen, Dingelsdorf, Oberuhldingen, Bermatingen, Gebrenberg 718 m, Kaltbrunn, Dettingen, THE PFAHLBAUTEN MUSEUM, Markdorf, Hepbach, Allensbach, Litzelstetten, Unteruhldingen, Baitenhausen, BADEN-, Hegne, MAINAU, Daisendorf, Niederzell, Riedetsweiler, Lupbach, Riedheim, Mittelzell, MEERSBURG, Stetten, Ittendorf, Efrizwelle, REICHENAU, Oberzell, Wollmatingen, WÜRTTEMBERG, Berlingen, Mannenbach, Staad, Hagnau am Bodensee, Kippenhausen, Schnetzenhausen, Salenstein, Immenstaad am Bodensee, Fischbach, Manzell, Tägerwilen, KONSTANZ, Kreuzlingen, Bottighofen, Scherzingen, Münsterlingen, Bodensee, Schönenbaumgarten, Altnau, Zuben, Güttingen, SWITZERLAND, Langrickenbach, Kesswil, Dünnershaus, Dozwil, Sommeri, Romanshorn, Salmsach, Amriswil, Egnach, Hagenwil, Erdhüsen, Frasnacht, Muolen, Neukirch, Arbon, Steinach, Roggwil

0 kilometres 5
0 miles 5

Above Tree-lined road to Reichenau, *see p239*

KEY

🚇 Drive route

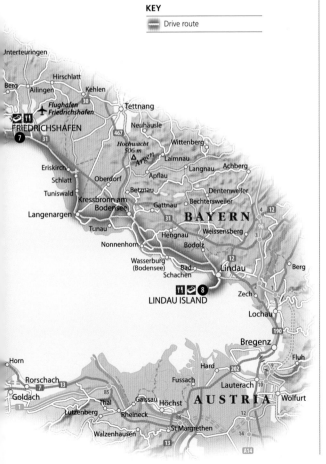

PLAN YOUR DRIVE

Start/finish: Konstanz to Lindau Island.

Number of days: 2–3 days, allowing a day to explore the Bodensee Islands.

Distance: 90 km (56 miles).

Road conditions: Well-paved roads.

When to go: This drive is good year round though in summer (June, July & August) traffic along the coastal roads can be heavy. Spring (April & May), when fruit trees are in bloom, is particularly attractive. Wine lovers should try to visit during autumn (September & October), when many festivals are held.

Opening times: Most attractions open daily. Shops are open from 9am to 5pm, Monday to Friday and close early on Saturdays. Most shops and services are closed on Sundays. Restaurants generally close around 10pm.

Main market days: Konstanz: Wed & Sat; **Friedrichshafen:** Tue, Fri & Sat.

Shopping: The Saturday market on Adenauerplatz in Konstanz sells fresh regional specialities, including home-made sausages and cheese.

Major festivals: Konstanz: Bodenseefestival (Bodensee festival), May; Konstanzer Internationale Musiktage (international music days of Konstanz), mid-Jun & mid-Jul; Seenachtsfest (late night festival), Aug; **Mainau:** Gräfliches Inselfest (count's island festival), May; Mainau Melodie (music festival), Jul; **Meersburg:** Winzerfest (winegrowers'festival), Jul; Bodensee Weinfest (wine festival), Sep.

DAY TRIP OPTIONS

Despite the need for a ferry to access the northern shore, Konstanz is the best Bodensee base. A day can be spent exploring **historic** Konstanz and the nearby **garden island** of Mainau, with the option of **swimming** before heading back to Konstanz. The high-lights of the north shore can be covered in a day and include **prehistoric dwellings**, a **Baroque church**, the **fairy-tale town** of Meersburg and the intriguing **Zeppelin Museum** in Friedrichshafen. For full details, *see p241*.

VISITING KONSTANZ

Parking
The most convenient car park is just off the Fischmarkt on Münzgasse.

Tourist Information
Bahnhofplatz 43, 78462; 07531 133 030; www.konstanz.de/tourismus; Nov–Mar: closed Sat & Sun

WALKING AROUND KONSTANZ

The Rhine promenade begins at the Archäologisches Landesmuseum in Konstanz and joins a lakeside path that leads to the ferry terminal at Staad, and beyond to Mainau, from where boats return to Konstanz. This enables a one-way hike of around two hours, with a string of beaches to stop and swim along the way. Take bus No. 1 from the ferry terminal to get back to Konstanz.

WHERE TO STAY IN KONSTANZ

Barbarossa *moderate*
A central, mid-range guesthouse with several elegantly furnished rooms.
Obermarkt 8–12, 78462; 07531 12 89 90; www.barbarossa-hotel.com

Hotel-Sonenhof *moderate*
Located close to the Swiss border, this basic hotel stands in a residential street.
Otto-Raggenbass-Strasse 3, 78462; 07531 222 57; www.hotel-sonnenhof-konstanz.de

Schifff am See *moderate*
A good waterfront option, close to the car ferry, this hotel has a fine restaurant.
William-Graf-Platz 2, 78464; 07531 310 41; www.ringhotel-schiff.de

Steigenberger Inselhotel *expensive*
This five-star hotel is housed in a former 13th-century Dominican monastery.
Auf der Insel 1, 78462; 07531 12 50; www.steigenberger.com

❶ Konstanz
Baden-Württemberg; 78462

The largest settlement on the Bodensee, Konstanz (Constance) avoided being bombed during World War II as it straddled the border of neutral Switzerland. As a result, its old town remains intact and is a reminder of the time when the town thrived as an imperial Free City. It became famous between 1414 and 1418 when the Council of Konstanz met here to restructure the Catholic Church. The town's picturesque lakefront is dotted with promenades and statues.

A two-hour walking tour

From the car park turn left down Fischmarkt and cross the main road, Konzilstrasse, to arrive at the lakefront. Here stands the **Konzilgebäude** (council building) ①, a conference and concert hall that began life as a granary and warehouse. Its name suggests that it probably served as a venue for the Council of Konstanz. Also linked to that era is the Imperia, a 9-m (30-ft) rotating statue of a woman at the end of the pier. It represents a courtesan in an Honoré de Balzac novel, who used her charms to manipulate the Catholic clergy during the Council. Back near the beginning of the pier, another statue commemorates Count Graf Ferdinand von Zeppelin (1838–1917), a pioneer of airships who was born in Konstanz. From here the lakefront promenade passes a series of **old warehouses** ②,

which have been converted into a restaurant district beside a yacht harbour. At the end of the promenade lies the aquarium complex of **Sea Life** ③ *(open daily)*. Walk back and continue to the opposite end of the promenade, cross the Stadtgarten to the Insel, an island which was long occupied by a Dominican priory that is today the Steigenberger Inselhotel. Cross the Konzilstrasse and turn right to a pedestrian underpass that resurfaces on the banks of the Rhine beside the **Rheintorturm** ④, a 15th-century defensive tower with a conical roof. The bridge over the Rhine leads to the **Archäologisches Landesmuseum** ⑤ or State Archaeology Museum *(closed Mon)*, which is housed in a former convent. Many of its finds are Roman, including 2nd-century bronzes of lion heads and sea leopards. Returning over the Rhine bridge and along the pedestrian underpass, follow Konzilstrasse before turning right down **Münsterplatz** ⑥, which is surrounded by old townhouses from as far back as the 15th century. The nearby Münster *(open daily)* commands attention – built of local sandstone, the church has oak doors that are known for their carvings of New Testament scenes. Later additions include the Baroque high altar and the Neo-Gothic spires, which can be climbed for views. From here turn left down

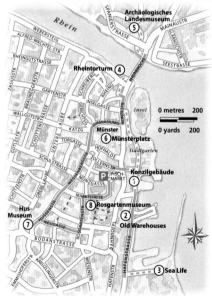

Wessenbergstrasse, which becomes Hussenstrasse, where the **Hus-Museum** ⑦ *(closed Mon)* occupies the house where the reformer Jan Hus stayed prior to his imprisonment. This museum documents his life and ideologies through displays. Turn left from here, then right down Neugasse and left along Rosengartenstrasse, which leads to the **Rosgartenmuseum** ⑧ *(closed Mon)*, the town's history museum. Its collection helps bring medieval Konstanz to life and includes the *Chronicle of the Council of Konstanz*, a richly illustrated book by Ulrich Richental, a local landowner. Turn right to Markstätte, the commercial hub of the town. Walk to the right along this and left down Brotlaube to return to the Fischmarkt car park.

🚗 *From the car park, turn left and left again on to Konzilstrasse. Follow signs for Reichenau/B33 turning left to cross causeway to the island. The museum is signposted with facilities for car park.*

② Reichenau
Baden-Württemberg; 78479
Even though the causeway to the island of Reichenau is only 2 km (1 mile) long, the island's sense of remoteness, together with a perfect climate, encouraged Benedictines to found a monastery here in AD 724. One of Europe's centres of learning in the 10th century, it was famous for its library and scriptorium, where monks would produce manuscripts. Copies can be purchased in the **Museum Reichenau** *(Apr–Oct: closed Mon; Jul & Aug: open daily, Nov–Mar: open Sat & Sun)*, which provides an introduction to the island's three surviving churches.

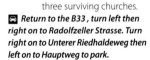
Pretty flowers in Reichenau

🚗 *Return to the B33, turn left then right on to Radolfzeller Strasse. Turn right on to Unterer Riedhaldeweg then left on to Hauptweg to park.*

③ Mainau
Baden-Württemberg; 78465
The thriving palm groves and flower gardens *(open daily)* of the island of Mainau are reminiscent of the Mediterranean but against an Alpine backdrop. The formal gardens here were planted in 1853 on the initiative of Grand Duke Friedrich I of Baden and his current descendant, the Swedish Count Bernadotte, continues the tradition. In summer, the Italian Rose Garden blooms, while in autumn, dahlias spring to life.

🚗 *Return to Unterer Riedhaldeweg and turn left on to it. In Staad, turn left on to the B33 to the dock for the Staad-Meersburg ferry.*

Above Vineyard with Bodensee in the background, Reichenau **Below** Cycling past the Benedictine monastery, Reichenau

EAT AND DRINK

KONSTANZ
Hafenhalle *inexpensive–moderate*
The largest of the harbourside restaurants, with a lively adjacent beer garden, Hafenhalle offers good local fish and game. During summer, stop here for Sunday breakfast and enjoy bands playing Dixieland jazz. *Hafenstrasse 10, 78462; 07531 211 26; www.hafenhalle.com*

Staader Fährhaus *moderate*
This stylish restaurant with a pleasant outdoor terrace beside the ferry terminal in Staad serves creative local fish dishes as well as a good selection of vegetarian food. *Fischerstrasse 30, 78464; 07531 361 67 63; www.staaderfaehrhaus.de*

Other options
Among the many cozy places to enjoy a drink in Konstanz are the **Brauhaus** *inexpensive (Johann Albrecht Konradigasse 2, 78462; 07531 250 45)*, a microbrewery with an array of beers and pub food. The **Niederburg Weinstube** *inexpensive (Niederburggasse 7, 78462; 07531 213 67)*, a rustic backstreet wine bar serves regional wines until midnight.

MAINAU
Schwedenschenke *moderate*
By day this restaurant is renowned for its Swedish meatballs, but by night it transforms into an elegant flagship of haute cuisine, offering a romantic setting in which to enjoy excellent fresh local perch and trout. *Insel Mainau, 78465; 07531 303 156; www.mainau.de*

Eat and Drink: inexpensive, under €20; moderate, €20–€40; expensive, over €40

Above left Vineyard topped by 18th-century Basilika Birnau Above right Meersburg harbour, an important ferry port Below Lakeside café in the town of Meersburg

WHERE TO STAY

MEERSBURG

Gasthof zum Bären *moderate*
A romantic 13th-century inn, with small rooms, enjoying a perfect location in the heart of the old town.
Marktplatz 11, 88709; 07532 432 20; www.baeren-meersburg.de

FRIEDRICHSHAFEN

Gasthof Rebstock *inexpensive*
Located a short walk northwest of the centre, this family-run guesthouse has clean and comfortable rooms. It has a beer garden and offers bike rentals.
Werastrasse 35, 88045; 07541 950 16 40; www.gasthof-rebstock-fn.de

Buchhorner Hof *moderate*
This traditional hotel provides bright rooms with Bodensee views and modern facilities.
Friedrichstrasse 33, 88045; 07541 20 50; www.buchhorn.de

Hotel Maier *moderate*
The elegant Hotel Maier is 5 km (3 miles) west of central Friedrichshafen. Rooms are of the bold boutique variety and have a satellite TV and other facilities.
Poststrasse 1–3, 88048; 07541 40 40; www.hotel-maier.de

LINDAU ISLAND

Bayerischer Hof *expensive*
This luxury hotel in a Neo-Classical building has a prime position on the lakefront beside the harbour. Its spacious rooms are decorated with 19th-century style furnishings. The hotel has fitness and spa facilities, which include a pool and a sauna.
Seepromenade, 88131; 08382 91 50; www.bayerischerhof-lindau.de

Where to Stay: inexpensive, under €70; moderate, €70–€150; expensive, over €150

④ Meersburg
Baden-Württemberg; 88709
Nestled between vineyards and with an atmospheric castle looming over its half-timbered pedestrian centre, Meersburg is fairy-tale Germany come to life. From its main street, Unterstadtstrasse, which runs parallel to the lakefront, Steigstrasse leads to the gates of the austere **Altes Schloss** *(open daily)*. With foundations laid by Merovingian King Dagobert I in AD 628, this is Germany's oldest castle. The Prince-Bishops of Konstanz, who used it as a summer residence

Annette von Droste-Hülshoff (1797–1848)

Perhaps the greatest-ever German female poet, Annette von Droste-Hülshoff spent her later years in the Altes Schloss in Meersburg. The dank castle was the perfect muse for her tortured Romantic verses, but it was probably the cause of her death too, for she died of pneumonia here in 1848. Her flowery Biedermeier quarters have been well preserved and remain intact.

from 1268, were inspired to build a cheerful-looking palace in the 18th century. Baroque architect Balthasar Neumann built the pastel-pink **Neues Schloss**, but this could only be enjoyed until secularization in 1802. It provides great views of the Bodensee.

🚗 *Turn left on to B31/Unteruhildingen then on to Meersburger Strasse. In Unteruhildingen, turn right on to main car park. Follow signs to the museum.*

⑤ The Pfahlbauten Museum
Baden-Württemberg; 88690
A reconstructed prehistoric hamlet, the Pfahlbauten Museum *(closed Dec–Feb)* features open-air re-creations of Stone and Iron Age dwellings based on archaeological remains found here. These suggest that structures were built by driving huge stakes into the ground. The interiors provide a glimpse of what life was like here between 4000 and 850 BC.

🚗 *Turn right out of the car park towards Oberuhldingen and turn left for Birnau; park in Basilika's car park.*

⑥ Basilika Birnau
Uhldingen-Mühlhofen; 88690
The Rococo **Basilika Birnau** *(open Wed & Sun)* was built between 1747–50 by a celebrity cast of designers, including architect Peter Thumb, sculptor Josef Anton Feuchtmayer, who crafted the altar, and fresco painter Gottfried Bernhard Göz. To the right of the main altar is a side altar dedicated to St Bernard of Clairvaux, whose words were said to be sweet as honey, as depicted by the statue of a cherub who sucks a finger he has dipped in a beehive.

🚗 *Return to Birnau and then take the B31 to Friedrichshafen.*

Turn right on to Eckenerstrasse and park at the car park, which is beside Seestrasse.

❼ Friedrichshafen

Baden-Württemberg; 88045
Although an industrial Bodensee town, Friedrichshafen also has a lakeside promenade. At its eastern end is the 22-m (72-ft) high Moleturm tower. To the west, the **Zeppelindenkmal**, an obelisk, and the **Zeppelinbrunnen** fountain, commemorate an aeronautical event. It was here on 2 July 1900 that Count Graf Ferdinand von Zeppelin launched his airships; within three decades, scheduled services began. A **Zeppelin Museum** *(May–Oct: open daily; Nov–Apr: closed Mon)* celebrates this achievement. Although the Zeppelin's popularity declined after the 1937 Hindenburg disaster, safer models have now been created. Trips on the Bodensee are run by the Deutsche-Zeppelin Reederei *(www.zeppelinflug.de)*.
🚗 *Turn right on to Eckenerstrasse, then get on to the B31 towards Lindau. Follow signs to Langenargen, then past Wasserburg to Lindau. Turn right on to Langenweg, then cross the roundabout onto Chelles-Allee to take the causeway*

to the island. At the roundabout, turn right on to Zwanzigerstrasse to park.

❽ Lindau Island

Bavaria; 88131
The old town of Lindau is crammed onto an island on the Bodensee. The Mediterranean feel here stems from the influence of Italian merchants who converted the town into a trading hub in the Middle Ages. The town's Marktplatz is graced by **Haus zum Cavazzen**, a Baroque patrician mansion with witty murals. It houses the Stadtmuseum *(Apr–Oct: closed Mon)*, which displays paintings with the family trees of the local nobility. From here, turn left along In der Grub to Schrannenplatz, where the 11th-century **Peterskirche** contains the only surviving frescoes of painter Hans Holbein the Elder. Beside it, the **Diebsturm**, or thieves' tower, once fortified the western limits of Lindau but later became a prison. Back on In der Grub, turn right on Schafgasse to Maximilianstrasse. Turn left along it and head to Reichsplatz, which leads to the old town hall, the Gothic **Altes Rathaus**. Its frescoes depict scenes from the imperial Diet held in 1496.

Left Elaborately arched pier, Friedrichshafen
Below left Cobbled street in the atmospheric town of Lindau

WINE TASTING

The region around Meersburg produces some fine wines. Taste wines at a vineyard such as the **Weingut Aufricht** *(Höhenweg 8, 88719; 07532 24 27; www.aufricht.de)*, just outside Meersburg en route to Friedrichshafen. Also visit the **Staatsweingut Meersburg** *(Seminarstrasse 60, 88719; 07532 446 744; www.staatsweingut-meersburg.de)* to the left of the Neues Schloss.

EAT AND DRINK

MEERSBURG
Winzerstube zum Becher *moderate*
A cozy traditional wine bar serving the finest regional food in town.
Höllgasse 4, 88709; 07532 90 09; closed Mon; www.zumbecher.de

Other options
The **Café Gross** *(Unterstadtstrasse 22, 88709; 07532 60 55)* is worth seeking out for wonderful home-made cakes.

FRIEDRICHSHAFEN
Lammgarten *inexpensive*
Located behind the yacht marina, this is good for Bodensee *Felchen* (whitefish).
Uferstrasse 27, 88045; 07541 246 08

Glückler *moderate*
A good place to enjoy *Zander*, Bodensee *Felchen* and trout.
Olgastrasse 23, 88045; 07541 221 64; www.weinstube-glueckler.de

Kurgarten *expensive*
A fine restaurant where Bodensee views accompany excellent international dishes.
Graf-Zeppelin-Haus, Olgastrasse 20, 88045; 07541 320 33

LINDAU ISLAND
Reutemann *moderate*
This harbourside eatery is known for its views and fine Bodensee fish.
Seepromenade, 88131; 08382 91 50

DAY TRIP OPTIONS

From Konstanz, all destinations on the northern shore of the Bodensee are best accessed using the ferry to Meersburg.

Coastal fun
Follow the walk around Konstanz ❶, then hop on a passenger ferry from its harbour to the gardens

of Mainau ❸. Pack swimming gear, as several beaches dot the way.

Frequent passenger ferries travel to Mainau from the dock at the southern end of the promenade in Konstanz.

Scenic north shore
Explore the prehistoric dwellings in the Pfahlbauten Museum ❺

before heading to the Basilika Birnau ❻ and the attractive castle in Meersburg ❹. Finally, visit the interesting Zeppelin Museum in Friedrichshafen ❼.

Turn right on to the B33 and then take the Staad-Meersburg ferry to Meersburg. Then follow the tour from there on.

Eat and Drink: inexpensive, under €20; moderate, €20–€40; expensive, over €40

The German Alps

Lindau to Schönau am Königsee

Highlights

- **"Mad" King Ludwig's vision**
  Visit the extravagant palaces of "Mad" King Ludwig, from fabulous Schloss Linderhof to Herrenchiemsee's extraordinary tribute to the Sun King

- **Faith and inspiration**
  Admire the remarkable works of art inspired by Bavaria's Catholicism, such as the beautiful Wieskirche

- **Natural splendour**
  Experience the region's scenic thrills, from crystal-clear mountain lakes to Germany's highest peak, the Zugspitze

- **Winter wonderland**
  Discover the Alps, the country's greatest winter sports playground

View of the breathtaking Alpine landscape around Berchtesgaden

The German Alps

From the balmy shores of Lake Constance (Bodensee) in the west to the gates of Salzburg in the east, the German Alps (Bayerische Alpen) offer some of the country's most thrilling landscapes. Through high-altitude passes and along Alpine lakeshores, this consistently beautiful route meanders deep into the mountains. The stunning scenery it passes is just one of its attractions. Regarded as Germany's winter playground, the region offers a wealth of activities, from high-altitude skiing at Garmisch-Partenkirchen to the more usual winter sports at Bayrischzell or Reit im Winkl; in summer, it is a paradise for walkers and cyclists. There are cultural highlights, too, such as the charming optical illusions of the *Lüftmalerei* paintings, the giddy excesses of "Mad" King Ludwig's palaces and the sumptuous interiors of Baroque and Rococo churches. Food lovers will enjoy the simple, hearty food, from Allgäu cheese and Swabian noodles to fresh fish and game in season.

KEY

⬛ Drive route

0 kilometres 15

0 miles 15

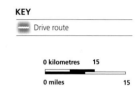

ACTIVITIES

Enjoy skiing on the Zugspitze's high-altitude pistes at Garmisch-Partenkirchen, with superb views as far as Italy and Switzerland

Ascend a mountain in a summer cable car at Walchensee to enjoy the fresh air, exhilarating walks and breathtaking views

Admire the falconry displays at Aschau im Chiemgau's Schloss Hohenaschau

Take a yachting course on the beautiful blue Chiemsee

Slide down into Berchtesgaden's salt mine

Above Pretty geraniums outside a guesthouse in Reit im Winkl, *see p252* **Right** Bavaria's largest lake, Chiemsee, a paradise for water sports enthusiasts, *see p252*

Above Beautiful scenery near Garmisch, the best-known resort town in the Bavarian Alps, *see p250*

PLAN YOUR DRIVE

Start/finish: Lindau to Schönau am Königsee.

Number of days: 5 days, allowing half a day to explore Lindau.

Distance: 461 km (286 miles).

Road conditions: Roads are well surfaced, but at times are steep and twisting. Ice and snow may be a problem in winter. There are occasional signposted roads with brown "Deutsche Alpenstrasse" signs.

When to go: The best weather is from May to October, while December to Easter is ideal for winter sports.

Opening times: Museums often close on Mondays, while shops remain closed on Sundays.

Major festivals: Immenstadt: Viehscheid (the departure of the cows), Sep; **Oberammergau**: Oberammergauer Passionsspiele (passion play), May–Oct, every ten years, next in 2020.

DAY TRIP OPTIONS

The German Alps can be explored in a series of day trips. Lindau or Bad Hindelang are the best bases to explore the Allgäu, while Füssen and Oberammergau are ideal for experiencing the richest concentration of **churches** and **palaces**. For **stunning lake** and **mountain scenery**, Tegernsee or Bad Tolz are excellent bases, while the **salt mining history** and **Nazi associations** of Berchtesgadener Land are easily explored from Berchtesgaden or Bad Reichenhall. For full details, *see p253*.

Above Cobbled street lined with houses in the town of Lindau

VISITING LINDAU

Parking
There is a paid car park (P5) on the island across the railway from the tourist office and Altstadt. Cross the causeway and follow signs to reach it.

Tourist Information
Alfred Nobel Platz 1, 88131; 08382 260 030; www.lindau.de; Apr–Oct: open daily; Nov–Mar: open Mon–Fri

WHERE TO STAY

LINDAU

Helvetia *expensive*
This harbourside four-star hotel offers themed suites and a spa. It also has its own yacht and boats can be hired.
Seepromenade 3, 88131; 08382 91 30; www.hotel-helvetia.com

Hotel Bad Schachen *expensive*
This classic, grand old hotel with lovely views offers an outdoor pool by the lake and a spa with an indoor pool.
Bad Schachen 1, 88131; 08382 29 80; www.badschachen.de; open Apr–Oct

IMMENSTADT

Gasthof Drei König *inexpensive*
A 200-year-old Gasthof (guesthouse) in the centre of Immenstadt offering double rooms with en suite showers.
Marienplatz 11, 87509; 08323 86 28; www.drei-koenig.de

BAD HINDELANG

Romantik Hotel Die Sonne *moderate*
Located in the centre of the town, this hotel's main building is 400 years old. Rooms have en suite bath or shower and there is an indoor pool and sauna.
Marktstrasse 15, 87541; 08324 89 70; www.sonne-hindelang.de

❶ Lindau
Bavaria; 88131

Occupying an island off the north shore of Lake Constance, the lake resort of Lindau prospered in the Middle Ages owing to its trade links with Italy across the Alps. The town's architectural legacy is a reminder of its early prosperity, and with its café-lined waterfront and breathtaking backdrop of the snow-capped Alps, Lindau is a delight to visit.

A two-hour walking tour

Park in the car park and cross the footbridge over the railway tracks to the main railway station. Continue past the station to the **Hafen** ①, or harbour, which is dominated by a mid-19th-century lighthouse and the statue of the Bavarian Lion, the symbol of Lindau. Pause here for cake or ice cream or simply to admire the lovely panorama of the Austrian and Swiss Alps. On the landward side of the harbour is the 13th-century **Mangturm** ②, a former lighthouse whose campanile-like architecture is a reminder of the town's Italian links. Continue along the waterfront, bearing left into Reichsplatz, which features the Lindavia Fountain and the step-gabled old town hall, the **Altes Rathaus** ③. Built between 1422 and 1436, it served as the venue of an imperial Diet or Reichstag in 1496. Turn right along Ludwigstrasse, at the

Epitaph of Andreas Bertsch, Stadtmuseum

end of which lies the town's **Theater** ④, housed in a 700-year-old former church of the Minorite order. Continue past it into Fischergasse, where a half-timbered passageway between No. 19 and No. 21 leads to the **Gerberschanze** ⑤, a fragment of the old town wall. Return to Fischergasse, turn right to reach the **Heidenmauer** ⑥, another surviving part of the town wall. Turn left into Schmiedgasse to the Marktplatz, which is dominated by two churches – the Protestant parish **Kirche von St Stephan** ⑦, with an interior dating from 1783 and the Catholic church of **Unserer Lieben Frau** ⑧, whose interior is designed in a florid southern German style. Facing the two churches across the square is the **Haus zum Cavazzen** ⑨, a Baroque mansion dating from 1730. Its interior houses the Stadtmuseum *(Apr–Oct: closed Mon)*. From the Marktplatz,

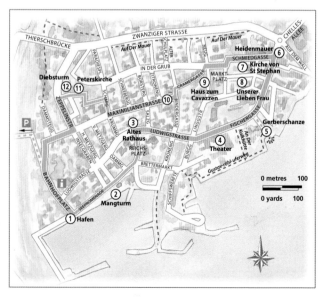

bear left along Cramergasse to **Maximilianstrasse** ⑩, Lindau's main street, lined with old patrician houses. Turn right into Schafgasse and left to the **Peterskirche** ⑪, an ancient church which now serves as the town's war memorial today. The interior contains the only known frescoes by Hans Holbein the Elder (c. 1460–1524). Next to it is the **Diebsturm** ⑫, or Thief's Tower, whose fairy-tale appearance belies its historical role as a jail. Take Zeppelinstrasse, turn right to return to the car park.

🚗 **Return to the mainland across the causeway. At the landward end, bear right. Follow signs for A96, leave the roundabout and get on to the B12. After Lindau, turn right on to the B31, which becomes the B308 to continue to Immenstadt. Park in the signposted P2 Zentrum or P4 Bahnhof.**

❷ Immenstadt

Bavaria; 87509

To the east of Immenstadt town lies the **Grosse Alpsee**, the Allgäu's largest natural lake. Popular in summer for water sports, visitors can hire pedal boats, rowing boats, sailing dinghies or try windsurfing (www.immenstadt. de) here. To the west lies Germany's longest summer toboggan run, the **Alpsee Bergwelt Sommerrodelbahn** (Apr–Nov: open daily; Dec–Mar: open Fri–Sun; www.alpsee-bergwelt.de).

The Viehscheid

Immenstadt's famous cheese is made with the milk produced by cows that graze the Alpine meadows above the town in summer. At the end of the season, in September, some 1,000 cows are brought down during the festival known as the Viehscheid. The herdsmen wear traditional folk dress, including *Lederhosen*.

🚗 **Continue along Sonthofener Strasse. Follow the B19/B308 to Sonthofen where the B308 leads to Bad Hindelang. Stay on the B308 to Reute. Park on the left next to the B308.**

❸ Bad Hindelang

Bavaria; 87541

This Alpine paradise by the Austrian border is made up of scattered settlements. The meadows here are among the richest in Germany for wild flowers, and include some 40 species of orchid. The town provides opportunities in summer for hiking and rock climbing. More than 60 hiking trails (tourist office; Am Bauernmarkt 1; 08324 89 20) are available here. Visitors can try the Salewa Klettersteig climbing course, which has, since 2008, ascended the 1,876-m (6,155-ft) Iseler peak (mountain guides' office; 08324 95 36 50). In winter, the ski resort **Oberjoch**, which lies to the east, has a reliable snow record.

🚗 **Continue on the B308/Jochstrasse to Oberjoch, follow the B310 and turn right on to the B309 to Nesselwang.**

Logo of an Allgäu cheese factory, Immenstadt

EAT AND DRINK

LINDAU

Ratsstuben *moderate*
Fresh seasonal produce, from Allgäu cheese to fish from the lake, paired with excellent Italian wine, is served at this simple but stylish hotel restaurant.
Ludwigstrasse 7, 88131; 08382 66 26; www.ratsstuben.li; closed Sun, Mon & Jan–Feb

Bayerischer Hof *expensive*
Local produce is cooked with an Italian flair at this plush hotel's dining room, which offers dishes such as carpaccio of Allgäu veal.
Bahnhofsplatz 2, 88131; 08382 91 50; www.bayerischerhof-lindau.de

IMMENSTADT

Gasthof Drei König *moderate*
There is a strong regional feel to the menu at this restaurant in the centre of Immenstadt, serving *Maultaschen* (Swabian ravioli) and *Kässpatzen* (noodles with Allgäu mountain cheese) alongside meat and fish options.
Marienplatz 11, 87509; 08323 86 28; www.drei-koenig.de

BAD HINDELANG

Chesa Schneider *moderate*
In a suitably rustic, pine-clad setting, the Romantik Hotel Die Sonne's restaurant serves an authentic version of Allgäu cooking. Home-made noodles, local cheese and fresh fish are served alongside the more sophisticated likes of venison *Schnitzel* (pork fillet).
Marktstrasse 15, 87541; 08324 89 70; www.sonne-hindelang.de

Right Idyllic pastures along the way to Füssen **Below left** *Lüftmalerei*, traditional Bavarian wall paintings, Oberammergau **Below right** Gilded statues and pool in the gardens in front of Schloss Linderhof

WHERE TO STAY

NESSELWANG

Brauerei-Gasthof Hotel Post
moderate
This family-run hotel opposite Nesselwang's parish church has 23 rooms with en suite baths or showers. It also has an attractive wood-panelled restaurant and its own brewery.
Hauptstrasse 25, 87484; 08361 309 10; www.hotel-post-nesselwang.de

FÜSSEN

Hotel Kurcafé *moderate–expensive*
This established hotel in the centre of Füssen offers well-equipped doubles and deluxe rooms with marble bathrooms and air conditioning. There is also a café and restaurant.
Prinzregentenplatz, 87629; 08362 930 180; www.kurcafe.com

OBERAMMERGAU

Alte Post *moderate*
A lovely old inn dating back to the early 17th century. Rooms have en suite baths or showers, LCD TV and Internet.
Dorfstrasse 19, 82487; 08822 91 00; www.altepost.com

ETTAL

Klosterhotel Ludwig der Bayer
moderate
Located opposite Ettal's magnificent abbey, this hotel is named after the abbey's founder. Rooms, suites and apartments are tastefully decorated; some have balconies. Facilities include an indoor pool, table tennis room and a bowling alley.
Kaiser Ludwig Platz, 82488; 08822 91 50; www.ludwig-der-bayer.de

④ Nesselwang
Bavaria; 87484

Set amid meadows at the foot of the 1,575-m (5,167-ft) Alpspitze, the village of Nesselwang is a centre for activity holidays, such as mountain biking and canyoning in summer and skiing in winter *(tourist office; Lindenstrasse 16, 08361 92 30 40)*. In 2003, Nesselwang opened Bavaria's first **Nordic Walking Park**, which is part of a 420-km (261-mile) network stretching into neighbouring districts. In winter, the **Alpspitzbahn** gondola serves the Alpspitze's mostly blue ski runs, which are generally for beginners. There's even floodlit evening skiing on the lower slopes. The village clusters around the imposing church of **St Andreas**, which was rebuilt in a Neo-Baroque style between 1904 and 1906 after falling into disrepair.

🚗 *Continue along the B309/Fussener Strasse, which becomes the B310/Pfronter Strasse just before Pfronten. Continue on the B310 to Füssen. Park in one of the signposted underground car parks close to the tourist office and the old town.*

⑤ Füssen
Bavaria; 87629

The main urban centre for southeastern Allgäu, Füssen is a charming town with an enchanting setting of lakes and mountains. The old town, or Altstadt, is dominated by the **Hohe Schloss**, a former summer palace of Augsburg's bishops, which houses two **art galleries** *(Apr–Oct: closed Mon; Nov–Mar: open Fri–Sun)*. Also worth visiting are the former Benedictine monastery of **Kloster St Mang** and the **Heilig Geist Spitalkirche**, or the Church of the Holy Ghost.

🚗 *Continue along Sebastianstrasse then take the B17 to Steingaden.*

> **Schloss Neuschwanstein**
>
> A visit to "Mad" King Ludwig II's *(see p207)* castle of Neuschwanstein *(open daily)* is worth a detour off the Alpenstrasse route. Perched on a crag above Hohenschwangau, the castle was inspired by Wagner's operas and only completed in 1884. To reach Hohenschwangau look out for the brown "Königsschlösser" signs along the B17.

Left House decorated with *Lüftmalerei*, Oberammergau **Below** Exterior of the pilgrimage church of Wieskirche

---

EAT AND DRINK

NESSELWANG

Brauerei-Gasthof Hotel Post
moderate
With its traditional tiled oven and wood-panelled ceiling, the Hotel Post's dining room is an attractive setting for hearty meals. Begin with pork with onions and caraway followed by beer goulash or *Schnitzel* (pork fillet) in brewer's malt and breadcrumbs.
Hauptstrasse 25, 87484; 08361 309 10; www.hotel-post-nesselwang.de

FÜSSEN

Gasthof zum Schwanen
inexpensive–moderate
This restaurant serves *Schnitzel* alongside regional specialities from Swabia and the Allgäu, including *Maultaschen* (Swabian ravioli) with Emmenthal and salad and *Kässpatzen* (cheese-topped noodles) with roast onion and salad.
Brotmarkt 4, 87629; 08362 61 74; closed Mon

OBERAMMERGAU

St Benoît *expensive*
Oberammergau's most elegant hotel, Maximilian, is the setting for the Michelin-starred St Benoît, a renowned gourmet restaurant. The cooking incorporates French, Mediterranean and Asian influences. The hotel has its own microbrewery, Maxbräu, which serves refined Bavarian food.
Hotel Maximilian, Ettaler Strasse 5, 82487; 08822 94 87 40; www.stbenoit. de; open Sun & Mon

---

In Steingaden turn right and at the next junction turn right again to Wies/ Wieskirche. There is paid parking close to the church.

⑥ Wieskirche

Bavaria; 86989
About 5 km (3 miles) from Steingaden, in the district of Pfaffenwinkel (priest's corner), lies the dazzling Rococo Wieskirche, a UNESCO World Heritage Site. Completed in 1754 by German architect Dominikus Zimmermann, this spectacular church is a masterpiece of 18th-century southern German architecture.

🚗 *Return to last junction, head east and pass Schwaig. Turn right on to the B23 for Oberammergau. There is free parking near the tourist office.*

Oberammergau's Passion Play
Performed in the last year of each decade – the next is due in 2020 – the Passion Play has its origins in a promise made by the villagers in 1633 during the Thirty Years' War. They pledged to perform a play about the life of Christ if God would spare them from the plague that was ravaging the surrounding district. The play is still performed by locals on an open-air stage in the town. During the years when the play is not being performed, it is still possible to tour the Passionstheater.

⑦ Oberammergau

Bavaria; 82487
Renowned worldwide for its Passion Play, Oberammergau is also worth a visit for its lovely setting in the Ammergau Alps, its strong tradition of handicrafts and woodcarving, and its southern German charm. The town's houses are decorated with some of the best *Lüftmalerei* work

in Bavaria, most notably on the 18th-century **Pilatushaus** *(open daily)* whose astonishing frescoes are the work of Franz Seraph Zwink (1748–92).

🚗 *Continue on the B23 to Ettal. There is free parking in front of Kloster Ettal.*

⑧ Ettal

Bavaria; 82488
Ettal, about 4 km (3 miles) from Oberammergau, was founded by Ludwig IV of Bavaria. It is best known for the Benedictine monastery of **Kloster Ettal**, one of the most grand of Bavaria's Baroque abbeys. The domed abbey church *(open daily)* assumed its present form between 1744 and 1753, when architect Joseph Schmuzer was commissioned to complete the fire-damaged church. The interior is deco-rated with Rococo stuccowork.

🚗 *Turn left from the western end of Ettal. Get on to Linderhof Strasse to Linderhof. Follow signs to the car park.*

⑨ Schloss Linderhof

Bavaria; 82488
In the early 1850s, Linderhof was bought by the Bavarian King Maximilian II. This mountain district appealed to his young heir, who later went on to become "Mad" King Ludwig and was responsible for Schloss Linderhof *(open daily)*. Set in terraced gardens, between Ettal and the Austrian border, Schloss Linderhof was originally built by Ludwig II as a hunting lodge for his father. It was transformed into its current Neo-Rococo appearance by Georg Dollmann between 1870 and 1872.

🚗 *Return to Ettal, turn right along the B23 then right at Oberau to get on the B2 for Garmisch-Partenkirchen. Look out for signposted car parks in Garmisch and in Partenkirchen.*

Right Yacht sailing on the Walchensee **Far right** Isar river, Bad Tölz **Below right** Bad Tölz's Marktstrasse, lined with houses with painted façades

ACTIVITIES AROUND TEGERNSEE

Mountain biking is a popular activity in Tegernsee (*www.tegernsee.com*). Every summer the town has a mountain biking festival (*www.mtb-festival.de*). The Gleitschirmschule Tegernsee offers tandem jumps and paragliding courses (*Tegernseerstrasse 88, 83700 Reitrain; 08022 25 56; www.paragliding-tegernsee.de*).

VISITING GARMISCH-PARTENKIRCHEN

Parking
The paid car park at the Kongresshaus is the most central in Garmisch.

Tourist Information
Richard Strauss Platz 2, 82467; 08821 18 07 00; www.gapa.de; mid-May–late Oct, mid-Dec–mid-Jan: open daily

WHERE TO STAY

GARMISCH-PARTENKIRCHEN

Atlas Grand Hotel *moderate*
Partenkirchen's oldest hotel is located on its main street. Rooms have en suite baths or showers.
Ludwigstrasse 49, 82467; 08821 936 30; www.atlas-grandhotel.com

Reindl's Partenkirchner Hof *expensive*
This five-star, traditional hotel has a welcoming rustic ambience.
Bahnhofstrasse 15, 82467; 08821 94 38 70; www.reindls.de

WALCHENSEE

Einsiedl *moderate*
A simple hotel with a beer garden and boats for hire nearby. Wi-Fi is available.
Walchensee, 82432; 08858 90 10; www.hotelamwalchensee.de

BAD TÖLZ

Posthotel Kolberbräu *moderate*
This family-run former coaching inn has 35 tastefully decorated rooms.
Marktstrasse 29, 83646; 08041 768 80; www.kolberbraeu.de

TEGERNSEE

Hotel Bayern *expensive*
Hotel Bayern's sleek and elegant rooms range in size and style. There is also an on-site spa.
Neureuthstrasse 23, 83684; 08022 18 20; www.dastegernsee.de

Where to Stay: inexpensive, under €70; moderate, €70–€150; expensive, over €150

⑩ Garmisch-Partenkirchen
Bavaria; 82467

Facing each other across the narrow Partnacher stream in the shadow of Germany's highest mountain, the 2,962-m (9,718-ft) **Zugspitze**, the twin towns of Garmisch and Partenkirchen together comprise Germany's best-known ski resort. The towns were amalgamated at the time of the 1936 Winter Olympics but still have quite distinct characters: Garmisch is cosmopolitan, while Partenkirchen preserves its old-fashioned Alpine charm. In Partenkirchen, composer **Richard Strauss's villa** (*closed Sat & Sun*) is now a small museum.

🚗 *Continue along the B2 to Krün, turn left on to the B11 for Walchensee. Park at signposted car parks along the route.*

Winter Sports
The towering Zugspitze provides a spectacular backdrop for Garmisch-Partenkirchen's pistes, which include Germany's only glacier skiing and the fearsome Kandahar Run, used for World Championship downhill races. The Zugspitze offers 22 km (14 miles) of high-altitude skiing at a height of almost 3,000 m (9,843 ft); for beginners, runs are graded blue (*www.zugspitze.de*). Due to the altitude of its pistes, the ski season here is a long one, beginning in November and continuing through to May.

⑪ Walchensee
Bavaria; 82432

Surrounded by impressive mountains, Walchensee lies 802 m (2,631 ft) above sea level and is among Bavaria's most beautiful lakes. Despite its scenic grandeur, it remains relatively undiscovered. In summer the lake offers everything from angling and swimming to windsurfing and sailing. Enjoy an excursion in the Herzogstandbahn cable car (*Am Tanneck 6, 82432; open daily*), which goes from the north end of Walchensee village to the top of the 1,731-m (5,679-ft) **Herzogstand** offering breathtaking panoramas of the surrounding landscape.

🚗 *Take the B11 to Kochel am See. Park on signposted car parks at the lake, city or museum.*

⑫ Kochel am See
Bavaria; 82431

To the north of Walchensee lies Kochel am See. The town is closely associated with artist Franz Marc (1880–1916), who, in the years before World War I, was a leading member of the Munich-based Blauer Reiter group of Expressionist painters. A villa overlooking the lake now houses the **Franz Marc Museum** (*closed Mon*), which displays about 200 of the artist's works.

🚗 *Continue along the B11 to Benediktbeuern. The abbey is well signposted and provides parking space.*

⑬ Benediktbeuern
Bavaria; 83671

Visible from a distance, the Bavarian onion-domed towers of the basilica of Benediktbeuern rise above an abbey complex of considerable size

and splendour. Founded around AD 725, the Benedictine abbey was rebuilt in Baroque style after 1669 and secularized in 1803; it is now home to the Salesians Don Boscos, a Roman Catholic order.

🚗 *Continue along the B11, bypassing Brichl and turn right on to the B472 for Bad Tölz. Park in one of the riverside car parks or on-street in the spa quarter (Kurzone) close to the tourist office.*

⑭ Bad Tölz

Bavaria; 83646

The town of Bad Tölz straddles the Isar river, with a leafy spa quarter on the west bank facing an attractive, hilly old town. The main street, **Marktstrasse**, owes its present appearance to the Munich architect Gabriel von Seidl, who in the early 20th century re-emphasized the street's Alpine character. To the south of Marktstrasse is the **Gries**, a quaint artisans' quarter.

🚗 *Take the B13/Lenggrieser Strasse. At Sylvensteinsee reservoir turn left on to the B307 and continue to Tegernsee. Park at signposted car park in Strandbad and Ortsmitte.*

⑮ Tegernsee

Bavaria; 83684

Crystal-clear Tegernsee is framed by wooded hills and mountains rising from its southern shore towards the Austrian border. It is among the most chic of Bavaria's mountain lakes, with a sprinkling of resorts along its shores, and has a reputation as an upmarket destination. The lake acts as a scenic backdrop to a range of activities, from mountain biking to paragliding.

🚗 *Take the B307/ Münchner Strasse. At Am See, turn right to Hausham then right again to the level crossing. Turn right on to the B307 for Schliersee. Park along the route on signposted car parks.*

⑯ Schliersee

Bavaria; 83727

Modest in size and appearance in comparison to Tegernsee, Schliersee shares the same lovely mountain backdrop. The lakefront is home to a modern spa complex, **Monte Mare** *(open daily)*, complete with a pool, sauna and whirlpool. Hourly cruises *(May–Sep: open daily)*, depart from the jetty in front of the spa complex for the island of Wörth in the centre of the lake.

🚗 *Continue along the B307 to Bayrischzell. For parking follow signs to Ortsmitte.*

⑰ Bayrischzell

Bavaria; 83735

Nestled at the foot of the 1,838-m (6,030-ft) **Wendelstein** is the rustic village of Bayrischzell. Wendelstein can be ascended by cable car *(open daily; departures hourly; www.wendel steinbahn.de)* from Osterhofen just west of the village, or by old-fashioned cog railway from Brannenburg in the northeast. To the east of the village lies the **Sudelfeld**, Germany's largest contiguous ski complex. It has 21 lifts and 31 km (19 miles) of red (intermediate) and blue (easy) pistes, though there are some black (advanced) runs too *(www.sudelfeld.de)*.

🚗 *Continue on the B307/Alpenstrasse and pass Oberaudorf to Niederaudorf. Turn left to Brannenberg along Rosenheimer Strasse. At Brannenberg turn right on to Nussdorfer Strasse to Neubeuern. Turn right to Frasdorf and get on to the Rosenheimer Strasse to reach Aschau im Chiemgau. Park at the car park near the tourist office.*

Above Diners at a monastery-café in Tegernsee **Below left** Boating on the Tegernsee **Below right** Lush pasture land in Bayrischzell

VISITING BAD TÖLZ

Parking
Park in one of the car parks on the riverside or on-street in the area around the tourist information office.

Tourist Information
Max Höfler Platz 1, 8346; 08041 786 70; www.bad-toelz.de; open Mon–Sat

EAT AND DRINK

BENEDIKTBEUERN

Der Klosterwirt *moderate*
Robust Bavarian fare characterizes the cooking at the Klosterwirt, which is located within the abbey complex.
Zeiler Weg 2, 83671; 08857 94 07; www.klosterwirt.de

BAD TÖLZ

Wirtshaus zum Starnbräu *moderate*
Beers from Munich's Hofbräuhaus brewery accompany the traditional Bavarian fare at the Starnbräu.
Marktstrasse 4, 83646; 08041 440 0030; www.starnbraeu.de

Right Twin-towered church in Aschau im Chiemgau **Below** View of picturesque Ruhpolding

WHERE TO STAY

ASCHAU IM CHIEMGAU

Residenz Heinz Winkler *expensive*
This five-star hotel occupies a historic inn; the main building dates back to 1405. Rooms and suites are furnished in traditional style, while the hotel's restaurant is one of Germany's best-known gourmet restaurants. There are spa facilities.
Kirchplatz 1, 83229; 08052 179 90; www.residenz-heinz-winkler.de

REIT IM WINKL

Unterwirt *expensive*
An old family-run hotel, Unterwirt exudes Alpine character, from its wooden ceilings to the traditional tiled ovens and country-style furnishings. There's a garden with an outdoor pool, a spa and a sauna. The menu of the hotel's restaurant offers *Leberkäse* (a form of meatloaf) and speciality meat served from its own butchery.
Kirchplatz 2, 83242; 08640 80 10; www.unterwirt.de

RUHPOLDING

Steinberger Hof
inexpensive–moderate
Nestled into the hillside, this traditional Alpine hotel has balconies with lovely views over the town. Some of the suites come equipped with a kitchen. The host family offers free skiing lessons in winter.
Steinberg 2, 83324; 08663 59 24; www.steinbergerhof.de

BERCHTESGADEN

Vier Jahreszeiten *moderate*
This family-run three-star hotel with mountain panoramas sits on the hillside close to the centre of town. Rooms are decorated in traditional style and have en suite bath or shower; many have balconies or mountain views.
Maximilianstrasse 20, 83471; 08652 95 20; www.hotel-vierjahreszeiten-berchtesgaden.de

⑱ Aschau im Chiemgau
Bavaria; 83229
This village is dominated by **Schloss Hohenaschau** *(guided tours: May–Oct: Tue–Fri, Sun & public hols)*, an 800-year old fortress remodelled during the Renaissance. It now houses the **Priental Museum**, which explores the history of the iron industry in the Prien Valley and is the venue for falconry displays *(open Tue–Fri & public hols)*. Nearby, the **Kampenwandbahn** gondola ascends the 1,669-m (5,476-ft) mountain, giving access to ski runs in winter and hiking trails in summer *(tourist office; Kampenwandstrasse 38; 08052 90 49 37)*.

🚗 *Take Bernauer Strasse. At Bernau, turn left for the B305. Cross the A8 and take Priener Strasse to the nearest town, Prien. Park at signposted car park in the town or at the harbour.*

⑲ Chiemsee
Bavaria; 83209
The blue waters of Bavaria's largest lake, the Chiemsee, are a paradise for yachtsmen in the summer months *(Chiemsee Yachtschule; 08051 17 40; www.dhh.de)*. Take a ferry to the lake's islands, **Herreninsel** and **Fraueninsel**. The former is the site of the **Schloss Herrenchiemsee** *(open daily)*, which was King Ludwig II's attempt to re-create Versailles. The castle is modelled after the original museum and is devoted to the life of Ludwig II.

🚗 *From Prien, return to Bernau. Continue on the B305 to Reit im Winkl. Follow signs to a car park.*

⑳ Reit im Winkl
Bavaria; 83242
Situated in a broad valley surrounded by mountains, Reit im Winkl is a charming Alpine town with chalet-style architecture and one of the best snow records of any German ski resort. Skiing was introduced to the area in the 19th century by foresters and Norwegian students; the **Skimuseum** *(open Tue, Wed & Fri)* documents the story in detail.

🚗 *Take the B305/Weitseestrasse to Waich, turn left on to Seehauserstrasse for Ruhpolding. In Ruhpolding, follow the car park routing system.*

㉑ Ruhpolding
Bavaria; 83324
Ruhpolding is the perfect spot to ascend in a cable car to the 1,672-m (5,485-ft) **Rauschberg**, which offers a panorama of 600 Alpine peaks. The town boasts 160 km (99 miles) of cross-country ski runs. South of the town is the **Holzknechtmuseum** *(May–Oct: closed Mon; Jan–Mar: open Wed; public hols)* with exhibits relating to the area's woodwork tradition.

🚗 *Return to the B305, turn left to Schneitzelreuth then left again on to the B21 for Bad Reichenhall. Park at signposted car parks in the town or at Alte Saline.*

㉒ Bad Reichenhall
Bavaria; 83435
A conservative German spa town, Bad Reichenhall is somewhat medicinal. The main focus of the town is the Kurpark, fringed by buildings such as the **Gradierhaus**, an outdoor saline inhaler originally intended to reproduce the health benefits of sea air. On the south side of the town is the former royal salt works, the **Alte Saline** *(May–Oct: open daily; Nov–Apr: open Tue–Fri & lst Sun;*

www.alte-saline-bad-reichenhall.de), with brine springs and a tunnel system.
🚗 *Return on the B21 to Unterjettenberg, turn left on to the B305 for Berchtesgaden. Park in the car park at Kur- und Kongresshaus.*

㉓ Berchtesgaden
Bavaria; 83471
Berchtesgaden was once an independent Prince-Bishopric living off the proceeds of the **Salzbergwerk**, or salt mine *(Bergwerkstrasse 83, 83471; open daily; www.salzzeitreise.de)*. The village has the atmosphere of a miniature capital city, notably on **Schlossplatz**, which is dominated by the Stiftskirche and the façade of the **Königliches Schloss** *(mid-May–mid-Oct: open Sun–Fri; mid-Oct–mid-May: open Mon–Fri)*, a former bishops' palace that now belongs to the Bavarian royal family, the Wittelsbachs.
🚗 *Continue on the Salzbergstrasse, up the steep ascent to Obersalzberg. Park at the Dokumentation Obersalzberg.*

㉔ Obersalzberg
Bavaria; 83471
A favourite holiday retreat of high-ranking Nazis, the mountain village of Obersalzberg is home to the **Dokumentation Obersalzberg** *(closed Mon)*. This museum occupies the site of Adolf Hitler's former mountain home and documents the rise, fall

and crimes of the Nazis. It ends with a visit to the warren of tunnels in which the Nazis planned to make their last stand. In summer, buses depart from the adjacent terminal for the ascent to the **Kehlsteinhaus**, or Eagle's Nest, the dictator's mountain-top tea room.
🚗 *Return to Berchtesgaden. Turn left on to the B305, then left at the round-about on to the B20 to Schönau am Königsee. Park away from the lake and complete the journey on foot.*

㉕ Schönau am Königsee
Bavaria; 83471
Around 4 km (2 miles) south of Berchtesgaden lies Schönau am Königsee, which is home to the 8-km (5-mile) long fjord-like lake, **Königsee**. The lake lies in the shadow of the 2,713-m (8,901-ft) **Watzmann** at the eastern limit of the Deutsche Alpen-strasse. The chapel of **St Bartholomä**, which stands at the foot of the moun-tain, can only be reached by boat. Tour boats *(daily, except 24 Dec)* depart from the village of Schönau for the chapel.

Above left Berchtesgaden, with the Alps in the background **Above top right** Chalet and signposts in Ruhpolding **Above right** River boat on Bavaria's largest lake, the Chiemsee **Centre left** Kehlsteinhaus or Eagle's nest, Obersalzberg

---

DAY TRIP OPTIONS
The region can be explored in a series of day trips.

Architectural haven
Visit the church of Wieskirche ❻, then head to Oberammergau ❼ to admire the façade paintings. Stop at Ettal ❽ to see the Baroque abbey.

From Wieskirche, follow directions to
Oberammergau, take the B23 to Ettal.

Lakes and mountains
Head to one of Bavaria's most beautiful lakes, the Walchensee ⓫, then stop by the Kochel am See ⓬. Next, visit the Tegernsee ⓯ and its pretty neighbour, Schliersee ⓰.

Follow the B11 to Kochel am See. Go past Benediktbeuern to the B472 to
Bad Tölz. Take the B13 and B307 to Tegernsee. Follow directions to Schliersee.

Historical associations
Learn about Berchtesgaden's ㉓ salt mining history, then visit the Nazi's holiday retreat at Obersalzberg ㉔.

Follow Salzbergstrasse from Berchtesgaden to the Dokumentation Obersalzberg.

Eat and Drink: inexpensive, under €20; moderate, €20–€40; expensive, over €40

General Index

Acknowledgments

Dorling Kindersley would like to thank the many people whose help and assistance contributed to the preparation of this book.

Contributors
Jürgen Scheunemann was born and raised in rural northern Germany and now lives in Berlin. A freelance journalist, he has also written and translated several travel guides on Asia, the US, Berlin and Germany.

James Stewart is a travel journalist and guidebook author for over 10 years. He writes for several publications, including *The Times*, *Guardian* and *Wanderlust*. He is the author of *Rough Guide to Tasmania* and co-author of *Rough Guide to Germany*. He has also contributed to *Rough Guide Make the Most of Your Time on Earth* and *Rough Guide Clean Breaks*.

Neville Walker is a travel writer and lives in London and Austria. He has written and updated guidebooks to Provence & the Côte d' Azur, Germany, Austria and Gran Canaria for a number of travel publishers, including Rough Guides. He also writes for publications such as the *Financial Times* and the *Guardian*.

Christian Williams grew up in Germany. He has been a freelance writer since 1997, and has written or co-written several travel guidebooks, including the Rough Guides to Berlin and Austria. He has also penned articles for various magazines and provided content for various travel websites.

Fact Checker
Claudia Himmelreich

Proofreader
Ankita Awasthi

Indexer
Hilary Bird

Editorial Consultant
Helen Townsend

Design and Editorial
Publisher Douglas Amrine
List Manager Vivien Antwi
Project Editors Michelle Crane, Georgina Palffy
Assistant Editor Vicki Allen
Project Designer Shahid Mahmood
Senior Cartographic Editor Casper Morris
Cartographer Stuart James
Senior DTP Designer Jason Little
Senior Picture Researcher Ellen Root
Production Controller Linda Dare

Special Assistance
Hugh Thompson and Debra Wolter for editorial; Alf Alderson, Philipp Erbslöh, Tino Gerdesius, Gisela Grunemann, Bridget Neumann and Alexandra Whittleton for test drives.

Revisions Team
Sreemoyee Basu, Joel Dullroy, Bharti Karakoti, Rada Radojicic, Ajay Verma

Photography
Alex Havret, Lynn McPeake, James Tye

Additional Photography
Sheeba Bhatnagar, Witold Danilkiewicz, Geoff Dann, Adam Hajder, Michael Jackson, Diana Jarvis, Dorota and Mariusz Jarymowicz, Jamie Marshall, Wojciech Medrzak, Tomasz Mysluk, Ian O'Leary, Pawel Wojcik.

Maps
Cartographic Production
Lovell Johns Ltd, www.lovelljohns.com

Source Data
Base mapping supplied by Kartographie Huber, www.kartographie.de

Elevation Data
SRTM data courtesy of ESRI

Picture Credits
The publisher would like to thank the following individuals, companies, and picture libraries for their kind permission to reproduce their photographs:

Placement Key: a=above; b=below/bottom; c=centre; f=far; l=left; r=right; t=top.

akg-images: historic-maps/Abraham Orte 28-29. **Alamy Images:** blickwinkel 208-209; Werner Dieterich 231tr; imagebroker 22bl, 129tl; Interfoto 56br; Werner Otto 134tr; Peter Widmann 55bl, 180-81. **Auf Schönburg. Burghotel und Restaurant :** Volker Linger 23tl. **Berlin Airports:** 10tr, 10bl. **Dorling Kindersley:** Michael Jackson 26tr; Schloss (Burg) Lichtenstein 229tr. **Masterfile:** 175br, 224-225; Robert Harding Images 248br. **Photolibrary:** Bahnmueller Bahnmueller 27br; Barbara Boensch 133br; DEA Picture Library 179tl; euroluftbild euroluftbild 98tl; Hendrik Holler 215tr; Stefan Kiefer 189tl; Werner Otto 39c, 52br, 134br, 190-191; Chris Seba 37tr; Siepmann 177bl; Konrad Wothe 21tl; Ernst Wrba 100tl. **Tourist Information Creglingen:** 195cl, 195br. **Richard Neville Walker:** 164br. **Wikipedia, The Free Encyclopedia:** Wolfgang Manousek - http://en.wikipedia.org/wiki/File:Building_in_germany.jpg 253cl; Public Domain 167c, 198cr.
Sheet Map:
Getty Images: Gavin Hellier.
Jacket images:
Front: Getty Images: Gavin Hellier.
Spine: 4Corners Images: SIME/Reinhard Schmidt.
Back: Corbis: Karl-Heinz Haenel tl; **Getty Images:** LOOK/Sabine Lubenow tr; Stone/John Lamb tc.

Phrase Book

IN AN EMERGENCY

Where is the telephone?	Wo ist das Telefon?	voh ist duss tel-e-fone?
Help!	Hilfe!	hilf-uh
Please call a doctor	Bitte rufen Sie einen Arzt	bitt-uh roof'n zee ine-en artst
Please call the police	Bitte rufen Sie die Polizei	bitt-uh roof'n zee dee poli-tsy
Please call the fire brigade	Bitte rufen Sie die Feuerwehr	bitt-uh roof'n zee dee foyer-vayr
Stop!	Halt!	hult

COMMUNICATION ESSENTIALS

Yes	Ja	yah
No	Nein	nine
Please	Bitte	bitt-uh
Thank you	Danke	dunk-uh
Excuse me	Verzeihung	fair-tsy-hoong
Hello (good day)	Guten Tag	goot-en tahk
Goodbye	Auf Wiedersehen	owf-veed-er-zay-ern
Good evening	Guten Abend	goot'n ahb'nt
Good night	Gute Nacht	goot-uh nukht
Until tomorrow	Bis morgen	biss morg'n
See you	Tschüss	chooss
What is that?	Was ist das?	voss ist duss
Why?	Warum?	var-room
Where?	Wo?	voh
When?	Wann?	vunn
Today	heute	hoyt-uh
Tomorrow	morgen	morg'n
Month	Monat	mohn-aht
Night	Nacht	nukht
Afternoon	Nachmittag	nahkh-mit-tahk
Morning	Morgen	morg'n
Year	Jahr	yar
There	dort	dort
Here	hier	hear
Week	Woche	vokh-uh
Yesterday	gestern	gest'n
Evening	Abend	ahb'nt

USEFUL PHRASES

How are you? (informal)	Wie geht's?	vee gayts
Fine, thanks	Danke, es geht mir gut	dunk-uh, es gayt meer goot
Until later	Bis später	biss shpay-ter
Where is/are?	Wo ist/sind...?	voh ist/sind
How far is it to...?	Wie weit ist es...?	vee vite ist ess
Do you speak English?	Sprechen Sie Englisch?	shpresh'n zee eng-glish
I don't understand	Ich verstehe nicht	ish fair-shtay-uh nisht
Could you speak more slowly?	Könnten Sie langsamer sprechen?	kurnt-en zee lung-zam-er shpresh'n

USEFUL WORDS

large	gross	grohss
small	klein	kline
hot	heiss	hyce
cold	kalt	kult
good	gut	goot
bad	böse/schlecht	burss-uh/shlesht
open	geöffnet	g'urff-nett
closed	geschlossen	g'shloss'n
left	links	links
right	rechts	reshts
straight ahead	geradeaus	g'rah-der-owss

MAKING A TELEPHONE CALL

I would like to make a phone call	Ich möchte telefonieren	ish mer-shtuh tel-e-fon-eer'n
I'll try again later	Ich versuche es später noch einmal	ish fair-zookh-uh es shpay-ter nokh ine-mull
Can I leave a message?	Kann ich eine Nachricht hinterlassen?	kan ish ine-uh nakh-risht hint-er-lahss-en
answer phone	Anrufbeantworter	an-roof-be-ahnt vort-er
telephone card	Telefonkarte	tel-e-fone-kart-uh
receiver	Hörer	hur-er
mobile	Handy	han-dee
engaged (busy)	besetzt	b'zetst
wrong number	falsche verbindung	falsh-uh fair-bin-doong

SIGHTSEEING

library	Bibliothek	bib-leo-tek
entrance ticket	Eintrittskarte	ine-tritz-kart-uh
cemetery	Friedhof	freed-hofe
train station	Bahnhof	barn-hofe
gallery	Galerie	gall-er-ree
information	Auskunft	owss-koonft
church	Kirche	keersh-uh
garden	Garten	gart'n
palace/castle	Palast/schloss	pallast/shloss
place (square)	Platz	plats
bus stop	Haltestelle	hal-te-shtel-uh
national holiday	Nationalfeiertag	nats-yon-ahl-fire tahk
theatre	Theater	tay-aht-er
free admission	eintritt frei	ine-tritt fry

SHOPPING

Do you have/ Is there...?	Gibt es...?	geept ess
How much does it cost?	Was kostet das?	voss kost't duss?
When do you open/ close?	Wann öffnen Sie? schliessen Sie?	vunn off'n zee shlees'n zee
this	das	duss
expensive	teuer	toy-er
cheap	preiswert	price-vurt
size	Grösse	gruhs-uh
number	Nummer	noom-er
colour	Farbe	farb-uh
brown	braun	brown
black	schwarz	shvarts
red	rot	roht
blue	blau	blau
green	grün	groon
yellow	gelb	gelp

TYPES OF SHOPS

antique shop	Antiquariat	antik-var-yat
pharmacy	Apotheke	appo-tay-kuh
bank	Bank	bunk
bakery	Bäckerei	beck-er-eye
bookshop	Buchhandlung	bookh-hant-loong
clothes shop boutique	Kleiderladen, Boo-teek-uh	klyder-lard'n boo-teek-uh
department store	Warenhaus	vahr'n-hows
drugstore	Drogerie	droog-er-ree
food shop	Lebensmittel-geschäft	lay-bens-mittel-gush-eft
glass, porcelain	Glas, Porzellan	glars, Port-sellahn
hairdresser	Friseur	freezz-er
market	Markt	markt
travel agency	Reisebüro	rye-zer-boo-roe
newspaper kiosk	Zeitungskiosk	tsytoongs-kee-osk
post office	Post	posst
shop/store	Geschäft/laden	gush-eft/lard'n
film processing shop	Photogeschäft	fo-to-gush-eft
self-service shop	Selbstbedienungs-laden	selpst-bed-ee-nungs-lard'n
shoe shop	Schuhladen	shoo-lard'n

STAYING IN A HOTEL

Do you have any vacancies?	Haben Sie noch Zimmer frei?	harb'n zee nokh tsimm-er-fry
with twin beds?	mit zwei Betten?	mitt tsvy bett'n
with a double bed?	mit einem Doppelbett?	mitt ine'm dopp'l-bet
with a bath?	mit Bad?	mitt bart
with a shower?	mit Dusche?	mitt doosh-uh
I have a reservation	Ich habe eine Reservierung	ish harb-uh ine-uh rez-er-veer-oong
key	Schlüssel	shlooss'l
porter	Pförtner	pfert-ner

EATING OUT

Do you have a table for…?	Haben sie einen Tisch für…?	*harb'n zee tish foor*
I would like to reserve a table	Ich möchte eine Reservierung machen	*ish mer-shtuh ine-uh rezer-veer-oong makh'n*
I'm a vegetarian	Ich bin Vegetarier	*ish bin vegg-er-tah-ree-er*
Waiter!	Herr Ober!	*hair oh-bare!*
The bill, please	Die Rechnung, bitte	*dee resh-noong bitt-uh*
breakfast	Frühstück	*froo-shtock*
lunch	Mittagessen	*mit-targ-ess'n*
dinner	Abendessen	*arb'nt-ess'n*
bottle	Flasche	*flush-uh*
dish of the day	Tagesgericht	*tahg-es-gur-isht*
main dish	Hauptgericht	*howpt-gur-isht*
dessert	Nachtisch	*nahkh-tish*
cup	Tasse	*tass-uh*
wine list	Weinkarte	*vine-kart-uh*
glass	Glas	*glars*
spoon	Löffel	*lerff'l*
teaspoon	Teelöffel	*tay-lerff'l*
tip	Trinkgeld	*trink-gelt*
knife	Messer	*mess-er*
starter (appetizer)	Vorspeise	*for-shpize-uh*
plate	Teller	*tell-er*
fork	Gabel	*gahb'l*

MENU DECODER

Aal	arl	eel
Apfel	upf'l	apple
Apfelschorle	upf'l-shoorl-uh	apple juice with sparkling mineral water
Apfelsine	upf'l-seen-uh	orange
Aprikose	upri-kawz-uh	apricot
Artischocke	arti-shokh-uh-	artichoke
Aubergine	or-ber-jeen-uh	aubergine (eggplant)
Banane	bar-narn-uh	banana
Beefsteak	beef-stayk	steak
Bier	beer	beer
Bockwurst	bokh-voorst	a type of sausage
Bohnensuppe	burn-en-zoop-uh	bean soup
Branntwein	brant-vine	spirits
Bratkartoffeln	brat-kar-toff'ln	fried potatoes
Bratwurst	brat-voorst	fried sausage
Brötchen	bret-tchen	bread roll
Brot	brot	bread
Brühe	bruh-uh	broth
Butter	boot-ter	butter
Champignon	shum-pin-yong	mushroom
Currywurst	kha-ree-voorst	sausage with curry sauce
Dill	dill	dill
Ei	eye	egg
Eis	ice	ice/ice cream
Ente	ent-uh	duck
Erdbeeren	ayrt-beer'n	strawberries
Fisch	fish	fish
Forelle	for-ell-uh	trout
Frikadelle	frika-dayl-uh	rissole/hamburger
Garnele	gar-nayl-uh	prawn/shrimp
gebraten	g'braat'n	fried
gegrillt	g'grilt	grilled
gekocht	g'kokht	boiled
geräuchert	g'rowk-ert	smoked
Geflügel	g'floog'l	poultry
Gemüse	g'mooz-uh	vegetables
Gulasch	goo-lush	goulash
Gurke	goork-uh	gherkin
Hammelbraten	hamm'l-braat'n	roast mutton
Hähnchen	haynsh'n	chicken
Hering	hair-ing	herring
Honig	hoe-nikh	honey
Kaffee	kaf-fay	coffee
Kalbfleisch	kalp-flysh	veal
Kaninchen	ka-neensh'n	rabbit
Karpfen	karpf'n	carp
Kartoffelpüree	kar-toff'l-poor-ay	mashed potatoes
Käse	kayz-uh	cheese
Kaviar	kar-vee-ar	caviar
Knödel	k'nerd'l	noodle
Kopfsalat	kopf-zal-aat	lettuce
Krebs	krayps	crab
Kuchen	kookh'n	cake
Lachs	lahkhs	salmon
Leber	lay-ber	liver
mariniert	mari-neert	marinated

Marmelade	marmer-lard-uh	marmalade, jam
Milch	milsh	milk
Mineralwasser	minn-er-arl-vuss-er	mineral water
Olive	o-leev-uh	olive
Petersilie	payt-er-zee-li-uh	parsley
Pfeffer	pfeff-er	pepper
Pfirsich	pfir-zish	peach
Pflaumen	pflow-men	plum
Pommes frites	pomm-fritt	chips/French fries
Quark	kvark	soft cheese
Rindfleisch	rint-flysh	beef
Rippchen	rip-sh'n	cured pork rib
Rührei	rhoo-er-eye	scrambled eggs
Saft	zuft	juice
Salat	zal-aat	salad
Salz	zults	salt
Salzkartoffeln	zults-kar-toff'l	boiled potatoes
Sauerkirschen	zow-er-keersh'n	cherries
Sauerkraut	zow-er-krowt	sauerkraut
Sekt	zekt	sparkling wine
scharf	sharf	spicy
Schaschlik	shash-lik	kebab
Schlagsahne	shlahgg-zarn-uh	whipped cream
Schnittlauch	shnit-lowhkh	chives
Schnitzel	shnitz'l	veal or pork cutlet
Schweinefleisch	shvine-flysh	pork
Spargel	shparg'l	asparagus
Spiegelei	shpeeg'l-eye	fried egg
Spinat	shpin-art	spinach
Tee	tay	tea
Tomate	tom-art-uh	tomato
Wassermelone	vuss-er-me-lohn-uh	watermelon
Wein	vine	wine
Weintrauben	vine-trowb'n	grapes
Wiener Würstchen	veen-er voorst-sh'n	frankfurter
Zander	tsan-der	pike-perch
Zitrone	tsi-trohn-uh	lemon
Zucker	tsook-er	sugar
Zwiebel	tsveeb'l	onion

NUMBERS

0	null	nool
1	eins	eye'ns
2	zwei	tsvy
3	drei	dry
4	vier	feer
5	fünf	foonf
6	sechs	zex
7	sieben	zeeb'n
8	acht	uhkht
9	neun	noyn
10	zehn	tsayn
11	elf	elf
12	zwölf	tserlf
13	dreizehn	dry-tsayn
14	vierzehn	feer-tsayn
15	fünfzehn	foonf-tsayn
16	sechzehn	zex-tsayn
17	siebzehn	zeep-tsayn
18	achtzehn	uhkht-tsayn
19	neunzehn	noyn-tsayn
20	zwanzig	tsvunn-tsig
21	einundzwanzig	ine-oont-tsvunn-tsig
30	dreißig	dry-sig
40	vierzig	feer-sig
50	fünfzig	foonf-tsig
60	sechzig	zex-tsig
70	siebzig	zeep-tsig
80	achtzig	uhkht-tsig
90	neunzig	noyn-tsig
100	hundert	hoond't
1,000	tausend	towz'nt
1,000,000	eine Million	ine-uh mill-yon

TIME

one minute	eine Minute	ine-uh min-oot-uh
one hour	eine Stunde	ine-uh shtoond-uh
half an hour	eine halbe Stunde	ine-uh hullb-uh shtoond-uh
Monday	Montag	mohn-targ
Tuesday	Dienstag	deens-targ
Wednesday	Mittwoch	mitt-vokh
Thursday	Donnerstag	donn-ers-targ
Friday	Freitag	fry-targ
Saturday	Samstag/ Sonnabend	zums-targ zonn-ah-bent
Sunday	Sonntag	zon-targ

Driver's Phrase Book

SOME COMMON ROAD SIGNS

Achtung	watch out
Anlieger frei	residents only
Autobahn	motorway
Autobahndreieck	motorway junction
Autobahnkreuz	motorway junction
Bahnübergang	level crossing
Baustelle	roadworks
bei Frost Glatteisgefahr	icy in cold weather
bitte einordnen	get in lane
Bundesautobahn	federal motorway
Bundesstrasse	A-road, trunk road
Durchgangsverkehr	through traffic
Einbahnstrasse	one-way street
eingeschränktes	restricted parking
Halteverbot	
Fahrradweg	cycle path
Frostschäden	frost damage
Fussgänger	pedestrians
Fussgängerzone	pedestrianized precinct
Gefahr	danger
gefährliche Kreuzung	dangerous junction
gefährliche Kurve	dangerous bend
Gegenverkehr hat Vorfahrt	oncoming traffic has right of way
gesperrt für Fahrzeuge aller Art	closed to all vehicles
Halteverbot	no stopping
Höchstgeschwindigkeit	maximum speed
keine Zufahrt	no entry
Kreuzung	crossroads
Kriechspur	crawler lane
kurvenreiche Strecke	bends
Landstrasse	A-road, B-road
langsam fahren	drive slowly
Nebel	fog
nur für Busse	buses only
Parken nur mit parkscheibe	parking disc holders only
Parkverbot	no parking
Radweg kreuzt	cycle track crossing
Raststätte	services area
rechts fahren	keep to the right
Sackgasse	no through road
schlechte Fahrbahn	bad surface
Schule	school
Schwerlastverkehr	heavy vehicles
Seitenstreifen nicht befahrbar	soft verges
Stadtmitte	town centre
starkes Gefälle	steep gradient
Stau	tailback, traffic jam
Steinschlag	falling rocks
Strassenbahn	tram
Überholen verboten	no overtaking
Umgehungsstrasse	bypass
Umleitung	diversion
Unebenheiten	uneven surface
verengte Fahrbahn	road narrows
Vorfahrt gewähren	give way
Vorfahrtsstrasse	drivers on this road have priority
Zoll	customs

DIRECTIONS YOU MAY BE GIVEN

an der nächsten Ausfahrt	at the next junction
an der nächsten Kreuzung	at the next crossroads
erste Strasse rechts	first on the right
geradeaus	straight on
links	on the left
links abbiegen	turn left
rechts	on the right
rechts abbiegen	turn right
vorbei an…	past the…
zweite Strasse links	second on the left

THINGS YOU'LL SEE

Ausfahrt	exit
Autowäsche	car wash
Benzin	petrol
bleifrei	lead free
Bremsflüssigkeit	brake fluid
Einfahrt	entrance, way in
geschwindigkeits-beschränkung	speed limit
Luftdruck	air pressure
Münztank	coin-operated pump
Öl	oil
Parkhaus	multi-storey car park
Parkplatz	car park
Parkschein entnehmen	take a ticket
PKW	private car
Reifendruck	tyre pressure
Reparaturwerkstatt	garage, repairs
unverbleit	unleaded
verbleit	leaded
Waschstrasse	car wash
Wasser	water
Zapfsäule	petrol pump

USEFUL PHRASES

I need some petrol/oil/water
Ich brauche Benzin/Öl/Wasser
ish browkhuh bentseen/url/Vasser

Fill it up, please!
Volltanken, bitte!
folltanken bittuh

20 litres of 4-star unleaded, please
Zwanzig Liter Super Bleifrei, bitte
tsvantsish leeter zooper bly-fry bittuh

Would you check the tyres, please?
Könnten Sie bitte die Reifen überprüfen?
kurnten zee bittuh dee rife-enooberproofen

Do you do repairs?
Machen sie Reparaturen?
makhen zee reparatooren

Can you repair the clutch?
Können sie die Kupplung Reparieren?
kurnen zee dee kooploong repareeren

There is something wrong with the engine
Mit dem Motor stimmt etwas nicht
mit daym mohtor shtimmt etvuss nisht

The engine is overheating
Der Motor ist heissgelaufen
dair mohtor ist hice-gulowfen

I need a new tyre
Ich brauche einen neuen Reifen
ish browkhuh ine-en noyen rife-en

Can you replace this?
Haben Sie dafür einen Ersatz?
hahben zee dafoor ine-en airsats

The indicator is not working
Der Blinker funktioniert nicht
dair blinker foonkts-yoneert nisht

How long will it take?
Wie lange wird das dauern?
vee lang-uh veert dass dowern

Where can I park?
Wo kann ich parken?
vo kan ish parken

Can I park here?
Kann ich hier parken?
kan ish heer parken

I'd like to hire a car
Ich möchte ein Auto mieten
ish murshtuh ine owto meeten

I'd like an automatic/a manual
Ich möchte ein Auto mit Automatik/mit Handschaltung
ish murshtuh ine owto mit owtomahtik/mit hantshaltoong

Can we hire a baby/child seat?
Können wir einen Baby/Kindersitz mieten?
kurnnen veer ine-nen Baibee/Kindairzits meeten

How much is it for one day?
Was kostet es pro Tag?
Vuss kostet ess pro tahk

Where is the nearest petrol station?
Wo ist die nächste Tankstelle?
vo ist dee naykstuh tankshtelluh

How do I get to…?
Wie komme ich nach…?

Is this the road to…?
Ist das die Strasse nach…?
ist dass dee shtrahssuh nahkh

Which is the quickest way to…?
Was ist der schnellste Weg Zum…?
vuss ist dair shnelstuh vayk tsoo

USEFUL WORDS

bonnet	**die Motorhaube**	*mohtorhowbuh*
boot	**der Kofferraum**	*kofferrowm*
brake	**die Bremse**	*bremzuh*
breakdown	**die Panne**	*pannuh*
car	**das Auto**	*owto*
car park	**der Parkplatz**	*parkplats*
(multistorey)	**das Parkhaus**	*parkhowss*
caravan	**der Wohnwagen**	*vohn-vahgen*
clutch	**die Kupplung**	*kooploong*
crossroads	**die Kreuzung**	*kroytsoong*
drive (verb)	**fahren**	*faren*
engine	**der Motor**	*mohtor*
exhaust	**der Auspuff**	*owss-poof*
fan belt	**der Keilriemen**	*kile-reemen*
garage (for repairs)	**die Werkstatt**	*vairkshtat*
(for petrol)	**die Tankstelle**	*tankshtelluh*
gear	**der Gang**	*gang*
gears/gear box	**das Getriebe**	*gutreebuh*
headlights	**die Scheinwerfer**	*shine-vairfer*
indicator	**der Blinker**	*blinker*
junction	**die Kreuzung**	*kroytsoong*
(motorway entry)	**die Auffahrt**	*owf-fart*
(motorway exit)	**die Ausfahrt**	*owss-fart*
licence	**der Führerschein**	*f√rer-shine*
lorry	**der Lastwagen**	*last-vahgen*
motorbike	**das Motorrad**	*motor-raht*
motorway	**die Autobahn**	*owtoh-bahn*
number plate	**das Nummernschild**	*noom-mern-shilt*
parking meter	**die Parkuhr**	*park-oor*
parking ticket	**der Strafzettel**	*shtrahf-tsettel*
petrol	**das Benzin**	*bentseen*
petrol station	**die Tankstelle**	*tankshtelluh*
rear lights	**das Rücklicht**	*rooklisht*
road	**die Strasse**	*shtrahssuh*
spark plug	**die Zündkerze**	*ts√nt-kairtsuh*
speed	**die Geschwindigkeit**	*gush-vindish-kite*
speedometer	**der Tacho(meter)**	*takho(mayter)*
steering wheel	**das Lenkrad**	*lenkraht*
tow	**abschleppen**	*apshleppen*
traffic lights	**die Ampel**	*ampel*
trailer	**der Anhänger**	*anheng-er*
tyre	**der Reifen**	*rife-en*
van	**der Lieferwagen**	*leefer-vahgen*
wheel	**das Rad**	*raht*
windscreen	**die Windschutz-**	*vint-shoots-scheibe shybuh*
windscreen wiper	**der Scheibenwischer**	*shyben-visher*

Road Signs

SPEED LIMITS AND GENERAL DRIVING INDICATIONS

Give way

Compulsory stop

Your route has priority

End of priority

You have priority at the next junction

Junction gives priority to traffic from the right

Give way to oncoming traffic

No overtaking

Roundabout

No access to vehicles over 3.8 m

No access to vehicles over 2 m

Obligatory minimum distance of 70 m

Speed limit

End of speed limit

Minimum speed limit

WARNING SIGNS

Unspecified danger

Succession of bends

Slippery road

Risk of rockfalls

Bumpy road

Road narrows

Road narrows on the left

Level crossing with barrier

Level crossing with no barrier

Steep descent

Wild animals

Children crossing or school

Pedestrian crossing

Road works

Risk of snow and ice